INTRODUCTION

TO

THE TALMUD

INTRODUCTION TO THE TALMUD

by Moses Mielziner

With a new bibliography, 1925-1967

by ALEXANDER GUTTMANN

BLOCH PUBLISHING COMPANY

New York

Fifth Edition

Library of Congress Catalogue
Card Number: 68-29908
ISBN: 0-8197-0015-0

PREFACE TO THE FOURTH EDITION

Ever since the publication of the third edition of Mielziner's Introduction to the Talmud in 1925, numerous books and essays have been written in the field of Talmud. This literature sheds new light on the spiritual and material life of the talmudic period, on literary problems relative to the talmudic sources, and on certain aspects of Jewish history. However, all this has invalidated relatively little of the important work done by the men of the Wissenschaft des Judentums since Z. Frankel and outlined concisely in Mielziner's book. The reprint of the book is therefore justified.

The principal, though inevitable, weakness of Mielziner's Introduction today is that it can not inform the student about the literature published since 1925. The present edition attempts to correct this weakness to a considerable extent by adding a selected list of relevant literature printed after 1924. Due to the close relationship between Talmud and Midrash, the bibliography includes midrashic literature, too, although Mielziner almost completely excluded this area. This new material will also make our bibliography more useful for readers of Strack's Introduction to the Talmud and Midrash, which was reprinted in 1959 without any supplementary literature.

Thanks are due to Dr. Samuel Sandmel who initiated and negotiated the publication of this new edition of Mielziner's Introduction, and to Dr. Fritz Bamberger who completed the arrangements with Bloch Publishing Company.

Alexander Guttmann

Hebrew Union College—Jewish Institute of Religion
Cincinnati, July 1967

PREFACE TO THE FIRST EDITION

The Talmud is undoubtedly one of the most remarkable literary productions of antiquity. In its twelve folio volumes it embodies the mental labors of the ancient Jewish teachers during a period of about eight hundred years. The attention of these teachers was directed particularly to expounding and developing the religious, moral and civil law of the Bible. The pages of this great work are, besides, replete with wise observations, ethical maxims, beautiful legends and parables, and exegetical explanations. We also find in it valuable historical and ethnographical material, as well as occasional references to the various branches of ancient knowledge and science.

The Talmud is also remarkable for the powerful influence it exerted upon the thought and life of the Jews during the Middle Ages, yes, even down to quite recent times. Its authority was second only to that of the Bible. Although modern Jews have emancipated themselves more or less from its authority, the Talmud still remains a venerable literary monument of a great and important epoch in the development of Judaism. At the same time, it is a valuable source of religious and ethical doctrines as well as of scientific investigation.

In our day, quite a general interest in this literary monument of antiquity is being awakened. This increasing interest is manifested not only by the publication of numerous works and monographs on Talmudical topics, but also by the fact that several universities and colleges abroad and in this country have established chairs for the study of this special branch of literature.

The present work which I have called "Introduction to the Talmud" is the result of many years' labor and of a long experience as professor of the Talmudical branches at the Hebrew Union College. It is intended to facilitate the exceedingly difficult study of an intricate subject. It is the first comprehensive work of its kind in the English language, yes, it might be said, in any modern language, if we except Prof. Herman L. Strack's "Einleitung in den Talmud", a book which, though treating our subject with scientific exactness and impartiality, was not intended to cover the whole ground as is attempted in the present publication.

Earlier works of this kind, from the eleventh century down to our time, have been written in Hebrew or rather in the Rabbinical idiom, and hence are accessible to Rabbinical scholars only. Valuable literary material, the result of keen critical research into our subject, has been published by some modern scholars, among whom may be named the late Z. Frankel, and I. H. Weiss.[1] The results reached by these scholars have been duly considered in our "Historical and Literary Introduction".

Regarding the second and third parts of this work, I had to rely almost entirely on my own researches. The only modern work on Talmudical Hermeneutics is Dr. H. S. Hirschfeld's "Halachische Exegese". But the usefulness of this learned work is greatly impaired by the fact that

[1] The literature on this subject is given further on in the chapter "Auxiliaries to the study of the Talmud" pp. 83—85.

the author cast it into a philosophical form to which the subject-matter does not readily lend itself.

It has been my endeavor to present the methods of the Talmudical interpretation of the Bible in the proper light. The application of the various hermeneutical rules is illustrated by numerous examples which have been carefully selected, and which will afford the student an opportunity of becoming familiar with some of the peculiarities of the Talmudical Law.

Part III of this Introduction is the first attempt at presenting the Methodology and Terminology of the Talmud in a strictly systematical way. It is, to some extent, an exposition of the Dialectics of the Rabbis, an analysis of their discussions and debates. The references and examples added to each of the technical terms and phrases show their prevalence in all sections of the Talmud. I may be pardoned in entertaining the hope that this portion of my work will be found a reliable guide through the labyrinth of Talmudical discussions.

The appended treatise "Outlines of Talmudical Ethics" is essentially the contents of my paper on that subject read at the World's Parliament of Religions in Chicago.

The alphabetical Register of the principal Tanaim and Amoraim, the Index of technical Terms and Phrases, and the "Key to the Abbreviations used in the Talmud and its commentaries" will, I hope, add to the usefulness of this work.

CINCINNATI, MARCH, 1894.

THE AUTHOR.

Preface to the Second Edition

Encouraged by the very favorable reception given to the first edition of this Introduction to the Talmud, I have carefully revised the work for the present new edition. The numerous typographical errors which had escaped the attention of the proofreader of the former edition have been corrected, and several pages of new matter have been appended which supplement the Bibliography of modern works and pamphlets on Talmudic Subjects.

CINCINNATI, O., NOVEMBER, 1902.

THE AUTHOR.

PREFACE TO THIRD EDITION

This edition — the third — of Mielziner's *Introduction to the Talmud,* may be briefly described as a reprint of the work originally published in 1894, with a section of additional Notes. The work itself is essentially an Introduction, in the elementary sense, intended for readers who desire to acquaint themselves with the "sea of the Talmud." It is, therefore, obvious that within the compass of a modest volume such as the present, nothing more than brief treatment is possible. The fact that the work is regarded as "indispensable to a proper understanding of Talmudical discussions"* explains sufficiently its popularity. It is hoped that this new, enlarged and revised edition will stimulate a wider interest in the study of the vast literature of the Talmud. In the bibliographical material, only the more important works are indicated. No attempt is made to give exhaustive lists of works on the many subjects referred to. The *Additional Notes* at the end of the book is the joint work of Dr. Joshua Bloch and Dr. Louis Finkelstein and, it is believed, they embody a fairly good summary of the results of modern research in Talmudic lore since the publication of the second edition of this work in 1903. The Index is the work of Morton M. Berman, a student of the Jewish Institute of Religion, New York. In the preparation of these notes additional help was received from Dr. Jacob Z. Lauterbach, Professor Talmud, Hebrew Union College.

J. B.

New York, December, 1924.

---

*C. Levias, A Grammar of the Aramaic Idiom contained in the Babylonian Talmud. Cincinnati, 1900, p. 2.

TABLE OF CONTENTS

PART I

HISTORICAL AND LITERARY INTRODUCTION

PART II

LEGAL HERMENEUTICS OF THE TALMUD

PART III

TALMUDICAL TERMINOLOGY AND METHODOLOGY

PART IV

INTRODUCTION
TO
THE TALMUD

PART I

HISTORICAL AND LITERARY INTRODUCTION

THE TALMUD AND ITS COMPONENT PARTS

§ 1.

The Talmud is the work which embodies the mental labors of the ancient Jewish teachers during a period of about eight hundred years (from about 300 before, to 500 after, the Christian era) in expounding and developing the civil and religious law of the Bible. Besides, it contains the theosophical views, ethical maxims and exegetical remarks of those teachers; it is interwoven with many valuable historical and ethnographical records and occasional references to the different branches of ancient knowledge and sciences.

The Talmud consists of two distinct works, the *Mishna*, as the text, and the *Gemara* as a voluminous collection of commentaries and discussions on that text.

The appellation Talmud, meaning the Study, properly refers to the Gemara only, but according to a literary usage established in later times, the name Talmud is applied also to the combined work of Mishna and Gemara.[1]

We have two compilations of the Gemara, different from each other in language as well as in contents. One originated in the Palestinian, and the other in the Babylonian schools. The latter is called תלמוד בבלי the Babylonian Talmud, and the former תלמוד ירושלמי the Palestinian Talmud. The Mishna text in both of them is the same, though occasionally offering slight variations.

---

[1] As a technical term the word תלמוד was applied by the ancient teachers to signify the method of deducing a law from the words of Scripture; compare the phrase תלמוד לומר, Maccoth I, 7, a. o. Subsequently the word was applied to the discussions of the teachers on the Mishna; compare Sanhedrin 24a: תלמודה של בבל. After the Mishna and Gemara had been combined in one work, it became customary to use the word as an appellation of the whole work.

CHAPTER I

THE MISHNA.

ITS ORIGIN, COMPILATION AND NAME

§ 2.

The Mishna is the authorized codification of the oral or unwritten law which, on the basis of the written law contained in the Pentateuch, developed during the second Temple and down to the end of the second century of the common era.

The oral law consisted partly of legal traditions and usages which had been handed down from time immemorial; partly of enactments (תקנות גזירות וסייגים) of the men of the Great Synod or the Sopherim, and subsequently of the Sanhedrin; and partly of the laws which proceeded from the discussions and decisions of the teachers, the Tanaim, in the Palestinian academies, established for the purpose of cultivating and transmitting that law. Its transmission was, for many centuries, confined to verbal communication, as it was considered a religious offence to reduce the tradition to writing.[1]

The cultivation of that law consisted mainly in the endeavor to found its provisions on a biblical basis and support, and to deduce therefrom new provisions for cases not yet provided for. This endeavor gave rise to discussions and a frequent conflict of opinions. Also the reports of these conflicting opinions were conscientiously preserved in the memory of subsequent teachers. Thus, in the course of time, the subject matter of the oral law accumulated to an immense bulk which, not yet in any way systematized, became almost too heavy to be preserved merely by the power of memory.

The first attempt towards bringing some order and system into this chaotic mass of traditions was made by Hillel, president of the Sanhedrin in the time of Herod, by arranging it into six principal divisions. His attempt was later resumed by the

[1] In order to assist their memory, however, some teachers had private scrolls on which they for their own use entered single theses of the tr ditional law. Such a scroll was called מגלת סתרים "Secret Scroll."

celebrated R. Akiba who subdivided the subject matter belonging to each of the six divisions, into homogeneous parts. Within each part again he grouped the single laws according to their inter-connection and according to certain mnemonical considerations. The work of R. Akiba was continued by his distinguished disciple R. Meir who completed the collection and improved its formal arrangement. But neither this compilation of R. Meir nor similar works of his colleagues succeeded in commanding general recognition, as every teacher in the various academies preferred to transmit and expound the accumulated material of the law according to a method and arrangement of his own.

Finally R. Jehuda Hanasi, flourishing towards the end of the second century, undertook the great task of establishing a general code of the oral law. By virtue of his eminent learning, his dignity as Patriarch and as head of a celebrated academy, he succeeded in accomplishing this task. Taking the unfinished work of R. Akiba and R. Meir as basis, and retaining, in general, its division and arrangement, he examined and sifted the whole material of the oral law, and completed it by adding the decisions which his academy gave concerning many doubtful cases. Unanimously adopted opinions he recorded without the names of their authors or transmitters, but where a divergence of opinions appeared, the individual opinion is given in the name of its author, together with the decision of the prevailing majority, or side by side with that of its opponent, and sometimes even with the addition of short arguments pro and con.

Like the former compilations of the oral law, this work of R. Jehuda was called *Mishna*. In order to distinguish it from that of R. Akiba and R. Meir it was originally designated the *Mishna of R. Jehuda*, but after having been generally accepted as the exclusively authorized code of the traditional law, it bears the simple name *Mishna* without any further modification.[1]

---

[1] Whether R. Jehuda Hanasi actually committed his Mishna to writing or not, is a question concerning which the scholars of ancient as well as of modern times express different opinions. In accordance with the principle mentioned in Talm. Gittin 60 b and Temura 14 b in the name of some teachers, that the oral law ought not to be

In later years of his life, R. Jehuda revised his work, and made several changes. Some additions were made by his disciples.[1]

Concerning the etymology and signification of the word מִשְׁנָה there is a difference of opinion. Some regard it as a feminine form of the Hebrew word מִשְׁנֶה (analogous to the double form מִקְנֶה and מִקְנָה), meaning *the second in rank*, hence a signification of the work containing the oral law which takes the second rank compared with the biblical law; which is considered the first. In this sense the word is taken not only by the fathers of the Church who rendered it by the term δευτέρωσις, but also by many modern scholars. Others derive it from the verb שנה *to repeat*, which in new Hebrew, like the Aramaic תנא received

---

written down דברים שבעל פה אי אתה רשאי לאמרן בכתב it is maintained by Sherira Gaon (according to one version in his Iggereth), by Rashi in his commentary on B. Metzia 33 a and Erubin 62 b, by Tosaphoth on Megilla 32 a, and by some other authorities of the Middle Ages that R. Jehuda compiled his great Mishna work in his mind without writing it down, and that it was transmitted only orally during many generations, until circumstances in the sixth century made it neccessary to commit it to writing. This view is accepted and defended even by some modern scholars, as Luzzatto, Rapaport, Jost, Graetz, Leopold Loew, and others.

More plausible is the opposite opinion holding that R. Jehuda Hanasi wrote out the Mishna in full. This opinion is shared in the Middle Ages by Samuel Hanagid, R. Nissim, R. Abraham b. David, Maimonides, and in modern times by Geiger, Frankel, Lebrecht, I. H. Weiss, and others.

The arguments in favor of the former opinion are found in Graetz' Geschichte der Juden IV, second edition, p. 494, and in Leopold Loew's Graphische Requisiten II, pp. 112-132; the contrary arguments in Frankel's Darke Hamischna p. 211: Weiss' Dor Dor III, 244-248. Compare also Hamburger's Real-Encycl. II, p. 796, and S. Adler's Kobetz al Yad, p. 54.

[1] Clear evidences of such additions by later hands are found in the last Mishna of Sota, where the death of Rabbi is mentioned, and in the last Mishna of Uk'tzin, where mention is made of R. Joshua b. Levi who flourished after Rabbi. As later additions and interpolations must also such passages as רבי אומר or דברי רבי be regarded which occasionally occur in the context of the Mishna, e. g. Nazir I, 4; IV, 5; Maccoth I, 8.

the meaning, *to relate, to teach, to transmit orally*. Mishna then means *the oral teaching*, the instruction in the traditional law, in contradistinction to מקרא the reading in the written law of the Bible.

THE DIVISION OF THE MISHNA.

§ 3.

The Mishna is divided into six main sections, termed *Sedarim* ("Orders" or "Series")[1]. A mnemonical sign of the sequence of these sections are the words זמן נקט (time he took), formed by the initials of their names.

I. *Zeraim* זרעים *Seeds* or productions of the land. This section embraces the ritual laws concerning the cultivation of the soil and its products. It is introduced by a treatise on prayer and benedictions.

II. *Moed* מועד *Festival*, treats of the laws concerning the Sabbath and all festivals.

III. *Nashim* נשים *Women*, regulations concerning marriage and divorce.

IV. *Nezikin* נזיקין *Damages*, embracing a great part of the civil and criminal law.

V. *Kodashim* קדשים *Sacred things*, treats of the sacrificial laws and the temple service.

VI. *Teharoth* טהרות *Purification*, the laws concerning the clean and unclean.

Each Seder (section) is subdivided into Masechtoth or treatises, of which each bears a name indicating its general contents[2].

The Mishna contains in all sixty three Masechtoth. Each Masechta is again subdivided into *Chapters*, called Perakim, and each Perek into paragraphs, of which each is termed *Mishna* or

---

[1] On account of this division of the Mishna into six series the whole Talmud is signified by the technical term ש״ס which is an abbreviation of the words ששה סדרים.

[2] The word מסכת or מסכתא is probably derived from נסך to *weave*, and means then a *web*, just as in Latin textus from texere, means a web, and then a composition of words and sentences.

Halacha. The latter term for a single paragraph is especially used in the Palestinian Talmud.

ORDER OF SUCCESSION, NAMES AND GENERAL CONTENTS OF THE MASECHTOTH.

§ 4.

Concerning the order in which the Masechtoth belonging to every section follow after each other, some difference appears between the separate Mishna edition (called Mishnayoth משניות)[1] and the arrangement of the Masechtoth as generally adopted in the editions of the Babylonian and the Palestinian Talmud. This is especially the case in the Sedarim II—VI, while in Seder I the order of succession is the same in all editions.

---

[1] Maimonides in the introduction to his Mishna commentary endeavors to find some reasons for the order of succession of the Masechtoth in each Seder. But his reasons are often rather forced. R. Sherira Gaon, in his celebrated epistle holds that the compiler of the Mishna did not have the intention to arrange the Masechtoth according to a strictly systematical order. This opinion is also expressed in the Gemara B. Kamma 102 a; Aboda Zara 7a : אין סדר למשנה בתרי מסכתות; though, on the other hand, the Gemara sometimes refers to a close connection of one Masechta with the preceding one, as in the beginning of Masecheth Sota : מכדי תנא מנזיר סליק מ"ט תנא סוטה; comp. also the beginning of Mas. Shebuoth and of Taanith.

Geiger (Wissenschaftliche Zeitschrift II, p. 487 ss.) shows that in the separate Mishna edition, at least in the Sedarim II—VI, the Masechtoth are simply arranged according to the number of Perakim of which they consist, so that the Masechtoth having the greater number stand first and are gradually followed by those having a lesser number of Perakim. Where the arrangement seemingly deviates from this rule, we can easily account for the deviation. Thus the three *Babas*, each having ten Perakim, are placed first in Seder Nezikin, because belonging together and having in all thirty Perakim. They are followed by Sanhedrin having eleven Perakim, and then by Maccoth which though consisting only of three Perakim is in its contents a continuation of the subject treated in Sanhedrin, forming with it fourteen Perakim.

The following is a full list of the Masechtoth belonging to each Seder and the number of their Perakim; besides the order of their succession in the separate Mishna edition as well as in the two compilations of the Talmud.

The letter G added to the number of the order of succession in this list indicates that there is Gemara to that Masechta in either of the two Talmud compilations.

I. SEDER ZERAIM, containing eleven Masechtoth.

Order of Succession in the Separate Mishna edition.	TALMUD Babli.	Jerushalmi.		Number of Perakim
1	1.G.	1.G.	*Berachoth*, ברכות, Benedictions or Prayers, treats of liturgical rules.	9
2	2	2.G.	*Peah*, פאה, Corner, treats of the corners and gleanings of the field, the forgotten sheaves, the olives and grapes to be left to the poor, according to Levit. XIX 9.10 and Deut. XXIV 19. 21.	8
3	3	3.G.	*Demai*, דמאי, The Uncertain, treats of corn bought from persons suspected of not having given thereof the tithes.	7
4	4	4.G.	*Khilayim*, כלאים, Mixtures, treats of the prohibited mixtures in plants, animals and garments, according to Levit. XIX, 19; Deutr. XXII, 9-11.	9
5	5	5.G.	*Shebiith*, שביעית, The Sabbatical year, according to Ex. XXIII, 11; Lev. XXV, 2-7; Deutr. XV, 1-11.	10
6	6	6.G.	*Therumoth*, תרומות, The Heave offerings for the priests, according to Numb. XVIII, 12.	11
7	7	7.G.	*Maaseroth*, מעשרות, The Tithes, to be given to the Levites, according to Lev. XXVII, 30-33; Num. XVIII, 21-24.	5
8	8	8.G.	*Maaser Sheni*, מעשר שני, The second Tithe, according to Deut. XIV, 22-26.	5
9	9	9.G.	*Challa*, חלה, The Dough, the portion to be given thereof to the Priests, according to Num. XV, 20. 21.	4
10	10	10.G.	*Orla*, ערלה, The Uncircumcised, treats of the fruits of a tree during the first four years after its planting, according to Lev. XIX, 23-25.	3

Order of Succession in the Separate Mishna edition.	TALMUD Babli.	Jerushalmi.		Number of Perakim
11	11	11.G.	*Biccurim*, בכורים, The First fruits to be brought to the Temple, according to Deut. XXVI, 1-11.	3
			II. SEDER MOED, containing twelve Masechtoth.	
1	1.G.	1.G.	*Sabbath*, שבת, treats of the labors prohibited on that day.	24
2	2.G.	2.G.	*Erubin*, ערובין, Combinations. This Masechta being a continuation of the preceding, treats especially of imaginary combinations of localities by which to extend the Sabbath boundary.	10
3	3.G.	3.G.	*Pesachim*, פסחים, treats of the laws relating to the feast of Passover and the paschal lamb.	10
4	11	5.G.	*Shekalim*, שקלים, treats of the half Shekel which, according to Ex. XXX, 12-16, every Israelite had to pay as a temple tax.	8
5	8.G.	4.G.	*Yoma*, יומא, the Day, i. e. the day of Atonement, according to Lev. XVI, 3-34.	8
6	9.G.	6.G.	*Succah*, סוכה, treats of the laws concerning the feast of Tabernacles, Lev. XXIII, 34-36.	8
7	4.G.	8.G.	*Betza* ביצה or *Yom tov* יום טוב, treats of the kinds of work which, according to Ex. XII, 16, were prohibited or permitted on the festivals. The name Betza (the egg) is taken from the first word in that Masechta.	5
8	7.G.	7.G.	*Rosh Hashana*, ראש השנה, Beginning of the year, treats of the feast of New Year.	4
9	10.G.	9.G.	*Taanith*, תענית, on the public fasts.	4
10	12.G.	10.G.	*Megilla*, מגילה, the Scroll, treats of the reading of the book of Esther on the feast of Purim.	4
11	5.G.	12.G.	*Moed Katon*, מועד קטן, Minor feast, treats of laws relating to the days intervening between the first and last days of Pesach and Succoth.	3
12	6.G.	11.G.	*Chagiga*, חגיגה, Feast offering, treats of the private offerings on the three feasts of pilgrimage, according to Deut. XVI, 16. 17.	3
			III. SEDER NASHIM, containing seven Masechtoth.	
1	1.G.	1.G.	*Yebamoth*, יבמות, Sisters-in-Law, treats of Levirate marriage, according to Deut. XXV, 5-10.	16

Order of Succession in the Separate Mishna edition.	TALMUD Babli.	Jerushalmi.		Number of Perakim
2	2.G.	3.G.	*Khethuboth*, כתובות, Marriage deeds, treats of dower and marriage settlements.	13
3	5.G.	4.G.	*Nedarim*, נדרים, Vows, treats of vows and their annulment, with reference to Num. XXX, 3-16.	11
4	6.G.	6.G.	*Nazir*, נזיר, the Nazarite, treats of the laws concerning him, according to Num. VI, 2-21.	9
5	7.G.	2.G.	*Sota*, סוטה, on the woman suspected of adultery, according to Num. V, 12-31.	9
6	4.G.	5.G.	*Gittin*, גיטין, on Divorces, based on Deut. XXIV, 1-5.	9
7	3.G.	7.G.	*Kiddushin*, קדושין, on Betrothals.	4

IV. SEDER NEZIKIN, containing ten Masechtoth.

1	1.G.	1.G.	*Baba Kama*, בבא קמא, First Gate, treats of Damages and Injuries, and their remedies, with reference to Ex. XXI, 28-37; XXII, 1-5.	10
2	2.G.	2.G.	*Baba Metzia*, בבא מציעא, Middle Gate, treats of laws concerning found property (Deut. XXII, 1-4), concerning trust (Ex. XXII, 6-14), concerning buying and selling (Lev. XXV, 14), lending (Ex. XXII, 24-26; Lev. XXV, 35-37) and concerning hiring and renting.	10
3	3.G.	3.G.	*Baba Bathra*, בבא בתרא, Last Gate, treats of laws concerning real estate and commerce, mostly based on the traditional law; besides of the laws concerning hereditary succession, based on Num. XXVII, 7-11.	10
4	5.G.	4.G.	*Sanhedrin*, סנהדרין, treats of the courts and their proceedings, and of the punishment of capital crimes.	11
5	7.G.	5.G.	*Maccoth*, מכות, Stripes, treats of false witnesses and their punishment (Deut. XIX, 16-19); of the cities of refuge (Num. XXXV, 10-32; Deut. XIX, 1-13) and of crimes punished by stripes (Deut. XXV, 1-3.	3
6	6.G.	6.G.	*Shebuoth*, שבועות, Oaths, treats of the different kinds of oaths, those made in private life as well as those administered in court, Lev. V, 4. 5. 21. 22; Ex. XXII, 6-10.	8

Order of Succession in the Separate Mishna edition.	TALMUD Babli.	TALMUD Jerushalmi.		Number of Perakim
7	8	Wanting	*Eduyoth*, עדיות, Testimonies, contains a collection of traditional laws and decisions gathered from the testimonies of distinguished teachers.	8
8	4.G.	7.G.	*Aboda Zara*, עבודה זרה, Idolatry, treats of laws concerning idols and the relation to the worshipers thereof.	5
9	10	Wanting	*Aboth*, אבות, Fathers or Sentences of the Fathers (the principal teachers), contains ethical maxims of the Mishna teachers.	5
10	9.G.	8.G.	*Horayoth*, הוריות, Decisions, treats of the consequences of acting according to erroneous decisions rendered by a religious authority, with reference to Lev. chapters IV and V.	3

V. SEDER KODASHIM, containing eleven Masechtoth.

Separate Mishna edition	Babli	Jerushalmi		Number of Perakim
1	1.G.		*Zebachim*, זבחים, Sacrifices, treats of the animal sacrifices and the mode of their offering, with reference to the first chapters of Leviticus.	14
2	2.G.	Wanting	*Menachoth*, מנחות, Meat-offering, treats of meat-and drink offerings, with reference to Lev. ch. II	13
3	4.G.		*Cholin*, (or Chullin) חולין, Profane things, treats of the traditional manner of slaughtering animals for ordinary use; besides of the dietary laws.	12
4	3.G.		*Bechoroth*, בכורות, The first born, treats of the laws concerning the first born of man and animals, according to Ex. VIII, 12.13 and Num. XVIII, 15–17.	9
5	5.G.		*Arachin*, ערכין, Estimations, treats of the mode in which persons or things dedicated to the Lord by a vow are legally appraised in order to be redeemed for ordinary use, according to Lev. XXVII, 2–27.	9
6	6.G.		*Themura*, תמורה, Exchange, treats of the laws concerning sanctified things having been exchanged, according to Lev. XXVII, 10–27.	7
7	7.G.		*Kherithoth*, כריתות, Excisions, treats of the sins subject to the punishment of excision, and their expiation by sacrifices.	6

Order of Succession in the Separate Mishna edition.	TALMUD Babli.	Jerushalmi.		Number of Perakim
8	8.G.	WANTING	*Me-ila*, מעילה, Trespass (Sacrilege), treats of the sins of violating or profaning sacred things, according to Lev. V, 15. 16.	6
9	10.G.	WANTING	*Thamid*, תמיד, The Daily Sacrifice, describes the Temple service connected with the daily morning and evening offering, according to Ex. XXIX, 38–41; Num. XXVIII, 2–8.	7
10	11.	WANTING	*Middoth*, מדות, Measurements, contains the measurements and description of the Temple, its courts, gates and halls, also description of the service of the priestly guards in the Temple.	5
11	9.		*Kinnim*, קנים, The bird's nests, treats of the sacrifices consisting of fowls, the offering of the poor, according to Lev. I, 14; V, 7; XII, 8.	3

VI. SEDER TEHAROTH, containing twelve Masechtoth.

1	2.	WANTING	*Khelim*, כלים, Vessels, treats of the conditions under which domestic utensils, garments etc. receive ritual uncleanness, according to Lev. XI, 33-35.	30
2	3.	WANTING	*Ohaloth*, אהלות, Tents, treats of tents and houses conveying the ritual uncleanness of a dead body, according to Num. XIX, 14.15.	18
3	4.	WANTING	*Nega-im*, נגעים, Leprosy, treats of the laws relating to leprosy of men, garments and dwellings, according to Lev. XIII and XIV.	14
4	5.	WANTING	*Parah*, פרה, The Heifer, treats of the laws concerning the red heifer and the use of its ashes for the purification of the unclean, according to Num. XIX.	12
5	6.	WANTING	*Teharoth*, טהרות, Purifications. The word is here used euphemistically, as the Masechta treats of some lesser degrees of uncleanness lasting only till sunset; e. g., Lev. XI, 24–28.	10
6	7.		*Mikvaoth*, מקואות, Wells, treats of the conditions under which wells and reservoirs are fit to be used for ritual purifications.	10
7	1.G.	1.G.	*Nidda*, נדה, The Menstruous, treats of the legal uncleanness arising from certain conditions in women, according to Lev. XV,	10

Order of Succession in the Separate Mishna edition.	TALMUD Babli.	Jerushalmi.		Number of Perakim
			19-31 and XII, 2-8.	
8	8.		*Mach-shirin*, מכשירין, Preparations, treats of liquids that, according to Lev. XI, 34. 38, prepare and dispose seeds and fruits to receive ritual uncleanness.	6
9	9.		*Zabim*, זבים, Persons suffering of running issues, treats of the uncleanness arising from such secretions, according to Lev. XV, 2-18.	5
10	10.		*Tebul Yom*, טבול יום, Immersed at day time, treats of the state of him who at day time immersed for his purification, while his perfect cleanness according to the law is not acquired before the setting of the sun.	4
11	11		*Yadayim*, ידים, Hands, treats of the ritual uncleanness of hands, according to the traditional law, and of their purification.	4
12	12		*Uk-tzin*, עוקצין, Stalks of Fruit, treats of stalks and shells of fruit in regard to conveying ritual uncleanness.	3

Remark 1. In connection with the main subject treated in each Masechta and generally indicated in its name, occasionally other more or less congenial subjects are treated. Thus, for instance, the last Perakim of Masecheth Megilla are devoted to laws cnncerning the sanctity of synagogues and the reading of Scriptures at the public service. In the first Perek of Kiddushin, after having set forth the different modes of contracting marriage, rules are incidently laid down concerning the legal modes of acquiring differentkinds of property, etc.

Remark 2. The Perakim belonging to each Masechta are designated in the separate Mishna edition simply by the letters of the Hebrew alphabet, and in the Talmud edition by ordinal numbers as well as by a certain name taken from the first word or words with which that Perek begins. Thus the first Perek of Berachoth is designated in the separate Mishna edition by פרק א' and in the Talmud edition by מאמתי ,פרק ראשון. In earlier rabbinical literature references to a certain Perek of the Mishna are generally made by giving only the name of that Perek without stating the Masechta to whieh it belongs, as

פרק המפקיד referring to the third Perek of Baba Metzia. An alphabetical list of the names of all Parakim with the indication of the Masechtoth to which they belong is found in the appendix to Masecheth Berachoth in the Talmud editions, immediately after Maimonides' Introduction to Seder Zeraim.

LANGUAGE OF THE MISHNA.

§ 5.

The language of the Mishna is New Hebrew, as developed during the period of the second Temple. The Hebrew having been supplanted by the Aramaic dialects as the language of common life, the ancient idiom was cultivated by the learned for liturgical and legal purposes. Many new words and phrases had to be coined to express new ideas and objects, and new grammatical forms and syntactical constructions adopted for the favored processes of legal dialectics. As far as possible use was made for this purpose of new derivations of the stock of Biblical words and of some genuine Hebrew roots which though not happening to occur in the Biblical literature still lingered in the memory of the people. Besides, recourse was had to the dominating languages. From the Aramaic especially some word roots and grammatical inflections, derivations and constructions were borrowed and modified according to the genius of the Hebrew idiom. Utensils and other objects and ideas till then unknown were designated by the same terms, used by that nation from which they had been borrowed. In this way, many Greek terms and with them also some Latin words more or less modified, were adopted and naturalized.[1]

---

[1] Modern works on the language of the Mishna are:

M. I. Landau, Geist und Sprache der Hebräer nach dem zweiten Tempelbau (Prague 1822).

A. Geiger. Lehr-und Lesebuch zur Sprache der Mishna (Breslau, 1845).

L. Dukes, Sprache der Mishna (Esslingen, 1845).

J. H. Weiss, Mishpat Leshon ha-Mishna (Vienna 1867).

Herm. L. Strack und C. Siegfried, Lehrbuch der neuhebraeischen Sprache und Literatur, Karlsruhe und Leipzig, 1884.

Salomon Stein, Das Verbum der Mischnasprache, Berlin 1888.

In this New Hebrew language, also called the *language of the sages* (לשון חכמים or לשנא דרבנן), are composed not only the Mishna but also the kindred works to be mentioned in the following chapter.

As to the style of expression, the Mishna is very brief and concise well calculated to impress itself upon the memory-

CHAPTER II

WORKS KINDRED TO THE MISHNA

§ 6.

There are several works which are kindred to the contents of the Mishna, and originated partly before and partly after its close, though their present shape belongs to a much later period. We refer to the *Tosephta*, the *Mechilta*, *Siphra* and *Siphre*. These works are very important from the fact that they throw much light on the Mishna in revealing the sources of many of its canons, and the reasons of its diverging opinions. For this purpose, they are frequently quoted in the Gemara. The following will briefly describe each of these works.

a. The Tosephta.

§ 7.

The word Tosephta (תוספתא) means Addition, Supplement, and, as indicated by this name, the work is intended to complete deficiencies of the Mishna. It is divided into Masechtoth, generally corresponding to those of the Mischna, but differing from them in the arrangement of their subject, and in the division of their Perakim. The latter are not subdivided into paragraphs. There are in all sixty Masechtoth and 452 Perakim. The Tosephta contains mainly the remnants of the earlier compilations of the Halacha made by R. Akiba, R. Meir, R. Nehemia, and others not adopted in the Mishna, and, besides, additions made, after R. Jehuda Hanasi's death, by his desciples R. Chiya, R. Oshaya, Bar Kappara and others. But we find in that work also many sayings and decisions of later Amoraim of the Babylonian and Palestinian schools. In its present shape it belongs to the fifth or sixth century.[1]

---

[1] The Tosephta is usually printed as an appendix to Alphasi's compendium of the Talmud. In the Vienna edition of the Babyl. Talmud (1860-72) the Masechtoth of the Tosephta are appended to the corresponding Mosechtoth of the Talmud. A separate revised edition of the whole Tosephta was published by Dr. Zuckermandel (Pasewalk and Treves, 1877-82). Dr. Adolph Schwartz is publishing a new edition of the

b. THE MECHILTA

§ 8.

The Mechilta, the Siphra and the Siphre have this in common, that they treat of the oral law not according to well arranged subjects, as is the case with the Mishna and the Tosephta, but rather in the form of a running commentary and discussion on the biblical passages from which the law is deduced or on which it is based.

The term Mechilta (מכילתא), being the Aramaic equivalent of the Hebrew word מדה, means originally "Measure", but in the rabbinical language it signifies the method of the traditional interpretation (Midrash), and then a collection of interpretations of the law.

The work bearing that particular name contains a collection of rabbinical interpretations on several sections of the second book of Moses; beginning with Ex. ch. XII, 1, it goes on till ch. XXIII, 19. Of the remaining chapters it comments only on XXXI, 12-17 and on XXXV, 1-3.

Though principally of a legal character (Midrash Halacha), it has also homiletical interpretations (Midrash Agada), especially on Ex. XIII, 17–XIX, 25.

The Mechilta is divided into nine main sections (Masechtoth), named according to the contents of the Bible passage which they expound, as מסכת דפסחא, מס' דבשלח etc. Each Masechta is subdivided into chapters (Parashoth), the total number of which is 77.

Passages from the Mechilta are occasionally quoted in the Talmud, without however mentioning the name of that book. In the post-Talmudic literature it is mentioned as מכילתא דר' ישמעאל. Some were therefore inclined to regard R. Ishmael

---

Tosephta with notes and text corrections, of which the first volume is out, Wilna 1891.

Critical researches on the Tosephta are found in Frankl's Darke Hamishna pp. 304-307 and in I. H. Weiss', Dor Dor etc. II pp. 217-225; also in I. H. Duenner's Wesen and Ursprung der Tosephta, Amsterdam 1874.

(flourishing in the beginning of the second century) as its author; but against this opinion speaks the circumstance that the names of teachers living much later are mentioned in the book. Modern scholars hold that the Mechilta was originally a collection of teachings of R. Ishmael and his school. This collection having been brought from Palestine to Babylon, received there many interpolations. In the form we possess it, the book belongs to the fourth or fifth century.[1]

c. THE SIPHRA.

§ 9.

The Siphra (ספרא i. e. the book), also called Torath Cohanim, is a collection of traditional interpretations of the whole book of Leviticus, introduced by an exposition of R. Ishmael's thirteen hermeneutic rules.

Different from the Mechilta, the style of the Siphra is generally more argumentative, defending the traditional interpretations against possible objections. Both names of this book are mentioned, and numerous passages thereof are quoted, in the Talmud. The authorship of its essential parts is there ascribed to R. Jehuda b. Ilai, a disciple of R. Akiba (סתם ספרא ר' יהודה Sanhed. 86), and according to this statement the collection originated in Palestine in the middle of the second century. But in the course of time it was considerably increased by additions from the hands of later teachers, especially those belonging to the school of Abba Areca and is therefore also called ספרא דבי רב.[2]

As before us, the book has two different divisions which are

---

[1] The latest editions of the Mechilta with critical introductions and annotations were published by I. H. Weiss (Vienna 1885) and by M. Friedmann (Vienna 1870.)

Critical researches on the Mechilta are also found in Frankel's Monatschrift 1853, pp. 388 398, and Geiger's *Urschrift* pp. 140, 152 sqq. and in his Zeitung 1871 pp. 8-28. I. H. Weiss Dor Dor II, pp. 225-231.

[2] The latest edition of the Siphra with the commentary of R. Abraham b. David of Posquieres (Rabed) and annotations by I H. Weiss was published Vienna 1862.

As to critical researches on the Siphra, see Frankel, Monatsschrift 1854 and I. H. Weiss, in his Introduction to the Siphra, and in his Dor Dor II p. 231-236.

rather bewildering, one according to the customary Sabbath lessons, Parashoth, subdivided into Perakim; the other according to sections named after their main contents and subdivided into chapters termed Parasha or Parashata.

d. The Siphre.

§ 10.

The Siphre, or, as its fuller title reads, ספרי דבי רב (the books of the school of Rab), comprises the traditional interpretations of the book of Numbers, beginning with chapter V, and of the whole book of Deuteronomy. The author of the Siphre on Numbers was evidently not the same as the author of that on the last book of the Pentateuch. The style of the former, being more argumentative and discoursive, often resembles that of the Siphra, while Siphre on Deuteronomy is generally brief, bearing more resemblance to the Mechilta. The passages anonymously given in the Siphre are ascribed in the Talmud to R. Simon b. Jochai, one of the distinguished disciples of R. Akiba (סתם ספרי ר' שמעון Sanhedrin 86a); but, as, on the one hand, many of those passages can be traced back to the school of R. Ishmael, and, on the other hand, teachers of a much later period are mentioned therein, it is the opinion of modern scholars that the Siphre before us is a composite of two different works which, like the Siphra, received its present shape in the Babylonian shools founded by Abba Areca.

The Siphre is divided into sections corresponding to those of the Sabbath lessons and subdivided into paragraphs, termed Piskoth. That on Numbers has 161, and that on Deuteronomy 357 Piskoth.[1]

e. Baraitha.

§ 11.

Besides the Tosephta, the Mechilta, the Siphra and the Siphre just described, other collections of a similar character existed during the Talmudical period. In the course of time

[1] The latest edition of the Siphre with annotations is that of M. Friedmann, Vienna 1864.

they perished, but many hundred fragmentary passages thereof are quoted in all parts of the Palestinian and Babylonian Gemara. Such a passage quoted from those lost collections as well, as from the Tosephta, Mechilta, Siphra and Siphre was termed *Baraitha* (ברייתא), or *Mathnitha Baraitha*, meaning an *extraneous* Mishna. This term was used in order to distinguish those passages from passages, in *our Mishna*, that is, the authorized Mishna of R. Jehuda Hanasi, compared with which they had but a subordinate value. The Baraithoth are often found to be conflicting with each other or with the authorized Mishna, and in this case the Gemara usually displays, great ingenuity and subtility in the attempt to reconcile them. In some instances, however, one or the other Baraitha is declared to be spurious.[1]

---

1 Some critical researches on the Baraitha are found in Frankel's Darke Hamishna p. 311-313, and in I. H. Weiss, Dor Dor II p. 239-244.

CHAPTER III

THE AUTHORITIES OF THE MISHNA

§ 12.

The authorities mentioned in the Mishna and Baraitha as having transmitted and developed the oral law belong to three different periods, namely:

1. The period of *Sopherim*
2. The period of *Zugoth*, and
3. The period of *Tanaim.*

a. Sopherim or scribes were the learned men who succeeded Ezra during a period of about two hundred years. To them many institutions and extensions of the Mosaic law are ascribed תקנות סופרים, דברי סופרים. The Sopherim are also called collectively אנשי כנסת הגדולה the Men of the Great Synod. According to tradition, this synod consisted of 120 members, but we have no record of their names with the exception of *Ezra*, its founder, and of *Simon the Just* (the high priest Simon I, between 310-292, or his grandson Simon II, between 220-202 B. C.) who is said to have been one of the last members of the Great Synod.

Antigonos of Sochô, a disciple of Simon the Just, was the connecting link between this and the following period.

b. The word *Zugoth* (זוגות), meaning the pairs (duumviri), is the appellation of the leading teachers from Jose ben Joezer till Hillel, of whom always two, at the same time, stood at the head of the Sanhedrin, one as president (Nasi), and the other as vice-president (Ab beth din).

The succession of these Zugoth was:

1. *Jose ben Joezer* and *Jose ben Jochanan*, flourishing at the time of the Maccabean wars of independence.
2. *Joshua b. Perachia* and *Nitai of Arbela*, flourishing at the time of John Hyrcan.

3. *Juda b. Tabai* and *Simon b. Shetach*, flourishing at the time of Alexander Janai and queen Salome.
4. *Shemaiah* and *Abtalion*, flourishing at the time of Hyrcan II.
5. *Hillel* and *Shamai*, flourishing at the time of king Herod.

c. With the disciples of Hillel and Shamai begins the period of *Tanaim*, which lasted about 210 years (from 10 to 220 Ch. Era). With the beginning of this period the title *Rabbi* (my teacher) for the ordained teachers, and the title *Rabban* (our teacher) for the president of the Sanhedrin came in use.

In the Mishna, the term Tana (תנא), meaning a teacher of the oral law, does not yet occur. Those teachers are there signified by generally adding the title of *Rabbi* to their names, or by calling them collectively חכמים the Sages, while the authorities of the preceding period are occasionally designated זקנים הראשונים the former elders. It is first in the Gemara that the term *Tana* (תנא) is applied to a teacher mentioned in the Mishna and Baraitha, in contradistinction to the *Amoraim*, expounders of the Mishna, as the teachers after R. Jehuda Hanasi are called.

The period of the Tanaim is generally divided into 5 or 6 minor sections or generations. The purpose of this division is to show which teachers developed their principal activity contemporaneously, though the actual lifetime of some of them extended to more than one generation.

The following chronological tables contain the names only of the more prominent teachers of each generation. Every table is followed by short biographical sketches of the teachers mentioned therein.[1]

---

[1] Fuller characteristics of the lives and teachings of the principal Tanaim are given in the following works:

Graetz, History of the Jews, Vol. IV.

Z. Frankel, Darke Hamishna.

I. H. Weiss, Zur Geschichte der juedischen Tradition, Vol. I. and II.

Jacob Bruell, Mebo Hamishna, Vol. I.

J. Hamburger, Real Encyclopaedie, Vol. II. Die Talmudischen Artikel.

M. Braunschweiger, Die Lehrer der Mishnah.

THE FIRST GENERATION OF TANAIM

§ 13.

The principal Tanaim of the first generation, which lasted about seventy years [1], from 10 to 80, C. E., are:

1. The School of Shamai, and the School of Hillel
2. Akabia ben Mahalalel.
3. Rabban Gamaliel the Elder.
4. Rabbi Chanina, Chief of the Priests.
5. R. Simon ben Gamaliel.
6. R. Jochanan ben Zaccai.

Characteristics and Biographical Sketches.

1. *The School of Shamai* and *the School of Hillel* were founded by the disciples of the great teachers whose names they bear. Following the principles of their masters, they differed widely in their opinions on many legal questions; the School of Shamai, in general, taking a rigorous, and the school of Hillel a more lenient view of the question. In their frequent controversies the School of Shamai, having been founded already during the life time of Hillel, is always mentioned first. Of individual teachers belonging to either of these two schools only a very few are occasionally mentioned by name. Both schools existed during the whole period of the first generation, and the antagonism of their followers extended even to the middle of the subsequent generation.

2. *Akabia ben Mahalalel.* Of this teacher who flourished shortly after Hillel only a few opinions and traditions are recorded. According to what is related of him in Mishna Eduyoth V, 6. 7, he was a noble character with unyielding principles.

3. *Rabban Gamaliel the Elder.* He was a son of R. Simon, and grandson of Hillel whom he succeeded in the office of Nasi. Many important ordinances (תקנות) of the Rabbinical law are ascribed to him He died eighteen years before the destruction of Jerusalem. The epithet "the Elder" generally added to his name, is to distinguish him

---

[1] This comparatively great length of the first generation is easily explained by the circumstance, that it refers to the duration of the prevailing Schools of Shamai and Hillel, and not, as in the subsequent generations, to that of the activity of a single leading teacher.

from his grandson Gamaliel of Jabne, who flourished in the following generation.

4. *Rabbi Chanina, Chief of the Priests,* or the proxy of the high-priest. He as well as "the court of Priests" ב"ד של כהנים are incidentally mentioned in the Mishna in connection with laws concerning the sacrifices and the temple service.

5. *R. Simon ben Gamaliel.* He was the son and successor of Rabban Gamaliel the Elder, and was executed by the Romans in the time of the destruction of Jerusalem. Belonging to the school of Hillel, his individual opinions in questions of law are but rarely recorded in the Mishna. He must not be confounded with his grandson who had the same name and belonged to the fourth generation of Tanaim.

6. *R. Jochanan b. Zaccai.* This distinguished teacher was one of the youngest disciples of Hillel, occupied a high position already before the destruction of Jerusalem, and afterwards became the founder and head of the celebrated academy of Jabne (Jamnia).

Of other authorities belonging to the first generation of Tanaim, mention must be made of *Admon, Chanan* and *Nachum the Mede,* who were civil judges before the time of the destruction of Jerusalem and whose legal opinions are occasionally recorded in the Mishna.

THE SECOND GENERATION OF TANAIM.

§ 14.

This generation lasted about forty years, from 80 to 120. The principal Tanaim belonging to it are:

1. Rabban Gamaliel II (of Jabne).
2. Rabbi Zadok.
3. R. Dosa (b. Harchinas).
4. R. Eliezer b. Jacob.
5. R. Eliezer (b. Hyrcanos).
6. R. Joshua (b. Chanania).
7. R. Elazar b. Azaria.
8. R. Juda b. Bathyra.

Characteristics and Biographical Sketches.

1. *Rabban Gamaliel II.* He was a grandson of Gamaliel the Elder; after the death of R. Jochanan b. Zaccai he became president of the

academy of Jabne,and like his ancestors, he bore the title Nasi (Prince); with the Romans, Patriarch. In order to distinguish him from his grandfather, he received the surname *Gamaliel of Jabne*, or the Second.

2. *R. Zadok.* Of him it is related that he, in anticipation of the destruction of the Temple, fasted for forty successive years. He then removed to Jabne where he as well as his son, R. Eliezer b. Zadok, belonged to the distinguished teachers.

3. *R. Dosa b. Harchinas* belonged to the school of Hillel, and removed with R. Jochanan b. Zaccai from Jerusalem to Jabne where he reached a very old age. He stood in such high esteem that his most distinguished colleagues appealed to his opinion in doubtful cases.

4. *R. Eliezer b. Jacob* was head of a school, and in possession of traditions concerning the structure and interior arrangements of the temple. He is also mentioned with commendation as to his method of instruction which was "concise and clear" (קב ונקי). There was also another Tana by a similar name who flourished in the fourth generation.

5. *R. Eliezer b. Hyrkanos,*in the Mishna called simply R. Eliezer, was one of the most distinguished disciples of R. Jochanan b. Zaccai who characterized him as "the lime cemented cistern that does not lose a drop". He was a faithful conservator of handed-down decisions and opposed to their slightest modification and to any new deductions to be made therefrom. His school was in Lydda, in South Judea. Though formerly a disciple of the Hillelites, he inclined to the views of the Shamaites and consequently came in conflict with his colleagues. Being persistent in his opinion, and conforming to it even in practice, he was excommunicated by his own brother-in-law, the patriarch Gamaliel II.

6. *R. Joshua b. Chanania,* in general called simply R. Joshua, was likewise one of the favored disciples of R. Jochanan b. Zaccai. Shortly before the destruction of the Temple he left Jerusalem with his teacher, after whose death he founded a separate school in *Bekiin.* As member of the Sanhedrin in Jabne, he participated conspicuously in its deliberations and debates. His discussions were mostly with *R. Eliezer* to whose unyielding conservatism he formed a striking contrast, as he represented the more rational and conciliatory element of that generation, and combined with great learning the amiable virtues

of gentleness, modesty and placability which characterized the Hillelites. As he, on several occasions, was humiliated by the Nasi Gamaliel II with whom he differed on some questions, the members of the Sanhedrin resented this insult of their esteemed colleague by deposing the offender from his dignity and electing another president. It was only through the interference of the appeased R. Joshua that R. Gamaliel, who apologized for his conduct, was again restored to his office.

7. *R. Elazar b. Azaria* descended from a noble family whose pedigree was traced up to Ezra the Scribe. Already while a young man, he enjoyed such a reputation for his great learning that he was made president of the academy at Jabne in place of the deposed R. Gamaliel. When the latter was reinstated, R. Elazar was appointed as vice-president. His controversies were mostly with R. Joshua, R. Tarphon, R. Ishmael and R. Akiba. On account of the noble virtues which he combined with his great learning he was compared to "a vessel filled with aromatic spices", and R. Joshua said of him: "a generation having a man like R. Elazar b. Azaria, is not orphaned".

8. *R. Juda b. Bathyra* had a school in *Nisibis* (in Assyria) already at the time when the temple of Jerusalem was still in existence. He was probably a descendant of the family Bene Bathyra who were leaders of the Sanhedrin under king Herod, and who resigned that office in favor of Hillel. Several other Tanaim had the same family name, as R. Joshua b. Bathyra, R. Simon b. Bathyra and one called simply Ben Bathyra.

Of other teachers belonging to the second generation we have yet to mention *R. Nechunia b. Hakana* who was the teacher of R. Ishmael, and *Nachum of Gimzo* who introduced the hermeneutic rule of רבוי ומעוט (extension and limitation) which was later further developed by his great disciple R. Akiba.

THE THIRD GENERATION OF TANAIM

§ 15.

Several Teachers of the third generation, which lasted from the year 120 till about 139, flourished already in the preceding one. The principal teachers are:

1. R. Tarphon.
2. R. Ishmael.
3. R. Akiba.
4. R. Jochanan b. Nuri.
5. R. Jose the Galilean.
6. R. Simon b. Nanos.
7. R. Juda b. Baba.
8. R. Jochanan b. Broka.

Characteristics and Biographical Sketches.

1. *R. Tarphon*, or Tryphon, of Lydda. He is said to have been inclined to the views of the School of Shamai. On account of his great learning he was called "the teacher of Israel"; besides, he was praised for his great charitable works. His legal discussions were mostly with his colleague R. Akiba.

2. *R. Ishmael* (b. Elisha) was probably a grandson of the high priest Ishmael b. Elisha who was condemned to death by Titus together with the patriarch Simon b. Gamaliel I. When still a boy, he was made a captive and brought to Rome, where R. Joshua who happened to come there on a mission, redeemed him at a high ransom and brought him back to Palestine. R. Nechunia b. Hakana is mentioned as one of his principal teachers. When grown to manhood, he became a member of the Sanhedrin and was highly revered by his colleagues. He is named among those who emigrated with the Sanhedrin from *Jabne* to *Usha*. His residence was in South Judea in a place called Kephar Aziz. His academical controversies were mostly with R. Akiba to whose artificial methods of interpreting the law he was strongly opposed, on the principle that the Thora, being composed in the usual language of man, must be interpreted in a plain and rational way. As guiding rules of interpretation he accepted only the seven logical rules which had been laid down by Hillel, which he however,

by some modifications and subdivisions, enlarged to thirteen. Of these thirteen rules we shall treat in the second part of this work. A separate school which he founded was continued after his death by his disciples and was known by the name of "Be R. Ishmael". Of the book *Mechilta* which is ascribed to R. Ishmael and his school we have spoken above (p. 18).

3. *R. Akiba* (b. Joseph) was the most prominent among the Tanaim. He is said to have descended from a proselyte family and to have been altogether illiterate up to the age of his manhood. Filled with the desire to acquire the knowledge of the law, he entered a school and attended the lectures of the distinguished teachers of that time, especially of R. Eliezer b. Hyrkanos, R. Joshua b. Chanania, and of Nachum of Gimzo. Subsequently he founded a school in B'ne Brak, near Jabne, and became a member of the Sanhedrin in the last mentioned city. Through his keen intellect, his vast learning and his energetic activity he wielded a great influence in developing and diffusing the traditional law. He arranged the accumulated material of that law in a proper system and methodical order, and enriched its substance with many valuable deductions of his own. His methodical arrangement and division of that material was completed by his disciple R. Meir, and later on became the groundwork of the Mishna compiled by R. Jehuda Hanasi. Besides, he introduced a new method of interpreting the Scriptures which enabled him to find a biblical basis for almost every provision of the oral law. This ingenious method, which will be described in the II Part of this book, was admired by his contemporaries, and notwithstanding the opposition of some of his colleagues, generally adopted in addition to the 13 hermeneutic rules of R. Ishmael. R. Akiba's legal opinions are very frequently recorded in all parts of the Mishna and in the kindred works. His academical discussions are mostly with his former teachers R. Eliezer, R. Joshua and with his colleagues R. Tarphon, R. Jochanan b, Nuri, R. Jose the Galilean and others.

R. Akiba died a martyr to religion and patriotism. Having been a stout supporter of the cause of Bar Cochba, he was cruelly executed by the Romans for publicly teaching the Law contrary to the edict of the emperor Hadrian.

4. *R. Jochanan b. Nuri* was a colleague of R. Akiba with whom he frequently differed on questions of the law. In his youth he seems to have been a disciple of R. Gamaliel II. for whose memory he always

retained a warm veneration. He presided over a college in Beth Shearim, a place near Sepphoris in Galilee.

5. *R. Jose the Galilean* was a very distinguished teacher. Of his youth and education nothing is known. At his first appearance in the Sanhedrin of Jabne, he participated in a debate with R. Tarphon and with R. Akiba and displayed such great learning and sagacity that he attracted general attention. From this debate his reputation as a teacher was established. He was an authority especially in the laws concerning the sacrifices and the temple service. His discussions were mostly with R. Akiba, R. Tarphon and R. Elazar b. Azariah. Of his domestic life it is related that he had the bad fortune of having an ill-tempered wife, who treated him so meanly that he was compelled to divorce her, but learning that she in her second marriage lived in great misery, he generously provided her and her husband with all the necessaries of life. One of his sons, R. Eleazar b. R. Jose the Galilean, became a distinguished teacher in the following generation and established the thirty two hermeneutic rules of the Agada.

6. *R. Simon b. Nanos*, also called simply Ben Nanos, was a great authority especially in the civil law, so that R. Ishmael recommended to all law students to attend the lectures of this profound teacher. His legal controversies were mostly with R. Ishmael and R. Akiba.

7. *R. Judah b. Baba*, who on account of his piety was called the *Chasid*, is noteworthy not only as a distinguished teacher but also as a martyr to Judaism. Contrary to the Hadrianic edict which, under extreme penalty, prohibited the ordination of teachers, he ordained seven disciples of R. Akiba as Rabbis, and for this act was stabbed to death by the Roman soldiers.

8. *R. Jochanan b. Broka* was an authority especially in the civil law. Also his son R. Ishmael was a distinguished teacher who flourished in the following generation. Of other teachers belonging to this generation the following are to be mentioned. *R. Elazar* (or Eliezer) of *Modin*, an authority in Agada interpretation. *R. Mathia b. Charash* who, formerly a disciple of R. Eliezer b. Hyrkanos, founded a school in the city of Rome and thus was the first teacher who transplanted the knowledge of the rabbinical law from Asia to Europe; further, several of R. Akiba's earlier disciples, especially (Simon) *Ben Zoma* and

(Simon) *Ben Azai*, both of whom, besides being distinguished in the law, were also deeply engaged in the theosophic speculations of those times.

THE FOURTH GENERATION OF TANAIM.

§ 16.

This generation extended from the death of R. Akiba to the death of the patriarch R. Simon b. Gamaliel II, from the year 139 to about 165. Almost all leading teachers of this generation belong to the latter disciples of R. Akiba.

1. R. Meir.
2. R. Jehuda (ben Ilai).
3. R. Jose (ben Chalafta).
4. R. Simon (b. Jochai).
5. R. Elazar (b. Shamua).
6. R. Jochanan the Sandelar.
7. R. Elazar b. Jacob.
8. R. Nehemia.
9. R. Joshua b. Korcha.
10. R. Simon b. Gamaliel.

Characteristics and Biographical Sketches.

1. *R. Meir*, the most prominent among the numerous disciples of R. Akiba, was a native of Asia Minor and gained a subsistence as a skilfull copyist of sacred Scripture. At first, he entered the academy of R. Akiba, but finding himself not sufficiently prepared to grasp the lectures of this great teacher, he attended, for some time, the school of R. Ishmael, where he acquired an extensive knowledge of the law. Returning then to R. Akiba and becoming his constant and favored disciple, he developed great dialectical powers. R. Akiba soon recognized his worth and preferred him to other disciples by ordaining him at an early date. This ordination was later renewed by R. Judah b. Baba. On account of the Hadrianic persecutions, R. Meir had to flee from Judea, but after the repeal of those edicts, he returned and joined his colleagues in re-establishing the Sanhedrin in the city of Usha, in Galilee. His academy was in Emmaus, near Tiberias, and for a time also in Ardiscus near Damascus where a large

circle of disciples gathered around him. Under the patriarch R. Simon b. Gamaliel II he occupied the dignity of a *Chacham* (advising Sage), in which office he was charged with the duty of preparing the subjects to be discussed in tne Sanhedrin. A conflict which arose between him and the patriarch seems to have induced him to leave Palestine and return to his native country, Asia Minor, where he died. R. Meir's legal opinions are mentioned almost in every Masechta of the Mishna and Baraitha. His greatest merit was that he continued the labors of R. Akiba in arranging the rich material of the oral law according to subjects, and in this way prepared the great Mishna compilation of R. Judah Hanasi. Besides being one of the most distingued teachers of the law, he was also a very popular lecturer (Agadist) who used to illustrate his lectures by interesting fables and parables. Of his domestic life it is known that he was married to Beruria the learned daughter of the celebrated teacher and martyr R. Chananiah b. Teradyon. The pious resignation which he and his noble wife exhibited at the sudden death of their two promising sons has been immortalized by a popular legend in the Midrash.

2. R. *Jehuda b. Ilai* is generally called in the Mishna simply R. Jehuda. After having received instruction in the law from his father who had been a disciple of R. Eliezer b. Hyrkanos, he attended the lectures of R. Tarphon and became then one of the distinguished disciples of R. Akiba. On account of his great eloquence he is called ראש המדברים "The first among the speakers". Also his piety, modesty and prudence are highly praised. He gained a modest subsistence by a mechanical trade, in accordance with his favored maxims: "Labor honors man", and "He who does not teach his son a trade, teaches him, as it were, robbery". Having been one of the seven disciples who after the death of R. Akiba were ordained by R. Juda b. Baba contrary to the Hadrianic edict, he had to flee. After three years he returned with his colleagues to Usha and became one of the prominent members of the resuscitated Sanhedrin. The patriarch R. Simon ben Gamaliel honored him greatly, and appointed him as one of his advisers. As expounder of the law he was a great authority, and is very often quoted in all parts of the Mishna and Baraitha. His legal opinions generally prevail, when differing from those of his colleagues R. Meir and R. Simon. To him is also ascribed the authorship of the essential

part of the Siphra. (See above p. 19). The Agada of the Talmud records many of his beautiful sayings which characterize him not only as a noble-hearted teacher, but also as a sound and clear-headed interpreter of Scriptures. He, for instance, denied the literal meaning of the resurrection of the dead bones spoken of in Ezekiel ch. XXXVII, but declared it to be merely a poetical figure for Israel's rejuvenation (Talm Sanhedrin 72 b.).

R. Jehuda had two learned sons who flourished as teachers in the following generation.

3. *R. Jose b. Chalafta*, in the Mishna called simply R. Jose, was from *Sepphoris* where already his learned father had established a school. Though by trade a tanner, he became one of the most distinguished teachers of his time. He was a disciple of R. Akiba and of R. Tarphon. Like his colleagues he was ordained by R. Juda b. Baba and, on this account, had to flee to the south of Palestine, whence he later on returned with them to Usha. For having kept silent, when in his presence R. Simon made a slighting remark against the Roman government, he was banished to Asia Minor. When permitted to return, he settled in his native city Sepphoris where he died in a high age. Besides being a great authority in the law, whose opinions prevail against those of his colleagues R. Meir, R. Jehuda and R. Simon, he was an historian to whom the authorship of the chronological book *Seder Olam* is ascribed.

4. *R. Simon b. Jochai* from Galilee, in the Mishna called simply R. Simon, was likewise one of the most distinguished disciples of R. Akiba whose lectures he attended during thirteen years. "Be satisfied that I and thy creator know thy powers", were the words with which this teacher comforted him, when he felt somewhat slighted on account of a certain preference given to his younger colleague R. Meir. He shared the fate of his colleagues in being compelled to flee after ordination. Afterwards, he joined them at the new seat of the Sanhedrin in Usha. On a certain occasion he gave vent to his bitter feeling against the Romans, which was reported to the Roman governor who condemned him to death. He, however, escaped this fate by concealing himself in a cave where he is said to have remained for several years together with his son, engaged in the study of the law, and subsisting on the fruit of the carob-trees which abounded there in the neighborhood. In the meantime political affairs had taken a

favorable turn so that he had no longer to fear any persecution; he left his hiding place and reopened his academy at *Tekoa*, in Galilee, where a circle of disciples gathered around him. He survived all his colleagues, and in his old age was delegated to Rome, where he succeeded in obtaining from the emperor (Marcus Aurelius) the repeal of some edicts against the Jewish religion.

In the interpretation of the law, R. Simon departed from the method of his teacher R. Akiba, as he inclined to the view of R. Ishmael that "the Thora speaks the common language of man", and consequently regarded logical reasoning as the proper starting point for legal deductions, instead of pleonastic words, syllables and letters. In accordance with this sound principle, he tried to investigate the evident motive of different biblical laws, and to make conclusions therefrom for their proper application. [1] In regard to treating and arranging the oral law, however, he followed the method of R. Akiba in subsuming various provisions under guiding rules and principles. R. Simon is regarded as the author of the *Siphre*, though that work in its present shape shows many additions by the hands of later authorities. (See above p. 20).

5. *R. Elazar b. Shamua*, in the Mishna simply *R. Elazar*, was among those of R. Akiba's disciples who in consequence of the Hadrian edicts went to the South, whence he went to Nisibis. He does not, however, appear to have joined his colleagues when they gathered again at Usha. He is regarded as a great authority in the law. The place of his academy is not known, but it is stated that his school was always overcrowded by disciples eager to hear his learned lectures. Among his disciples was also the later patriarch R. Jehuda. On a journey, he visited his former colleague R. Meir at Ardiscos. in Asia Minor, and with him had discussions on important questions of the law which are recorded in the Mishna and Baraitha.

6. *R. Jochanan the Sandelar* had this surname probably from his trade in sandals. Born in Alexandria in Egypt, he came to Palestine to attend the lectures of R. Akiba, and was so faithful a disciple that he visited this teacher even in prison, in order to receive instruction from him. His legal opinions are occasionaly recorded in the Mishna as well as in the Tosephta and Baraitha.

---

[1] See Talm. B. Metzia 115 a and Sanhedrin 21 a.

7. *R. Elazar* (or Eliezer) *b. Jacob* was a disciple of R. Akiba and later a member of the Sanhedrin in Usha. This teacher must not be confounded with a former teacher by that name who flourished in the second generation (See above p. 26).

8. *R. Nechemia* belonged to the last disciples of R. Akiba and was an authority especially in the sacrificial law and in the laws concerning levitical purification. His controversies are mostly with R. Juda b. Ilai. He is said to have compiled a Mishna-collection which was embodied in the Tosephta.

9. *R. Joshua b. Korcha* is supposed by some to have been a son of R. Akiba who, on one occasion, is called by such a surname (meaning the bald head); but this supposition is very improbable, for it would be strange that the son of so illustrious a man should not rather have been called by his father's proper name, and that he should never have alluded to his celebrated parent or to any of his teachings. [1]

R. Joshua b. K. belonged to the authorities of this generation, though only a few of his opinions are recorded in the Mishna.

10. *R. Simon b. Gamaliel* was the son and successor of the patriarch Gamaliel II of Jabne. In his youth, he witnessed the fall of Bethar, and escaped the threatened arrest by flight. After the death of the emperor Hadrian, he returned to Jabne where he in connection with some teachers, reopened an academy, and assumed the hereditary dignity of a patriarch. As the returning disciples of R. Akiba, who were the leading teachers of that generation, preferred Usha as the seat of the new Sanhedrin, R. Simon was obliged to transfer his academy to that city, and appointed R. Nathan as Ab Beth-din (vice-president) and R. Meir as Chacham (advising sage, or speaker). Both of these two officers had to retire however, when found planning his deposal on account of some marks of distinction introduced in order to raise the patriachal dignity. He did not enjoy the privilege of his predecessors to be titled *Rabban* (our teacher), but like the other teachers, he was simply called Rabbi (my teacher) [1], probably because many of his contemporaries were

[1] That R. Akiba had a son by the name of R. Joshua is stated in a Baraitha (Pesachim 112a and Shebuoth 6a); but the identity of this son with R. Joshua b. Korcha is conclusively disproved by the Tosaphist Rabenu Tam in his remarks on Sabbath 150a and B Bathra 113a.

[1] There are, however, some passages in the Mishna and Gemara in which he is called Rabban, as Gittin 74a; B. Bathra 113a; Arachin 28a.

superior to him in learning. Still, his legal opinions, which are frequently quoted in the Mishna and Baraitha, give evidence that he was a man of considerable learning and of sound and clear judgment as well as of noble principles. He introduced several legal provisions for the protection of the rights of women and slaves and for the general welfare of the community. All his opinions expressed in the Mishna, with the exception of only three cases, are regarded by later teachers as authoritative (Halacha). His discussions recorded in the Mishna and Baraitha are mostly held with his celebrated son R. Jehuda Hanasi. R. Simon b. Gamaliel appears to have been acquainted also with the Greek language and sciences.

Of other authorities belonging to this generation, we have to mention: *Abba Saul, R. Elazar b.Zadok.* and especially *R. Ishmael the son of R. Jochanan b. Broka.*

Apart from the great circle of teachers mentioned above, the disciples of R. Ishmael b. Elisha formed a school in the extreme South of Judea (Darom) where they continued the methods of their teacher. Of this separate school, called *Debe R. Ishmael*, only two members are mentioned by name: *R. Josiah and R. Jonathan.*

THE FIFTH GENERATION OF TANAIM.

§ 17.

This generation extends from the death of R. Simon b. Gamaliel II to the death of R. Jehuda Hanasi (from 165 to about 200.)

The following are the most prominent teachers of this generation.

1. R. Nathan (the Babylonian).
2. Symmachos.
3. R. Jehuda Hanasi (the patriarch), called simply Rabbi.
4. R. Jose b. Juda.
5. R. Elazar b. Simon.
6. R. Simon b. Elazar.

Characteristics and Biographical Sketches.

1. *R. Nathan* was the son of one of the exilarchs in Babylon, and probably received his education in his native country. For some

unknown reasons he emigrated to Judea, and on account of his great learning he was appointed by the patriarch R. Simon b. Gamaliel to the dignity of Ab-Beth-din (chief Justice or vice-president) in the Sanhedrin of Usha. He had to retire from this office because of his and R. Meir's dissension with the patriarch, but was soon reinstated and became reconciled with the Synhedrial president who held him in high esteem. Also the succeeding patriarch R. Jehuda, with whom he had many discussions on questions of the law, speaks of him with great respect. R.Nathan was not only an authorityin the rabbinical law, especially in jurisprudence,but appears also to have been well versed in mathematics, astronomy and other sciences. To him is ascribed the authorship of Aboth de R. Nathan, which is a kind of Tosephta to Pirke Aboth.

2. *Symmachos* was a prominent disciple of R. Meir and distinguished for his great dialectical powers. After the death of his teacher, he as well as other disciples of R. Meir were excluded from the academy of R. Jehuda Hanasi, as they were charged of indulging in sophistical disputations in order to display their dialectical sagacity, instead of seeking after truth. Nevertheless the Mishna as well as the Tosephta makes mention of the opinions of Symmachos. His renown lay in the rabbinical jurisprudence in which he laid down certain principles often referred to in the Talmud.

3. *R. Jehuda (Juda) Hanasi,* by way of eminence simply called *Rabbi,* was a son of the patriarch R. Simon b. Gamaliel II, and is said to have been born on the same day when R. Akiba was executed. His principal teachers were R. Simon b. Jochai and R. Elazar b. Shamua under whose guidance his intellectual capacity and splendid talents early developed. Beside his immense knowledge of the whole range of the traditional law, he had a liberal education in secular branches and was especially acquainted with the Greek language which he preferred to the Syriac, the popular language of Palestine at that time. After the death of his father he succeeded him in the dignity of patriarch, and became the chief authority eclipsing all other teachers of that generation. Though blessed with great riches, he preferred to live in a simple style and applied his wealth to the maintenance of his numerous pupils and to charitable works. The seat of his academy was first at Beth-Shearim, afterward at Sepphoris and also at Tiberias. Among his most distinguished disciples were: R. Chiya; (Simon) bar Kappara;

Levi bar Sissi; R. Abba Areca, later called Rab; Mar Samuel, and many others. He is said to have been in a friendly relation with one of the Roman emperors, either Marcus Aurelius or, more probably, Lucius Verus Antoninus. By virtue of his authority R. Jehuda abolished several customs and ceremonies which though sanctified by age had become impracticable through the change of times and circumstances. His most meritorious work by which he erected for himself a monument of enduring fame was the completion of the Mishna compilation which henceforth became the authoritative code of the traditional law and superseded all similar compilations made by former teachers.

4. *R. Jose ben Juda* (b. Ilai) belonged to the great teachers of that generation and was a friend of R. Jehuda Hanasi. His legal opinions are frequently recorded in the Mishna as well as in the Tosephta.

5. *R. Elazar b. Simon* (b. Jochai) was a disciple of R. Simon b. Gamaliel and of R. Joshua b. Korcha. Although an authority in the rabbinical law to whom even the patriarch sometimes yielded, he incurred the severest censure of his colleagues for having, on a certain occasion, lent his assistance to the Romans in persecuting some Jewish freebooters.

6. *R. Simon b. Elazar* (probably E. b. Shamua) was a disciple of R. Meir whose opinions he often quotes. He established several important principles, especially in the civil law.

THE SIXTH GENERATION OF TANAIM

§ 18.

To this generation belong the younger contemporaries and disciples of R. Juda Hanasi. They are not mentioned in the Mishna, but in the Tosephta and Baraitha, and are therefore termed semi-Tanaim, who form a connecting link between the period of Tanaim and that of the Amoraim. Their names are:

1. Plimo.
2. Ise b. Juda.
3. R. Elazar b. Jose.
4. R. Ishmael bar Jose.
5. R. Juda b. Lakish.
6. R. Chiya.
7. R. Acha.
8. R. Abba (Areca).

The most prominent among these semi-Tanaim were R. Chiya and R. Abba (Areca).

1. *R. Chiya* (bar Abba) the elder, which epithet is to distinguish him from a later Amora by the same mame, was a Babylonian who came at an already advanced age to Palestine where he became the most distinguished disciple and friend of R. Jehuda Hanasi. He and his disciple R. Oshaya (or Hoshaya) are regarded as the principal authors or compilers of the Tosephta (see above p. 17).

2. *R. Abba* (Areca) a nephew of R. Chiya was likewise a Babylonian and a disciple of R. Jehuda Hanasi, after whose death he returned to his native country where, under the historical name of Rab, he became the principal Amora. (See the following chapter).

Of other distinguished teachers flourishing in this generation and in the beginning of the period of the Amoraim we have to mention especially *R. Janai* (the elder) and *R. Jonathan* (the elder). The former lived in Sepphoris and was one of the teachers of R. Jochanan bar Naphachi, the greatest among the Palestinian Amoraim.

CHAPTER IV

THE EXPOUNDERS OF THE MISHNA

§ 19.

As the Mishna compilation of R. Jehuda Hanasi became the authoritative code of the oral Law, the activity of the teachers was principally devoted to expounding this code. This was done as well in the academies of *Tiberias*, *Sepphoris*, *Caesarea* in Palestine, as in those of *Nahardea*, *Sura*, and later of *Pumbaditha* and some other seats of learning in Babylonia. The main object of the lectures and discussions in those academies was to interpret the often very brief and concise expression of the Mishna, to investigate its reasons and sources, to reconcile seeming contradictions, to compare its canons with those of the Baraithoth, and to apply its decisions and established principles to new cases not yet provided for. The teachers who were engaged in this work which finally became embodied in the Gemara, are called *Amoraim*, meaning speakers, interpreters, expounders. [1] They were not as independent in their legal opinions and decisions as their predecessors, the Tanaim and semi-Tanaim, as they had not the authority to contradict Halachoth and principles accepted in the Mishna or Baraitha. The Palestinian Amoraim having generally been ordained by the Nasi had the

---

[1] In a more restricted meaning the term *Amora*(from אמר to say, to speak) signifies the same as *Methurgeman* (מתורגמן the interpreter), that is the officer in the academies who, standing at the side of the lecturer or presiding teacher, had to announce loudly and explain to the large assembly what the teacher just expressed briefly and in a low voice.

The term *Tana*, which generally applies only to the teachers mentioned in the Mishna and Baraitha, is in the period of Amoraim sometimes used also to signify one whose special business it was to recite the memorized Baraithoth to the expounding teachers. In this sense the term is to be understood in the phrase: תני תנא קמיה דפלוני Betza 29b. and often.

title of *Rabbi*, while the Babylonian teachers of that period had only the title of *Rab* or of *Mar*.

The period of Amoraim extends from the death of R. Jehuda Hanasi to the compilation of the Babylonian Talmud, that is, from the beginning of the third to the end of the fifth century. This period has been divided by some into six, by others into seven minor periods or generations which are determined by the beginning and the end of the activity of the most prominent teachers flourishing during that time.

The number of Amoraim who are mentioned in the Talmud amounts to several hundreds. The most distinguished among them, especially those who presided over the great academies are contained in the following chronological tables of the six generations of Amoraim.[1]

THE FIRST GENERATION OF AMORAIM.

§ 20.

A. Palestinian (219-279).	B. Babylonian (219-257).
1. R. Chanina bar Chama.	1. Abba Areca, called simply Rab.
2. R. Jochanan (bar Napacha)	
3. R. Simon ben Lakish (Resh Lakish).	2. (Mar) Samuel.
4. R. Joshua ben Levi.	

Biographical Sketches.

A. PALESTINIAN AMORAIM.

During this generation R. Gamaliel III and R. Judah II were successively the patriarchs.

1. *R. Chanina bar Chama* (born about 180, died 260) was a disciple of R. Jehuda Hanasi whose son and successor R. Gamaliel III bestowed

[1] Some scholars count the semi-Tanaim as the first generation, and have consequently seven instead of six generations. The period of Palestinian Amoraim being much shorter than that of the Babylonian, ends with the third generation of the latter. Frankel in his מבוא הירושלמי, treating especially of the Palestinian Amoraim, divides them also into six generations.

on him the title of Rabbi. He then presided over his own academy in Sepphoris and stood in high regard on account of his learning, modesty and piety. As teacher he was very conservative, transmitting that only which he had received by tradition, without ever allowing himself an independent decision. Of his prominent contemporaries are: R. *Ephes* who reopened a school at Lydda in South Judea; *Levi b. Sissi* (called simply Levi) who though not presiding over an academy, was a distinguished teacher,and later emigrated to Babylonia; further *Chizkia* who was a son of R. Chiya the Elder and whose teachings are frequently quoted in the Talmud. This Chizkia who had not the title of Rabbi must not be mistaken for a R. Chizkia who belonged to the third generation.

2. *R. Jochanan* bar Napacha, in general called simply R. Jochanan (born about 199; d. 279), was in his early youth a disciple of R. Jehuda Hanasi, later of R. Oshaya in Caesarea, also of R. Janai and especially of R. Chanina b. Chama. He then founded his own academy in Tiberias which henceforth became the principal seat of learning in the holy land. By his great mental powers he excelled all his contemporaries and is regarded the chief Amora of Palestine. In expounding the Mishna he introduced an analytical method, and laid down certain rules for the final decision in such cases in which the Tanaim expressed opposite opinions. His legal teachings ethical aphorisms, and exegetical remarks, transmitted by his numerous disciples, form the principal elements of the Gemara. He is supposed to have laid the foundation of the Palestinian Talmud, though, in its present shape, this work can not have been compiled before at least one century after R. Jochanan's death.[1]

3. *R. Simon b.Lakish,* whose name is generally abbreviated in Resh Lakish, was a man who combined great physical strength with a noble heart and a powerful mind. It is said, that in his youth, he was compelled by circumstances to gain his livelihood as a gladiator or soldier

[1] As to further characteristics of this and the other prominent Amoraim, the following works may be consulted: Graetz, History of the Jews, vol. IV; Z. Frankel, Mebo; I. H. Weiss, Dor Dor, vol III; I. Hamburger, Real Encyclopädie, vol II. Besides, J. Fürst, "Kultur und Literaturgeschichte der Juden in Asien", which treats especially of the Babylonian academies and teachers during the period of the Amoraim.

until making the acquaintance of R. Jochanan who gained him for the study of the law and gave him his sister in marriage. Having developed extraordinary mental and dialectical powers, he became R. Jochanan's most distinguished friend and colleague. In the interpretation of the Mishna and in legal questions they differed however very often, and their numerous controversies are reported in the Babylonian Talmud as well as in the Palestinian. Also in his Agadic teachings, Resh Lakish was original and advanced some very rational views.

4. *R. Joshua b. Levi* presided over an academy in Lydda. He is regarded as a great authority in the law, and his decisions prevail even in cases where his celebrated contemporaries, R. Jochanan and Resh Lakish differ from him. Though himself a prolific Agadist, he disapproved the vagaries of the Agada and objected to their being written down in books. The circumstance that, on a certain occasion, his prayer for rain proved to be efficient, probably gave rise to the mystic legends with which the fancy of later generation tried to illustrate his great piety.

To other celebrities flourishing in this generations belongs R. *Simlai* of Lydda who later settled in Nahardea. He was reputed less as teacher of the Halacha than for his ingenious and lucid method of treating the Agada.

B. BABYLONIAN AMORAIM.

1. *Abba Areca* (or Aricha) was the real name of the chief Babylonian Amora who, by way of eminence, is generally called *Rab* (the teacher). He was born about 175 and died 247. As an orphaned youth he went to his uncle the celebrated R. Chiya in Palestine to finish his studies in the academy of R. Jehuda Hanasi. The mental abilities which he displayed soon attracted general attention. After the death of R. Jehuda, Abba returned to his native country and in the year 219 founded the academy in Sura where 1200 pupils flocked around him from all parts of Babylonia. His authority was recognized even by the most celebrated teachers in Palestine. Being regarded as one of the semi-Tanaim he ventured in some instances even to dispute some opinions accepted in the Mishna, a privilege otherwise not accorded to any of the Amoraim.[1] Most of his decisions, especially in ritual questions, obtained legal sanction, but in the civil law his friend

[1] רב תנא הוא ופליג, Erubin 50b and often.

Samuel in Nahardea was his superior [1]. Over one hundred of his numerous disciples, who transmitted his teachings and decisions to later generations are mentioned in the Talmud by their names.

2. *Samuel*, or Mar Samuel, was born about 180 in Nahardea, died there 257. His father, Abba bar Abba, and Levi b. Sissi were his first teachers. Like Rab he went to Palestine and became a disciple of Rabbi Jehuda Hanasi from whom, however, he could not obtain the ordination. After his return to Nahardea, he succeeded R. Shela in the dignity of president of the academy (Resh-Sidra) in that city. Besides the law, he cultivated the sciences of medicine and astronomy. As Amora he developed especially the rabbinical jurisprudence in which he was regarded as the greatest authority [2]. Among other important principles established by him is that of "*Dina d'malchutha Dina*", that is, the civil law of the government is as valid for the Jews as their own law. The most friendly and brotherly relation prevailed between Samuel and Rab, although they often differed in questions of the law. After Rab's death (247), his disciples recognized Samuel as the highest religious authority of Babylonia. He died about ten years later, leaving behind numerous disciples, several of whom became the leading teachers in the following generation.

A distinguished contemporary of Samuel was *Mar Ukba*, at first head of the court in Kafri, and later Exilarch in Naharde[illegible].

---

[1] הלכתא כרב באיסורי וכשמואל בדינין Bechoroth 49b.

[2] Mar Samuel made also a compilation of Baraithoth which is quoted in the Talmud by the phrase תנא דבי שמואל. Betza 29a and Moed Katon 18b; see Rashi's remark to the first mentioned passage.

THE SECOND GENERATION OF AMORAIM

§ 21.

A. Palestinian (279-320)	B. Babylonian (257-320).
1. R. Elazar b. Pedath.	1. Rab Huna.
2. R. Ame.	2. Rab Juda bar Jecheskel.
3. R. Assi.	3. Rab Chisda (or Chasda).
4. R. Chiya bar Abba.	4. Rab Shesheth.
5. Simon bar Abba.	5. Rab Nachman b. Jacob.
6. R. Abbahu.	
7. R. Zera (Zeira).	

Remarks and Biographical Sketches.

A. PALESTINIAN AMORAIM.

The patriarchate during this generation was successively in the hands of R. Gamaliel IV and R. Judah III.

1. *R. Elazar ben Pedath*, generally called simply R. Elazar, like the Tana R. Elazar (ben Shamua) for whom he must not be mistaken, was a native of Babylonia and a disciple and later an associate of R. Jochanan whom he survived. He enjoyed great authority and is very often quoted in the Talmud.

2 and 3. *R. Ame* and *R. Assi* were likewise Babylonians, and distinguished disciples of R. Jochanan. After the death of R. Elazar they became the heads of the declining academy in Tiberias. They had the title only of ,,Judges, or the Aaronites of the Holy Land" and subordinated themselves to the growing authority of the teachers in Babylonia. Rabbi Assi is not to be confoundend with his contemporary, the Babylonian Amora Rab Assi, who was a colleague of Rab Saphra and a disciple of Rab in Sura. [1]

4 and 5. *R. Chiya bar Abba* and *Simon bar Abba* were probably brothers. They had immigrated from Babylonia and became disciples of R. Jochanan. Both were distinguished teachers, but very poor. In questions of the law they were inclined to rigorous views.

6. *R. Abbahu* of Caesarea, disciple of R. Jochanan, friend and colleague of R. Ame and R. Assi, was a man of great wealth and of a liberal education. He had a thorough knowledge of the Greek

[1] See Tosaphoth Chullin 19a.

language, and favored Greek culture. Being held in high esteem by the Roman authorities, he had great political influence. He seems to have had frequent controversies with the teachers of Christianity in Caesarea. Besides being a prominent teacher whose legal opinions are quoted in all parts of the Palestinian and Babylonian Talmud, he was a very popular lecturer.

7. *R. Zeira* (*or Zera*) was a Babylonian and a disciple of Rab Juda bar Jecheskel, but dissatisfied with the hair splitting method prevailing in the academies of his native country, he emigrated to Palestine where he attended the lectures of R. Elazar b. Pedath in Tiberias, and tried, in vain, to unlearn his former method of study. Having been ordained as Rabbi, he became one of the authorities in Palestine together with R. Ame, R. Assi and R. Abbahu.

B. BABYLONIAN AMORAIM.

1. *Rab Huna* (born 212, died 297) was a disciple of Rab, whom, after Mar Samuel's death. he succeeded as president of the academy in Sura. In this office he was active for forty years. He employed fifteen assistants to repeat and explain his lectures to his 800 disciples. Highly revered for his great learning and his noble character, he enjoyed an undisputed authority to which even the Palestinian teachers R. Ame and R. Assi voluntarily subordinated themselves.

2. *Rab Juda bar Jecheskel,* generally called simply R. Juda (or Jehuda), was a disciple of Rab and also of Samuel. The latter teacher, whose peculiar method he adopted and developed, used to characterize him by the epithet שיננא "the acute". He founded the academy in Pumbaditha, but after R. Huna's death he was chosen as his successor (Resh Methibta) at Sura, where after two years (299) he died in an advanced age.

3. *Rab Chisda* (or Chasda) belonged to the younger disciples of Rab after whose death he attended also the lectures of R. Huna. But from the latter teacher he soon separated on account of a misunderstanding between them and established a school of his own. At the same time, he was one of the Judges in Sura. After Rab Juda's death R. Chisda, though already above 80 years old, became head of the academy in Sura and remained in this office for about ten years

4. *Rab Shesheth,* a disciple of Rab and Samuel, was member of the court in Nahardea. After the destruction of that city he went to

Mechuza; later he settled in Silhi where he founded an academy. Being blind, he had to rely upon his powerful memory. He was R. Chisda's opponent in the Halacha, and disapproved the hair splitting dialectical method which had come in vogue among the followers of Rab Juda in Pumbaditha.

5. *Rab Nachman b. Jacob*, called simply Rab Nachman, was a prominent disciple of Mar Samuel. By his father-in-law, the exilarch Abba bar Abuha, he was appointed chief justice in Nahardea. After Mar Samuel's death he succeeded him as rector of the academy in that city. When two years later (259) the city of Nahardea was destroyed, R. Nachman settled in Shechan-Zib. He is regarded as a great authority especially in the rabbinical jurisprudence in which he established many important principles. Among others, he originated the rabbinical oath termed שבועת היכת, that is, the purging oath imposed in a law suit on the claimee even in cases of general denial on his part (כופר הכל).

Of other teachers belonging to this generation who, though not standing at the head of the leading academies, are often quoted in the Talmud, the following must be noted:

a. *Rabba bar bar Chana* who was a Babylonian and son of Abba bar Chana. After having attended the academy of R. Jochanan in Palestine, he returned to his native country where he frequently reported the opinions of his great teacher. He is also noted for the many allegorical narratives ascribed to him in the Talmud.

b. *Ulla* (b. Ishmael) was a Palestinian who frequently travelled to Babylonia where he finally settled and died. Although without the title of Rabbi or Rab, he was regarded as a distinguished teacher whose opinions and reports are often mentioned.

THE THIRD GENERATION OF AMORAIM.

§ 22.

A. Palestinian (320-359).	B. Babylonian (320-375).
1. R. Jeremiah.	1. Rabbà bar Huna.
2. R. Jonah.	2. Rabba bar Nachmani.
3. R. Jose.	3. Rab Joseph (bar Chiya).
	4. Abaye.
	5. Raba.
	6. Rab Nachman bar Isaac.
	7. Rab Papa.

Remarks and Biographical Sketches.

A. PALESTINIAN AMORAIM.

The patriarch of this period was Hillel II who introduced the fixed Jewish calendar.

In consequence of the persecutions and the banishment of several religious teachers under the emperors Constantin and Constantius, the Palestinian academies entirely decayed. The only teachers of some prominence are the following:

1. *R. Jeremiah* was a Babylonian and disciple of R. Zeira whom he followed to Palestine. In his younger days, when still in his native country, he indulged in propounding puzzling questions of trifling casuistry by which he probably intended to ridicule the subtile method prevailing among some of the contemporary teachers, and on this account he was expelled from the academy. In the holy land he was more appreciated and after the death of R. Abbahu and R. Zeira was acknowledged as the only authority in that country.

2. *R. Jonah* was a disciple of R. Ila (Hila) and of R. Jeremiah. His opinions are frequently quoted especially in the Palestinian Talmud.

3. *R. Jose* (bar Zabda), colleague of the just mentioned R. Jonah, was one of the last rabbinical authorities in Palestine.

It is probable that the compilation of the Palestinian Talmud was accomplished about that time, though it cannot be stated by whom.

B. Babylonian Amoraim.

1. *Rabba* (or Rab Abba) *bar Huna* was not, as erroneously supposed by some, the son of the exilarch Huna Mari, but of Rab Huna, the disciple and successor of Rab. After the death of R. Chisda (309) he succeeded him in the dignity of president of the academy in Sura. Under his presidency, lasting 13 years, this academy was eclipsed by that of Pumbaditha, and after his death it remained deserted for about fifty years until Rab Ashe restored it to its former glory.

2. *Rabba bar Nachmani*, in the Talmud called simply Rabba, was born 270 and died 330. He was a disciple of Rab Huna, Rab Juda and Rab Chisda, and displayed from his youth great dialectical powers on account of which he was characterized as "the uprooter of mountains". Selected as head of the academy of Pumbaditha, he attracted large crowds of hearers by his ingenious method of teaching. In his lectures which commented on all parts of the Mishna he investigated the reason of the laws and made therefrom logical deductions. Besides, he tried to reconcile seeming differences between the Mishna, the Baraithoth and the traditional teachings of later authorities. He also liked to propound puzzling problems of the law in order to test and sharpen the mental powers of his disciples. A charge having been made against him by the Persian government that many of his numerous hearers attended his lectures in order to evade the poll-tax, he fled from Pumbaditha and died in solitude.

3. *Rab Joseph* (bar Chiya) was a disciple of Rab Juda and Rab Shesheth, and succeeded his friend Rabba in the dignity of president of the academy in Pumbadita, after having once before been elected for this office which he declined in favor of Rabba. On account of his thorough knowledge of the sources of the Law, to which he attached more importance than to ingenious deductions, he was called *Sinai.* Besides being a great authority in the rabbinical law, he devoted himself to the Targum of the Bible, especially of the prophetical books. In his old age he became blind. He died in the year 333 after having presided over the academy of Pumbaditha only for three years.

4. *Abaye*, surnamed *Nachmani* (b. 280. d. 338), was a son Kaylil and a pupil of his uncle Rabba bar Nachmani, and of Rab Joseph. He was highly esteemed not only for his profound knowledge of the law and his mastership in Talmudical dialectics, but also for his integrity

and gentleness. After Rab Joseph's death he was selected as head of the academy in Pumbaditha, but under his administration which lasted about five years, the number of hearers in that academy decreased considerably, as his more talented colleague *Raba* had founded a new academy in Machuza which attracted greater crowds of pupils. Under these two Amoraim the dialectical method of the Babylonian teachers reached the highest development. Their discussions, which mostly concern some very nice distinctions in the interpretation of the Mishna in order to reconcile conflicting passages, fill the pages of the Talmud.[1] In their differences concerning more practical questions the opinion of Raba generally prevails, so that later authorities pointed out only six cases in which the decision of Abaye was to be adopted against that of his rival.[2]

5. *Raba* was the son of Joseph b. Chama in Machuza. He was born 299 and died 352. In his youth he attended the lectures of Rab Nachman and of R. Chisda. Later, he and Abaye were fellow-students in the academy of Rabba bar Nachmani. Here he developed his dialectical powers by which he soon surpassed all his contemporaries. He opened an academy in Machuza which attracted a great number of students. After Abaye's death this academy supplanted that in Pumbaditha and during Raba's lifetime became almost the only seat of learning in Babylonia. His controversies with his contemporaries, especially with his rival colleague Abaye, are very numerous. Wherever an opinion of Abaye is recorded in the Talmud, it is almost always followed by the contrary view and argument of Raba.

6. *Rab Nachman b. Isaac* was a disciple of Rab Nachman (b. Jacob) and afterwards an officer as Resh Calla in the academy of Raba. After the death of the latter he was made president of the academy in Pumbaditha which now resumed its former rank. In this capacity he remained only four years (352–356) and left no remarkable traces of his activity. Still less significant was the activity of his

---

[1] The often very subtile argumentations of these two teachers became so proverbial that the phrase הויות דאביי ורבא "the critical questions of Abaye and Raba" is used in the Talmud as a signification of acute discussions and minute investigations, so in Succah 28a.

[2] הלכתא כוותיה דאביי בי"ע"ל ק"ג"ם Baba Metzia 21b; Sanhedrin 27a; Erubin 15a; Kidd. 52a; Gittin 34a.

successor *R. Chama* from Nahardea who held the office for twenty one years (356-377).

7. *Rab Papa* (bar Chanan), a disciple of Abaye and Raba, founded a new school in Nares, in the vicinity of Sura, over which he presided for nineteen years (354–375). He adopted the dialectical method of his former teachers without possessing their ingenuity and their independence, and consequently did not give satisfaction to those of his hearers who had formerly attended the lectures of Raba. One of his peculiarities was that he frequently refers to popular proverbs (אמרי אינשי). [1]

THE FOURTH GENERATION OF BABYLONIAN AMORAIM (375-427).

§ 23.

A. Sura.	B. Pumbaditha.	C. Nahardea.
1. Rab Ashe.	1. Rab Zebid.	Amemar.
	2. Rab Dime.	
	3. Rafram.	
	4. Rab Cahana.	
	5. Mar Zutra.	

Remarks and Biographical Sketches.

A. *Rab Ashe*, (son of Simai bar Ashe) was, at the age of twenty, made president of the reopened academy of Sura, after the death of Rab Papa, and held this office for fifty two years. Under his presidency, this academy, which had been deserted since the time of Rabba bar Huna, regained its former glory with which Rab had invested it. Combining the profundity of knowledge which formerly prevailed in this academy with the dialectic methods developed in that of Pumbaditha, he was generally recognized as the ruling authority, so that his contemporaries called him by the distinguishing title of *Rabbana* (our teacher). Invested with this great authority, Rab Ashe was enabled

[1] This Rab Papa must not be mistaken for an elder teacher by the same name, who had ten sons, all well versed in the law, one of whom, Rafram, became head of the academy of Pumbaditha in the following generation. Neither is Rab Papa identical with Rab Papi, a distinguished lawyer who flourished in a former generation.

to assume the task of sifting, arranging and compiling the immense material of traditions, commentaries and discussions on the Mishna which, during the two preceding centuries, had accumulated in the Babylonian academies. In the compilation and revision of this gigantic work which is embodied in the Gemara, he was occupied for over half a century, and still he did not complete it entirely but this was done, after his death, by his disciples and successors.

B. During the long period of Rab Ashe's activity at the academy in Sura, the following teachers presided successively over the academy in Pumbaditha.

1. *Rab Zebid* (b. Oshaya) who succeeded Rab Chama and held the office for eight years. (377-385).

2. *Rab Dime* (b. Chinena) from Nahardea, presiding only for three years (385-388).

3. *Rafram bar Papa* the elder, in his youth a disciple of Raba, succeeded R. Dime (388-394).

4. *Rab Cahana* (b. Tachlifa), likewise a disciple of Raba, was one of the former teachers of R. Ashe. In an already advanced age he was made president of the academy of Pumbaditha, and died in the year 411. This Rab Cahana must not be mistaken for two other teachers of the same name, one of whom had been a distinguished disciple of Rab, and the other (Rab Cahana b. Manyome) a disciple of Rab Juda b. Jecheskel.

5. *Mar Zutra* who, according to some historians, succeeded Rab Cahana as rector of the school in Pumbaditha (411-414) is probably identical with Mar Zutra b. Mare, who shortly afterwards held the high office as Exilarch. In the rectorship of Pumbaditha he was succeeded by *Rab Acha bar Raba* (414-419): and the latter by *Rab Gebiha* (419-433).

C. *Amemar*, a friend of Rab Ashe, was a distinguished judge and teacher in Nahardea. When his former teacher Rab Dime became president of the academy in Pumbaditha, he succeeded him in the rectorship of that of Nahardea from 390 to about 422. With him this once so celebrated seat of learning passed out of existence.

THE FIFTH GENERATION OF BABYLONIAN AMORAIM (427-468)

§ 24.

A. Sura.	B. Pumbaditha.
1. Mar Jemar (Maremar).	1. Rafram II.
2. Rab Ide bar Abin.	2. Rechumai.
3. Mar bar Rab Ashe.	3. Rab Sama b. Rabba.
4. Rab Acha of Difte.	

Remarks and Biographical Sketches.

A. 1. *Mar Jemar* (contracted to Maremar), who enjoyed high esteem with the leading teachers of his time, succeeded his colleague and friend Rab Ashe in the presidency of the academy in Sura, but held this office only for about five years (427–432).

5. *Rab Ide* (or Ada) *bar Abin* became, after Mar Jemar's death, president of the academy at Sura and held this office for about twenty years (432–452). He as well as his predecessor continued the compilation of the Talmud which Rab Ashe had commenced.

3. *Mar bar Rab Ashe*, whose surname was Tabyome, and who, for some unknown reasons, had been passed over in the election of a successor to his father, was finally made president of the academy in Sura and filled this office for thirteen years (455–468). In his frequent discussions with contemporary authorities he exhibits independence of opinion and great faculties of mind.

4. *Rab Acha of Difte*, a prominent teacher, was on the point of being elected as head of the academy of Sura, but was finally defeated by Mar bar Rab Ashe who aspired to that office which his father had so gloriously filled for more than half a century.

B. The academy of Pumbaditha which had lost its earlier influence, had during this generation successively three presidents, of whose activity very little is known, namely:

1. *Rafram II* who succeeded Rab Gebihah, from 433 to 443.
2. *Rab Rechumai*, from 443-456.
3. *Rab Sama b. Rabba*, from 456–471.

Toward the end of this generation, the activity of both academies was almost paralyzed by the terrible persecutions which the Persian King Firus instituted against the Jews and their religion.

THE SIXTH AND LAST GENERATION OF BABYLONIAN AMORAIM (468-500).

§ 25.

A. Sura.	B. Pumbaditha.
1. Rabba Thospia (or Tosfaah).	Rab Jose.
2. Rabina.	

Remarks and Biographical Sketches.

A. 1. *Rabba of Thospia*[1] succeeded Mar bar Rab Ashi as rector of the Suran academy just at the time when the Persian King Firuz had ordered the Jewish jurisdiction to be abolished and the academical assemblies to be prohibited. It is but natural that under such circumstances the academical activity of this Rabbi which lasted only about six years could not amount to much.

2. *Rabina* (contraction of Rab Abina) bar Huna,[2] who succeeded Rabba of Thospia, entered his office which he held from 488 to 499. under more favorable circumstances, since the persecution had ceased after the death of Firuz and the academies were reopened. He consequently developed a great activity, the object of which was to complete and close the compilation of the Talmud begun by Rab Ashi. In this task he was assisted by Rab Jose, the school head of Pumbaditha, and by some associates.

With the close of the Talmud and the death of Rabina (499) ended the period of the Amoraim. The Babylonian teachers who flourished during the subsequent half century are called *Saboraim* (רבנן סבוראי). They did not assume the authority to contradict the decisions established by the Amoraim, but merely ventured to express an opinion (סבר, to reason, think, suppose, opine) and to fix the final decision in cases where

[1] Regarding the correct name and native place of this Rabbi see Leopold Löw's "Lebensalter" p. 376, note 54, and Neubauer Géogr. du Talm., p. 332.

[2] This head of the Suran Academy is by chronographers usually called Rabina II, in order to distinguish him from a former teacher Rabina who was a disciple of Raba and flourished in the fourth generation. In the Talmud, both of them are called simply Rabina, and only from the connection it is to be seen whether it refers to that elder teacher or to the last of the Amoraim.

their predecessors, the Amoraim, disagreed. They gave the Talmud a finishing touch by adding those final decisions, also numerous, especially Agadic, passages.

B. *Rab Jose* presided over the academy in Pumbaditha 475-520. As Rabina was the last Amora for Sura, so Rab Jose was the last for Pumbaditha. Flourishing still for a number of years after the close of the Talmud,he was at the same time the first of the Saboraim,and must be considered as the most prominent among them.

Of Rab Jose's contemporaries and successors who like himself formed the connecting link between the period of Amoraim and that of the Saboraim, and whose opinions and controversies are still recorded in the Talmud, the following two must be mentioned: *Rab Achai b. Huna* and *Rab Samuel b. Abbahu*.

CHAPTER V

THE GEMARA

Classification of its contents into Halacha and Agada.

§ 26.

Tne collection of the commentaries and discussions of the Amoraim on the Mishna is termed *Gemara*. This term, derived from the verb נמר which in Hebrew means *to finish*, *to complete*, and in the Aramaic also *to learn*, *to teach*, signifies either the *completion*, the *supplement* (to the Mishna), or is identical with the word *Talmud* which is often used in its place, meaning, the *teaching*, *the study*.

Besides being a discursive commentary on the Mishna, the Gemara contains a vast amount of more or less valuable material which does not always have any close connection with the Mishna text, as legal reports, historical and biographical informations, religious and ethical maxims and homiletical remarks.

The whole subject matter embodied in the Gemara is generally classified into *Halacha* and *Agada*.

To *Halacha*[1] belongs that which has bearing upon tne law, hence all expositions, discussions and reports which have the object of explaining, establishing and determining legal principles and provisions. The principal branches of the Halacha are indicated by the names of the six divisions of the Mishna, and by those of the Masechtoth belonging to each division. See above pages 9-14.

The *Agada*[2] comprises every thing not having the character

---

[1] *Halacha* (הלכה) means *custom, usage practice*; then, an *adopted rule*, a *traditional law*. In a more extended meaning, the term applies to matters bearing upon that law.

[2] *Agada* or *Aggada* (הגדה, אגדתא, אגדה, derived from נגד which in the Hebrew *Hiphil* or Aramaic *Aphel* form signifies to *narrate*, to *tell*, to *communicate*) means that which is related, *a tale*, a *saying*, an individual utterance which claims no binding authority. Regarding this term, see W. Bacher's learned and exhaustive article, "The origin of the word Hagada (Agada)" in the Jewish Quarterly Review (London)

of Halacha, hence all historical records, all legends and parables, all doctrinal and ethical teachings and all free and unrestrained interpretations of Scripture.

According to its different contents and character, the Agada may be divided into:

1. *Exegetical* Agada, giving plain or homiletical and allegorical explanations of Biblical passages.

2. *Dogmatical* Agada, treating of God's attrributes and providence, of creation, of revelation, of reward and punishment, of future life, of Messianic time, etc.

3. *Ethical* Agada, containing aphorisms, maxims, proverbs, fables, sayings intending to teach and illustrate certain moral duties.

4. *Historical* Agada, reporting traditions and legends concerning the lives of biblical and post-biblical persons or concerning national and general history.

5. *Mystical* Agada, refering to Cabala, angelology, demonology, astrology, magical cures, interpretation of dreams, etc.

6. *Miscellaneous* Agada, containing anecdotes, observations, practical advices, and occassional references to various branches of ancient knowledge and sciences.

Agadic passages are often, by the way, interspersed among matters of Halacha, as a kind of diversion and recreation after the mental exertion of a tiresome investigation or a minute discussion on a dry legal subject. Sometimes, however, the Agada appears in larger groups, outweighing the Halacha matter with which it is loosely connected; f. i. Berachoth, 54a–64a; Sabbath 30a–33b; Megilla 10b–17a; Gittin 55b–58b; 67b–70a; Sota 9a–14a; B. Bathra 14b–17a; 73a–76a; Sanhedrin, Perek Chelek.

There are two compilations of the Gemara which differ from each other in language as well as in contents; the one made in Palestine is called *Jerushalmi*, the Jerusalem Gemara or Talmud;

Vol IV, pp. 406-429. As to fuller particulars concerning Halacha and Agada, see Zunz' G. Vortraege pp. 57-61 and 83 sq.; also Hamburger's Real Encyclopädie II, the articles Halacha and Agada.

the other originating in Babylonia is called *Babli*, the Babylonian Gemara or Talmud:

COMPILATION OF JERUSHALMI, THE PALESTINIAN TALMUD.

§ 27.

As no academy existed in Jerusalem after the destruction of the second temple, the customary appellation *Jerusalem* Talmud is rather a misnomer. More correct is the appellation the Palestinian Talmud (תלמוד ארץ ישראל) or the Gemara of the teachers of the West (גמרא דבני מערבא).

Maimonides in the introduction to his Mishna commentary ascribes the authorship of the Palestinian Talmud to the celebrated teacher R. Jochanan who flourished in the third century. This statement, if literally taken, cannot be correct, since so many of the teachers quoted in that Talmud are known to have flourished more than a hundred years after R. Jochanan. This celebrated Amora may, at the utmost, have given the first impulse to such a collection of commentaries and discussions on the Mishna, which was continued and completed by his successors in the academy of Tiberias. In its present shape the work is supposed to belong to the fourth or fifth century. Some modern scholars assign its final compilation even to a still later period namely after the close of the Babylonian Talmud. [1]

The Palestinian Gemara, as before us, extends only over thirty nine of the sixty three Masechtoth contained in the Mishna, namelly all Masechtoth of Seder Zeraim, Seder Moed, Nashim and Nezikin with the exception of Eduyoth and Aboth. But it has none of the Masechtoth belonging to Seder Kodashim, and of those belonging to Seder Teharoth it treats only of Masecheth Nidda. (see above pages 12-14).

Some of its Masechtoth are defective; thus the last four

[1] Critical researches on this subject are found in Geiger's Jued. Zeitschrift f. Wissenschaft 1870; Z. Frankel Mebo, p. 46 sq. and in Wiesner's Gibeath Jeruschalaim (Vienna 1872).

I. H. Weiss (Dor Dor III, p. 114 sq.) regards R. Jose (bar Zabda) who was a colleague of R. Jonah and one of the last authorities in Palestine, as the very compiler of the Pal. Talmud which in the following generation was completed by R. Jose bar Bun (Abun).

Perakim of Sabbath and the last Perek of Maccoth are wanting. Of the ten Perakim belonging to Masecheth Nidda it has only the first three Perakim and a few lines of the fourth.

There are some indications that elder commentators were acquainted with portions of the Palestinian Gemara which are now missing, and it is very probable that that Gemara originally extended to all or, at least, to most of the Masechtoth of the Mishna. The loss of the missing Masechtoth and portions thereof may be explained partly by the many persecutions which interrupted the activity of the Palestinian academies, partly by the circumstance that the Pelestinian Gemara did not command that general attention and veneration which was bestowed on the Babylonian Gemara.

Compilation of Babli, the Babylonian Talmud.

§ 28.

The compilation of the Babylonian Talmud is generally ascribed to Rab Ashe who for more than fifty years (375-427) officiated as head of the academy in Sura. It is stated that it took him about thirty years to collect, sift and arrange the immense material of this gigantic work. During the remaining second half of his activity he revised once more the whole work and made in it many corrections. This corrected edition is termed מהדורא בתרא the *latter revision*, and the former מהדורא קמא the *first revision.* [1]

[1] See Baba Bathra fol 157b.

Those scholars who maintain that the Mishna was not written down by R. Jehuda Hanasi, but that he merely arranged it orally (see above p. 5, note), maintain the same in regard to Rab Ashe's compilation of the Gemara, without being able to state when and by whom it was actually commited to writing. Against this opinion it has been properly argued that it must be regarded as absolutely impossible for a work so voluminous, so variegated in contents and so full of minute and intricate discussions, as the Talmud, to have been orally arranged and fixed, and accurately transmitted from generation to generation. On the strength of this argument and of some indications found in the Talmud, Z. Frankel (in his Mebo p. 47) even regards it as very probable that Rab Ashe in compiling the Gemara made use of some minor compilations which existed before him, and of some written records and memoranda containing short abstracts of the academical discussions in the preceding generations. Collecting

But Rab Ashe did not succeed in finishing the gigantic work. It was continued and completed by his disciples and successors, especially by the last Amoraim Rabina II who from 488 to 499 presided over the academy in Sura, and R. Jose, the school-head of Pumbaditha. Some additions were made by the Saboraim, and perhaps even by some still later hands.

The Gemara of the Babylonian Talmud covers only thirty seven Masechtoth of the Mishna, namely:

Of Zeraim only one, Berachoth, ommitting the remaining ten Masechtoth;

Of Moed eleven, omitting only Shekalim which in our Talmud editions is replaced by the Palestinian Gemara;

Of Nashim all of the seven Masechtoth beloning to that division;

Of Nezikin eight, omitting Eduyoth and Aboth;

Of Kodashim nine, omitting Middoth and Kinnim. In Thamid only chapters I. II. IV are provided with Gemara, but not chapters III. V. VI and VII.

Of Teharoth only Nidda; omitting eleven Masechtoth.

There being no traces of the Gemara missing to twenty six Masechtoth, it is very probable that this part of the Gemara has never been compiled, though those Masechtoth have undoubtedly also been discussed by the Babylonian Amoraim, as is evident from frequent references to them in the Gemara on the other Masechtoth. The neglect of compiling these discussions may be explained by the circumstance that those Masechtoth mostly treat of laws which had no practical application outside of Palestine. This is especially the case with the Masechtoth of Zeraim, except Berachoth, and those of Teharoth, except

and arranging these records he partly enlarged them by fuller explanations, partly left them just as he found them. Some traces of such memoranda, made probably by R Ashe's predecessors, are still found in numerous passages of the Talmud. We refer to the mnemonical signs and symbols (סימנים) which every now and then are there met with (in brackets) as headings of discussions and indicating either the names of the teachers to be quoted or the order of the subjects to be discussed. A critical investigation on these often very enigmatic *Simanim* is found in Jacob Brüll's דורש לציון Die Mnemotechnik des Talmuds (Vienna 1864).

Nidda. It was different with the Masechtoth belonging to Kodashim which, though treating of the sacrificial laws, are fully discussed in the Babylonian Talmud, as it was a prevailing opinion of the Rabbis that the merit of being engaged with the study of those laws was tantamount to the actual performance of the sacrificial rites (See Talm. Menachoth 110a).

The absence of Gemara on the Masechtoth Eduyoth and Aboth is easily accounted for by the very nature of their contents which admitted of no discussions.

THE TWO GEMARAS COMPARED WITH EACH OTHER.

§ 29.

The Palestinian and the Babylonian Gemaras differ from each other in language and style as well as in material and in the method of treating the same, also in arrangement.

As regards the language, the Palestinian Gemara is composed in the West Aramaic dialect which prevailed in Palestine at the time of the Amoraim.

The language of the Babylonian Gemara is a peculiar idiom, being a mixture of Hebrew and East Aramaic with an occasional sprinkling of Persian words. Quotations from Mishna and Baraitha and sayings of the elder Amoraim are given in the original, that is, the New Hebrew (Mishnic) language, while forms of judicial and notary documents and popular legends of later origin are often given in the Aramaic idiom.

Although the Palestinian Gemara extends to two more Masechtoth than the Babylonian, its total material amounts only to about one third of the latter. Its discussions are generally very brief and condensed, and do not exhibit that dialectic acumen for which the Babylonian Gemara is noted. The Agada in the Palestinian Gemara includes more reliable and valuable historical records and references, and is, on the whole, more rational and sober, though less attractive than the Babylonian Agada which generally appeals more to the heart and imagination. But the latter, on many occasions, indulges too much in gross exaggerations, and its popular sayings, especially those evidently interpolated by later hands, have often an admixture of superstitious views borrowed from the Persian surroundings.

The arrangement of the material in the two Talmuds differs in this, that in the Babylonian, the Gemara is attached to the single paragraphs (מתניתא) of the Mishna, while in the Palestinian all paragraphs (there termed הלכות) belonging to one Perek of the Mishna, are generally placed together at the head of each chapter. The comments and discussions of the Gemara referring to the successive paragraphs, are then marked by the headings הלכה א' הלכה ב' and so on.

The two Gemara collections make no direct mention of each other as literary works. But the names and opinions of the Palestinian authorities are very often quoted in the Babylonian Gemara; and in a similar way, though not to the same extent, the Palestinian Gemara mentions the views of the Babylonian authorities. This exchange of opinions was effected by the numerous teachers who are known to have emigrated or frequently travelled from the one country to the other.

The study of the Babylonian Talmud, having been transplanted from its native soil to North Africa, and the European countries (especially Spain, France, Germany and Poland), was there most sedulously and religiously cultivated in the Jewish communities, and gave rise to an immense Rabbinical literature. The Palestinian Talmud never enjoyed such general veneration and attention. Eminent Rabbis alone were thoroughly conversant with its contents, and referred to it in their writings. It is only in modern times that Jewish scholars have come to devote more attention to this Talmud, for the purpose of historical and literary investigations.

CHAPTER VI

APOCRYPHAL APPENDICES TO THE TALMUD

§ 30.

Besides the Masechtoth contained in the Mishna and the two Gemaras, there are several Masechtoth composed in the form of the Mishna and Tosephta, that treat of ethical, ritual, and liturgical precepts. They stand in the same relation to the Talmud as the Apocrypha to the canonical books of the Bible. When and by whom they were composed, cannot be ascertained. Of these apocryphal treatises, the following are appended to our editions of the Talmud:

1. *Aboth d'Rabbi Nathan* אבות דרבי נתן, divided into 41 chapters and a kind of Tosephta to the Mishnic treatise "Pirke Aboth," the ethical sentences of which are here con siderably enlarged and illustrated by numerous narratives. In its present shape, it belongs to the post-Talmudic period, though some elements of a Baraitha of R. Nathan (who was a Tana belonging to the fourth generation) may have been embodied therein.[1]

2. *Sopherim* סופרים the Scribes, containing in 21 chapters rules for the writing of the scrolls of the Pentateuch, and of the book of Esther; also Masoretic rules, and liturgical rules for the service on Sabbath, Feast and Fast days. R. Asher already expressed (in his Hilchoth Sepher Thora) the opinion that this Masecheth Sopherim belongs to the period of the Gaonim.[2]

---

[1] Compare Zunz, Gottesd. Vortraege, p. 108, sq.—Solomon Taussig published in his נוה שלום (Munich 1872) from a Manuscript of the Library in Munich a recension of the Aboth d'Rabbi Nathan which differs considerably from that printed in our Talmud editions. The latest edition of Aboth d. R. N. in two recensions from MSS. with critical annotations was published by S. Schechter (Vienna 1887).

[2] See Zunz, GD. V. p. 95, sq. The latest separate edition of Masecheth Sopherim from a MS. and with a German commentary was published by Joel Mueller, (Leipsic 1878).

3. *Ebel Rabbathi* אבל רבתי (the large treatise on Mourning), euphemistically called שמחות *Semachoth* (Joys), is divided into 14 chapters, and treats, as indicated by the title, of rules and customs concerning burial and mourning. It is not identical with a treatise under the same title, quoted already in the Talmud (Moed Katon 24a; 26a; Kethuboth 28a), but seems to be rather a reproduction of the same with later additions.[1])

4. *Callah* כלה (the bride, the woman recently married). This minor Masechta, being likewise a reproduction of a Masechta by that name, mentioned already in the Talmund (Sabbath 114 a; Taanith 10b; Kiddushin 49b; Jer. Berachoth, II, 5.), treats in one chapter of the duties of chastity in marriage and in general.

5. *Derech Eretz* דרך ארץ (the conduct of life), divided into 11 chapters, the first of which treats of prohibited marriages, and the remaining chapters, of ethical, social and religious teachings. References to a treatise by that name, are made already in the Talmud (B. Berachoth 22a and Jer. Sabbath VI, 2.)

6. *Derech Eretz Zuta* דרך ארץ זוטא (the conduct of life, minor treatise), containing 10 chapters, replete with rules and maxims of wisdom.[2]

7. *Perek Ha-shalom* פרק השלום (chapter on Peace) consists, as already indicated by the title, only of one chapter, treating of the importance of peacefulness.

Remark:–Beside these apocryphal treatises appended to our editions of the Talmud under the general title of מסכתות קטנות "Minor Treatises," there are seven lesser Masechtoth which were published by Raphael Kirchheim from an ancient manuscript. (Frankfort on the Main 1851.)

---

[1] See Zunz, G. V. p. 90, and N. Brüll "Die talm. Tractate über Trauer um Verstorbene (Jahrbücher für Jüd. Geschichte und Literatur I (Frankfurt a. M.) p. 1-57. M. Klotz just published "Der Talm. Tractat Ebel Rabbathi nach Handschriften bearbeitet, überzetzt und mit Anmerkungen versehen" Frankf. on the Main, 1892.

[2] On both of these Masechtoth Derech Eretz see Zunz GD. V. pp. 110-112. See also: Abr. Tawrogi "Der Talm. Tractat Derech Erez Sutta Kritisch bearbeitet, übersetzt und erläutert" (Berlin 1885).

CHAPTER VII

COMMENTARIES ON THE TALMUD

THE NECESSITY FOR SUCH COMMENTARIES

§ 31.

The Talmud offers to its students great difficulties, partly on account of the peculiar idiom in which it is written and which is intermixed with so numerous, often very mutilated, foreign words; partly on account of the extreme brevity and succinctness of its style, the frequent use of technical terms and phrases, and mere allusions to matters discussed elsewhere; partly also, on account of the circumstance that, in consequence of elliptical expressions, and in the absence of all punctuation marks, question and answer, in the most intricate discussions, are sometimes so closely interwoven, that it is not easy to discern at once, where the one ends and the other begins. To meet all these difficulties, which are often very perplexing, numerous commentaries have been written by distinguished Rabbis. Some of the commentaries extend to the whole Talmud, or a great portion thereof; others exclusively to the Mishna, or some of its sections. The following are the most important commentaries which are usually printed in our Talmud, and in the separate Mishna editions.

A. COMMENTARIES ON THE BABYLONIAN TALMUD.

§ 32.

1. The celebrated *Rabbenu Chananel* (ר"ח) of Kairwan (Africa), flourishing in the beginning of the eleventh century, wrote a commentary on the greater portion of the Talmud, which is often quoted by later commentators, and is now printed in the latest Talmud edition of Wilna.

2. *Rashi* רש"י, as the prince of commentators is generally called from the initials of his name, Rabbi Solomon Isaaki, of Troyes (1040—1105), wrote a commentary on almost the whole of

the Babylonian Talmud, which is printed in all editions thereof. It is a true model of concise, clear and systematic commentation. By a few plain words it often sheds light upon the obscurest passages, and unravels the most entangled arguments of the Talmudical discussions. As if anticipating the slightest hesitation of the unexperienced student, it offers him at once the needed explanation, or at least a hint that leads him the right way. It has truly been said that but for this peerless commentary of Rashi, the Babylonian Talmud would have remained as neglected as the Palestinian. An additional merit of that commentary is the fact that it very often establishes the correct version of the corrupted Talmud text. Such corrections are generally headed by the initials ה״ג (standing for הכי גרסינן "thus we are to read").

3. Supplements and additions to Rashi's commentary. The commentary on some Masechtoth, not being finished by Rashi, was completed in his spirit by his relatives and disciples. His son-in-law R. Jehuda b. Nathan completed that on Maccoth from fol. 19b.; his grandson R. Samuel b. Meir רשב״ם completed that on B. Bathra from fol. 29a. The last mentioned author, besides, added his commentary to Rashi's on the last Perek of Pesachim. The missing commentary of Rashi on Nedarim from fol. 22b. is supplemented by that of his predecessor, the celebrated Rabbenu Gershom.[1] To this commentary on Nedarim two others are added in our Talmud editions, one by Rabbenu Nissim (ר״ן) and the other by R. Asher הרא״ש, both flourishing in the fourteenth century.

4. *Tosaphoth* (meaning Additions) are a collection of annotations printed in all Talmud editions on the exterior margin of the page, while the interior margin on the opposite side of the Talmud text is generally assigned to Rashi's commentary. They are not, like the latter, a running commentary, but rather separate remarks and discussions on some passage of the text, intended to elucidate its meaning. Sometimes the explanations

[1] Some bibliographers maintain that also the commentary on *Nazir* and *Meilah*, ascribed to Rashi, does not belong to him, but to his disciples.

given in the commentaries of R. Chananel and Rashi are criticised and corrected. The latter of these two commentaries is, by way of excellence, generally designated as *Contros* (קינטרוס *commentarius*). The Tosaphoth often display great acumen and hair-splitting dialectics in finding, and again harmonizing, apparent contradictions between passages of the Talmud. Such questions of contradiction are generally introduced by the phrases: ואם תאמר (abbrev. וא"ת) "if thou wilt say or object..", or תימה "it is astonishing that..", or תימא "thou mayest say or object.. or קשה "here is the difficulty that....," and the final solution of the question or difficulty by ויש לומר (abbr. וי"ל) "but it may be said in answer to this....."

The numerous authors of these Tosaphoth (בעלי תוספות The Tosaphists, the glossarists) flourished during the 12th and 13th centuries in France and Germany. To the first among them belong the nearest relatives and disciples of Rashi, namely his two sons-in-law R. Meir b. Samuel and R. Jehuda b. Nathan (ריב"ן); his grandsons R. Isaac b. Meir (ריב"ם), R. Samuel b. Meir (רשב"ם)- and R. Jacob b. Meir, called Rabbenu Tam (ר"ת) and a nephew of the latter, R. Isaac b. Samuel, of Dampierre (ר"י הזקן).

Other authorities frequently mentioned in the Tosaphoth are: R. Jehuda b. Isaac, of Paris, called Sir Leon (12th century); R. Perez b. Elias in Corbeil (13th century).[1]

The Tosaphoth printed in our Talmud editions are merely extracts of older collections, namely of "Tosaphoth Sens" by R. Samson b. Abraham of Sens (abbrev. רשב"א, not to be confounded with the same abbreviation of R. Solomon b. Adereth) who flourished in the beginning of the 13th eentury, and principally of "Tosaphoth Tuch" or Touques by R. Eliezer of Tuch, (Touques), second part of that century.

A collection of "former Tosaphoth" תוספות ישנים on Yoma is, in some editions, appended to that Masechta. R. Moses of Coucy, the author of S'mag, is supposed to have been the originator of that collection.

---

[1] A full list of the Tosaphists is given by Zunz, Zur Geschichte und Literatur, pp. 29-60.

An anonymous author of the 14th century, excerpted from all Tosaphoth the practical results of their remarks and discussions. These paragraphed excerpts called פסקי תוספות (Decisions of the Tosaphoth) are in our Talmud editions appended to each Masechta.

Remark 1. References to certain passages in Rashi as well as Tosaphoth are usually made by citing the beginning words, or the catch words (דבור המתחיל abbrev. ד"ה) of that passage.

Remark 2. Of the great number of later commentaries and super-commentaries, generally published in separate volumes, the following are appended to some Talmud editions:

a. חכמת שלמה or חידושי מהרש"ל by *Solomon Luria* (מהרש"ל), in the XVI century. This shorter commentary is valuable especially on account of its numerous critical emendations in the reading of the Talmud text as well as of Rashi and Tosaphoth.

b. חידושי מהרש"א, Novellae, i. e. new comments by *R. Samuel Edels* (of Posen, died in the year 1631). In these explanatory and dialectical comments on Talmudical passages, and on Rashi and Tosaphoth, the author often displays a high degree of sagacity and penetration.

c. חידושי מהר"ם, Novellae, i. e. new comments by *R. Meir Lublin* (Rabbi in Cracow and Lemberg, died in the year 1616). These likewise very sagacious comments refer mostly to the Tosaphoth.

B. COMMENTARIES EXCLUSIVELY ON THE MISHNA.

§ 33.

1. The first to write a commentary on the whole Mishna was *Moses Maimonides* [XII century]. He commenced it in the 23rd year of his age, in Spain, and finished it in his 30th year, in Egypt. This commentary was written in Arabic, manuscripts of which are to be found in the Bodleian Library at Oxford, and in some other libraries. From the Arabic it was translated into Hebrew by several scholars, flourishing in the XIII century, namely Seder Zeraim, by Jehuda Charizi; Seder Moed, oy Joseph Ibn Alfual; Seder Nashim, by Jacob

Achsai (or Abbasi[1]). Seder Nezikin, by Solomon b. Joseph, with the exception of Perek Chelek in Sanhedrin and Masecheth Aboth, including the ethical treatise Sh'mone Perakim, introducing the latter, which were translated by Samuel Ibn Tibbon; Seder Kodashim, by Nathanel Ibn Almuli; the translator of Seder Teharoth is not known. These translations are appended to all Talmud editions, behind each Masechta under the heading of פירוש המשניות להרמב"ם.

The characteristic feature of this commentary of Maimonides consists in this, that it follows the analytical method, laying down at the beginning of each section the principles and general views of the subject, and thereby throwing light upon the particulars to be explained, while Rashi in his Talmud commentary adopted the synthetical method, commencing with the explanation of the particulars, and thereby leading to a clear understanding of the whole of the subject matter.

2. Several distinguished Rabbis wrote commentaries on single sections of the Mishna, especially on those Masechtoth to which no Babylonian Gemara (and hence no Rashi) exists. Of these commentaries the following are found in our Talmud editions:

a. פירוש הר"ש on all Masechtoth of Seder Zeraim, except Berachoth, and all Masechtoth of Seder Teharoth, except Nidda, by *R. Simson* of *Sens* (XII century), the celebrated Tosaphist.

b. פירוש הרא"ש, on the same Masechtoth, by *R. Asher b. Yechiel* (XIII cemtury) the author of the epitome of the Talmud which is appended to all Masechtoth.

c. פירוש ר"ש on Masecheth Middoth, by *R. Shemaya* who is supposed to have been a disciple of Rashi.

d. פירוש הראב"ד on Masecheth Eduyoth, by *R. Abraham b. David* (XII cent.), the celebrated author of critical annotations on Maimonides' Talmudical code.

e. Commentary on the Masechtoth Kinnim and Tamid by an anonymous author.

3. *R. Obadya of Bertinoro* in Italy, and Rabbi in Jerusalem (d. in the year 1510), wrote a very lucid commentary on the whole Mishna which accompanies the text in most of our separate

[1] See Graetz, Geschichte d. J. vol. VII, p. 302.

Mishna editions. He follows the synthetic method of Rashi, and adds to each paragraph of the Mishna the result of the discussion of the Gemara.

4. תוספות יו"ט Additional Comments by *Yom Tob Lipman Heller*, Rabbi of Prague and Cracow (XVII century). These comments likewise extending to all parts of the Mishna, and accompanying its text on the opposite side of Bartinoro's commentary in most of our Mishna editions, contain very valuable explanations and critical remarks.

5. Of shorter commentaries to be found only is some special editions of the Mishna text the following may be mentioned:

a. עץ חיים, by *Jacob Chagiz*, Rabbi in Jerusalem (XVII century), the author of a Talmudical terminology *Techilath Chochma.*

b. מלא כף נחת, by Senior Phoebus (XVIII cent.). This commentary is an abstract of Bertinoros and Yom Tob Lipman Heller's commentaries.

c. כף נחת, by *Isaac Ibn Gabbai* in Leghorn (XVII century), is generally based on the commentaries of Rashi and Maimonides.

C. COMMENTARIES ON THE PALESTINIAN TALMUD.

§ 34.

The Palestinian Talmud was not as fortunate as the Babylonian in regard to complete and lucid commentaries. Most of the commentaries on the former extend only to some sections or parts thereof, and none of them dates further back than to the sixteenth century.

The first commentary on the whole Palestinian Talmud by an anonymous author, appeared in the Cracow edition of the year 1609, and is reprinted in the latest Krotoschin edition. It is a brief and insufficient commentary.

2. שדה יהושע, a commentary on 18 Masechtoth by *R. Joshua Benveniste* (XVII century).

3. קרבן עדה and additions, called שירי קרבן on Seder Moed, Nashim and part of Nezikin by *R. David Fraenkel*, Rabbi in Dessau and later in Berlin, (teacher of Moses Mendelssohn, XVIII century).

4. פני משה and מראה הפנים, a double commentary on the whole Jerushalmi *by R. Moses Margolioth* (XVIII century). This double commentary and the preceding of David Fraenkel are embodied in the Shitomir edition (1860-67).

5. אהבת ציון on Berachoth, Peah and Demai by *Z. Frankel* (Vienna 1874 and Breslau 1875).

6. Commentary on Seder Zeraim and Mosecheth Shekalim by *Solomon Syrileio* (or *Serillo*), an exile from Spain. Of this commentary only Berachoth was published from a MS. with annotations by M. Lehmann (Frank. on the Main 1875).

Regarding some other commentaries on single parts of the Palestinian Talmud see Z. Frankel, Mebo Ha-Jerushalmi 134a-136a.

CHAPTER VIII

EPITOMES AND CODIFICATIONS OF THE TALMUD

INTRODUCTORY.

§ 35.

Since the Babylonian Talmud was considered by most of the Jewish communities in all countries as the source of the rabbinical law by which to regulate the religious life, it is but natural that already at a comparatively early period attempts were made to furnish abstracts of the same for practical purposes. This was done partly by epitomes or compendiums which, retaining the general arrangement and divisions of the Talmud, bring its matter into a narrower compass by omitting its Agadic and unnecessary passages, and abridging the legal discussions; and partly by codes in which the results of the discussed legal matter is presented in a more systematic order. The first attempts in this direction were made by R. Jehudai Gaon of Sura (VIII century) in his book *Halachoth Ketuoth* (abridged Halachoth), and by R. Simon of Kahira (—IX century) in his (*Halachoth Gedoloth*. Both of these two works which afterwards coalesced into one work still extant under the latter title, were however eclipsed by later master works of other celebrated Rabbinical authorities.

A. EPITOMES.

§ 36.

The principal epitomes or compendiums of the Talmud are by the following authors:

1. *R. Isaac Alfasi* (after the initials called "Rif", born in 1013 near the city of Fez in Africa, died in 1103 as Rabbi at Lucena in Spain) wrote an excellent compendium which he called "Halachoth" but which is usually called by the name of its author אלפסי or רי"ף. In this compendium he retains the general arrangement, the language and style of the Talmud, but omits, besides the Agada, all parts and passages which

concern laws that had become obsolete since the destruction of the temple. Besides, he condensed the lengthy discussions, and added his own decision in cases not clearly decided in the Talmud.

Remark. Alfasi's compendium comprises in print three large folio volumes in which the text is accompanied by Rashi's Talmud commentary and, besides, by numerous commentaries, annotations and glosses, especially those by R. Nissim b. Reuben (ר"ן); by R. Zerachia Halevi (Maor); by R. Mordecai b. Hillel; by R. Joseph Chabiba (Nimuke Joseph), and by some other distinguished Rabbis.

2. *R. Asher b. Jechiel* (הרא"ש), a German Rabbi, later in Toledo, Spain, where he died in 1327, wrote a compendium after the pattern of that of Alfasi and embodied in the same also the opinions of later authorities. This compendium is appended in our Talmud editions to each Masechta, under the title of the author רבינו אשר.

R. Jacob, the celebrated son of this author, added to that compendium an abstract of the decisions contained in the same, the קיצור פיסקי הרא"ש.

B. CODES.

§ 37.

1. *Mishne Thora* משנה תורה "Repetition of the Law", by R. Moses Maimonides (רמב"ם) flourishing in the XII century. This is the most comprehensive and systematically arranged Code of all the Laws scattered through the two Talmuds, or resulting from the discussions in the same. Occasionally also the opinions of the post Talmudic authorities, the Gaonim, are added.

This gigantic work, written throughout in Mishnic Hebrew in a very lucid and attractive style, is divided into *fourteen* books, hence its additional name Sepher Ha-yad (יד having the numerical value of 14), and by way of distinction, it was later called "Yad Hachazaka", the strong hand. Every book is, according to the various subjects treated therein, divided into Halachoth, the special names of which are given at the head of each of those fourteen books. The Halachoth are again subdivided into chapters (Perakim), and these into paragraphs.

Remark. This Code is usualy published in four large folio volumes and provided with the following annotations and commentaries:

a. *Hasagoth Rabed* השגות הראב"ד Critical Remarks, by *R. Abraham b. David*, of Posquieres, a contemporary and antagonist of Maimonides.

b. *Migdal Oz* מגדל עוז, the *Tower of Strength*, defending Maimonides' Code against the censures of the critic named above, by *Shem Tob Ibn Gaon*, of Spain (beginning of XIV century).

c. *Hagahoth Maimuniyoth* הגהות מימוניות, Annotations, by *R. Meir Ha-Cohen*, of Narbonne (XIV century).

d. *Maggid Mishne*. a commentary, generally referring to the Talmudical sources of the decisions in Maimonides' Code, by *Don Vidal di Tolosa* (XIV century).

e. *Khesef Mishne*, כסף משנה, a commentary like the preceding, by *R. Joseph Karo*, the author of the Shulchan Aruch (XVI century).

In some editions the following two commentaries are also appended.

Lechem Mishne לחם משנה, by *R. Abraham de Boton*, of Szafed, XVI century.

Mishne l'melech משנה למלך, *by Jehuda Rosanes*, Rabbi in Constantinople, d. 1727.

2. ס'מצות גדול (abbrev. סמ"ג), the great Law book, by the Tosaphist *R. Moses* of *Coucy*, in France (XIII century). This work arranges the Talmudical law according to the 613 precepts which the Rabbis found to be contained in the Pentateuch, and is divided into עשין commendatory, and לאווין prohibitory laws.

Remark. A similar work, but on a smaller scale, is ס' מצות קטן (סמ"ק), also called *Amude Golah*, by *R. Isaac b. Joseph*, of Corbeil. (d. 1280).

3. *Turim* טורים (the Rows of Laws), by *R. Jacob*, son of that celebrated R. Asher b. Jechiel who was mentioned above. The work is divided into four parts, called: *Tur Orach Chayim*, treating of Liturgical Laws; *Tur Yore Dea*, treating of the Ritual Laws; *Tur Eben Ha-ezer* on the Marriage Laws, and *Tur Choshen Mishpat* on the Civil Laws. Each of these four books is subdivided according to subjects under appropriate headings, and into chapters, called Simanim. This

code differs from that of Maimonides in so far as it is restricted to such laws only which were still in use outside of Palestine, and as it embodies also rules and customs which were established after the close of the Talmud. Besides, it is not written in that uniform and pure language and in that lucid style by which the work of Maimonides is characterized.

Remark. The text of the Turim is generally provided with the commentaries *Beth Joseph*, by R. Joseph Karo, and *Darke Moshe*, by *R. Moses Isserles.*

4. *Shulchan Aruch*, שלחן ערוך (the prepared table), by *R. Joseph Karo* (XVI century), the same author who wrote the commentaries on the codes of Maimonides and of R. Jacob b. Asher. Taking the last mentioned code (Turim) and his own commentary on the same as basis, and retaining its division into four parts as well as that into subjects and chapters, he subdivided each chapter (Siman) into paragraphs (סעיפים) and so remodeled its contents as to give it the proper shape and style of a law book. This Shulchan Aruch together with the numerous annotations (הגהות) added to it by the contemporary R. Moses Isserles (רמ"א) was up to our time regarded by all rabbinical Jews as the authoritative code by which all questions of the religious life were decided.

Remark. The glosses and commentaries on the Shulchan Aruch are very numerous. Those usually printed with the text in the folio editions are the following, all belonging to the seventeenth century:

a. *Beer ha-Gola*, giving the sources of that code, by Moses Ribkes in Amsterdam.

b. *Ture Zahab* (ט"ז) commentary on all parts of the code, by R. David b. Samuel Halevi.

c. *Sifthe Cohen* (ש"ך) on Jore Dea and Choshen Mishpat, by R. Sabbathai Cohen.

d. *Magen Abraham* (מ"א) on Orach Chayim, by R. Abram Gumbinner.

e. *Beth Samuel* on Eben Ha-ezer by R. Samuel b. Uri, of Furth.

f. *Chelkath Mechokek* on Eben Ha-ezer, by R. Moses of Brisk.

Constant references to the four Codes mentioned above are made in the marginal glosses which are found on every page of the Talmud, under the heading of "*En Mishpat, Ner Mitzwah*". It is the object of these glosses to show, at every instance when a law is quoted or discussed in the Talmud, where the final decision of that law is to be found in the various codes. The authorship of these marginal glosses is ascribed to R. Joshua Boas Baruch (XVI century). The same scholar wrote also the glosses headed *Thora Or* which are found in the space between the Talmud text and Rashi's commentary, and which indicate the books and chapters of the biblical passages quoted in the Talmud, besides, the very important glosses on the inner margins of the pages, headed *Massoreth Ha-shas* (מסורת הש"ס) which give references to parallel passages in the Talmud. The last mentioned glosses were later increased with critical notes by Isaiah Berlin (Pik), Rabbi in Breslau (d. 1799).

C. COLLECTIONS OF THE AGADIC PORTIONS OF THE TALMUD.

§ 38.

While the above mentioned Compendiums and Codes are restricted to abstracting only the legal matter (Halacha) of the Talmud, *R. Jacob ibn Chabib*, flourishing at the beginning of the sixteenth century, collected all the Agadic passages especially of the Babylonian Talmud. This very popular collection which is usually printed with various commentaries has the title of *En Jacob* (עין יעקב; in some editions it is also called עין ישראל).

R. Samuel Jafe, flourishing in the latter part of that century, made a similar Collection of the Agadic passages of the Palestinian Talmud with an extensive commentary under the title of יפה מראה (Vienna, 1590 and Berlin 1725-26). An abridged edition with a short commentary was published under the title of ס' בנין ירושלים (Lemberg, 1860).

CHAPTER IX

MANUSCRIPTS AND PRINTED EDITIONS OF THE TALMUD

A. Manuscripts.

§ 39.

In consequence of the terrible persecutions of the Jews during the Middle Ages, and the destruction of their libraries, so often connected therewith, and especially in consequence of the vandalism repeatedly perpetrated by the Church against the Talmud,[1] only a very limited number of manuscripts of the same have come down to our time. Codices of single *Sedarim* (sections) and *Masechtoth* (tracts or treatises) are to be found in various libraries of Europe, especially in the Vatican Library of Rome, and in the libraries of Parma, Leyden, Paris, Oxford, Cambridge, Munich, Berlin and Hamburg. The only known complete manuscript of the Babylonian Talmud, written in the year 1369, is in possession of the Royal Library of Munich. A fragment of Talmud Pesachim, of the ninth or tenth century, is preserved in the University Library of Cambridge, and was edited with an autotype fascimile, by W. H. Lowe, Cambridge 1879.

The Columbia College in the city of New York, lately acquired a collection of manuscripts containing the treatises *Pesachim*, *Moed Katon*, *Megilla* and *Zebaehim* of the Babylonian Talmud. These manuscripts came from Southern Arabia, and date from the year 1548.[2]

---

[1] It is stated that at the notorious *auto-da-fe* of the Talmud, held in the year 1249, at Paris, twenty four cart-loads of Talmud tomes were consigned to the flames. Similar destructions of the Talmud were executed by the order of Pope Julius III, in the year 1553, first at Rome, then at Bologne and Venice, and in the following year in Ancona and other cities. Among the 12,000 tomes of the Talmud that were burned at Cremona, in the year 1559 (see *Graetz Geschichte d. Juden* X. p. 382), were undoubtedly also numerous Manuscripts, though most of them may have been printed copies.

[2] See *Max L. Margolis*, "The Columbia College MS. of Meghilla examined," New York 1892.

Manuscripts of the *Mishna* or of single Sedarim thereof, some of which dating from the thirteenth century, are preserved in the libraries of Parma, of Berlin, of Hamburg, of Oxford and of Cambridge. That of the last mentioned library was edited by W. H. Lowe: "The Mishna on which the Palestinian Talmud rests," etc., Cambridge, 1883.

Of the *Palestinian Talmud* the only manuscript, of considerable extent, is preserved in the Library of Leyden. See S. M. Schiller-Szinessy, "Description of the Leyden MS. of the Palestinian Talmud." Cambridge 1878. Fragments of the Palestinian Talmud are also found in some other libraries, especially in those of Oxford and Parma.

Fuller information concerning MSS. of the Talmud is given in F. Lebrecht's "Handschriften und erste Ausgaben des Babyl. Talmud," Berlin 1862. See also M. Steinschneider's "Hebräische Bibliographie," Berlin, 1862 and 1863.

B. THE TALMUD IN PRINT.

a. The Mishna editions.

§ 40.

Already as early as the year 1492, the first edition of the Mishna together with the commentary of Maimonides appeared in Naples. It was followed by several editions of Venice (1546-50, and 1606), of Riva di Trento (1559) and of Mantua (1559-63). In the last mentioned editions the commentary of Obadia di Bertinoro is added. The editions which have since appeared are very numerous. Those which appeared since the seventeenth century are generally accompanied, besides Bertinoro's commentary, by תוספות י"ט by Lipman Heller or some other shorter commentaries.

b. The Babylonian Talmud.

§ 41.

The first complete edition of the Babylonian Talmud was published by Daniel Bomberg in 12 folio volumes, Venice

1520-23.[1] Besides the text, it contains the commentary of Rashi, the Tosaphoth, the Piske-Tosaphoth, the compendium of Asheri, and the Mishna commentary of Maimonides. This original edition served as model for all editions which subsequently appeared at Venice, Basel, Cracow, Lublin, Amsterdam, Frankfort on-the-Oder, Berlin, Frankfort on-the-Main, Sulzbach, Dyhernfurt, Prague, Warsaw, and recently at Vienna and Wilna. The later editions were greatly improved by the addition of valuable literary and critical marginal notes and appendices by learned rabbis. But the Basel and most of the subsequent editions down almost to the present time, have been much mutilated by the official censors of the press, who expunged from the Talmud all those passages which, in their opinion, seemed to reflect upon Christianity, and, besides, changed expressions, especially names of nations and of sects, which they suspected as having reference to Christians.[2]

The Amsterdam editions, especially the first (1644-48), escaped those mutilations at the hand of the censors, and are on this account considered very valuable. Most of the passages which have elsewhere been eliminated or altered by the censors, have been extracted from the Amsterdam edition, and published in separate small books. Of these the following two may be mentioned: קבוצות ההשמטות (s.l.) and חסרונות הש"ס, Koenigsberg, 1860.

A critical review of the complete editions of the Babylonian Talmud and of the very numerous editions of single Masechtoth

---

[1] Prior to this first complete edition, a number of single Masechtoth of the Babyl. Talmud had already been published by Gershom of Soncino, between the years 1484 and 1519, at Soncino and at Pesaro.

[2] Words mostly changed are: instead of גוי (gentile) כותי (a Samaritan) or כושי (an Aethiopian); instead of מין (a heretic) צדוקי (a Sadducee) or אפיקורוס (an Epicurean); instead of נכרי (an alien, a Non Israelite) עכו"ם (an idolater); instead of או"ה (the nations of the world)—בבליים (Babylonians) or כנענים (Canaanites); instead of רומאי (the Romans) ארמאי (Syrians) or פרסאי (Persians); instead of רומי (Rome) העיר (the city) etc.

In the more recent editions, however, except those appearing under Russian censorship, the original readings have mostly been restored.

since the year 1484, was published by Raphael Rabbinovicz, in his Hebrew pamphlet, מאמר על הדפסת התלמוד Munich 1877.[1]

The same author also collected and published very rich and important material for a critical edition of the Babylonian Talmud from the above mentioned manuscript in the Royal Library of Munich and other manuscripts, as well as from early prints of single Masechtoth in various libraries. The title of this very extensive work, written in Hebrew, is *Dikduke Sopherim*, ס'דקדוקי סופרים with the Latin title: Variae lectiones in Mishnam et in Talmud Babylonicum, etc., Munich 1868-86. The fifteen volumes in octavo which have appeared of this valuable work comprise only three and a half Sedarim of the six Sedarim of the Talmud. It is to be regretted that in consequence of the death of the learned author the completion of this important work has been suspended.

c. The Palestinian Talmud.

§ 42.

Of the Palestinian Talmud (Jerushalmi) only four complete editions appeared:

1. The first edition, published by Daniel Bomberg, Venice 1523-24, in one folio volume, without any commentary.

2. The *Cracow* edition, 1609, with a short commentary on the margin.

3. The *Krotoshin* edition, 1866, with a commentary like that in the Cracow edition, but added to it are marginal notes, containing references to parallel passages in the Babylonian Talmud, and corrections of text readings.

4. The *Shitomir* edition, 1860-67, in several folio volumes, with various commentaries.

Besides these four complete editions, several parts have been published with commentaries.

---

[1] This instructive pamphlet is also reprinted as an appendix to vol. VIII of Dikduke Sopherim.

CHAPTER X

AUXILIARIES TO THE STUDY OF THE TALMUD

A. Lexicons

§ 43.

1. The *Aruch* (הערוך) by *R. Nathan b. Jechiel*, of Rome, flourishing in the eleventh century. This oldest Lexicon for both Talmuds and the Midrashim, on which all later dictionaries are based, still retains its high value, especially on account of its copious quotations from the Talmudical literature by which many corrupted readings are corrected. It received many valuable additions (מוסף הערוך) at the hand of Benjamin Mussaphia (XVII century). These additions, generally headed by the initials אמר בנימין=א"ב, mostly explain the Greek and Latin words occurring in the Talmud and Midrash. The edition by M. Landau (Prague 1819-24, in five 8vo volumes) is increased by numerous annotations and supplied with definitions in German. The latest and best edition of that important work is:

2. *Aruch Completum* (ערוך השלם) by *Alexander Kohut*, vol. 1-VIII. Vienna and New York, 1878-1892. In this edition the original lexicon of Nathan b. Jechiel is corrected by collating several ancient Mss. of the work, and, besides, considerably enlarged by very valuable philological and critical researches and annotations.

3. *Lexicon Talmudicum* by *Joh. Buxtorf*, Basel, 1640. Of this work written in Latin, a new corrected and enlarged edition was published by *B. Fischer*, Leipsic, 1869-75.

4. Neuhebraisches und chald. *Wörterbuch über die Talmudim* und Midrashim, by *J. Levy* in four volumes. Leipsic 1876-89.

5. *A Dictionary of the Talmud* Babli and Yerushalmi and the Midrashic Literature, by *M. Jastrow*. London and New York, 1886-1903, in two volumes.

Remark. There are, besides, several small dictionaries, mostly abstracts of the Aruch, and useful for beginners. Special mention deserves *M. Schulbaum*, Neuhebräisch-deutsches Wörterbuch, Lemberg, 1880.

B. GRAMMARS.

§ 44.

The modern works on the Grammar of the *Mishna* have already been mentioned above p. 15 in the Note to the paragraph speaking of the Language of the Mishna. The first attempt at compiling a Grammar of the peculiar dialect of the Babylonian Gemara was made by:

S. D. Luzzatto in his "Elementi grammaticali del Caldeo Biblico e del dialetto Talmudico Babilonese". Padua, 1865.

Two translations of this work appeared, namely:

1. Grammatik der bibl. chaldaeischen Sprache und des Idioms des Talmud Babli. Ein Grundriss von S. D. Luzzatto, mit Anmerkungen herausgegeben von *M. S. Krüger*. Breslau, 1873.

2. Luzzatto's Grammar of the bibl. Chaldaic Language and of the idiom of the Talmud Babli, translated by *J. Goldammer*, New York, 1876.

Caspar Levias. Grammar of the Aramaic Idiom contained in the Babylonian Talmud. Cincinnati, 1900.

I. Rosenberg. Das Aramäische Verbum in babyl. Talmud. Marburg, 1888.

C. CHRESTOMATHIES.

§ 45.

A. B. Ehrlich. Rashe Perakim, Selections from the Talmud and the Midrashim. New York, 1884.

B. Fischer. Talmudische Chrestomathie mit Anmerkungen, Scholien und Glossar. Leipsic, 1884.

Ph. Lederer. Lehrbuch zum Selbstunterricht im babyl. Talmud, 3 parts, Pressburg, 1881-88.

A. Singer. המדריך Talmudische Chrestomathie für den ersten Unterricht im Talmud, 2 parts. Pressburg, 1882.

D. INTRODUCTORY WORKS AND TREATISES

a. OLDER WORKS

§ 46.

1. *Samuel Hanagid*, of Granada (XI century), was the first to write an introduction to the Talmud. Only a part of his work has come down to our time, and is appended to the first volume of our Talmud editions under the heading מבוא התלמוד.

2. *Moses Maimonides* opens his Mishna commentary on Seder Zeraim with an introduction to the Talmud, especially to the Mishna.

This introduction of Maimonides as well as that of Samuel Hanagid have been translated into German by *Pinner* in his Translation of Talm. Berachoth.

3. ס' כריתות (Methodology of the Talmud), by *Samson of Chinon* (XIV century). Constantine (1515), Cremona, (1558), Verona (1657).

4. הליכות עולם, by *Jeshua b. Joseph Halevi*, of Toledo, (XV century).

This work was translated into Latin by Constantin L'Empereur, under the title Clavis Talmudica. Leyden, 1634.

In the editions of Venice (1639), and of Livorno (1792) the Halichoth Olam is accompanied by two complementary works: כללי התלמוד, by Joseph Karo, and יבין שמועה, by Solomon Algazi.

Abstracts of the works 3 and 4 are added to Samuel Hanagid's Mebo Hatalmud in the appendix to our Talmud editions.

5. דרכי הגמרא Methodology of the Talmud by *Isaac Campanton*, of Castilia (XV century), published in Venice (1565) Mantua (1593), Amsterdam (1754). A new edition was published by Isaac Weiss, Vienna, 1891.

6. תחלת חכמה (Methodology of the Talmud), by *Jacob Chagiz* (XVII century). Verona 1647. Amst. 1709.

b. MODERN WORKS IN HEBREW.

§ 47.

J. Abelsohn. זכרון יהודה, Methodology of the Mishna and Rules of Halacha. Wilna, 1859.

Jacob Brüll. מבוא המשנה, Introduction to the Mishna; 2 volumes. Frankf. o. M. 1876-85. Vol. I treats of the lives and methods of the teachers from Ezra to the close of the Mishna, and vol. II of the Plan and System of the Mishna.

Zebi Hirsch Chajes. מבוא התלמוד, Introduction to the Talmud. Lemberg, 1845.

Z. Frankel. דרכי המשנה, Hodegetica in Mishnam etc., Leipsic, 1859. A little Supplement to this important work was published under the title of "Additamenta et Index ad librum Hodegetica in Mischnam". Leipsic, 1867.

Z. Frankel. מבוא הירושלמי, Introductio in Talmud Hierosolymitanum. Breslau, 1870.

Joachim Oppenheim. תולדות המשנה, the genesis of the Mishna. Pressburg, 1882.

J. H. Weiss. דור דור ודורשיו with the German title: Zur Geschichte der jüdischen Tradition. Vienna, 1871-83. Vol I and II treat of the period to the close of the Mishna, and Vol. III of that of the Amoraim.

J. Wiesner. גבעת ירושלים, Investigations concerning the origin and the contents of the Palestinian Talmud. Vienna, 1872.

c. WORKS AND ARTICLES IN MODERN LANGUAGES.

§ 48.

S. Adler. The article *Talmud* in Johnson's Encyclopedia, New York. Reprinted in the author's collective work "Kobetz al Yad". New York, 1886: pp. 46-80.

J. S. Bloch. Einblicke in die Geschichte der Entstehung der Talmudischen Literatur. Vienna, 1884.

N. Brüll. Die Entstehungsgeschichte des babyl. Talmuds als Schriftwerkes (in Jahrbücher für Jüd. Geschichte u. Literatur II pp. 1-123).

Sam. Davidson. The Article *Talmud* in John Kitto's Cyclopaedia.

J. Derenbourg. Article *Talmud* in Lichtenberg's Encyclopedie des sciences religieuses. Paris, 1882. XII pp. 1007-1036.

Z. Frankel. Beiträge zur Einleitung in den Talmud (in Monatschrift für Geschichte und Wissenschaft des Judenthums X, pp. 186-194; 205-212; 258-272).

J. Hamburger. Articles *Mischna* and *Talmud* in Real Eycyclopädie für Bibel und Talmud. Strelitz 1883. Vol II pp. 789-798 and 1155-1167.

D. Hoffmann. Die erste Mischna und die Controversen der Tanaim. Berlin, 1882.

B. Pick. Article *Talmud* in Clintock and Strong's Cyclopaedia of theological Literature. Vol. X, pp. 166-187.

Ludw. A. Rosenthal. Ueber den Zusammenhang der Mischna. Ein Beitrag zu ihrer Entstehungsgeschichte. Strasburg, 1890.

S. M. Schiller-Szinessy. Article *Mishnah* in Encyclopedia Britannica, 9th Edition, vol. XVI, and Article *Talmud* in vol. XXIII.

Hermann L. Strack. Einleitung in den Thalmud. Leipsic, 1887. This work of the celebrated Christian scholar which treats of the subject with thoroughness, exactness and impartiality, is a reprint of the article *Talmud* in Herzog's Real Encyclopädie für protestant. Theologie. Second Edition, vol. XVIII.

d. HISTORICAL WORKS.

Of modern historical works which, treating of the Talmudical period shed much light upon the genesis of the Talmud, the following are very important:

Julius Fürst. Kultur und Literaturgeschichte der Juden in Asien (Leipsic, 1849), treats of the Baoylonian academies and teachers during the period of the Amoraim.

I. M. Jost. Geschichte des Judenthums und seiner Secten (Leipsic 1857-59). Vol II, pp. 13-222 treat of the period from the destruction of the temple to the close of the Talmud.

H. Graetz. Geschichte der Juden, Vol. IV, second edition, Leipsic, 1866. This volume has been translated into English by James K. Gutheim: History of the Jews from the Downfall of the Jewish State to the conclusion of the Talmud. New York, 1873.

G. Karpeles. Geschichte der jüdischen Literatur. Berlin, 1886. pp. 265-332.

e. ENCYCLOPEDICAL WORKS.

§ 50.

Jsaac Lamperonti, physician and Rabbi in Ferrara (XVIII century) wrote in the Hebrew language a very extensive and useful Encyclopedia of the Talmud and the Rabbinical Decisions, under the title of פחד יצחק. Five folio volumes of this work, comprising the letters א-מ, were published at Venice (1750) and Livorno (1840). The remaining volumes have lately been published in 8vo at Lyck (1864-1874) and Berlin (1885-1889), where also a new edition of the former volumes appeared.

Solomon Rapaport. ערך מלין, an encyclopedical work in Hebrew of which only one volume, containing the letter א, appeared (Prague 1852).

J. Hamburger. Real Encyclopaedie für Bibel und Talmud, Abtheilung II. Die Talmudischen Artikel A-Z. Strelitz, 1883. Three Supplements to this valuable work appeared Leipsic 1886-92.

f. SOME OTHER BOOKS OF REFERENCE.

§ 51.

Simon Peiser. נחלת שמעוני. Onomasticon of Biblical persons and of the Mishna teachers quoted in the Talmud and in Midrash (Wandsbeck 1728).

Malachi ben Jacob (XVIII century), יד מלאכי. This book is a Methodology of the Talmud, alphabetically arranged. Livorno, 1767, Berlin, 1852.

A. Stein. Talmudische Terminologie; alphabetisch geordnet. Prague, 1869.

Jacob Brüll. דורש לציון Die Mnemonotechnik des Talmud. Vienna, 1864.

This little book explains the *Simanim*, i. e. the mnemonical signs and symbols so often met with in the Talmud which are intended to indicate the sequence of the discussing teachers or of their arguments. See above p. 60, Note.

Israel Mash. מלין דרבנן Rabbinical Sentences, alphabetically arranged. Warsaw, 1874.

S. Ph. Frenkel. ציון לדרש. Index of the Agadic passages of the Talmud. Krotoschin, 1885.

Moses Halevi. ציונים. Legal and ethical maxims of the Talmud, alphabetically arranged. Belgrade, 1874.

Wiesner. Scholien, wissenschaftliche Forschungen aus dem Gebiete des babyl. Talmud. I Berachoth; II Sabbath; III Erubin and Pesachim. Prague, 1859-67.

CHAPTER XI

TRANSLATIONS OF THE TALMUD

A. The Mishna.

§ 52.

a. Latin Translations.

The learned Dutch *G. Surenhusius* published (Amsterdam, 1698-1703) a Latin version of the Mishna and of the commentaries of Maimonides and Obadia Bertinoro with annotations by several Christian scholars.

Remark. Prior to this publication of Surenhusius, a Latin version of some single Masechtoth of the Mishna was published by various Christian Scholars, as *Sabbath* and *Erubin* by Seb. Schmidt (Leipsic, 1661); *Shekalim*, by Joh. Wülfer (Altdorf, 1680); *Aboda Zara* and *Tamid*, by C. Peringer (Altdorf, 1680).

b. German Translations.

Johann Jacob Rabe. Mishnah übersetzt und erläutert. Anspach, 1760-63.

I. M. Jost, the celebrated Jewish historian, published (Berlin 1832-34) a new German translation in Hebrew characters with short introductions and annotations, together with the vocalized Mishna text and the commentary כף נחת.

A. Sammter. Mischnajoth, vokalisirter Text mit deutscher Uebersetzung und Erklärung. Berlin, 1886—.

c. English Translations.

W. Walton. Translation of the treatises Sabbath and Erubin, London, 1718.

D. A. de Sola and *M. I. Raphall*. Eighteen treatises from the Mishna translated. London, 1843.

Joseph Barclay published under the title "The Talmud" a translation of eighteen treatises of the Mishna with annotations. London, 1878.

C. Taylor. Sayings of the Jewish Fathers (the treatise Aboth). Cambridge, 1877.

Remark. The treatise Aboth has been translated into almost all of the European languages.

B. THE BABYLONIAN TALMUD

§ 53.

To translate the Mishna is a comparatively easy task. Its generally plain and uniform language and style of expression, and its compendious character could easily enough be rendered into another language especially when accompanied by some explanatory notes. But it is quite different with the Gemara, especially the Babylonian. There are, of course, also passages in the Gemara which offer no great difficulties to a translator who is sufficiently familiar with the idiom in which the original is composed. We refer to the historical, legendary and homiletical portions (Agadas) which the compilers have interspersed in every treatise. The main part of the Gemara, however, which is essentially of an argumentative character, giving minute reports of discussions and debates on the law, this part, so rich in dialectical subtilities, and so full of technicalities and elliptical expressions, offers to the translator almost insurmountable difficulties. Here a mere version of the original will not do; neither will a few explanatory foot notes be sufficient. It would sometimes require a whole volume of commentary to supplement the translation of a single chapter of the original, in order to render fully and clearly the train of thought and dialectical arguments so idiomatically and tersely expressed therein.[1] This

[1] A striking analogy to this difficulty of translating the legal discussions of the Talmud is found in an other branch of legal literature, as may be seen from the following Note which a learned jurist kindly furnished me: "The Year Books of the English Law, sometimes called the *Black Letter Books*, written in the quaint French Norman, which was the court-language of that day, have always been more or less a sealed book, except to experts in historical antiquities. By the effort of the Selden Society these Reports are being translated from time to time into the English; but to the uninitiated, even in English, these reports are gibberish, and none but those thoroughly versed in legal antiquities, and who have so to speak imbibed from a thousand other sources the spirit of the laws of that day, will be much benefited by this translation. It will take volumes of commentary, a hundred times more bulky than the text, to make this mine of English common law of any value to the general practitioner, not to speak of the laity. "It is caviar to the general public."

explains why the various attempts at translating the whole of the Babylonian Talmud have, thus far, proven a failure, so that as yet only comparatively few Masechtoth of this Talmud have been translated, and these translations are in many cases not intelligible enough to be fully understood by the reader who is not yet familiar with the original text and with the spirit of the Talmud.

a. LATIN TRANSLATIONS OF SINGLE MASECHTOTH.

Blasius Ugolinus published in volume XIX of his Thesaurus antiquitatum sacrarum (Venice 1756) a translation of the Masechtoth Zebachim and Menachoth, and in vol. XXV (1762) the Masecheth Sanhedrin.

G. E. Edzard published (Hamburg, 1705) a Latin translation of the first two Perakim of Aboda Zara.

b. GERMAN TRANSLATIONS.

Johann Jacob Rabe. Der Tractat *Brachoth* nach der Hierosolymitan und Babylonischen Gemara übersetzt uud erläutert. Halle, 1777.

C. *M. Pinner.* Tractat *Berachoth.* Text mit deutscher Uebersetzung und Einleitung in den Talmud. Berlin, 1842.

Ferd. Christian Ewald. Aboda Sarah, ein Tractat aus dem Talmud übersetzt. Nürenberg, 1856 and 1868.

A. Sammter. Tractat *Baba Mezia.* Text mit deutscher Uebersetzung und Erklärung. Berlin, 1876.

M. Rawicz. Der Tractat *Megilla* nebst Tosafoth ins Deutsche übertragen. Frankfort on the Main, 1883.

M. Rawicz. Der Tractat *Rosch ha-Schanah* ins Deutsche übertragen. Frankf. on the Main, 1886.

M. Rawicz. Der Tractat *Sanhedrin* übertragen und mit erläuternden Bemerkungen versehen. Frankf. 1892.

D. O. Straschun. Der Tractat *Taanith* ins Deutsche übertragen. Halle, 1883.

August Wünsche. Der Babyl. Talmud in seinen haggadischen Bestandtheilen übersetzt, 2 volumes. Leipsic, 1886-88.

Isaak Levy. Der achte Abschnitt aus dem Tractate Sabbath

(Babli und Jeruschalmi) übersetzt und philologisch behandelt. Breslau, 1892.

c. FRENCH TNANSLATIONS.

I. Michel Rabbinowicz, this translator of several parts of the Babyl. Talmud adopted the proper method in presenting the mental labor embodied in that work. In selecting a treatise for translation he followed the example of Alphasi (see above p. 72) in his celebrated epitome of the Talmud, in omitting all digressions from the main subject, and all episodic Agadas which the compilers interspersed among the stern dialectical discussions. The main part thus cleared from all disturbing and bewildering by-work, is then set forth in a clear and fluent translation which combines correctness with the noted ease and gracefulness of the French language. Necessary explanations are partly given in short foot-notes, and partly, with great skill, interwoven into the translation of the text. An understanding of the intricate dialectical discussions is greatly facilitated by appropriate headings, such as: Question; Answer; Rejoinder; Reply; Objection; Remark, etc. Besides, each treatise is prefaced by an introduction, in which the leading principles underlying that part of the Talmud are set forth. Of this lucid translation the following parts have appeared:

1. Législation criminelle du Talmud, containing the treatise of *Sanhedrin* and such portions of *Maccoth* as refer to the punishment of criminals. Paris, 1876.

2. Législation civile du Talmud, traduction du traité *Kethuboth*. Paris, 1880.

3. Nouveau Commentaire et traduction du traité *Baba Kamma*. Paris, 1873.

4. Nouveau Commentaire et traduction du traité *Baba Metzia*. Paris, 1878.

5. Nouveau Commentaire et traduction du traité *Baba Bathra*. Paris, 1879.

6. La médicine, les païens etc. This volume contains such portions of thirty different treatises of the Talmud as refer to medicine, paganism, etc. Paris, 1879.

M. Schwab, added to the first volume of his French translation of the Palestinian Talmud, (Paris, 1871) also a translation of Berachoth of the Babyl. Talmud.

d. English Translation.

A. W. Streane. Translation of the treatise *Chagiga.* Cambridge, 1891.

C. The Palestinian Talmud.

§ 54.

a. Latin Translation.

Blasius Ugolinus published in volumes XVII-XXX of his Thesaurus antiquitatum sacrarum (Venice 1755-65) the following treatises in Latin: Pesachim (vol XVII); Shekalim, Yoma, Succah, Rosh Hashanah, Taanith, Megilla, Chagiga, Betza, Moed Katan (vol. XVIII); Maaseroth, Maaser Sheni, Challah, Orlah, Biccurim (vol. XX); Sanhedrin, Maccoth (vol. XXV); Kiddushin, Sota, Kethuboth (vol. XXX).

b. German Translations.

Joh. Jacob Rabe, besides translating Berachoth in connection with that treatise in the Babylonian Gemara, as mentioned above, published: Der Talmudische Tractat *Peah,* übersetzt und erläutert. Anspach, 1781.

August Wünsche. Der Jerusalemische Talmud in seinen haggadischen Bestandtheilen zum ersten Male in's Deutsche übertragen. Zurich, 1880.

c. French Translation.

Moise Schwab. Le Talmud de Jerusalem traduit pour la première fois X volumes. Paris, 1871-90.

d. English Translation.

M. Schwab, the author of the French translation just mentioned, published in English: The Talmud of Jerusalem. Vol. I Berachoth. London, 1886.

CHAPTER XII

BIBLIOGRAPHY

OF MODERN WORKS AND MONOGRAPHS ON TALMUDIC SUBJECTS.

(Arranged with reference to subjects and in alphabetical order of authors).

§ 55.

AGADA.

W. Bacher. Die Agada der Tannaiten. Strasburg, Als. 1884.

" Die Agada der Babylonischen Amoräer, Strasburg, Als. 1878.

" Die Agada der Palästinischen Amoräer, Strasburg, Als. 1891.

S. Back. Die Fabel im Talmud u. Midrasch (in Monatsschrift f. Geschichte u, Wissenschaft d. Judenthums, XXIV, 1875; XXV, 1876; XXIX 1880; XXX, 1881; XXXII, 1883; XXXIII, 1884).

M. Grünbaum. Beiträge zur vergleichenden Mythologie aus der Haggada (in Zeitschrift d. D. Morgenl. Gesellschaft, vol. XXXI, 1877).

M. Güdemann. Mythenmischung in der Haggada (in Monatschrift f. Geschichte u. Wissenschaft d. Judenthums, vol. XXV, 1876).

D. Hoffmann. Die Antonius Agadoth im Talmud (in Magazin für Wissenschaft des Judenthums, vol. XIX, 1892).

ARCHAEOLOGICAL.

Ad. Brüll. Trachten der Juden im nachbiblischen Alterthum Frankf. on the M. 1873.

Franz Delitzsch. Jüdisches Handwerkerleben zur Zeit Jesu, Elangen, 1879. Translated by B. Pick "Jewish Artisan Life." New York, 1883.

M. H. Friedländer. Die Arbeit nach Bibel u. Talmud. Brünn, 1891.

L. Herzfeld. Metrologische Voruntersuchungen, Geld und Gewicht der Juden bis zum Shluss des Talmuds (in Jahrbuch für Geschichte der Juden u. des Judenthums, vol. III pp. 95-191, Leipsic, 1863).

Alex. Kohut. Ist das Schachspiel im Talmud genannt? (Z. d. D. M. G. XLVI, 130-39).

Leopold Löw. Graphische Requisiten und Erzeugnisse bei den Juden, Leipsic, 1870-71.

" " Die Lebensalter in der Jüd. Literatur. Szegedin, 1875.

B. Zuckerman. Ueber Talmudische Münzen u. Gewichte. Breslau, 1862.

" Das jüdische Maassystem. Breslau, 1867.

BIOGRAPHICAL.

Sam. Back. Elischa ben Abuja, quellenmässig dargestellt. Frankf. on the M., 1891.

A. Blumenthal. Rabbi Meir, sein Leben u. Wirken. Frankf. 1889.

M. Braunschweiger. Die Lehrer der Mischna, ihr Leben u. Wirken. Frankf. on the M., 1890.

S. Fessler. Mar Samuel, der bedeutendste Amora, Breslau, 1879.

M. Friedländer. Geschichtsbilder aus der Zeit der Tanaiten u. Amoräer. Brünn, 1879.

S. Gelbhaus. R. Jehuda Hanasi und die Redaction der Mischna. Vienna, 1876.

D. Hoffmann. Mar Samuel, Rector der Academie zu Nahardea. Leipsic, 1873.

Armand Kaminka. Simon b. Jochai (chapter in the author's Studien zur Geschichte Galilaeas. Berlin, 1890).

Raphael Lévy. Un Tanah (Rabbi Meïr), Etude sur la vie et l'enseignement d'un docteur Juif du II siècle. Paris 1883.

M. I. Mühlfelder. Rabh. Ein Lebensbild zur Geschichte des Talmud, Leipsic, 1873.

J. Spitz. Rabban Jochanan b. Sakkai, Rector der Hochschule zu Jabneh. Berlin, 1883.

I. Trenel. Vie de Hillel l'Ancient. Paris, 1867.

H. Zirndorf. Some Women in Israel (pp. 119-270 portraying distinguished women of the Talmudic age). Philadelphia, 1892.

CHRONOLOGY AND CALENDAR

L. M. Lewisohn. Geschichte u. System des jüdischen Kalenderwesens. Leipsic, 1856.

B. Zuckermann. Materialien zur Entwickelung der altjüdischen Zeitrechnung. Breslau 1882.

CUSTOMS.

Joseph Perles. Die jüdische Hochzeit in nachbiblischer Zeit. Leipsic, 1860.

" " Die Leichenfeierlichkeiten im nachbiblischen Judenthum. Breslau, 1861.

Remark. An English translation of both of these two monographs is embodied in "Hebrew Characteristics", published by the American Jewish Publication Society. New York, 1875.

M. Fluegel. Gedanken über religiöse Bräuche und Anschauungen. Cincinnati, 1888.

DIALECTICS.

Aaron Hahn. The Rabbinical Dialectics. A history of Dialecticians and Dialectics of the Mishna and Talmud, Cincinnati. 1879.

EDUCATION.

Blach-Gudensberg. Das Paedagogische im Talmud. Halberstadt. 1880.

M. Duschak. Schulgesetzgebung u. Methodik der alten Israeliten. Vienna, 1872.

Sam. Marcus. Zur Schul-Paedagogik des Talmud. Berlin, 1866.

Joseph Simon. L'èducation et l'instruction d'après la Bible et le Talmud Leipsic, 1879.

J. Wiesen. Geschichte und Methodik der Schulwesens im talmudischen Alterthum. Strasburg, 1892.

ETHICS.

M. Bloch Die Ethik der Halacha, Budapest, 1886.

Herman Cohen. Die Nächstenliebe im Talmud. Ein Gutachten. Marburg, 1886.

M. Duschak. Die Moral der Evangelien u. des Talmuds. Brünn 1877.

H. B. Fassel. Tugend-und Rechtslehre des Talmud. Vienna, 1848.

E. Grünebaum. Die Sittenlehre des Judenthums andern Bekentnissen gegenüber. Strasburg, 1878.

M. Güdemann. Nächstenliebe. Vienna, 1890.

Alex. Kohut. The Ethics of the Fathers. A series of lectures. New York, 1885.

L. Lazarus. Zur Charakteristik der talmudischen Ethik. Breslau, 1877.

Marc. Lévy. Essai sur la morale de Talmud. Paris 1891.

Luzzatto. Israelitische Moraltheologie, deutsch von L. E. Igel, Breslau, 1870.

S. Schaffer. Das Recht und seine Stellung zur Moral nach talmudischer Sitten, und Rechtslehre. Frankf. on the M., 1889.

N. J. Weinstein. Geschichtliche Entwickelung des Gebotes der Nächstenliebe innerhalb des Judenthums, kritisch beleuchtet. Berlin, 1891.

EXEGESIS.

H. S. Hirschfeld. Halachische Exegese. Berlin, 1840.

" " Die Hagadische Exegese. Berlin, 1847.

S. Waldberg. Darke Hashinnuyim, on the methods of artificial interpretation of Scriptures in the Talmud and Midrash. (in Hebrew) Lemberg, 1870.

GEOGRAPHY AND HISTORY.

A. Berliner. Beiträge zur Geographie u. Ethnographie Babyloniens im Talmud u. Midrasch. Berlin 1883.

J. Derenbourg. Essai sur l'histoire et la géographie de la Palestine d'après les Talmuds et les autres sources rabbiniques. Paris, 1867.

H. Hildesheimer. Beiträge zur Geographie Palästinas. Berlin, 1886.

Armand Kaminka. Studien zur Geschichte Galilaeas. Berlin, 1890.

Ad. Neubauer. La géographie du Talmud. Mémoire couronné par l'académie des inscriptions et belles-lettres. Paris, 1868.

LAW.

a. IN GENERAL.

Jacques Levy. La jurisprudence du Pentateuque et du Talmud. Constantine, 1879.

S. Mayer. Die Rechte der Israeliten, Athener und Römer. Leipsic, 1862-66.

I. L. Saalschütz. Das Mosaische Recht, nebst den vervollständigenden thalmudisch-rabbinischen Bestimmungen. 2-nd Edition. Berlin, 1853.

S. Schaffer. Das Recht u. seine Stellung zur Moral nach talmudischer Sitten-und Rechtslehre. Frankf. on the M., 1889.

I. M. Wise. The Law (in the Hebrew Review, Vol. I pp. 12-32. Cincinnati, 1880).

b. JUDICIAL COURTS.

J. Selden. De Synedriis et praefecturis juridicis veterum Ebraeorum. London, 1650; Amsterd. 1679; Frankf., 1696.

E. Hoffmann. Der oberste Gerichtshof in der Stadt des Heiligthums. Berlin, 1878.

c. EVIDENCE IN LAW.

I. Blumenstein. Die verschiedenen Eidesarten nach mosaisch-talmudischem Rechte. Frankf. on the M., 1883.

Z. Frankel. Der Gerichtliche Beweis nach mosaisch-talmudischem Rechte. Berlin. 1846.

D. Fink. "Miggo" als Rechtsbeweis im bab. Talm. Leipsic, 1891.

d. CRIMINAL LAW.

O. Bähr. Das Gesetz über falsche Zeugen, nach Bibel u. Talmud. Berlin, 1862.

P. B. Benny. The Criminal Code of the Jews. London, 1880.

M. Duschak. Das mosaisch-talmudische Strafrecht. Vienna, 1869.

J. Fürst. Das peinliche Rechtsverfahren im jüd. Alterthum. Heidelberg, 1870.

E. Goitein. Das Vergeltungsprinzip im bibl. u. talmudischen Strafrecht (in Zeitschrift für Wissenschaft d. J. Vol. XIX.

S. Mendelsohn. The Criminal Jurisprudence of the ancient Hebrews compiled from the Talmud and other rabbinical writings. Baltimore, 1891.

Julius Vargha. Defense in criminal cases with the ancient Hebrews, translated from the first chapter of the author's large work "Vertheidigung in Criminalfällen", and publisched in the Hebrew Review, Vol. I pp. 254-268. Cincinnati, 1880.

I. Wiesner. Der Bann in seiner geschichtlichen Entwickelung auf dem Boden des Judenthums. Leipsic, 1864.

Thonisson. La peine de mort dans le Talmud. Brussels, 1886.

e. CIVIL LAW.

M. Bloch. Die Civilprocess-Ordnung nach mosaisch-rabbinischem Rechte. Budapest. 1882.

H. B. Fassel. Das mosaisch-rabbinische Civilrecht. Gr. Kanischa, 1852-54.

" " Das mosaisch-rabbinische Gerichtsverfahren in civilrechtlischen Sachen. Gr. Kanischa, 1859.

L. Auerbach. Das jüdische Obligationsrecht. Berlin, 1871.

S. Keyzer. Dissertatio de tutela secundum jus Talmudicum. Leyden 1847.

f. INHERITANCE AND TESTAMENT.

L. Bodenheimer. Das Testament. Crefeld, 1847.

Eduard Gans. Grundzüge des mosaisch-talmudischen Erbrechts (in Zunz' Zeitschrift für die Wissenschaft des Judenthums p. 419 sq.).

Moses Mendelssohn. Ritualgesetze der Juden, betreffend Erbschaften Vormundschaft, Testamente etc. Berlin, 1778, and several later editions.

Joh. Selden. De Successionibus in bona defuncti ad leges Hebrae orum. London, 1646; Frankf., 1696.

g. POLICE LAW.

M. Bloch. Das mosaisch-talmudische Polizeirecht. Buda Pest, 1878. Transated into English by I. W. Lilienthal in the Hebrew Review Vol. I, Cincinnati 1881.

h. LAW OF MARRIAGE AND DIVORCE.

P. Buchholz. Die Familie nach mos.-talmud. Lehre. Breslau, 1867.

M. Duschak. Das mosaisch-talmudische Eherecht. Vienna, 1864.

Z. Frankel. Grundlinien des mosaisch-talmud. Eherechts. Breslau, 1860.

S. Holdheim. Die Autonomie der Rabbinen und das Princip der jüdischen Ehe. Schwerin, 1847.

L. Lichtschein. Die Ehe nach mosaisch-talm. Auffassung. Leipsic, 1879.

M. Mielziner. The Jewish Law of Marriage and Divorce in ancient and modern times, and its relation to the law of the State. Cincinnati, 1884.

Joh. Selden. Uxor Ebraica sive de nuptiis et divortiis etc. London, 1646.

I. Stern. Die Frau im Talmud. Zürich, 1879.

i. Laws Concerning Slavery.

M. Mielziner. Verhältnisse der Sklaven bei den alten Hebräern nach biblischen und talmudischen Quellen, Copenhagen, (Leipsic), 1859.

An English translation of this treatise was published by Prof. H. I. Schmidt in the Gettysburg Evang. Review vol XIII, No 51, and reprinted in the Am. Jew's Annual. Cincinnati, 1886.

I. *Winter.* Stellung der Sklaven bei den Juden. Breslau, 1886.

Zadok-Kahn. L'esclavage selon la Bible et le Talmud. Paris, 1867,

" " Sklaverei nach Bibel u. Talmud. Deutsch von Singer. Berlin, 1888.

LINGUISTICS.

A. Berliner. Beiträge zur hebräischen Grammatik im Talmud u. Midrasch. Berlin, 1879.

Ad. Brüll Fremdsprachliche Redensarten u. Wörter in den Talmuden u. Midraschim. Leipsic, 1869.

N. Brüll. Fremdsprachliche Wörter in den Talmuden u. Midraschim (in Jahrbücher für jüd. Geschichte u. Literatur I, 123-220). Frankf. o. M., 1874.

Jos. Perles. Etymologische Studien zur Kunde der rabbinischen Sprache und Alterthümer. Breslau, 1871.

G. Rülf. Zur Lautlehre der aramäisch-talmudischen Dialecte. Breslau, 1879.

Mich. Sachs. Beiträge zur Sprach-und Alterthumsforschung. 2 volumes. Berlin, 1852-54.

MATHEMATICS.

B. Zuckermann. Das Mathematische im Talmud. Beleuchtung und Eläuterung der Talmudstellen mathematischen Inhalts. Breslau, 1878.

MEDICINE, SURGERY etc.

Jos. Bergel. Die Medizin der Talmudisten. Leipsic, 1885.

Joach. Halpern. Beiträge zur Geschichte der talm. Chirurgie. Breslau, 1869.

A. H. Israels. Collectanea Gynaecologica ex Talmude Babylonico. Gröningen, 1845.

L. Katzenelsson. Die Osteologie der Talmudisten. Eine talmudisch-anatonische Studie (in Hebrew). St. Petersbourg, 1888.

R. I. Wunderbar. Biblisch-talmudische Medicin, 2 volumes. Riga (Leipsic), 1850-60.

NATURAL HISTORY AND SCIENCES.

Jos. Bergel. Studien über die naturwissenschaftlichen Kenntnisse der Talmudisten. Leipsic, 1880.

M. Duschak. Zur Botanik des Talmud. Buda Pest, 1870.

L. Lewysohn. Die Zoologie des Talmuds. Frankf. on the M., 1858.

Imm. Löw. Aramäische Pflanzennamen. Leipsic, 1881.

PARSEEISM IN THE TALMUD.

Alexander Kohut. Was hat die talm. Eschatologie aus dem Parsismus aufgenommen? (in Z. d. D. M. G. vol. XXI pp 552-91).

" " Die jüdische Angelologie und Daemonologie in ihrer Abhängigkeit vom Parsismus. Leipsic, 1866.

" " Die talmudisch-midraschische Adamssage in ihrer Rückbeziehung auf die pers. Yima und Meshiasage, in Z. d. D. M. G. XXV pp. 59-94.

" " Die Namen der pers. u. babylonischen Feste im Talmud (in Kobak's Jeschurun, vol. VIII, 49-64). The same subject in Revue. des Etudes Juives, Vol. XXIV.

POETRY.

S. Sekles. The Poetry of the Talmud. New York, 1880.

PROVERBS, MAXIMS, PARABLES.

L. Dukes. Rabbinische Blumenlese. Leipsic, 1844.

" " Rabbinische Spruchkunde. Vienna, 1851.

J. R. Fürstenthal. Rabbinische Anthologie. Breslau, 1834.

Giuseppe Levi. Parabeln, Legenden u. Gedanken aus Talmud u. Midrasch, aus dem Italienischen ins Deutsche übetragen von L. Seligmann. Leipsic, 1863.

Löwenstein. Sentenzen, Sprüche u. Lebensregeln aus dem Talmud, Berlin, 1887.

PSYCHOLOGY

M. Jacobson. Versuch einer Psychologie des Talmud. Hamburg, 1878.

I. Wiesner. Zur talmudischen Psychologie (in Magazin für jüdische Geschichte und Literatur, Vol. I, 1874, and II, 1875).

RELIGIOUS PHILOSOPHY AND HISTORY.

M. Friedländer. Ben Dosa und seine Zeit, oder Einfluss der heidnischen Philosophie auf das Judenthum u. Christenthum. Prague, 1872.

M. Güdemann. Religionsgeschichtliche Studien. Leipsic, 1876.

M. Joel. Blicke in die Religionsgeschichte zu Anfang des II Jahrhunderts. Breslau, 1880.

A. Nager. Die Religionsphilosophie des Talmud. Leipsic, 1864.

SUPERNATURALISM AND SUPERSTITION.

Gideon Brecher. Das Transcendentale, Magik und magische Heilarten im Talmud. Vienna, 1850.

David Joel. Der Aberglaube und die Stellung des Judenthums zu demselben. 2 parts. Breslau, 1881-83.

Alex. Kohut. Jüdische Angelologie u. Daemonologie in ihrer Abhängigkeit vom Parsismus. Leipsic, 1866.

Sal. Thein. Das Princip des planetarischen Einflusses nach der Anschauung des Talmud. Vienna, 1876.

S. Wolffsohn. Oneirologie im Talmud, oder der Traum nach Auffassung des Talmuds. Breslau, 1874.

POPULAR TREATISES AND LECTURES ON THE TALMUD.

Tobias Cohn. Der Talmud. Ein Vortrag. Vienna, 1866.

Emanuel Deutsch. What is the Talmud? (in the Quarterly Review for October, 1867, reprinted in the Literary Remains, New York, 1874).

M. Ehrentheil. Der Geist des Talmud. Breslau, 1887.

Karl Fischer. Gutmeinung über den Talmud. Vienna, 1883.

Sams. Raph. Hirsch. Beziehung des Talmuds zum Judenthum und zur sozialen Stellung seiner Bekenner. Frankf. o. M., 1884.

P. I. Hershon. Talmudic Miscellany. London, 1880.

P. L. Hershon. Treasures of the Talmud. London, 1882.

Abram S. Isaacs. Stories from the Rabbis. New York. 1893.

A. Jellinek Der Talmud. Zwei Reden. Vienna, 1865.
Der Talmndjude. 4 Reden. Vienna, 1882-83.

M. Joel. Gutachten über den Talmud. Breslau, 1877.

Albert Katz. Der wahre Talmudjude. Die wichtigsten Grundsätze des talmudischen Schriftthums über das sittliche Leben des Menschen. Berlin, 1893.

S. Klein. Die Wahrheit über den Talmud, (aus dem Französischen "La veritè sur le Talmud", übersetzt von S. Mannheimer, Basel, 1860.

Isidore Loeb. La Controverse sur le Talmud sous Saint Louis, Paris, 1881.

H. Polano. The Talmud, Selections from the contents of that ancient book. London, 1876.

Ludwig Philippson. Zur Characteristik des Talmuds (in "Weltbewegende Fragen". Vol. II, pp. 349-416. Leipsic, 1869).

Em. Schreiber. The Talmud. A series of (4) Lectures. Denver, 1884.

L. Stern. Ueber den Talmud. Vortrag. Wurzburg, 1875.

J. Stern. Lichtstrahlen aus dem Talmud. Zurich, 1883.

A. A. Wolff. Talmudfjender (the Enemies of the Talmud),in Danish. Copenhagen, 1878.

August Wünsche. Der Talmud. Eine Skizze. Zurich, 1879.

CHAPTER XIII

OPINIONS ON THE VALUE OF THE TALMUD

§ 57.

No literary monument of antiquity has ever been subject to so different and opposite views and opinions, as the Talmud. Its strict followers generally looked upon it as the very embodiment of wisdom and sagacity, and as a work whose authority was second only to that of the Bible. In the non-Jewish literature it was often decried as "one of the most repulsive books that exist", as "a confused medley of perverted logic, absurd subtileties, foolish tales and fables, and full of profanity, superstition and even obscenity", or at the most, as "an immense heap of rubbish at the bottom of which some stray pearls of Eastern wisdom are hidden."

It is certain that many of those who thus assumed to pass a condemning judgment upon the gigantic work of the Talmud never read nor were able to read a single page of the same in the original, but were prompted by religious prejudice and antagonism, or they based their verdict merely on those disconnected and often distorted passages which Eisenmenger and his consorts and followers picked out from the Talmud for hostile purposes.

Christian scholars who had a deeper insight into the Talmudical literature, without being blinded by religious prejudices, expressed themselves quite differently on the character and the merits of that work, as may be seen from the following few quotations.

Johann Buxtorf, in the preface to his Lexicon Chald. et Talmudicum, says: "The Talmud contains many legal, medical, physical, ethical, political, astronomical, and other excellent documents of sciences, which admirably commend the history of that nation and time; it contains also luminous decisions of antiquity; excellent sayings; deep thoughts, full of grace and sense; and numerous expressions which make the reader not only better, but also more wise and learned, and which, like unto flashing jewels, grace the Hebrew speech not less than all those Greek and Roman phrases adorn their languages."

Other favorable opinions expressed by Christian scholars of the sixteenth to eighteenth centuries are collected in Karl Fischer's "Gutmeinung über den Talmud der Hebräer." Vienna, 1883.

Of such scholars as belong to our time, the following may be quoted here.

The late *Prof. Delitzsch* in his "*Jüdisches Handwerkerleben zur Zeit Jesu*" says:

"Those who have not in some degree accomplished the extremely difficult task of reading this work for themselves, will hardly be able to form a clear idea of this polynomical colossus. It is an immense speaking-hall, in which thousands and tens of thousands of voices, of at least five centuries, are heard to commingle. A law, as we all know from experience, can never be so precisely formulated that there does not remain room for various interpretations; and question upon question constantly arises as to the application of it to the endless multiplicity of the existing relations of life. Just imagine about ten thousand decrees concerning Jewish life classified according to the spheres of life, and in addition to these, about five hundred scribes and lawyers, mostly from Palestine and Babylon, taking up one after another of these decrees as the topic of examination and debate, and, discussing with hair-splitting acuteness, every shade of meaning and practical application; and imagine, further, that the fine-spun thread of this interpretation of decrees is frequently lost in digressions, and that, after having traversed long distances of such desert-sand, you find, here and there, an oasis, consisting of sayings and accounts of more general interest. Then you may have some slight idea of this vast, and of its kind, unique, juridic codex, compared with whose compass all the law-books of other nations are but Lilliputians, and beside whose variegated, buzzing market din, they represent but quiet study-chambers."

J. Alexander, in his book on *The Jews*; their *Past, Present* and *Future* (London, 1870), says:

"The Talmud, as it now stands, is almost the whole literature of the Jews during a thousand years. Commentator followed upon commentator, till at last the whole became an immense bulk; the original Babylonian Talmud alone consists of 2947 folio pages. Out of such literature it is easy to make quotations which may throw an odium over the whole. But fancy if the production of a thousand years of English literature, say, from the "History" of the venerable Bede to Milton's "Paradise Lost," were thrown together into a number of uniform folios, and judged in like manner; if because some superstitious monks wrote silly "Lives of Saints," therefore the works of John Bunyan should also be considered worthless. The absurdity is too obvious to require another word from me. Such, however, is the continual treatment the Talmud receives both at the hand of its friends and of its enemies. Both will find it easy to quote in behalf of their preconceived notions, but the earnest student will rather try to weigh the matter impartially, retain the good he can find even in the Talmud, and reject what will not stand the test of God's word."

The impartial view of the Talmud taken by modern Jewish scholars may be seen from the following opinion expressed by the late *Prof. Graetz* in his "History of the Jews" (vol. IV. 308 sq.).

"The Talmud must not be considered as an ordinary literary work consisting of twelve folios; it bears not the least internal resemblance to a single literary production; but forms a world of its own which must be judged according to its own laws. It is, therefore, extremely difficult to furnish a specific sketch of the Talmud, seeing that a familiar standard or analogy is wanting. And however thoroughly a man of consummate talent may have penetrated its spirit and become conversant with its peculiarities, he would scarcely succeed in such a task. It may, in some respects, be compared with the Patristic literature, which sprang up simultaneously. But on closer inspection, this comparison will also fail...

The Talmud has at different times been variously judged on the most heterogeneous assumptions; it has been condemned and consigned to the flames, simply because it was presented in its unfavorable aspect without taking into consideration its actual merits. It cannot be denied that the Babylonian Talmud labors under some defects, like any other mental product which pursues a single course with inexorable consistency and undeviating dogmatism. These defects may be classified under four heads: the Talmud contains some unessential and trivial subjects, which it treats with much importance and a serious air; it has adopted from its Persian surroundings superstitious practices and views, which presuppose the agency of intermediate spiritual beings, witchcraft, exorcising formulas, magical cures and interpretations of dreams and, hence, are in conflict with the spirit of Judaism; it further contains several uncharitable utterances and provisions against members of other nations and creeds; lastly it favors a bad interpretation of Scripture, absurd, forced and frequently false commentations. For these faults the whole Talmud has been held responsible and been denounced as a work devoted to trifles, as a source of immorality and trickery, without taking into consideration that it is not a work of a single author who must be responsible for every word, and if it be so, then the whole Jewish people was its author. Over six centuries are crystallized in the Talmud with animated distinctness, in their peculiar costumes, modes of speech and of thought, so to say a literary Herculaneum and Pompeii, not weakened by artistic imitation, which transfers a colossal picture to the narrow limits of a miniature. It is, therefore, no wonder, if in this world sublime and mean, great and small, serious and ridiculous, Jewish and heathen elements, the altar and the ashes, are found in motley mixture. Those odious dicta of which Jew-haters have taken hold, were in most cases nothing else but the utterances of a momentary indignation, to which an individual had given vent and which were preserved and embodied in the Talmud by over-zealous disciples, who were unwilling to omit a single expression of the revered ancients. But these utterances are richly counterbalanced by the maxims of benevolence and philanthropy towards every man, regardless of creed and nationality, which are also preserved in the Talmud. As counterpoise to the rank superstition, there are found therein sharp warnings against superstitious, heathen practices (Darke Emori), to which subject a whole section, under the name of *Perek Emorai*, is devoted.[1]

"The Babylonian Talmud is especially characterized and distinguished from the Palestinian, by high-soaring contemplations, a keen understanding, and flashes of thought which fitfully dart through the mental horizon. An incalculable store of ideas and incentives to thinking is treasured in the Talmud, but not in the form of finished themes that may be appropriated in a semi-somnolent state, but with the fresh coloring of their inception. The Babylonian Talmud leads into the laboratory of thought, and its ideas may be traced from their embryonic motion up to a giddy height, whither they at times soar into the region of the incomprehensible. For this reason it became, more than the Jerusalemean, the national property, the vital breath, the soul of the Jewish people——".

WHY STUDY THE TALMUD?

§ 58.

Some years ago, the author addressed the Classes of the Hebrew Union College on this question. An abstract of that address may find here a proper place for the benefit of younger students:

Upon resuming our labors for a new scholastic year, I wish to address the students regarding that branch of instruction which I have the privilege of teaching in the collegiate classes of this institution. I wish to answer the question:

FOR WHAT PURPOSE DO WE STUDY THE TALMUD?

There was a time—and it is not so very long since it passed by—there was a time when such a question would scarcely have entered into the mind of one who was preparing for the Jewish ministry. For the Talmud was then still regarded as the embodiment of all religious knowledge and Jewish lore. Its authority was considered second only to that of the Bible, its study regarded as a religious service, a God-pleasing work in

---

[1] Sabbath 66a; Tosептha ch. VII, VIII.

which all pious and literate men in Israel were engaged, even those who did not aspire to a rabbinical office. He, to whom the Talmud was a *terra incognita* was looked upon as an *Am Ha'arets*, a rustic and illiterate man, who had no right to express an opinion in religious matters. How then could he who wanted to become a religious guide and leader in Israel ask, for what purpose is the Talmud to be studied? The Talmudic literature was the very source of the Jewish law. By it all conditions of the religious and moral life were ordered. How could a rabbi expect to be able to answer and decide the many religious questions laid before him daily, without a thorough acquaintance with that source?

But it is quite different in our time, which looks upon the Talmud with less reverential eyes. The mere study of its literature is not any longer considered a religious act that secures eternal bliss and salvation; neither is the Talmud any longer regarded as the highest authority by whose dicta questions of religion and conscience are to be finally decided.

Of what use is the study of the Talmud in our time? Is it nowadays absolutely necessary even for the Jewish theologian, for a Jewish minister, to cultivate this hard and abstruse branch of literature? Would it not be more useful if our students instead of devoting a part of their valuable time to this obsolete and antiquated study would apply it to some other branch of knowledge which is of more import to, and has more bearing upon the present time?

It sometimes seemed to me as if I could read this question from the faces of some of our students during the Talmudic instruction, especially when we just happened to have before us some abstruse passages in the Talmud in which seemingly quite indifferent and trifling subjects are minutely treated in lengthy discussions, or where the whole train of thought widely differs from modern conception and modern ways of thinking.

Nay, I have even heard such a question from the lips of men who take great interest in our college, of earnest and judicious men who are highly educated and versed in our literature and who themselves in their youth imbibed spiritual draughts from the Talmudic fountain. Why trouble our students with that irksome and useless branch of literature, why not instead of it rather take up other subjects of more modern thought?

Let us, therefore, shortly consider the question: For what purpose do we study the Talmud, or why is that study indispensable for every one who prepares for the Jewish ministry?

In the first place, my young friends, I wish to call your attention to the fact that the Talmud is a product of the mental labors of our sages and teachers during a period of eight hundred to one thousand years, and that the pages of this voluminous literary work offer a natural reflection of whatever the Jewish mind has thought, perceived and felt during that long period under the most different circumstances and times, under joyful and gloomy events, under elevating and oppressing influences.

I beg you to consider furthermore what a powerful and decided influence this gigantic literary work after its final conclusion has exercised upon the mind and the religious and moral life of the professors of Judaism during fourteen centuries up to our time. Consider, how it is to be ascribed to their general occupation with, and veneration for the Talmud that our ancestors during the dark centuries of the Middle Ages did not become mentally hebetated and morally corrupted, in spite of the degradation and systematic demoralization which they had been exposed to. For while the study of the more dialectic part of that literature preserved their intellectual powers ever fresh and active and developed some of the greatest minds, the reading of those popular sayings and impressive moral and religious maxims with which the Talmudic writings are so amply provided, fostered even within our masses that unshaken faithfulness and that unparalleled firmness of character by which they resisted all persecutions and all alluring temptations.

Take all this into consideration, and you will perceive that none can expect to know and understand Judaism as historically developed, without knowing the Talmud, without being familiar with the spirit of that vast literature which proved such a powerful agency in the development of Judaism and in its preservation.

Let me also tell you, that he is greatly mistaken who imagines that modern Judaism can entirely discard and disregard the Talmud in religious questions. Although its authority is not any longer respected as absolutely binding, albeit under the changed circumstances in which we are living, many laws and customs treated and enjoined in the Talmud have become obsolete and impracticable, and though many religious views expressed by the Talmudists are rejected as incompatible with modern thoughts and conceptions, it is a fact, that Judaism nowadays still rests on the foundation which is laid down in the Talmud. Thus for instance, the elements of our ritual prayers and the arrangement of our public service, our festive calendar and the celebration of some of our holiest festivals, the marriage law and innumerable forms and customs of the religious life are, though more or less modified and fashioned according to the demands of our time, still on the whole permeated and governed by the Talmudic principles and regulations.

You can therefore never expect to have a full and clear insight into our relgious institutions without being able to go to the source from which they emanated.

I could also speak of the great importance of the Talmud in so far as it contains a vast fund of informations which are of decided value to general history and literature and to different branches of science, but I will remind you only of its great significance in regard to two branches of knowledge which are of vital import to Jewish theology and the Jewish ministry. I refer to the interpretation of the Bible and to Ethics.

The great value of the Talmud for Bible exegesis and Bible criticism is generally acknowledged even by non-Jewish scholars.

In regard to its value for Ethics I shall quote here a passage from an elaborate and lucid article on the Talmud which the venerable Rabbi Dr. Samuel Adler in New York published lately in one of the American Encyclopedias. He says:

"With the consideration of the ethical significance of the Talmud we approach the highest level, the crowning portion of the whole work. Not but that we meet with passages that must be rejected by a pure morality; prevailing views and embittering experiences have certainly exercised a disturbing influence on the ethical views of various spiritual heroes of the Talmud; but these are isolated phenomena, and disappear, compared with the moral elevation and purity of the overwhelming majority of the men of the Talmud, and compared with the spirit that animates the work as a whole. What is laid down as the moral law in the Talmud can still defy scrutiny at the present day; and the very numerous examples of high moral views and actions on the part of the Talmudists are such as can not be found in any work of antiquity, and must still excite the admiration of the reader of the present day, in spite of the ceremonial fetters which they bore, and in spite of the occasional narrowness of their point of view."

To impress you the more with the necessity of the Talmudic studies for a clear conception of Judaism and its history, I could also quote the opinions of many of our greatest scholars, but shall confine myself only to a quotation from the writings of two of our most renowned scholars whom none will suspect of having been biased by a too great predilection for the Talmud; one is the late Dr. Geiger, and the other our great historian, the late Dr. Jost.

Geiger (*Das Judenthum und seine Geschichte* I. p. 155) in speaking of the Talmud and the rabbinical literature, says:

"Gigantic works, productions of gloomy and brighter periods are here before us, monuments of thought and intellectual labor; they excite onr admiration. I do not indorse every word of the Talmud, nor every idea expressed by the teachers in the time of the Middle Ages, but I would not miss a tittle thereof. They contain an acumen and power of thought which fill us with reverènce for the spirit that animated our ancestors, a fulness of sound sense, salutary maxims—a freshness of opinion often bursts upon us that even to this day exercises its enlivening and inspiring effect."

Jost in his *Geschichte des Judenthum's und seiner Secten* II., 202, characterizes the Talmud by the following masterly words:

"The Talmud is a great mine, in which are imbedded all varieties of metals and ores. Here may be found all kinds of valuables, the finest gold and rarest gems, as also the merest dross. Much has been unearthed that has realized countless profit to the world. The great spiritual work whose outcome has been apparent in the advancement of religion has shown that the Talmud is not only of incalculable value in the pursuit of wisdom, but that it has a self-evident significance for all times, which can not be shown by any mere extracts from its pages, and that it can not be disregarded on the plea of its antiquity as valueless in the knowledge of the Jewish religion. Indeed it is and must remain the chief source of this knowledge, and particularly of the historical development of the Jewish religion. More than this, it is the abode of that spirit which has inspired that religion, these many centuries, that spirit from which even those who sought to counteract it could not escape. It is and will remain a labyrinth with deep shafts and openings, in which isolated spirits toil with tireless activity, a labyrinth which offers rich rewards to those who enter impelled by the desire to gain, not without hidden dangers to those who venture wantonly into its mazes and absorb its deadly vapors. Religion has created this work, not indeed to give utterance in an unsatisfactory way to the great questions of Deity and Nature, Mortality and Eternity, and not to carry on controversies upon the proper formulation of articles of faith, but to give expression to a religion of deed, a religion designed to accompany man from the first steps in his education until he reaches the grave, and beyond it; a guide by which his desires and actions are to be regulated at every moment, by which all his movements are to be guarded, that takes care even of his food and drink, of his pleasures and pains, of his mirth and sorrow, and seeks to elevate him, at all times, to an enunciation of the purest faith.

It is thus that this spirit, which breathes from the Talmud, enters into the nation's inmost life. It offers repeated recitals of the various modes of thinking, practising, believing, of the true and false representations, of hopes and longings, of knowledge and error, of the great lessons of fate, of undertakings and their consequences, of utterances and their effects, of persons and their talents and inaptitudes, of words and examples, of customs, both in matters of public worship and private life; in short, of all the happenings, past or cotemporary, in the time which the Talmud comprises, *i. e.*, a period of nearly one thousand years, excluding the Bible times.

Hence, also, its great value to antiquarians in the frequent allusions to facts, opinions and statements, to modes of expression and grammatical construction, to peculiarities of every kind, which at the same time afford a view of the development of mankind, such as no other work of the past gives.

To treat the Talmud with scorn because of its oddnes, on account of much that it contains that does not conform to our maturer modes of thinking, because of its evident errors and misconceptions—errors from ignorance or errors in copying,—to throw it overboard, as it were, as useless ballast, would be to insult all history, to deprive it of one of its strongest limbs, to dismember it.

To dam up its channels by taking away the Talmud, would be to close the access to the head waters and living sources of the Jewish religion, and thus leave her again in a desert land, after the tables of the law have already called forth a world of life and activity. It would be turning one's back, as it were, denying and disregarding one's own. There is a historical justification for the sharply defined modes of worship and religious forms that have their embodiment in set words and in fixed deeds. For this we must look to the Talmud. Judaism is rooted in the Talmud and would be tossed about in mid-air if torn from its soil, or require a new planting and a new growth."

In conclusion, my young friends, let me say this:

If our College had no other purpose than to graduate common Sabbath school teachers who should be able to occasionally deliver popular though superficial lectures, the study of the

Talmud as well as that of our rabbinical and philosophical literature, might have been stricken from the course of your studies. But our College has a higher aim and object. Its object is to educate future guides and leaders of our congregations, to educate banner-bearers of Judaism, representatives and cultivators of Jewish knowledge and literature.

You can never expect to answer this purpose without a thorough knowledge of, and familiarity with, that vast literature that offers us the means to follow and understand the religious formation, the growth and the entire course of development of Judaism from its beginning to the present time."

PART II

LEGAL HERMENEUTICS OF THE TALMUD

LEGAL HERMENEUTICS OF THE TALMUD

INTRODUCTION

a. Definition.

§ 1.

Hermeneutics is the science of interpretation or of explaining the meaning of an author's words, according to certain rules. The term is especially applied to the exegesis or interpretation of the sacred Scripture.

Although hermeneutics and exegesis are synonyms, as both words from which they are derived ἑρμηνεύειν and ἐξηγεῖσθαι mean to *explain*, *interpret*, still literary usage makes that difference between them, that the term *hermeneutics* refers to that branch of science which establishes the principles and rules of interpretation, while *exegesis* is the actual application of those principles and rules.

By Legal Hermeneutics of the Talmud we understand an exposition of those principles and rules which the teachers of the Talmud established in their interpretation of the Biblical Law.

b. Methods of Interpretation.

§ 2.

The Ta'mud distinguishes between two methods of Scriptural interpretation, one which is termed *Peshat*, and the other *Derash*.

Peshat (פשט) is the plain interpretation, where a law or a passage in Scripture is explained in the most natural way according to the letter, the grammatical construction, and the spirit of the passage. Hence the talmudic phrase: פשטיה דקרא the plain meaning, the immediate and primary sense of a Scriptural passage (Chullin 6a).

Derash (from דרש to search, investigate) is that method by which it is intended, for certain reasons, to interpret a passage in a more artificial way which often deviates from the plain and natural meaning. The result of this method of interpretation is termed מדרש that which is searched out, the artificial deduction, as זה מדרש דרש פ׳ this artificial interpretation was made by that certain teacher, Mishna Shekalim VI, 6.

As an illustration of these two methods of interpretation we refer to the following passage in Deut. XXIV, 16. לא יומתו אבות על בנים וגו׳,

"The fathers shall not be put to death for the children, neither shall the children be put to death for the fathers." The plain and natural meaning of this passage is that the family of a criminal shall not be involved in his punishment. But the artificial interpretation of the Rabbis which is also adopted in the Targum Onkelos takes the word על in the sense of בעדות *through the testimony*, and explains this passage to the effect that the testimony of relatives must never be accepted in a criminal or civil case. Talm. Sanhedrin fol. 27b.

c. TWO KINDS OF MIDRASH.

§ 3.

There are two kinds of Midrash. Where the interpretation bears on the enactment or determination of a law, be it a ritual, ceremonial, civil, or criminal law, it is called מדרש הלכה Interpretation of *Halacha*, or legal interpretation.

But where the Midrash does not concern legal enactments and provisions, but merely inquires into the meaning and significance of the laws or where it only uses the words of Scripture as a vehicle to convey a moral teaching or a religious instruction and consolation, it is called מדרש אגדה Interpretation of the Agada, homiletical interpretation.

The following examples will illustrate both kinds of Midrash.

1) In Lev. XIX, 3 the law reads: איש אמו ואביו תיראו "Ye shall fear every man his mother, and his father". In the interpretation of this passage the Rabbis explain that the ex-

pression איש *every man* must here not be taken in its literal sense, as if referring to the man (the son) only, and not also to woman (the daughter), for the plural form "ye shall fear" includes the daughter as well as the son in this divine injunction of filial respect and obedience:

איש אין לי אלא איש אשה מנין ?
כשהוא אומר תיראו הרי כאן שנים
Talm. Kiddushin 30b.

This is Midrash Halacha, as it concerns the determination of the law.

Commenting on the same passage, the Rabbis further explain why in this passage the first place is given to the mother, while in the decalogue where filial love to parents is commanded, the father is mentioned first. The reason offered is, that as a rule children fear the father, but love the mother more particularly. (Ibid. fol. 31a.) This explanation belongs rather to the Agada.

2) In Exodus XX, 25 the law reads: "And if thou wilt make me an altar of stone, thou shalt not build it (אתהן) of hewn stone: for if thou lift up thy iron tool upon it, thou hast polluted it."

The Midrash Halacha of this passage emphasizes the objective pronoun אתהן and concludes that the prohibition of hewn stones is restricted to the altar only, but in building the temple such stones may be used:

בו אי אתה בונה גזית אבל אתה בונה גזית בהיכל
Mechilta, Yithro XI.

The Midrash Agada to this passage explains ingeniously the reason why the application of iron is here called a pollution of the altar; it is because iron abridges life, the altar prolongs it; iron causes destruction and misery, the altar produces reconciliation between God and man; and therefore the use of iron cannot be allowed in making the altar. (Mechilta ibid.; compare also Mishna Middoth III, 4.)

The hermeneutic rules for Midrash Agada resemble in many respects those of Midrash Halacha, in others they differ. We propose to treat here especially of the Hermeneutics of the Halacha.

ORIGIN AND DEVELOPMENT OF MIDRASH HALACHA.

a. CIRCUMSTANCES THAT NECESSITATED ARTIFICIAL INTERPRETATION.

§ 4.

Ever since the time of Ezra, the Scribe, and especially since the religious and political revival under the Maccabees, the law embodied in the Pentateuch was generally looked upon as the rule of Israel's life. But side by side with this *written law*, תורה שבכתב, went an *unwritten*, *oral* law תורה שבעל פה.

This consisted partly of a vast store of religious and national customs and usages which had been established in the course of several centuries and handed down orally from generation to generation; partly of decrees and ordinances enacted according to exigencies of the changed times and circumstances by the *Sopherim* and the succeeding authorities, the Sanhedrin.

As long as the validity of this oral law had not been questioned, there was no need of founding it on a Scriptural basis. It stood on its own footing, and was shielded by the authority of tradition. From the time hovever when the Sadducean ideas began to spread, which tended to undermine the authority of the traditional law and reject everything not founded on the Scriptures, the effort was made by the teachers to place the traditions under the shield of the word of the Thora. To accomplish this task, the plain and natural interpretation did not always suffice. More artificial methods had to be devised by which the sphere of the written law could be extended so as to offer a basis and support for every traditional law and observance, and, at the same time, to enrich the substance of this law with new provisions for cases not yet provided for. This artificial interpretation which originated in the urgent desire to ingraft the traditions on the stem of Scripture or harmonize the oral with the written law, could, of course, in many instances not be effected without strained constructions and the exercise of some violence on the biblical text,[1] as is illustrated in the following example.

It was a rule of law established by tradition, firstly, that judicial decisions are rendered by a majority of votes; secondly that in capital cases, the majority of one vote was sufficient for the acquittal, but for the condemnation a majority of at least two votes was required; thirdly that in taking the votes in a criminal case, it must be commenced from the youngest judge, in order that his opinion and vote shall not be influenced by that of his older colleagues.

When the question came up to find a biblical basis for these rules, reference was made to the following passage in Ex. XXIII, 2 which reads:

לא תהיה אחרי רבים לרעות
ולא תענה על רב לנטות אחרי רבים להטות

"Thou shalt not follow the many to evil, neither shalt thou speak in a case to deviate after the many to pervert justice".

In its simple sense this passage is a warning for the judge as well as for the witness not to be influenced by the unjust

---

[1] This effort to base traditional institutions and usages on the written law is not without a certain parallel-though under quite different circumstances and influences—in the history of jurisprudence among other nations, as may be seen from the following interesting notice in Lieber's "Legal and Political Hermeneutics," page 239. Speaking of the law which grew up in the course of centuries by the combination of the *lex scripta*, or Roman law, with the customs of the various nations that received it, he says: "A favorite field for the exercise of professional ingenuity was the interpretation of the Roman law in such manner as to find therein formal written authority for the institutions, rules and usages that the Germanic races had inherited from their ancestors. For a century past it has been one of the chief tasks of the continental jurists, and especially of the class among them known as Germanists, to restore these remains of national law to their original shape, free from the distortions and disguises forced upon them by this Romanizing process."

opinion of the multitude in a law suit, but to follow his own conviction in giving his vote or his testimony. But the artificial interpretation forced upon this passage a different meaning. By separating the last three words אחרי רבים להטות from the context and forming them as a separate sentence:the Rabbis found therein an express biblical precept "to lean to the majority", that is, to decide doubtful cases by a majority of votes. The first part of the passage "thou shalt not follow the many to evil" was interpreted to mean "do not follow the simple majority (of one) for *condemnation*, as for the acquittal, but it requires at least a majority of two votes to condemn the accused (Mishna Sanhedrin I, 6)

The word ריב in the middle part of the passage, being here exceptionally written in the text without a mater lectionis רב, so as to admit the word to be read *Rabh* (the superior), one of the Babylonian teachers made use of this circumstance to interpret לא תענה על רב "thou shalt not express thy opinion after the superior", hence the younger members of a criminal court have to vote first (Talm. Sanhedrin 36a).

Conclusions derived by authoritative interpretations from the Mosaic Law were, in general, endowed with the same authority and sanctity as the clear utterances of that Law, and termed מן התורה or, in the Aramaic form, מדאורייתא (derived from the Biblical law).

In many instances, however, the Talmudic teachers freely admit that the meaning which they put upon the text was not the plain and natural interpretation; that "the natural sense of a passage must never be lost sight of"[2], and that their strain-

[1] Maimonides (ס' המצוות שורש ב') holds that laws derived from the Mosaic law by means of the hermeneutic rules are, in general, not to be regarded as *biblical laws* (מן התורה) except when expressly characterized as such in the Talmud. But this somewhat rational view is strongly criticized by Nachmanides (in his annotations to that book) who shows that from the Talmudical standpoint every law which the Rabbis derived by the authoritative interpretation from sacred Scripture, has the character and sanctity of a Mosaic Law.

[2] אין המקרא יוצא מידי פשוטו Sabbath 63a; Yebamoth 11b; 24a.

ed interpretation must be regarded merely as an attempt "to provide an established custom and law with a Biblical support".[1]

Remark. There are some legal traditions of an ancient date mostly concerning the ritual law, for which the Rabbis were unable to find a biblical support or even a mere hint. They are termed הלכה למשה מסיני "traditional laws handed down from Moses on Sinai". That this phrase is not to be taken literally, but often as merely intended to designate a very old tradition the origin of which cannot be traced, is evident from Mishna Eduyoth VIII, 7. Maimonides in the introduction to his Mishna Commentary enumerates the traditions mentioned in the Talmud by that appellation to the number of twenty three. This enumeration, however has been found not to be quite correct, as the traditions designated by that name actually amount to the number of fifty five. Compare Herzfeld, Geschichte des Volkes Israel II, 227-232.

b. THE EARLIEST COLLECTION OF HERMENEUTIC RULES.

§ 5.

Hillel the Elder. who flourished abount a century before the destruction of the second temple, is mentioned as having been the first to lay down certain hermeneutic rules (מדות), seven in number, for the purpose of expounding the written law and extending its provisions. Some of these rules were probably already known before Hillel, though not generally applied; but it was his merit to have fixed them as standard rules of legal interpretation. The headings of his seven rules are:

1. קל וחומר, the inference from minor and major.
2. גזירה שוה, the analogy of expressions.
3. בנין אב מכתוב אחד, the generalization of one special provision.
4. בנין אב משני כתובים, the generalization of two special provisions.

[1] הלכתא נינהו ואסמכינהו רבנן אקראי Erubin 4b; Succah 28a; Kidd. 9a. Compare also the phrase: קרא אסמכתא בעלמא Berachoth 41b; Yoma 80b; B. Metzia 88b and elsewhere very often used.

5. כלל ופרט, the effect of general and particular terms.

6. כיוצא בו ממקום אחר, the analogy made from another passage.

7. דבר הלמד מענינו, the explanation derived from the context.

These seven rules of Hillel having later been embodied in the system of R. Ishmael, their fuller contents and application will be explained in the exposition of the single rules of that system.[1]

c. A NEW METHOD OF INTERPRETATION INTRODUCED BY NAHUM.

§ 6.

Besides the seven rules of Hillel which were generally adopted, some other peculiar methods of interpreting the Scripture were introduced by succeeding teachers for the sake of making new deductions from the written law. Thus *Nahum of Gimzo*, a contemporary of R. Johanan ben Zaccai, originated a method which is termed רבוי ומיעוט the *extension* and *limitation.* According to this method certain particles and conjunctions employed in the Mosaic law were intended to indicate the extension or limitation of its provisions, so as to include the additions of tradition, or exclude what tradition excludes. As extensions were regarded especially the words: גם, את, אף and כל, and as limitations the words: אך, מן and רק.

This method is illustrated by the following examples:

1) The word את which marks the direct objective case agrees in form with the preposition את *with.* Hence this word in the passage Deut. X, 20: את י"י אלהיך תירא is interpreted לרבות תלמידי חכמים "It is to include the wise men", who are to be revered along with God (Pesachim 22b.).

2) The principle that "acts done through our agent are as if done by ourselves", is derived from the passage Numbers XVIII, 28: כן תרימו גם אתם "Thus ye also shall offer an

[1] These seven rules of Hillel are quoted in Tosephta Sanhedrin ch. VII; Aboth of R. Nathan ch. XXXVII and in the introductory chapter of the Siphra.

heave offering", by interpreting: גם לרבות את השליח "this *also* is to include your *agent*; he may offer your heave offering in your place". Kiddushin 41b.

3) That the rigorous precepts of the Sabbath do not apply to cases where life is in danger (פיקוח נפש), is derived from the limiting word אך in the passage Exod. XXXI, 13: אך את שבתותי תשמורו: "merely my Sabbaths you shall keep" by interpreting אך לחלק, this "*merely*" excludes such cases. Yoma 85b.

d. DEVELOPMENT OF THIS METHOD BY R. AKIBA.-

§ 7.

This new method of R. Nahum of Gimzo was not generally approved by his contemporaries. One of its opponents was R. Nehunia ben Hakana who insisted upon retaining only the rules of Hillel.[1] But in the following generation, the celebrated *R. Akiba* resumed the method of his former teacher Nahum of Gimzo, and developed it into a system. The underlying principle of that system was that the language of the *Thora* differs from human language. The latter often uses more words, to express ideas, than necessary; superflous words being inserted either for the sake of grammatical form or for the sake of rhetorical flourish and emphasis. Not so the language in which the divine law was framed. Here not a word, not a syllable and not even a letter is superfluous, but all is essential and of vital importance to define the intention of a law and to hint at deductions to be made therefrom. According to this principle the indication of an extension and limitation of the law is not confined to those few particles pointed out by Nahum of Gimzo, but every word or part thereof which is not absolutely indispensable to express the sense of the law is designed to enlarge or restrict the sphere of its provisions.

Thus R. Akiba and the followers of his system found indications for the intended extension of a law in the repetition of

[1] See Talm. Shebuoth 26a.

a word[1]; in the absolute infinitive joined with the finite forms of a vero;[2] in the conjunction או[3] and in the conjunctive ו. Indications for an intended limitation of the law are found by laying stress either on a demonstrative pronoun,[5] or on the definite article ה[6], or on the personal pronoun added to a verb[7], or on a pronominal suffix[8] or on any noun[9] or verb[10] occurring in that law.

The new hermeneutic rules which R. Akiba thus added to those of Hillel and Nahum offered entirely new ways and means to find a Scriptural basis for the oral laws, and to enrich its substance with many valuable deductions.

e. R. ISHMAEL'S RULES.

§ 8.

The ingenious system of R. Akiba, though received with admiration by many of his contemporaries, had also its opponents. One of the most prominent among these was R. Ishmael b. Elisha. He claimed: דברה תורה כלשון בני אדם "The divine Law speaks in the ordinary language of Men". Therefore, no special weight ought to be attached to its turns of speech and repetitions so customary in human language. He consequently rejected most of the deductions which R. Akiba based on a seemingly pleonastic word, superfluous syllable or letter, and

---

[1] f. i. Pesachim 36a: מצות מצות ריבה; Yebamoth 70a: איש איש לרבות הערל compare also Shebuoth 4b: ונעלם ונעלם.

[2] Sanhedrin 64b הכרת תכרת; B. Metzia 31 a. b. השב תשיבם, שלח תשלח, עזב תעזוב etc.

[3] Sanhedrin 34b: או זבח לרבות; B. Kamma 53b: או לרבות את הכלים

[4] Sanhedrin 51b: בת ובת לרבות; Yebamoth 68b: ר"ע דדריש ווין; compare also Kethuboth 103a: ויו יתירה לרבות את אחיך הגדול.

[5] Horioth 9a: זה קרבן זו ואין אחרת; Chulin 42a: זאת החיה, חיה אחרת לא.

[6] Pesachim 5a: נכתוב קרא ראשון, הראשון למה לי ש"מ (למיעוט).

[7] Maccoth 2b: הוא ינוס, הוא ולא זוממין; compare also Horioth 12b: ת"ל והוא.

[8] Kiddushin 17b: ועבדו לעולם ולא את הבן; Sanhedrin 46a ותלית אתו ולא אותה

[9] Kiddushin 18a: בגניבתו ולא בכפילו; Sanhedrin 52a: איש פרט לקטן.

[10] Gittin 20a: וכתב ולא חקק; Kiddushin 64a: ולא יחלל, חללים עושה ואין ממזרים.

admitted only such deductions which could be justified by the spirit of the passage of law under consideration. As standard rules for interpretation he recognized only those laid down by Hillel which he however enlarged to thirteen by subdividing some of them, omitting one, and adding a new one of his own.

The thirteen rules of R. Ishmael are:

1. קל וחומר identical with Hillel's Rule I.
2. גזירה שוה identical with Hillel's Rule II.
3. בנין אב contraction of Hillel's Rules III and IV.

4 כלל ופרט
5 פרט וכלל } subdivision of Hillel's Rule V.
6 כלל ופרט וכלל

7. 8. 9. 10 and 11 are modifications of Hillel's Rule V.

12 דבר הלמד מענינו ודבר הלמד מסופו with some addition identical with Hillel's Rule VII.

13 שני כתובים המכחישים זה את זה, this rule is not at all found among Hillel's.

Among those rules of R. Ishmael, the sixth rule of Hillel "the analogy made from another passage" is omitted, but this omission is seeming only, since that rule was, under differnt names: היקש (the analogy) and מה מצינו (as we find-analogy) included partly in the rule of גזירה שוה, partly in that of בנין אב, as will be seen further on in the fuller exposition of these two rules.

R. Ishmael's thirteen rules were generally adopted as the authoritative rules of rabbinical interpretation without however supplanting the methods of R. Akiba which continued to be favored by many sf the Rabbis and were applied even by some of the immediate disciples of R. Ishmael.[1]

Remark. R. Eliezer, son of R. Jose the Galilean, again enlarged the hermeneutic rules to the number of thirty two. But as his rules mostly refer to the homiletical interpretation, they do not strictly belong to our subject. The Talmud though incidentally praising the eminence of this teacher (Chulin 89), nowhere mentions his rules. But in

[1] Compare B. Kamma 84a: דבי ר' ישמעל קרא יתירא דרשי; also Kiddushin 43: דבי ר' ישמעאל תנא או לרבות.

the Agadic interpretation of the Amoraim, some of his rules are applied. A *Baraitha* of R. Eliezer containing his thirty two rules is not mentioned in the Rabbinical writings before the tenth century. This Baraitha is embodied in the books: *Sefer Kerithoth* and *Halichoth Olam* of which we shall speak in the following paragraph.

LITERATURE ON THE HERMENEUTIC RULES.

§ 9.

The thirteen rules of R. Ishmael are collected in the introductory chapter of the Siphra.

R. Abraham b. David of Posquieres (ראב״ד), in the XII century, wrote some valuable annotations on that chapter in his commentary on the Siphra.

R. Solomon b. Isaac (רש״י), the celebrated commentator of the Talmud, in the XI century, occasionally explained, in his lucid way, the single rules where they are applied in the Talmudical discussions.[1]

Of standard works treating of the hermeneutic rules we mention:

ס' כריתות by *R. Samson of Chinon*, in the XIV century.

ס' הליכות עולם by *R. Jeshua b. Joseph Halevi*, flourishing in the XV century, in Spain.

An abstract of the two last mentioned works is found in an appendix to מסכת ברכות in the usual Talmud editions.

ס' מדות אהרן by *Aaron b. Chayim*, XVI century. This very valuable treatise forms the first part of the author's greater work called קרבן אהרן which is a commentary on the Siphra.

ס' יבין שמועה by *R. Solomon b. Abraham Algazi*, XVII century.

---

[1] A separate treatise on the hermeneutic rules, ascribed to this commentator and published in Kobak's "Ginze Nistaroth" 1·11 under the title of פירוש רשי על המדות seems to be spurious. It is, at most, a compilation of his various incidental remarks on the single rules found in his commentary on the Talmud.

ס' תחלת חכמה, by *Jacob Chagiz* XVII, century.

Of modern works on our subject the following deserve to be mentioned:

Halachische Exegese by *H. S. Hirschfeld*, Berlin, 1840.

תל־פיות by *Mordechai Plongian*, Wilna, 1849. This Hebrew book treats exclusively of the rule of Gezera Shava.

Palaestinische und alexandrinische Schriftforschung by *Z. Frankel*, Breslau, 1854.

EXPOSITION OF R. ISHMAEL'S HERMENEUTIC RULES

CHAPTER I

THE INFERENCE OF KAL VE-CHOMER

The rule which occupies the first place in the hermeneutic system of Hillel as well as in that of R. Ishmael, is termed קל וחומר. This rule is very frequently used in the Talmudic discussions. It has quite a logical foundation, being a kind of syllogism, an inference *a fortiori.*

I. Definition.

§ 10.

In the Talmudic terminology the word קל (light in weight) means that which, from a legal point of view, is regarded as being less important, less significant, and חומר (heaviness) that which is comparatively of great weight and importance. By the term קל וחומר then is meant an inference from the less to the more important, and *vice versa*, from the more to the less important.

For the sake of convenience, we shall use the word *minor* instead of קל, and *major* instead of חומר; but we must caution against confounding the meaning of these words with that of the terms major and minor, commonly used in logic in regard to syllogisms.

II. Principle.

§ 11.

The principle underlying the inference of קל וחומר is, that the law is assumed to have the tendency to proportionate its effect to the importance of the cases referred to, so as to be more rigorous and restrictive in important, and more lenient and permissive in comparatively unimportant matters. Hence, if a certain rigorous restriction of the law is found regarding a matter of minor importance, we may infer that the same restriction is the more applicable to that which is of major importance, though that restriction be not expressly made in the law for this case. And on the other hand, if a certain allowance is made by the law regarding a thing of major importance, we may properly conclude that the same allowance is the more applicable to that which is of comparatively minor importance[1].

Thus, for instance, שבת is in some respects regarded as being of more importance (חמור) than יו"ט (a common holiday). If, therefore, a certain kind of work is permitted on שבת, we justly infer that such a work is the more permissible on יו"ט; and *vice versa*, if a certain work is forbidden on יו"ט it must all the more imperatively be forbidden on שבת. Mishna Betza V. 2:

כל אלו ביו"ט אמרו ק"ו בשבת

III. BIBLICAL PROTOTYPE.

§ 12.

The inference, drawn in Scripture (Numbers xii. 14) on a certain occasion is regarded as a prototype of this manner of drawing indifferences which is employed in the Talmudic Halacha. Miriam had been punished with leprosy as a sign of the Lord's disfavor, and when the question arose how long she ought to be shut out of the camp in consequence of that disfavor, the answer was; "If her father had but spit in her face, should she not be ashamed (shut up) seven days? Let her be shut out from the camp seven days." Here an inference is made from minor to major, namely, from a human father's to the Lord's disfavor.

IV. TALMUDIC TERMS.

§ 13.

Every קל וחומר contains two things, A and B, standing in certain relations to each other and having different degrees

[1]Modern jurisprudence admits also a certain argument which is quite analogous to the principle of Kal ve-chomer, as may be seen from the following maxim, quoted by Coke on Littleton, 260: "Quod in minori valet, valebit in majori; et quod in majori non valet nec valebit in minori." "What avails in the less, will avail in the greater; and what will not avail in the greater, will not avail in the less."

of importance. Of these two things, A, which in Talmudic terminology is called מלמד (teaching) is expressly subject to a certain law or restriction, which by way of inference is to be transferred to B, termed למד (learning).

An inference is termed דין (a judgment); to make an inference דון (to judge). The peculiar law found in the מלמד is called נדון (to be judged from), while the law finally transferred to the למד is termed הבא מן הדין (the result of the inference).

Thus, in the biblical inference mentioned above, the *father's* disfavor is the מלמד, the *Lord's* disfavor is למד. The punishment in consequence of a father's disfavor (הלא תכלם שבעת ימים) is the נדון, and the final decision derived from this inference (תסגר שבעת ימים) is הבא מן הדין.

V. LOGICAL AND FORMAL ARRANGEMENT.

§ 14.

Logically, every ק"ו (like every syllogism) has three propositions, of which two are the *Premises* and one the *Conclusion*.

The *first premise* states, that two certain things, A and B, stand to each other in the relation of major and minor importance.

The *second premise* states that with one of these two things (A) a certain restrictive or permissive law is connected.

The *conclusion* is that the same law is the more applicable to the other thing (B).

The *first premise* is termed תחלת דין *the outset of the inference*, or עיקרא דדינא, the *most essential part of the inference*; while the final conclusion is called סוף דין the *end of the inference*.

The *formal* arrangement of these three propositions differs, however, from this logical order, as a ק"ו is usually expressed by two compound propositions, one of which is the *antecedent* and the other the *consequent*, as in case of an inference from minor to major:

מה פלוני ש··· (קל) אסור (חייב)

פלוני ש··· (חמור) אינו דין שאסור (שחייב)

"If A which in this or that respect is of minor importance, is subject to a certain severity of the law; ought not B, which is of major importance, be the more subject to the same severity?" Or, in case of an inference frome major to minor:

מה פלוני ש··· (חמור) מותר (פטור)
פלוני ש··· (קל) לא כל שכן (אינו דין שפטור)

"If a certain allowance is made by the law in the case of A, which is of major importance; ought not the same allowance be the more made in the case of B, which is of minor importance?"

VI. ILLUSTRATIONS OF INFERENCES FROM MINOR TO MAJOR.

§ 15.

a. In Exodus xxii. 13, the law is laid down that if a man borrow of his neighbor an animal or a thing, and the animal die or the object be destroyed, the borrower must restore the loss. But it is not expressly mentioned in this law whether the borrower was also responsible in cases when the borrowed animal or thing is *stolen.* The liability in this eventuality is then proved by way of an inference from the law regarding a (paid) depositary who, according to Exodus xxii. 9—11, *is not* bound to make restitution when the animal intrusted to his care died or became hurt, and yet *is* held responsible in case the intrusted thing was stolen (ואם גנב יגנב מעמו ישלם) The inference is made in the following way:

מה שומר שכר שפטור משבורה ומתה חייב בגניבה
שואל שחייב בשבורה ומתה אינו דין שחייב בגניבה

"If the depositary, though free from responsibility for damage and death, is still bound to restore the thing stolen from him, ought not the borrower, who is responsible for damage and death, to be the more bound to restore the thing stolen from him?" In this inference the depositary is *minor*, the borrower *major*. Baba Metzia 95a.

b. By a similar inference it is proved that a depositary has to make restitution in cases where the intrusted thing has become *lost*, though the law only speaks of his responsibility for theft (Exodus xxii. 11):

מה גניבה שקרובה לאונס משלם
אבידה שקרובה לפשיעה לא כל שכן

"If he has to make restitution for the *theft*, which is almost an accident (as the greatest vigilance may not always prevent it), how much the more is restitution to be made for *losing* (the intrusted object), which is almost a trespass (since he was deficient in the necessary care and vigilance). Here גניבה is minor, אבידה major. Baba Metzia 94b.

VII. ILLUSTRATION OF AN INFERENCE FROM MAJOR TO MINOR.

§ 16

While the Sadducees took the law "Eye for eye" etc., (Exodus xxi. 24), literally as jus talionis, the rabbinical interpretation was, that a limb was not actually to be maimed for a limb, but that the harm done to the injured person was estimated and a pecuniary equivalent paid by the offender. Among other arguments in support of this interpretation one of the rabbis applied the inference from major to minor, referring to the law (Exodus xxi. 29—30), by which, under certain circumstances, the proprietor of a beast which is notably dangerous and which has killed a person, is judged liable to the death penalty; but the capital punishment could be redeemed by money. Now, if the law expressly admits a pecuniary compensation in a case where the guilty person deserved capital punishment, how much the more is a pecuniary compensation admissible in our case where it does not concern capital punishment:

מה במקום שענש הכתוב מיתה לא ענש אלא ממון
כאן שלא ענש מיתה דין הוא שלא יענש אלא ממון

Mechilta to Exodus xxi. 24.

XIII. RESTRICTIONS IN THE APPLICATION OF INFERENCES.

§ 17

Conclusions made by an inference are restricted by three rules: 1-st, דיו לבא מן הדין להיות כנדון "It is sufficient that the result derived from an inference be equivalent to the law from which it is drawn"; that is to say, the law transferred to B (the major), must never surpass in severity the original law in A (the minor), from which the inference was made.

Thus, in the inference made in the Scripture in regard to Miriam, we might have expected that the time of her exclusion from the camp should be more than seven days, since the Lord's disfavor is of more consequence than a human father's; nevertheless, Scripture says, "Let her be shut out from the camp seven days," which is just as long as she would have felt humiliated if her father had treated her with contumely. On this passage the restrictive rule just mentioned is founded. An ample application of this rule is found in Mishna Baba Kamma II. 5.

2d. Another restrictive rule is אין עונשין מן הדין "The inference from minor to major is not to be applied in the *penal* law."

The reason for this rule lies in the possibility that the conclusions drawn by inference might have been erroneous, so that the infliction of a penalty derived from such a conclusion would not be justified.[2]

An application of the rule אין עונשין מן הדין is made in Talmud Maccoth 5b, to refute an objection to the rabbinical interpretation of the law, that the punishment of false witnesses (Deuteronomy xix. 19), is to take place only when the judgment against the falsely accused party has not yet been executed. The objection to this interpretation was raised by way of an inference from minor to major:

לא הרגו נהרגין הרגו אין נהרגין... לאו קו"ח הוא?

[1]Quite analogous to this rabbinical rule is that established in modern law, "that penal statutes must be construed strictly. They can not, therefore, be extended by their spirit or by equity to any other offenses than those clearly described and provided for." (See Bouvier's Law Dictionary, article Penal Statutes).

[2]According to Talmudic interpretation, however, this rule is derived from the Scripture, in which the law sometimes finds it necessary to expressly mention a case in which the punishment is to be inflicted, though it could have been easily found by a mere inference from another case. Thus, for instance, in regard to the law, Exodus xxi. 33, we read in Mechilta: וכי יפתח איש אין לי אלא פותח כורה מנין ת"ל כי יכרה איש עד שלא יאמר יש לי בדין אם הפותח חייב הכורה לא כל שכן הא אם אמרת כן ענשת מן הדין לכך נאמר כי יכרה ללמד שאין עונשין מן הדין

In Talmud Maccoth 5 *b*, the same principle is proved in a similar way from Leviticus xx. 17.

"If the witnesses are to be put to death, though their false testimony has not caused the death of the innocent, how much the more when it really had fatal consequences?"

But this quite logical objection is removed by the axiom אין עונשין מן הדין "No penalty can be inflicted which is based upon an inference."

3d. A third restrictive rule in the application of inferences of קו"ח is laid down in Mishna Yadaim III. 2:

אין דנין דברי תורה מדברי סופרים וכו'

or as the rule is expressed more concisely in Talmud Sabb. 132, and Nazir 57: אין דנין ק"ו מהלכה "No inferences must be made from traditional laws to establish a new law."[1]

IX. REFUTATION OF INFERENCES.

§ 18.

Not every קו"ח offered in the Talmudic discussions of the law is correct and valid. We sometimes find there very problematic and even sophistical inferences set forth merely as suppositions or hypotheses; these are, however, finally refuted. A refutation of a קו"ח is called פירכא.

Refutations may be made in two different ways: *a.* Either the correctness of the *premise in the antecedent* is disputed by showing that A (מלמד) which was supposed to be of minor importance (קל) is in some other respects really of major importance (חמור); or *b.* The correctness of the *conclusion in the consequent* is diputed by showing that the peculiar law connected with A (מלמד) can not be transferred to B (למד) as it is not transferred to C, which in certain respects is like B.

The first kind of refutation is called פירכא אעיקרא דדינא a *refutation* of the *most essential part of the inference*, and the second kind is termed פירכא אסוף דינא *refutation of the final conclusion* of the inference. The styles of expression in these two

---

[1]R. Akiba, however, did not accept this restrictive rule, but attempted to make inferences even from traditional laws to establish a new law. See Sabbath 132a. Compare also Talm. Jer. Kiddushin 1, 2: ר" עקיבא אית ליה למד מן למד

kinds of refutation are quite different. A refutation of the premise is usually expressed in the following way:

מה לפלוני שכן (חמור בכך וכך)
תאמר בזה (שאינו חמור בכך וכך)

"Why has A that particular severe provision of the law? Because it is of *major* importance in this or that respect. But how will you apply it to B, which is not so important in the same respect?"

The refutation of the final conclusion is usually expressed by the words, פלוני יוכיח שכן. "The case of C proves it;" viz.: that such a conclusion can not be admitted, since C is of equal importance with B, and still the restriction of A, which is intended to be transferred to B, is not applied to C.

X. ILLUSTRATION OF THE DIFFERENT KINDS OF REFUTATION.

§ 19.

1. It is well known that the law, "thou shalt not seethe a kid in its mother's milk," is, according to Talmudic interpretation, a general prohibition against boiling any kind of meat in any kind of milk. After having demonstrated that בשר בחלב (meat, which in contradiction to this law had been boiled with milk), is forbidden to be eaten (אסור באכילה), it is undertaken to prove that it is likewise forbidden to make any other use of it (אסור בהנאה). One of the rabbis tried to prove this by way of an inference from ערלה (the fruits of a tree during the first three years, which fruits were deemed forbidden to be used in any way אסור בהנאה). The inference was made in the following way:

מה ערלה שלא נעבדה בה עבירה אסורה בהנאה
בשר בחלב שנעבדה בו עבירה אינו דין שאסור בהנאה

"If those fruits, regarding which no law had been violated, are forbidden to be used in any way, ought not meat and milk, which, in violation of a law, have been boiled together, the more be forbidden to be used in any way?"

The premise in this inference is that ערלה is of *minor*

importance (קל) compared with בב"ח; but this premise is disputed by demonstrating that in certain respects it was, in fact, of *major* importance, since those fruits had at no time before been permitted to be used, while in regard to בב"ח there had been a time (namely, before being boiled together), when the use of each of these components was allowed:

מה לערלה שכן לא היתה לה שעת ההיתר (לפיכך אסורה בהנאה)
תאמר בב"ח שהיה לו שעת ההיתר

Chullin 115b; Mechilta to Exodus XXIII. 19.

2. Refutation of the conclusion in the inference. An illustration of this kind of refutation is furnished in Mishna Pesachim vi. 1, 2. There the law is laid down that if the eve of פסח happened to fall on a Sabbath, the sacrificial acts with the Paschal lamb, as the slaughtering, sprinkling, etc., were allowed, though such acts are otherwise regarded as labor (מלאכה), while certain preparatory acts (as carrying the lamb to the temple, etc.), though not regarded as real labor, but only as שבות (incompatible with a day of rest), are not allowed. This restriction is disputed by R. Eliezer, on the ground of the following inference:

מה אם שחיטה שהוא משום מלאכה דוחה את השבת
אלו שהן משום שבות לא ידחו את השבת?

"If slaughtering, though a real labor, abrogates the Sabbath, ought not things not regarded as real labor the more abrogate the Sabbath?"

But this logical conclusion is refuted by R. Joshua:

יו"ט יוכיח שהתירו בו משום מלאכה ואסור בו משום שבות

"A common holiday proves that this conclusion is not admissible, for on such a day some real labors (as cooking, baking, etc.), are permitted, while at the same time certain actions, which fall under the category of שבות, are positively prohibited."

XI REINSTATEMENT OF A REFUTED INFERENCE.

§ 20.

When an inference has been refuted in one of the two ways just mentioned, the attempt is sometimes made to defend and retain it by removing the objection raised in the refutation. If the arguments proffered for this purpose are found to be correct, the original inference is reinstated; if not, the refutation is sustained and the inference finally rejected.

Thus, for instance, in regard to R. Eliezer's inference, which R. Joshua refuted by the objection יו"ט יוכיח, R. Eliezer, in turn, attempted to remove this objection by asking: מה ראייה רשות למצוה "What can that which is *voluntary* prove against a *command*?" That is to say, if שבות actions are not allowed on יו"ט, it must be remembered that they concern only voluntary or private affairs, while the prohibition of such actions in regard to the Paschal lamb concerns a religious duty which is expressly commanded.

R. Joshua was silenced by this point of argumentation, and seemed to be willing to withdraw his objection to R. Eliezer's inference; but now R. Akiba appeared in the arena to defend R. Joshua's objection by showing that a difference between רשות and מצוה could not be admitted. He said הזאה תוכיח שהיא מצוה והיא משום שבות ואינה דוחה את השבת "The *sprinkling* (by which an unclean person was declared to be again clean) may prove it, because this also is an act belonging to the category of שבות, and at the same time concerns a *command* (since the performance of this act would make the person fit to bring his Paschal offering), and still it is not to be done on a Sabbath-day; therefore, you should not wonder that in our case those other acts (the carrying of the Paschal lamb, etc.), though concerning a מצוה and only שבות, are not to be done on a Sabbath day."

A repeated attempt of R. Eliezer to reinstate his inference by disputing R. Akiba's new objection, having been frustrated by the latter's counter-arguments, the inference was finally rejected.

XII. SOPHISTICAL INFERENCES.

§ 21.

In conclusion, we wish to call attention to some sophistical inferences of ק"ו mentioned in the Talmudic literature, which are refuted simply by an argument *ad absurdum*.

One of these inferences is quoted in the Mishna Yadaim iv. 7: "The Sadducees said, We have a strong argument against you Pharisees. You teach that one is responsible for a damage caused by his ox or ass, but not responsible for a damage caused by his slave or his bondwoman; is this not contrary to a simple rational inference?"

מה אם שורי וחמורי שאיני חייב בהם מצות הרי אני חייב בנזקן
עבדי ואמתי שאני חייב בהם מצות אינו דין שאהי חייב בנזקן

"If I be responsible for my animals regarding which I have no religious obligation, how much more must I then be responsible for the damage caused by my servants, regarding whom I have a religious obligation?"

The Pharisees promptly answered: "No! I am responsible for my animals, which have no free will and deliberation, but not for my slaves, who have knowledge and deliberation. If I offend them, they may go and deliberately set fire to my neighbor's property. Should I then be bound to pay?"

Another still more sophistical ק"ו is mentioned in Mass. Derech Eretz Rabba, chapter I. A certain Jose b. Tadai, of Tiberias, tried, in the presence of R. Gamaliel, to ridicule the application of inferences in ritual laws by the following paralogism:

מה אשתי שאני מותר בה אני אסור בבתה
אשת איש שאני אסור בה אינו דין שאהיה אסור בבתה

"If the marriage with one's own daughter is prohibited, although the marriage with her mother is permitted, how much more unlawful must it be to marry another married woman's daughter, since the marriage with her mother, a married woman, is positively prohibited?"

The fallacy in this inference is that the conclusion contradicts the premise. The premise is that the marriage with one's own wife is lawful, while according to the conclusion any marriage would be prohibited. But R. Gamaliel answered caustically: "Go, thou, and take care of the high-priest, in regard to whom it is written, Only a virgin fron among his people he shall marry; I shall then take care of all Israel." That is to say, show me, in the first place, how, according to the inference, the high-priest could enter a marriage, as Scripture expressly permits him to do, and I shall prove the same permission for all Israelites.

According to another version, R. Gamaliel excommunicated the scoffing questioner, remarking: אין דנין דבר לעקור דבר מן התורה "No inference can be admitted in which the conclusion contradicts the law."

A masterpiece of sophistical inferences is recorded in Sanhedrin 17. Referring to a tradition, according to which none could aspire for membership in the ancient Sanhedrin, without having given a proof of his dialectic ability by demonstrating, for instance, the cleanness of those eight reptiles which the law (Leviticus xi. 29, 30), expressly declares to be unclean, one of the Amoraim jokingly remarked: "If I had been living at the time when the Sanhedrin was still in existence, I might have aspired for membership by offering the following inference:

ומה נחש שממית ומרבה טומאה טהור
שרץ שאינו ממית ומרבה טומאה אינו דין שיהא טהור

"If a serpent, though killing men and beasts, and thus increasing ritual uncleanness, still is regarded a clean animal;[1] ought not a reptile that does not kill and increase uncleanness be the more regarded clean?"

This inference, though merely intended to display dialectic acumen, is earnestly refuted by the following argumentum *ad absurdum*: If, according to the first premise of this inference, a serpent ought to be unclean on account of its capability to kill a person, then any wooden instrument by which a person can be killed ought to be unclean.

This inference and its refutation are of some intrest as an instance which shows clearly that many of the Talmudic discussions on the law had no other purpose than to be a mental tournament, in which the rabbis and their disciples delighted to exercise their intellectual powers and exhibit their skill and acuteness in the art of reasoning and debating.

---

[1]The serpent is, of course, unclean in respect to food, but it is *clean* in as far as it does not belong to those eight reptiles concerning which the law ordained: "Whosoever doth touch them, when they are dead, shall be unclean until the even."

CHAPTER II

THE ANALOGY OF GEZERA SHAVA

Rule II

Introductory

§ 22.

Analogy, in the ordinary sense of the word, denotes such resemblance between things, as enables us to assume of one what we know of the other. Although conclusions drawn from analogy do not in general afford *certainty*, but only some degree of probability at best, much recourse is often taken to such conclusions in every branch of human knowledge, especially when all other means of argumentation fail.

The argument from analogy is also admitted as an aid in modern legal interpretation, either to determine an ambiguous expression in a law, or to decide a case not expressly provided for therein, or to supply a defect in one law by reference to the fuller contents of another law.

The analogy between two laws may be either *real* or *formal* It is real when these laws are of the same nature and the cases treated of in them resemble each other in material points and in important relations. It is formal, when the resemblance consists merely in some external points and relations, as in the wording of the laws or in the connection in which they are set forth. Arguments from a real analogy existing between different laws are very often applied in the Rabbinical interpretation. Such an analogy is termed מה מצינו of which we shall speak in the following chapter. But the Rabbis also admit the argument from a formal or external analogy. Whether also this kind of argumentation be in accordance with logical reasoning, depends upon the nature of the conclusion which is intended to be drawn therefrom. If the external relations upon which the argument proceeds, imply also an internal relation which has a bearing on the conclusion, it is logical and valid, otherwise it is not. There are especially two rules of Talmudical interpretation in which use is made of this kind of analogy. These are termed: 1. Gezera Shava; 2. Hakkesh.

A. GEZERA SHAVA.

I.—TERM, CLASSIFICATION AND FORMULA.

§ 23.

The term Gezera Shava (גזירה שוה) means literally either a similar section (part) or a similar decision (decree). In the Talmudic phraseology it denotes an *analogy of expressions*, that is, an analogy based on identical or similar words occurring in two different passages of Scripture. The Gezera Shava is used: *first*, as an exegetical aid to determine the meaning of an ambiguous expression in a law; *second*, as an argument in construing laws with reference to each other, so that certain provisions connected with one of them may be shown to be applicable also to the other. We have, then, two kinds of Gezera Shava, and in order to distinguish them clearly we propose to call the former the *exegetical* and the latter the *constructional* Gezera Shava. The usual formula for both kinds of Gezera Shava is:

נאמר כאן . . . . ונאמר להלן . . . .
מה להלן . . . . אף כאן

Here is said: . . . . . . There is said:. . . .

As there, ... so here.

II.—THE EXEGETICAL GEZERA SHAVA.

§ 23.

The theory of the exegetical Gezera Shava is expressed in the Talmudical phrase sometimes used in connection with this kind of analogy: ילמוד סתום מן המפורש "the indefinite is to be explained by the definite," that is to say, if an expression in one passage of Scripture is used ambiguously, its meaning is to be ascertained from another passage, where the same expression occurs in a connection in which it is clearly defined.

This quite rational theory is also adopted in modern scientific exegesis in reference to *parallel passages*, and is in some measure admitted even in the legal interpretation of statutes and documents.[1]

Examples of exegetical Gezera Shava:

1. In Levit. xvi. 29 the law relating to the Day of Atonement enjoins תענו את נפשותיכם "Ye shall afflict your souls," without defining the nature of this affliction. But the expression ענה occurs in other passages in a connection where it evidently refers to the suffering of want and hunger, as for instance in the passage ויענך וירעיבך Deut. viii. 3. (Compare also Psalm xxxv. 13 עניתי בצום נפשי). Hence the expression in our passage is to be taken in the meaning which tradition has put on it, *i. e.*, as a term of *fasting*.

נאמר כאן תענו את נפשותיכם
ונאמר להלן ויענך וירעיבך
מה להלן עינוי רעבון
אף עינוי שנאמר כאן עינוי רעבון

Siphra to Levit. xvi., and Talmud Yoma, 74.

2. In the law restricting the time of slavery, Exod. xxi. 2, the expression עבד עברי is somewhat ambiguous, as it might mean either a *servant of a Hebrew* (a heathen slave belonging to an Israelite) or a *Hebrew servant* (an Israelite who has been sold as a slave). That the expression is to be taken in the latter sense (the word עברי being here used as an adjective and

[1] "One of the chief rules in ascertaining the meaning of doubtful words is to try first to ascertain the meaning—from other passages of the same text in which the ambiguous word occurs, so used that it leaves no doubt—by parallels." Francis Lieber, "Legal and Political Hermeneutics," page 91.—The following rule of interpretation, which is quoted in "Broom's Legal Maxims," page 586, comes still nearer to the character of Talmudical Gezera Shava: "Where an act of Parliament has received a judicial construction putting a certain meaning on its words, and the Legislature in a subsequent act in *pari materia* uses the same words, there is a presumption that the Legislature used those words intending to express the meaning which it knew had been put upon the words before, and unless there is something to rebut that presumption the act should be so construed, even if the words were such that they might originally have been construed otherwise."

not as a noun) is proved by a reference to Deut. xv. 12, where in a repetition of the same law the servant is called אחיך העברי "thy Hebrew brother."[1]

נאמר כאן עבד עברי ונאמר לחלן אחיך העברי
מה להלן בבן ישראל הכתוב מדבר
אף כאן בבן ישראל הכתוב מדבר

Mechilta to Exodus XXI.

III.—THE CONSTRUCTIONAL GEZERA SHAVA.

§ 25

While the exegetical analogy is limited to the purpose of ascertaining the meaning of an ambiguous word, the constructional Gezera Shava intends to supply an omission in one law by the more explicit provisions of another law. For this purpose use is made of an identical characteristic word occurring in both laws. By showing that this characteristic word has some bearing on certain provisions made in one case, it is argued that the same provisions must apply also in the other case.

IV.—ILLUSTRATIONS.

§ 26.

1. Hillel, the elder, who first mentioned this rule of interpretation, applied it in the following case: The eve of the Pesach festival once happened to be on a Sabbath, and the question was whether it should be permitted to sacrifice the Paschal lamb on such a day. Among other arguments to prove the permission, Hillel referred also to the rule of Gezera Shava. He argued: In the law concerning the *daily offering* it is said (Num. xxiii. 2) that it was to be brought במועדו "in its due season," and also in the law regarding the Paschal lamb we

[1]The ancient versions, as well as the modern commentaries on the Bible, fully coincide with the Rabbinical interpretation of this expression. Strange enough, Saalschuetz, in his "Mosaisches Recht," page 702, tries to defend the other interpretation so promptly refuted by the Rabbis, and claims that עבד עברי refers to a certain class of heathen slaves in the service of a Hebrew. Compare Mielziner's "Die Verhaeltnisse des Sklaven bei den alten Hebraern," page 23.

read: The children of Israel shall keep the Passover במועדו "in its due season." (Num. ix. 2.) But concerning the daily offering the law expressly provides that it was to be brought also on the Sabbath day. (Num. xxviii. 10.) The expression במועדו then means that the offering must take place at the appointed time under all circumstances, even on a Sabbath; therefore, the same expression במועדו in regard to the Paschal lamb likewise enjoins that the offering take place at the time appointed, even on a Sabbath day.

נאמר מועדו בפסח ונאמר מועדו בתמיד
מה מועדו האמור בתמיד דוחה את השבת
אף מועדו האמור בפסח דוחה את השבת

Pesachim, page 66 a.

2. Another example, taken from the civil law, may here be added to illustrate the application of the Gezera Shava in construing a law which appears to be defective.

In Exod. xxii. 6-8, and 9-12, are contained two different laws concerning the safe-keeping of the property of a fellowman. The traditional interpretation correctly distinguishes between these two laws. The first treats of a gratuitous guardian, while the other refers to a paid depositary who has a greater responsibility than the former. Now, the first law seems to be somewhat defective. It provides that if the objects intrusted have been stolen from the house of the guardian "he shall be brought to the judges—that he has not put his hand to his neighbor's goods," but nothing is said of the way in which he was to prove this, neither is it said whether he was free from making restitution if he succeeded in proving this. The Rabbis supply this defect by means of a Gezera Shava. They refer to the second law in which (verse 10) the same phrase occurs, "that he has not put his hand to his neighbor's goods." Here the phrase is introduced by the words, "an oath of the Lord shall be between them both," and is followed by the words, "and shall not make restitution." Hence, according to this analogy, the phrase in the first case must also be supplied viz.: He shall be brought before the judges *to take an oath*[1] that he did not act fraudulently, which oath frees him from making restitution.

נאמרה שליחות יד למטה ונאמרה שליחות יד למעלה
מה להלן לשבועה אף כאן לשבועה

Mechilta to Exod. xxii., and Baba Metzia 41b.

The examples given above illustrate the process and character of most of the Gezeroth Shavoth which are quoted in the Talmud in the name of the great authorities of the Mishnic period. The external analogy (the parity of expressions) from which the argumentation proceeds, is there generally of such a nature as to imply also an internal or real analogy which justifies the conclusion to be drawn from it.

Usually the two words which form the basis for a Gezera Shava are exactly alike, but sometimes even such words are used for this purpose which, though different in expression, are identical in their meaning. Thus, for instance, a certain analogy is occasionally formed on the basis of the expressions ושב הכהן "the priest shall *return*" (Levit. xiv. 39), and ובא הכהן "the priest shall *come*" (*ibid.*, 44), since the verb "to return" is almost identical with the verb "to come" (as the former means to come again.)

ושב הכהן ובא הכהן, זו היא שיבה זו היא ביאה

Siphra to Levit xiv., and very often quoted in the Talmud.

V.—THE EXORBITANT GEZERA SHAVA.

§ 27

There is a peculiar kind of Gezera Shava sometimes resorted to, especially by Amoraim, which is quite different from the rational character of the analogies generally used by the Tanaim. Its peculiarity consists in this, that the argument from a parity of expressions is also admitted in cases where the two laws or passages, compared with each other, have nothing in common except a single, often very insignificant word

[1]The Septuagint already supplied the passage in this way by adding to "he shall appear before the judges" the words καὶ ὀμεῖται "and he shall swear."

which has not the least natural bearing on the conclusion to be drawn therefrom.

It is obvious that arguments from such mere verbal analogies easily result in what is termed in Logic a *fallacy*, or *sophistical conclusion.* It must, however, be stated that the Amoraim never used such purely verbal analogies for the purpose of deducing a new law from Scripture, but merely as an attempt to find a Scriptural support for an opinion expressed by one of the authorities in the Mishna.[1]

This kind of Gezera Shava is externally characterized by being usually introduced by this peculiar formula אתיא־מ־־־ or גמר־מ־־־ "that is derived from," followed by the two identical words on which the analogy in question is assumed to be based.

VI. ILLUSTRATIONS OF EXORBITANT USES OF GEZERA SHAVA.

§ 28.

a. In Mishna Sanhedrin I. 1, it is stated that criminal cases involving corporal punishment (stripes) could be decided by a minor court of three judges, but according to the opinion of R. Ishmael, such cases required a higher criminal court of twenty-three judges. The reason for this divergence of opinion was, probably, that this Rabbi regarded the infliction of corporal punishment as too serious a matter to be left to the decision of a civil court of three; as a criminal case it ought, like a case of capital punishment, to be judged by the higher court of twenty-three. But the Gemara, commenting on this Mishna, wants to know the Scriptural ground on which R. Ishmael based his analogy, and in answer to this question the Babylonian Amora, R. Ashi, thinks that he can find such a basis in the word רשע "the guilty" or criminal, which occurs as well in the law referring to corporal punishment (Deut. xxv. 2) as in that regarding the execution of capital punishment. (Num. xxxv. 31.)

אתיא רשע רשע מחייבי מיתות

Talmud Sanhedrin 10.

---

[1]Compare Z. Frankel's "Palaestinishe und Alexandrinische Schrift forshung," page 20.

b. Mishna Kiddushin I. 1 lays down the law that one of the means to contract marriage was כסף, that is, the giving of a piece of money or its value to the woman, with the express intention of engaging her for this consideration as his wife. The Gemara asks for a Biblical basis of this law, and the following answer is given: The Law, in speaking of marriage, uses the expression כי יקח איש אשה "if a man *take* a wife" (Deut. xxii. 13); but לקח "to *take*" also means "to *acquire*" property,[1] and is used elsewhere in connection with money given in consideration for the acquisition of property נתתי כסף השדה קח ממני (Gen. xxiii. 13); hence also a wife is acquired by means of money.

גמר קיחה קיחה משדה עפרון

Talmud Kiddushin 2a.

As to illustrations of Gezeroth Shavoth of a still more decidedly sophistical character, we refer to the following two examples in which an argument from analogy is based, in one instance, on an identical *pronoun* (לה) and in the other on an identical *adverb* (שם), occurring in two laws or passages of totally different nature and contents.[2]

כל מצוה שהאשה חייבת בה עבד חייב בה
דגמר לה לה מאשה

Talmud Chagiga, 4a.

[1]In the Pentateuch, however, the word לקח nowhere has the meaning of "to acquire or to buy;" it occurs in this meaning only a few times in some of the other books of the Bible (2 Sam. iv. 6; Prov. xxxi. 16, and Nehem x. 32), but in the Talmudic idiom it is almost exclusively used in this sense.—The formality of contracting marriage by means of a piece of money was probably of a late origin, and was perhaps influenced by a similar Roman custom—the nuptials by *coemptio*. The probability of such an influence gains some ground if we compare the expression of the Mishna האשה נקנית בשלשה דרכים בכסף בשטר בביאה with the corresponding expression used by Gajus I., § 110, in speaking of the Roman custom: "Feminae olim tribus modis in manum conveniebant: usu, farreo, coemptione." It is moreover evident that the civil law of the Mishna, though in doctrines and principles so widely different from the Roman law, adopted several legal formalities from the latter and modified them according to the leading Jewish principles.

[2]A very extensive use of this kind of Gezera Shava was made especially in the Agada (the homiletical explanation of moral and historical passages of Scripture), where it was not restricted by any rules. There it gave rise to many of those most fanciful interpretations and legendary narratives quoted in the Midrash and Talmud.

מנלן דמת אסור בהנאה
אתיא שם שם מעגלה ערופה

Aboda Zara 29b.

VII. RESTRICTIONS IN THE USE OF GEZERA SHAVA.

§. 29.

The exorbitancies which some teachers permitted themselves to make use of in the application of the Gezera Shava, served only to demonstrate the weakness of the theory of basing arguments upon an analogy of expressions. It having been found that such arguments easily run into vague fallacies, this whole theory seems to have been slighted by many. That such must have been actually the case is evident from the repeated admonitions which several prominent teachers addressed to their contemporaries: "Do not look slightingly upon arguments from the analogy of Gezera Shava, since very important injunctions of the traditional law can derive their Scriptural authority in no other way than by means of such an analogy."[1]

But as an arbitrary application of the analogy of Gezera Shava could easily lead to misuse, it was found necessary to subject it to some restrictions. This was done by the following rules:

1. The identical expression occurring in two different laws must at least in one of them be מופנה "empty," that is, seemingly *superfluous*, or pleonastic, and not already engaged for another deduction of the traditional interpretation, to enable it to be used for an analogy of Gezera Shava. Thus, for instance, in Deut. xxiii. 3, the law provides that a *bastard* "shall not enter into the congregation of the Lord, *even to the tenth generation.*" Immediately after this law follows another, with a similar provision, in regard to an Ammonite or Moabite: "*Even to the tenth generation* they shall not enter into the congregation of the Lord *for ever.*" The identical expression in both cases are the characteristic words, "even to the tenth generation." But in the second case this expression seems to be somewhat superfluous, or "empty," since the emphatic words "for ever" which

[1] לעולם אל תהי גזירה שוה קלה בעיניך וכו׳ Talmud Kherithoth, 5a. This admonition is there repeated in the name of four different teachers.

are added here exclude even the *latest* generations of an Ammonite or Moabite from the congregation. The expression is then assumed to have been used here for the purpose of intimating an analogy of Gezera Shava. As the phrase, "even to the tenth generation," is here clearly defined to mean *for ever* or the latest generations (*ten* being a round number taken to signify perfection and completeness), so the identical expression in the former law must be likewise taken in this sense—a bastard and his descendants are *for ever* disqualified from entering the community of Israel.[1]

מופנה להקיש ולדון גזירה שוה
מה דור עשירי האמור כאן עד עולם
אף דור עשירי האמור להלן עד עולם.

Siphre to Deut., section 259; compare also Talmud Jebamoth, 78b. An other example is found in Tal. Chagiga 9a.

A Gezera Shava in this case is termed מופנה מצד אחד "empty on one side," and is regarded admissible, but may still be rejected for certain reasons. Only when the identical expression is found to be superfluous in both laws under consideration, מופנה משני צדדין, is the analogy regarded as irrejectable. But if no pleonasm is recognizable in either of the two passages of the law, no analogy can be formed between them because of an identical expression occuring in each of them. Baba Kama 25b; Jebamoth 70a; Nidda 22b; Sabbath 131a.[2]

2. The second restrictive rule is less artificial and answers the purpose better than the former. It is this: אין אדם דן ג"ש מעצמו (Pesachim 66; Nidda 19b) "No one is permitted to reason from a Gezera Shava of his own." While the application of the logical inferences of Kal Vechomer could be left to the discretion of the teachers of the law, the use of the un-

[1]That is, according to Rabbinical interpretation, they are not permitted to intermarry with Israelites.

[2]The Talmud further makes many nice distinctions in regard to this מופ:ה, which however, are too intricate and subtle to be treated here. Those who take an interest in the details of this subject will consult with advantage Dr. H. S. Hirschfeld: Halachische Exegese p. 462—467.

certain conclusions from an analogy of expression had necessarily to be restrained. Such an analogy must be sustained by the authority of tradition in order to be valid and conclusive, or as a post-Talmudic addition to this rule explains: "One must have received the analogy from his teacher, and the teacher from his teachers, up to the time of the highest legislative authority."

This rule, however, hardly meant to say, as many interpreters understand it, that either the special application of a Gezera Shava in a certain case must have been handed down, or the identical expression on which the analogy is based must have been pointed out by tradition. If so, it is difficult to perceive how so many controversies could have been raised in the Talmud in which analogies of Gezera Shava are set forth and disputed, or withdrawn and replaced by others.

The true meaning of that rule seems rather to be that no new laws are to be deduced from Scripture by means of a Gezera Shava, but that such analogies could be only applied for the purpose of offering a biblical support to a law which already had the sanction of tradition. Such a support might be found in one way or another, and hence arose the difference of opinion in regard to some analogies.[1]

B. HECKESH.

VIII. TERM AND THEORY.

§ 30.

There is another kind of analogy, somewhat similar to Gezera Shava, which, though not expressly mentioned among the thirteen rules of R. Ishmael, was generally adopted and very frequently applied in the Talmudic interpretation of the law; it is termed Heckesh.

The word היקש, derived from the verb הקיש, to compare, means originally a *comparison*, an *analogy*, in which general sense it also occurs;[2] but in the Talmudic terminology it usually denotes a particular kind of analogy, based

[1] Compare Frankel: "Ueber palaestinische und Alexandrinische Schriftforshung p. 16, Note 6 and p. 20.

[2] For instance, Talmud Jerushalmi Pesachim vi. 1.

on the close connection of two subjects in one and the same passage of the Law.

The theory of this peculiar analogy is that where two subjects are connected in the law by a common predicate, the same provisions otherwise made in regard to one of them are under certain circumstances applicable also to the other.

Within certain limits this theory is not inconsistent with logical reasoning, since the connection of two subjects by a common predicate indicates that they in some respects have a relation to each other. In modern rules of legal interpretation also is a maxim: "Coupling words together shows that they ought to be understood in the same sense."[1] But in their endeavor to provide every traditional law with a Biblical support, the rabbis sometimes carried also this theory beyond its legitimate limits and beyond the natural scope of the written law.

IX. ILLUSTRATIONS.

§ 31.

The following examples will illustrate the different modes in which the theory of Heckesh is applied:

a. According to the traditional law, women are exempted from the performance of all periodical rites and religious duties incumbent on male Israelites. In regard to *prohibitory* commandments, however, no difference is made between man and woman. Her obligation in this respect is derived by the analogy of Heckesh from the words of Scripture (Numbers v. 6). "When a *man* or *woman* shall commit any sin," etc., in which passage women are placed in one category with men in regard to a trespass against the law.

איש או אשה כי יעשו מכל חטאת האדם
השוה הכתוב אשה לאיש לכל עונשין שבתורה

Kiddushin 35a.

b. Among other rules and regulations concerning civil and criminal courts, the traditional law provides that the sessions of a court must be opened in *day time* only; and further,

[1]Copulatio verborum indicat acceptionem in eodem sensu. Bacon, Max. Reg. 3; Broom, Max. 3d, Lond. edition, 523.

that *blindness* disables a man from acting as one of the judges. The reason for these two provisions is obvious enough. But their Biblical support is offered by R. Meir in the following more ingenious than natural deduction. He says: The Law, in speaking of the judicial functions of certain priestly courts, enjoins that "by their word shall every *controversy* and every *injury* be decided" יהיה כל ריב וכל נגע (Deuteronomy xxi. 5). "Controversy" refers to civil litigations, and "injnry" refers to the plague of leprosy (which in Leviticus xiii. 3, is termed נגע and was to be investigated by the priest). Both kinds of cases being connected in this law, they must be analogous to each other also in regard to their investigation. As the *blind* would not be the proper man, and *night* not the proper time for the investigation of a case of leprosy (Leviticus xiii. 6), so ought *day* to be the proper time for the trial of any case of litigation, and the *blind* not be admitted to judge such a case.

מקיש ריבים לנגעים
מה נגעים ביום ולא בסומין אף ריבים וכו׳

Sanhederin 34, b.

e. The traditional permission to cut off the sheaf of the first fruits for the purpose of the wave offering on the 16th day of Nissan, even if that day happened to be on a Sabbath, is based by R. Ishmael on the following passage (Exodus xxxiv. 21), בחריש ובקציר תשבות "In the time of *ploughing* and *reaping* thou shalt rest on the seventh day." Ploughing is under all circumstances an optional (private) act, since it is nowhere commanded to be done for a religious purpose. Hence, also the prohibition of reaping on a Sabbath day refers only to the optional reaping for private purposes, but not where it is to be done in fulfillment of a religious duty:

מה חריש רשות אף קציר רשות
יצא קציר העומר שהיא מצוה

Mishna Shebiith I. 4. Menachoth 72.

X. HECKESH FROM PREDICATES.

§ 32.

The analogy of Heckesh is also made from two predicates

belonging to one subject. In this case, the verbs constituting the common predicate are treated as verbal nouns. Such a Heckesh is, for instance, applied to prove that a wife may be taken in matrimony by means of a written contract of marriage which is handed to her. The law (Deuteronomy xxiv. 2), in speaking of a case where a divorced woman contracts a second marriage, uses the words: ויצאה והיתה "when she has *departed* out of his house she may *become* another man's wife." As the *departing* out of his house (divorce) is by means of a written document (bill of divorcement), so, also, the *becoming* a wife may be effected by means of a document written for that purpose.

מקיש הויה ליציאה
מה יציאה בשטר אף הויה נמי בשטר

Talmud Kiddushin 5. As to other examples compare B. Kamma, 71*a*,, and Chagiga, 4*b*.

XI. HECKESH IRREFUTABLE.

§ 33.

Arguments from Heckesh are, in general, regarded as being more conclusive than those from Gezera Shava, the latter admitting of a refutation, but not the former.[1] But as Gezera Shava, so also Heckesh could be applied only for the purpose of supporting a traditional law.

[1] אין משיבין על ההיקש Menachoth 82*b*; Baba Kamma 106*b*. Concerning the prevalence of one or the other of these two kinds of analogy in cases where they seem to be in conflict with each other, compare the divergence of opinions in Gittin 41, and Zebachim 48.

CHAPTER III

THE GENERALIZATION OF SPECIAL LAWS

Rule iii, Binyan Ab.

I. Theory and Term.

§ 34.

It is an established principle of modern interpretation of laws: "When the law is special, but its reason general, the law is to be understood generally"[1]. This principle is also applied in the rabbinical legal interpretation, as may be seen from the following example: In Deut. xxiv, 6, the law provides "No man shall take the mill or the upper millstone as pledge: for he taketh a man's life to pledge." This law is special, prohibiting certain specified utensils, the hand-mill and the mill-stones, to be taken as pledges.

The reason, however, which the law expressly assigns to this prohibition is general; by taking away from the poor debtor these utensils, so essential for daily domestic use, you are depriving his family of the means of preparing their food. Hence the Rabbis feel justified in generalizing this law, so that "Everything which is used for preparing food is forbidden to be taken as pledge."[2] In a similar way the special law: "Thou shalt not plow with an ox and an ass together" (Deut. xxii, 10) is generalized by the Rabbis so as to equally prohibit the yoking together of any two other animals of different species and strength. Ox and ass are here mentioned especially as being those animals ordinarily employed in agriculture. And not only in plowing, but also for any other purpose it is prohibited to yoke such different animals together.[3] From the quite rational principle just illustrated, developed the Rabbinical rule of

---

[1] Quando lex specialis, ratio autem generalis, generaliter lex est intelligenda.

[2] לא ריחים ורכב בלבד אלא כל דבר שעושין בו אוכל נפש שנאמר כי נפש הוא חובל. Mishna B. Metzia ix, 13.

[3] See Siphre P. 131; compare also Mishna Khilayim viii, 2.

generalizing special laws. According to the theory of this rule it is not even necessary to investigate whether the reason of a certain law is general or not, but any special law found in the Mosaic legislation is assumed to be applicable to all similar or analogous cases. Only where Scripture, in some of those ways which are defined by the Rabbis, indicates that the law in question is provided exclusively for the particular case mentioned therein, it is not applicable to similar cases. But otherwise, the provisions of the law are to be taken in a comprehensive and general sense, and the particular case expressly mentioned is to be regarded only as an illustrative example for its application.[1]

This theory is termed *Binyan Ab* (בנין אב), the construction of a leading rule i. e. the *Generalization of a special law.*[2]

II. METHOD OF GENERALIZING A LAW.

§ 35.

In Generalizing a special law so as to make it applicable to other cases, the Rabbis apply the following method:

They try to point out in the special case some characteristic peculiarities which taken together are the probable reason for the provision made by the law for this case. Any other case having the same peculiarities is regarded as an analogous case, subject to the same provision of the law.

The formula of this method is usually:

מה (דבר פלוני) מיוחד ש... אף כל... (כיוצא בו).

[1] A somewhat similar view is expressed by a modern law-writer, the celebrated Frenchman *Toullier* in his *Le Droit Civil Francais suivant l'ordre du Code*, liv 3. t. I. c. 1. "It is analogy which induces us, with reason, to suppose that, following the example of the Creator of the Universe, the lawgiver has established *general* and uniform laws, which it is unnecessary to repeat in all analogous cases."

[2] In the application of this theory sometimes the phrase is used: זה בנה אב "this (special case) establishes the general rule or law", f. ex. Sanhederin 30a; B. Kamma 77b. Sota 2b. In this phrase, the word אב meaning *father*, *chief*, *ruler* is taken in the sense of *principal* or *general rule* (compare the terms אבות נזיקין, אבות מלאכות). Hence בנה אב to build or construct a general rule, and בנין אב the construction of a general rule, the generalization of a special law.

"As A (the case mentioned in the law) being characterized by (that and that certain peculiarity) is subject here to a certain provision, so any case similar to it (by having the same pecularities), is subject to the same provision.

Where it is to be shown why the generalized law does not apply to a certain not quite analogous case, the formula is:

מה (דבר פלוני)... אף כל... יצא...

"As A (having those certain peculiarities) is here subject to that provision, so any other case (similar to it by having the same peculiarities). The case of B however is excepted from that provision, because of its not having the same peculiarities."

ILLUSTRATIONS.

§ 36.

a. In Leviticus chapter xi and Deut. chap. xiv, the law treats of clean and unclean animal food. Concerning the quad rupeds, fishes and flying insects, general rules are given pointing out certain criteria by which to distinguish between the clean and the unclean. For the distinction between clean and unclean fowls, however, no general rule is given, but there is merely a list of nineteen or twenty specified birds which are unclean. To have a general rule also for this kind of animals was the more necessary as many of the specified fowls can not easily be identified. The Rabbis therefore tried to find such a rule by generalizing the eagle which stands at the head of the specified list of unclean fowls. The eagle, they say, has four peculiarities: 1. it has not a "prolonged toe"; 2. it has no crop; 3. the inner coat of its gizzard cannot easily be peeled off from the fleshy part: 4. it "strikes" with its claws the prey in eating it. Hence any fowl resembling it in these peculiarities, is to be regarded as unclean.[1]

b. In Deut. ch xix, the law contains some particulars supplementary to a former law concerning the cities of refuge

---

[1] מה נשר מיוחד שאין לו אצבע יתירה וזפק ואין קורקבנו נקלף ודורס ואוכל טמא אף כל כיוצא בו טמא Talmud Chullin 61a.

which were designed to serve partly as a protection, partly as a punishment and atonement for him who unintentionally had committed a homicide. In this connection the special provision is made, that when a man goes *into a forest* with his neighbor to hew wood, and the iron of the axe slips out from the handle and accidentally kills the neighbor, the slayer shall flee into one of those cities.

This special provision is, of course, generalized by the Rabbis, so as to be applicable to analogous cases, e. g. if one in breaking down a wall kills a man accidentally by one of its falling stones. If, however, such an accident happened in private premises, where the man who was killed had no right to enter, he who unintentionally caused his death is entirely acquitted, without having to flee to the city of refuge; for "as the *forest* mentioned in the law is a public place which the slayer and the slain man equally had a right to enter, so that law applies only to accidents occurring on places which both of them were permitted to enter, but not in private premises, where the man who was killed was neither permitted nor expected to be."[1]

Remark. Where it is not intended to raise a special provision to a general law applicable to all similar cases, but merely to draw from it an analogy for one single similar case, there the method is termed מה מצינו (abbrev. מ"מ), from the phrase by which such an analogy is usually introduced: . . . מה מצינו "as we find concerning . . . so here"; e. g. Yebamoth 7b: מ"מ מאשת אח Nedarim 4b: מ"מ מנדרים.

Incorrectly the מ"מ is sometimes termed בנין אב, as in Menachoth 76a; ב"א מחביתי כה"ג; see Rashi 's commentary on that passage.

III. GENERALIZATION OF TWO SPECIAL PROVISIONS.

§ 37.

In the instances of Binyan Ab mentioned above, the general law is drawn merely from one special provision. Such generalization is qualified as בנין אב מכתוב אחד "a general law drawn from one passage (or provision)." But sometimes it is formed by a combination of two special provisions found either in one and the same passage or in two different passages of Scripture. In this case it is termed ב"א משני כתובים "a

[1] Mishna Maccoth II, 3. מה היער רשות לניזק ולמזיק ליכנס לשם אף כל רשות לניזק ולמזיק ליכנס לשם יצא חצר בעל הבית שאין רשות ל לכנס

general rule drawn from two provisions"[1] It makes no essential difference whether the two provisions are found in the same or in different passages, as the same method is applied in either case.

The method of generalizing two special provisions, so as to make of them one general law, is indicated by the formula always used for this purpose. It is:

לא הרי זה כהרי זה ולא הרי זה כהרי זה
הצד השוה בהן....

"Behold, this case is not like the other, and the other not like this; the common peculiarity is...." That is to say, first a difference between the two special provisions is stated, and then again those points are set forth which are common to both of them, and which form their characteristic peculiarity. Any other case having the same peculiarity is then subject to the same law.

Remark. The reason why a difference of the two special provisions has first to be demonstrated before generalizing them, is explained in the following way:

It is a Talmudic rule of interpretation that שני כתובים הבאים כאחד אין מלמדין "wherever two provisions of the law are found in Scripture which are so identical that one of them is seemingly superfluous, as it might as well have been derived from the other by way of an analogy, then no further deduction from either of them can be admitted" (Kiddushin 24a and elsewhere). In making a Binyan Ab by a combination of two special provsions it is therefore necessary first to show that they are not so identical as to be regarded as שני כתובים הבאים כאחד, but that they really do differ in some points.

---

[1] This definition is according to the opinion of R. Abraham b. David (Rabed) in his exposition of the hermeneutic rules. Some commentators, however, call the generalization of one special provision of a law: מה מצינו; the generalization of two provisions if found in one passage: ב"א מכתוב אחד, and if found in two different passages of Scripture: ב"א משני כתובים.

ILLUSTRATION OF GENERALIZING TWO SPECIAL PROVISIONS.

§ 38.

In Exodus XXI, 26 and 27, the law provides, that "if a man smite the *eye* of his servant and destroy it, he shall let him go free for his eye's sake. And if he smite out his servant's *tooth*, he shall let him go free for his tooth's sake."

Here two provisions are made, one concerning the eye and one concerning the tooth of the servant. Though different in their nature, eye and tooth have that in common that they are essential parts of the human body and the loss of them cannot be restored. Hence the Rabbis draw from these two provisions the general law that the mutilation of any member of the servant's body in consequence of brutal treatment on the part of the master, causes the immediate manumission of that slave.[1]

IV. GENERALIZING SEVERAL SPECIAL PROVISIONS.

§ 39.

There are some instances where a *Binyan Ab* is formed by a combination of three or even four different special provisions. The method of operation in such cases is just the same as in the case of generalizing two provisions.

An example of a combination of four different provisions for the purpose of forming one general rule is furnished in the first Mishna of Baba Kamma. There, reference is made to four principal damages provided for in the law: 1) the damage caused by a *goring beast* (Exod. XXI, 28. 35. 36.); 2) the damage caused by an uncovered *pit* (Exod. XXI, 33. 34.) 3) the damage caused by *depasturing* foreign fields (Exod. xxii. 4) and 4) damage caused by unguarded *fire* (ibid. verse 5.).

Of these four provisions the general law is formed that a man is responsible and has to make restitution for any damage

---

[1] לא הרי השן כהרי עין ולא הרי עין כהרי השן הצד השוה שבהן שהן ראשי אברים שאין יכולין לחזור אף כל ראשי אברים שאין יכולין לחזור יוצא עליהן בן חורין
Mechilta Mishpatim P. ix; cf. also Talmud Kidd. 24a.

caused by his neglect to guard that property which is under his care and liable to do damage.[1]

V. RECAPITULATION.

§ 40.

Briefly recapitulating this whole chapter on Generalization, we shall find that according to the Talmudical view every provision of the Mosaic law is, as far as possible, to be taken as a general law, applicable to all analogous cases. A plain application of a special provision to one analogous case is termed מה מצינו. The generalization of special provisions, so as to make them applicable to all analogous cases is termed בנין אב the construction of a general rule. If such a general rule is derived merely from one special provision, it is termed בנין אב מכתוב אחד. A general rule formed by a combination of two (or more) special provisions which, though different, have some characteristic points in common, is termed בנין אב משני כתובים. These common characteristics are termed הצד השוה.

---

[1] לא הרי השור כהרי המבעה ולא הרי מבעה כהרי השור ולא זה וזה שיש בהן רוח חיים כהרי האש שאין בו רוח חיים ולא זה וזה שדרכן לילך ולהזיק כהרי הבור שאין דרכו לילך ולהזיק הצד השוה שבהן שדרכן להזיק ושמירתן עליך

Examples of Binyan Ab formed of three provisions are found in Sanhedrin 66a; Maccoth 4b; Chullin 65b.

CHAPTER IV

THE GENERAL AND THE PARTICULAR

INTRODUCTORY

§ 41.

In order to understand the different hermeneutic rules under this heading, it is necessary to have a clear conception of the meaning of the two talmudical terms פרט and כלל.

כלל means the *General*, that which comprehends a class of objects; that which is applicable to a number of things agreeing in a certain point in common.

פרט means the *Particular* or the Special, that which singles out an individual from among a number or class.

Hence, any general term or any noun with the adjective כל "all" "whatsoever", is regarded as כלל; while any term denoting only a single object is taken as פרט.

The law usually speaks either in general or in particular terms. as: "He that smiteth a *man*, so that he die, shall be put to death" (Ex. XXI, 12); "Thou shalt not eat *any abominable thing*" (Deut. XIV, 3). In these two cases the terms are general. But in the law: "Thou shalt not seethe the *kid* in its *mother's milk*" (Ex. XXIII, 19), the terms are particular.[1]

It is obvious that where the law speaks in general terms it intends to refer to everything included in those terms. Where, however, it uses particular terms, the whole tenor of the law will decide whether it refers exclusively to the single objects mentioned and enumerated or also to others of a similar nature.

But it sometimes occurs that the law uses both kinds of terms together, so that either 1) the general is succeeded by

---

[1]The terms כלל and פרט are applied by the Rabbis even to *verbs*. A verb denoting an indefinite act, as to *do*, to *take*, is regarded as כלל, while a verb denoting a special kind of act, as to *bake*, is a פרט; e. g. Kiddushin 2ib. ולקחת-כלל; Menachoth 55b: לא תאפה-פרט, לא תעשה-כלל.

particulars, כלל ופרט, or 2) the particulars are succeeded by a general, פרט וכלל, or 3) one general term preceding and another succeeding the particulars, כלל ופרט וכלל. In each of these three cases the contents of either the general or that of the particulars are modified in some way. These modifications are defined by the following three rules.

RULE IV. GENERAL AND PARTICULAR.

§ 42.

כלל ופרט אין בכלל אלא מה שבפרט.

In the case of General and Particular, the general includes nothing but the particular.

That is, when a general term is followed by an enumeration of particulars, the law is assumed to refer exclusively to the enumerated particulars. The particulars are then not regarded as a mere illustrating example of the preceding general, but an indication that the contents of the latter are restricted solely to that of the particulars.[1]

The following examples will illustrate the application of this rule:

a. In Levit I, 2. The law defines the offerings to be brought on the altar by the following words: "you shall bring your offering of the *beast* (מן הבהמה), of the *herd* or of the *flock*." The general term is here "*the beast* (בהמה) which otherwise includes any kind of quadrupeds, both wild and tame (cf. Deut. XIV, 4. 5); but the special terms "*herd* and *flock*" limit the offering to these domesticated animals. The law is then to be construed in the following way: of the beast, viz. only of the herd and of the flock you shall bring your offering.[2]

---

[1] Somewhat analogous to this Rabbinical rule of interpretation is the following rule of construction of modern laws: "Where a general enactment is followed by a special enactment on the same subject, the latter enactment overrides and controls the earlier one". See Broom's Legal Maxims p. 650.

[2] בקר וצאן אמרתי לך ולא חיה. Tal. Zebachim 34a.

b. In Deut. XXII, 11 the law reads: "Thou shalt not wear a *mingled* stuff (שעטנז), wool and linen together". Here the general term שעטנז, meaning a mixture of different sorts, is followed by the particulars "wool and linen together;" hence the Rabbis regard the prohibition of wearing a garment of mingled stuff to be restricted to a mixture of wool and linen.[1]

c. In Levit. XVIII, 6 sq. the law on prohibited marriages begins with the general terms: "None of you shall approach to any that is near of kin to him—". According to this general interdiction the intermarriage with any degree of relationship would be prohibited. But as the general is followed by a specification of prohibited degrees, the interdiction is to be restricted to these specified degrees.[2]

RULE V. PARTICULARS AND GENERAL.

§ 43.

פרט וכלל נעשה הכלל מוסיף על הפרט ומרבינן הכל.

In the case of Particulars and General, the general term adds to the contents of the particulars, and we include everything (belonging to this general).

That is to say, where particular terms are followed by a general term, it is assumed that the law refers to anything included in the general,[3] the particulars being regarded merely as illustrative examples of that general.

---

[1] See Mishna Khilayim X, 1, and the commentary of Obadiah Bertinoro.

[2] Siphra in loco: איש איש אל כל שאר בשרו וגו'-כלל
ערות אביך וערות אמך וגו'—פרט
כלל ופרט ואין בכלל אלא מה שבפרט

It is true, the rabbinical law adds some extensions to the biblical list of prohibited degrees, but these extensions are not regarded as biblical, but as שניות 'secondary prohibitions' made by the authority of the Sopherim. See *Mielziner* 'The Jewish Law of Marriage and Divorce', p. 37.

[3] In a somewhat similar case, the modern rules of construction take just the opposite view, as may be seen from the following quotation in Broom's Legal Maxims p. 650: 'It is said to be a good rule of

This rule is applied in the following law in Exodus XXII, 9: "If a man delivereth to his neighbor an ass, or an ox, or a sheep, or any beast to keep, and it die, etc."

Here the enumerated particular terms *ass*, *ox*, *sheep* are followed by the general term "*any beast*". Hence this law refers to any kind of animal which is delivered to be guarded.[1]

RULE VI. GENERAL, PARTICULAR AND GENERAL.

§ 44.

A case of one general preceding and another following the particular can, in some respects, be regarded as an combination of the two former cases, namely of *General and Particular* and of *Particular and General*, and the rule for this combination is, consequently, a kind of amalgamation of the two rules given above concerning these two cases. While in the case of General and Particular (Rule IV) the general includes nothing but the strict contents of the particular, and in the case of Particular and General (Rule V) the contents of the particular are extended to the whole comprehension of the general, it is held that a particular between two general terms is to be extended only as far as to include that which is similar to the contents of this particular, or as the rule is expressed in the talmudic phraseology:

כלל ופרט וכלל אי אתה דן אלא כעין הפרט.

---

construction that "where an Act of Parliament begins with words which describe things or persons of an inferior degree and concludes with general words, the general words shall not be extended to any thing or person of a higher degree", that is to say, where a particular class [of persons or things] is spoken of, and general words follow, the class first mentioned is to be taken as the most comprehensive, and the general words treated as referring to matters ejusdem generis with such class, the effect of general words when they follow particular words being thus restricted'.

[1] Mechilta on this passage:

אין לי אלא שור או חמור או שה
שאר כל בהמה מנין ? ת"ל וכל בהמה
שכל הכלל שמוסיף על הפרט הכל בכללו

In a case of General, Particular and General, do include only that which resembles the particular.

An example illustrating the application of this rule is furnished in Ex. XXII, 8, where the law is laid down that in all cases when a person has been found guilty of having embezzled property, that person shall pay the double amount of the embezzlement. This law is introduced by the words: "For any matter of trespass (General), for ox; for ass, for sheep, for raiment (Particulars), for anything lost (General)... he shall pay double to his neighbor."

Applying the rule of General, Particular and General, the Rabbinical interpretation of this law is to the effect that the restitution of the *twofold* value is to be made only for such em bezzled property which resembles the particular (the specified objects: ox, ass, sheep, raiment) in this that it is *movable* property, and that it is an object of *intrinsic* value. Hence the fine of double payment for the embezzled property does not apply where it concerns *real estate* which is not movable, and neither where it concerns *bills* or *notes* which have no intrinsic but only a representative value.[1]

Remark 1. In regard to the limitation of "that which resembles the particulars" (כעין הפרט), the Talmud expresses two opinions which differ from each other slightly.

According to one opinion it is assumed that in a connection of *General, Particular and General* כללא קמא דוקא "the first general is prevailing and deciding," so that such a connection is to be treated mainly in accordance with the rule for כלל ופרט viz. that the general comprises nothing but the strict contents of the particular. These contents are, however, in our case modified by the succeeding general, so that it now comprises

[1] Baba Kamma 62 b:
על כל דבר פשע — כלל
על שור על חמור על שה ועל שלמה — פרט
על כל אבידה — חזר וכלל
מה הפרט מפורש דבר המטלטל וגופו ממון
אף כל דבר המטלטל וגופו ממון
יצאו קרקעות שאינן מטלטלין
יצאו שטרות שאע"פ שמטלטלין אין גופן ממון

Other examples are furnished in Nazir 35 b; Shebuoth 4 b; 43 a.

anything which resembles the particular, at least, in three points (בשלשה צדדין).

But the other opinion assumes that in a connection of *General, Particular and General* כללא בתרא דוקא "the last general is prevailing and deciding". Hence, such a connection is to be treated rather in accordance with the rule for פרט וכלל, so that the contents of the particular are extended to everything comprised in the general. This extension is, however, in our case modified by the first general in as far as it excludes that which resembles the particular only in one point (צד אחד), while anything resembling it in more than one point (בשני צדדין) is included. See Talm. Erubin 28a; compare also Rashi on Chullin 65b sub voce וכ"ת.

Remark 2. Two general terms either preceded or followed by a particular are, according to some authorithies, also treated as a case of General, Particular and General:

כל מקום שאתה מוצא שני כללים הסמוכין זה לזה
הטל פרט ביניהן ודונן בכלל ופרט וכלל

Chullin 66 b; B. Kamma 64 b.

Remark 3. The rule of General and Particular applies only when both are found in one and the same passage of the law, but not when in different passages:

כלל ופרט המורחקין זה מזה לא דרשינן בכלל ופרט

B. Kamma 85 a; Menachoth 55 b.

CHAPTER V

MODIFICATIONS OF THE RULES OF GENERAL AND PARTICULAR.

The Rules VII-XI contain five different modifications of the preceding rules concerning the General and Particular.

First Modification. Rule VII.

§ 45

כלל שהוא צריך לפרט ופרט שהוא צריך לכלל

There is a general that requires the Particular, and a Particular that requires the General.

That is to say, the preceding rules of General and Particular do not apply to cases where either the general needs the supplement of the particular, or where the particular necessarily requires the supplement of the general in order to express a full and clear meaning. For, an ambiguous general term cannot be treated as a general; neither can an indefinite special term be regarded as a particular.

Thus, in Leviticus XVII,13 the law enjoins that he who taketh in hunting any beast or fowl that may be eaten, shall pour out the blood thereof וכסהו בעפר "*and cover it with dust*".

In this passage the word וכסהו might have been taken as a general expression, since there are various ways of covering a thing; בעפר again is a particular term, and according to the rule of Klal u-Phrat (Rule IV) the interpretation of this law would be, that the blood must be covered with *dust* and with nothing else.

But the general expression כסה is ambiguous, as it admits of different meanings; it means as well *to cover* (i. e. to overlay, to envelop), as also to *hide* (to conceal, to withdraw from the sight). Without the addition of בעפר we might suppose that the law only intended to enjoin that such blood be put out of sight or concealed in a closed vessel. Hence the expression

וכסהו is "a General that requires the Particular", to express that the meaning is to overlay it with something.

Consequently the rule of K'lal u-Phrat cannot be applied here, and the term בעפר is not necessarily to be taken in its strictest sense, but may be extended so as to include anything resembling the dust.[1]

The same passage can also serve to illustrate the second part of our rule. The special term בעפר without the general expression וכסהו would have been quite meaningless, as no verb would be there indicating what to do with the dust. Hence it is "a Particular that requires the supplement of the General". Another, somewhat intricate, example in Talmud Bechoroth 19a.

SECOND MODIFICATION. RULE VIII.

§ 46.

כל דבר שהיה בכלל ויצא מן הכלל ללמד
לא ללמד על עצמו יצא אלא ללמד על הכלל כלו יצא.

When a single case, though already included in a general law, is expressly mentioned, then the provision connected with it, applies to all other cases included in that general law.

This rule is illustrated by the two following cases:

a. The practice of witchcraft was according to the general law in Ex. XXII, 17 (מכשפה לא תחיה) a capital crime. The nature of the capital punishment is, however, not defined in this general law. But in regard to a certain kind of witchcraft, namely אוב וידעוני (having a familiar spirit and being a wizard) the law specifies the punishment as that of stoning (Lev. XX, 27). Hence this punishment applies to the practice of any kind of witchcraft[2].

---

[1]Tal. Chullin 88b: אימא וכסהו כלל, עפר פרט
עפר אין מידי אחרינא לא ?
משום דהוה כלל הצריך לפרט
ואין דנין אותו בכלל ופרט.

[2]Talm. Sanhederin 67b: אוב וידעוני בכלל מכשפים היו
ולמה יצאו ? להקיש אליהם ולומר לך
מה אוב וידעוני בסקילה אף מכשף בסקילה.

b. Deut. XXII 1-3, the law treats of the duty to restore found property to its owner. After having enjoined this duty concerning animals found going astray, it is added: "And so shalt thou do with his *garment*; and so shalt thou do with every lost thing of thy brother's, which he hath lost, and thou hast found..."In interpreting this law the Rabbis say:Why is*garment* expressly mentioned, though contained in the general term of "every lost thing"? It is to indicate of what nature the found things must be concerning which it is your duty to advertise in order to restore them to their owner. Every garment had certainly an owner and, besides, it has some marks by which he could identify it. So the duty of advertising found things refers only to such property which obviously had an owner who will reclaim it and which has certain marks by which he might be able to identify it.[1]

THIRD MODIFICATION. RULE IX.

§ 47.

כל דבר שהיה בכלל ויצא לטעון טוען אחד שהוא כענינו יצא להקל ולא להחמיר.

Wherever a single case, though already included in a general law, is expressly mentioned with a provision similar to the general, such a case is mentioned for the purpose of alleviating, but not of aggravating.

An example is furnished in Ex.XXXV,3: "you shall kindle no fire throughout your habitations on the Sabbath day". Now kindling fire being regarded as a labor, is included in the general prohibition of doing any labor on the Sabbath day. Since here expressly mentioned, it is for the purpose of alleviating this special case by exempting it from the rigor of the general law in regard to labor on the Sabbath day, so that he

[1]Mishna B. Metzia II, 5: אף השמלה היתה בכלל כל אלה ולמה יצאת? להקיש אליה לומר לך מה שמלה מיוחדת שיש בה סימנים ויש לה תובעים אף כל דבר שיש בו סימנים ויש לו תובעים חייב להכריז

Other examples are furnished in Tal. Yehamoth 7a, and Kherithoth 2b.

who kindles fire on that day, transgresses only a prohibitory law, but is not subject to that severe punishment which the preceding verse appoints for other kinds of labor.[1]

FOURTH MODIFICATION. RULE X.

§ 48.

כל דבר שהיה בכלל ויצא לטעון טוען אחר שלא כענינו יצא להקל ולהחמיר.

Wherever a single case, though included in a general law, is separately mentioned with a provision differing from that contained in the general, such a case is mentioned for the purpose of alleviating as well as of aggravating.

This rule may be illustrated by the passage in Ex. XXI, 28-32. There the law provides that if a man or woman has been killed by a beast that had not been duly guarded by the proprietor, though its savage nature was known to him, that proprietor, besides losing the mischievous animal, had to pay (to the bereaved family) such an indemnification as may be laid upon him by the court. After this general provision the law adds that if a male or female slave was killed by such a vicious animal, its proprietor has to pay to the master of the slave an indemnification of *thirty* shekels. Now the case of male or female slave, though included in the preceding general law of man and woman, is here separately mentioned with a provision different from the general in this, that the amount of the indemnification is fixed. This separate provision is for the purpose of alleviating as well as aggravating; *alleviating* in the case of the actual value of the killed slave being

[1]Talm. Sabbath 70a, and Sanhederin 35b: הבערה ללאו יצאת.

There is however another opinion represented by R. Nathan who, interpreting this special prohibition of "kindling fire" according to the second modification (Rule VIII), holds: הבערה לחלק יצאת, this special prohibition of one kind of labor is an indication that each of several labors done on a Sabbath-day is to be regarded as a separate desecration of that day, for which the transgrassor, under circumstances, had to bring a separate sin-offering. Talm. ibid.

more, and *aggravating* in the case of its being less than thirty shekels.

See Mechilta, Mishpatim, Parsha XI and Mishna B. Kamma IV, 5.

FIFTH MODIFICATION. RULE XI.

§ 49.

כל דבר שהיה בכלל ויצא מן הכלל לדון בדבר החדש
אי אתה מחזירו לכללו עד שיחזירנו הכתוב לכללו בפירוש

Wherever a single case, though included in a general law, is excepted from it by an entirely new provision, such a case is not to be brought again under the general law, unless this be expressly indicated in the Scripture.

An illustrating example is furnished in Lev. XIV, 11-16. One of the two sacrifices which the healed leper had to bring for his purification was a *trespass-offering* (אשם). But while the blood of trespass-offerings in general was sprinkled only on the altar, the offering of the healed leper made an exception in this, that some of its blood was applied to the person of him that was to be cleansed (verse 25). This peculiar way of sprinkling is דבר החדש the entirely new (extraordinary) provision by which this sacrifice is excepted from the general law of trespass-offerings. Hence it would have to be excepted also from the other ordinances and rites regarding trespass-offerings, had not the Scripture expressly brought it again under the general law by adding (verse 13 כחטאת האשם הוא) that this offering was otherwise to be sacrificed as a trespass-offering in the usual way. Talm. Zebachim 49a.

CHAPTER VI

RULES XII AND XIII

THE EXPLANATION FROM THE CONTEXT. RULE XII

§ 50.

דבר הלמד מענינו ודבר הלמד מסופו

A word (or passage) *is to be explained from its connection or from what follows.*

That is to say, the true meaning of a law or of a clause in a law is sometimes to be interpreted by considering the whole context in which it stands or by looking to that which follows.[1]

Examples:

a. Explaining an ambiguous word from the context:

The word תנשמת occurs in Levit. XI,18, among the names of unclean fowls, and again in verse 30 among the creeping things on earth. Hence, it is concluded, that the law does not refer to the same animal, but in the former place to a certain kind of bird (namely according to LXX the *swan*, and according to the Talmud, to the *bat*), and in the other place to the *mole*.[2]

b. Explaining the meaning of a passage from the context.

In Ex. XVI, 29, we read: "Abide you every man in his place, let no man go out of his place on the seventh day." If taken out of its connection, this passage would contain an injunction that no Israelite shall leave his place on the Sabbath day. But if we look to the context, we find that it refers to

[1]Compare the following rule of modern jurisprudence with reference to the mode of construing deeds and written instruments: *Ex antecedentibus et consequentibus fit optima interpretatio.* "A passage will be best interpreted by reference to that wich precedes and follows it". (Broom, Legal Maxims 577). Compare also the maxim: *Noscitur a sociis* "The meaning of a clause may be ascertained by reference to the meaning of expressions associated with it" (ibi. 588).

[2]Chullin 63a: תנשמת באות שבעופות, דבר הלמד מענינו וכו׳
תנשמת באות שבשרצים וכו׳

the *manna* gatherers, prohibiting them to go out on the Sabbath day with the intention to seek manna.[1]

c. Interpreting a clause in a law by a clause which follows: In Deut. XIX, 5 relating to the cities of refuge for the manslayer, the law says: "Lest the avenger of the blood pursue the slayer and overtake him and slay him ; *and he is not worthy of death* etc." This last clause is somewhat ambiguous, whether referring to the *blood avenger* or to the manslayer. The latter interpretation is supported by the clause following it: "*in as much as he hated him not in time past.*"[2]

RECONCILIATION OF CONFLICTING PASSAGES. RULE XIII.

§ 51.

שני כתובים המכחישים זה את זה
עד שיבא הכתוב השלישי ויכריע ביניהם

Two passages contradicting each other are, if possible, to be reconciled by a third one.[3]

As an instance of contradictory passages we may refer to Ex. XIII, 6 and Deut. XVI, 8. While the former passage enjoins: "*Seven* days shalt thou eat unleavened bread," the latter passage says: "*Six* days thou shalt eat unleavened bread."

In a plain way, the contradiction between these two pas-

---

[1]This plain interpretation according to the context is also adopted by *Rashi* in his commentary on this passage. Talmudical interpretation, however, disregarded in this case the context, and deduced from the words of this passage the general prohibition that no Israelite shall, on a Sabbath-day, go farther than 2000 cubits from the place of his abode (תחום שבת "the Sabbath way"); for that was the distance of the holy tabernacle from the remotest part of the Israelitish camp in the desert. See Talm. Erubin 51a.

[2]Maccoth 10b: ולו אין משפט מות, ברוצח הכתוב מדבר
אתה אומר ברוצח או אינו אלא בגואל הדם?
כשהוא אומר והוא לו שונא לא מתמול שלשום
הוי אומר ברוצח הכתוב מדבר.

[3] Compare the following rule of interpretation established in modern jurisprudence (Potter, Dwarris treatise on statutes p. 144): "Where there is a discrepancy or disagreement between two statutes, such interpretation should be given that both may, if possible, stand together."

sages may be removed by taking the latter passage in the sense that six days unleavened bread shall be eaten, but that on the seventh, besides this observance, a holy convocation shall be held; or, that unleavened bread shall be eaten during six days *besides* the first, the celebration of which had been treated more fully in the preceding verses.

In a more artificial way, the rabbinical interpretation tries to reconcile the contradictory passages according to our Rule by referring to a third passage, namely Lev. XXIII, 14 where the law enjoins that no use whatsoever was allowed to be made of the new corn until the offering of an *Omer* of the first produce of the barley harvest had taken place on the morning after the first day of Pesach. Hence unleavened bread prepared of the new corn was to be eaten only during the six remaining days of that festival. Referring to this circumstance, the passage in Deut. XVI, 8 speaks of six days, while the passage in Ex XIII, 6 refers to the unleavened bread prepared of the produce of the former year's harvest which might be eaten during seven days.[1]

Remark. Some of the Rabbis however, apply in their interpretation of Deut. XVI, 8 the Rule VIII and arrive at the conclusion that, just as, according to this passage, the eating of unleavened bread on the *seventh* day was optional, so it was also optional on the first six days, so that it was not obligatory to eat just that which is properly called *unleavened bread* (Matza), provided that nothing is eaten which is leavened (Chametz). Only on the first eve of this festival the eating ot such unleavened bread was regarded as obligatory, as the law concerning the paschal-lamb on the eve expressly enjoins (Ex. XII, 8) "with unleavened bread and with bitter herbs they shall eat it."[2]

---

[1] Mechilta, Bo, VIII (compare also Talmud Menachoth 66a):
כתוב אחד אומר ששה וכתוב אחד אומר שבעה
ביצד יתקימו שני מקראות הללו ?
אלא ששה מן החדש שבעה מן הישן.

[2] Pesachim 120a: מה שביעי רשות אף ששת ימים רשות

CHAPTER VII

ADDITIONAL RULES

A. Juxtaposition

§ 52.

A peculiar kind of analogy which has some similarity to *Heckesh* (above p. 152) is that called סמוכין *contiguous passages*, or the *analogy* made from the *juxtaposition* of two laws in Scripture.

The theory of this rule is that the meaning of a law is sometimes explained from another law or passage which is placed near by, either preceding or following it.[1]

The following examples will illustrate this rule:

1. The word *Mamzer* (usually translated a *bastard*) in the law Deut. XXIII, 3: "A Mamzer shall not enter the congregation of the Lord" denotes, according to rabbinical interpretation, one born of incest or adultery. This interpretation is based on the circumstance that a preceding law (ib. verse 1.) interdicts an incestuous connection.[2]

2. The law prohibits *every labor* on Sabbath, without specifying the occupations included in that interdiction, thus leaving a wide scope to individual opinion on the nature of Sabbatical labor. Tradition, in order to prevent arbitrariness in so important a point, tried to fill out this void by a detailed definition of the nature of work, and minutely specified the labors which are allowed and which are forbidden on Sabbath. The Talmud distinguishes thirty nine chief labors אבות מלאכות, comprising all those occupations which were necessary for the

---

1 This rule was probably introduced by R. Akiba, see Siphre, Numbers 131: ר"ע אומר כל פרשה שסמוכה וכו'

2 Yebamoth 49a.

לא יקח איש את אשת אביו
וסמיך ליה לא יבוא ממזר

construction of the holy tabernacle. This is based on the circumstance that Scripture repeatedly (Exod. XXXI 1–17; XXXV, 1 sq.) brought the Sabbath law in juxtaposition with the description of the tabernacle.[1]

Remark. The theory of סמוכין which Ben Azai, one of R. Akiba's disciples, even applied in the construction of criminal laws, was not generally adopted. R. Jehuda ben Ilai, another disciple of R. Akiba, is especially mentioned as having been opposed to its general application. He strongly objected to a deduction based by the former on that theory in the case of a certain capital crime, remarking with astonishment: "How, shall we inflict the punishment of stoning upon a criminal because two laws are incidentally in juxtaposition?" (Yebamoth 4a; Sanhedrin 67b.).

He admitted the analogy from juxtaposition only in certain cases, especially in regard to laws found in the book of Deuternomy where the laws are evidently arranged according to a certain plan, while in regard to the other books of the Pentateuch it is held : אין מוקדם ומאוחר בתורה "there is no certain order for the sequence of the laws" (Pesachim 6b), hence no analogy must there be based on the juxtaposition of two laws (Sanhedrin ibid.).

§ 53.

Another kind of סמוכין consists in the method of separating the final part of a clause or sentence and connecting it with the beginning of the following clause or sentence, and in this way artificially forming a new sentence, the sense of which is to support a certain traditional law.

This peculiar method may be illustrated by the following examples.

1. It was a traditional rule of law, based on common sense, that a judge was unfit to sit in court when known to nourish inimical feelings either against the defendant or against one of his fellow judges. In the absence of an express passage

[1] Talm. Sabbath 49b: אבות מלאכות כנגד עבודת המשכן; see Rashi's Commentary on this passage. Other examples of this kind of analogy are found in Pesachim 96a; Yebamoth 4a.

in the Mosaic law bearing on this rule, the Rabbis construed an artificial support in the following way. In Numbers XXXV, 23, in the law about unintentional murder, it is said..... "whereas he was not his enemy, and did not seek his harm". These words plainly refer to the slayer and the slain man, but by connecting them with the beginning of the following sen tence (verse 24): "the congregation (i. e. the court) shall judge...", the new sentence is construed: Being no enemies and not seeking his harm, they shall judge as a court.[1]

2. In Lev. XXIII, 22 we read:... "and the gleaning of thy harvest *thou shalt not gather* ; *unto the poor* and the stranger shalt thou leave them." By closely connecting the end of the first clause with the beginning of the next clause, the sentence is formed : "*thou shalt not gather unto the poor*", intimating that the owner of the field has no right to gather the gleaning in behalf of a certain poor and thereby depriving the other poor of their claim to that gleaning warranted them by the laws.[2]

B. RESTRICTIVE RULES IN THE APPLICATION OF ANALOGY.

§ 54

By way of a plain analogy, particular provisions of the law concerning a certain case are in the Talmud often transferred to another case. This method is termed מה מצינו; (compare above p. 159). The phrases used in this process are either.... ילפינן מן or ....גמרינן מן, we derive, learn (this provision) from (that other case of...).

The use of analogy for such purpose presupposes consistency in the law, so that its provisions in one case were intended to apply also to an another similar case. But though the two cases from the comparison of which an analogy is drawn need not to be alike in all respects, still they must, at least, belong to the same sphere of the law. The provisions con

[1] והוא לא אויב לו ולא מבקש רעתו ושפטו וגו'
חד לדיין (רשונא לא ידון)
אידך לשני ת"ח ששונאין זא"ז שאין יושבין בדין כאחד
Talm. Sanhedrin 29a: compare Rashi's commentary.

[2] Tal. Gittin 12a: לא תלקט לעני, לא תסייע את העני

nected with the one case cannot be applied to another case which is totally different in its legal nature. Hence the following restrictive rules in the application of analogy:

1. אסורא מממונא לא ילפינן
ממונא מאסורא לא ילפינן

In a ritual case we do not apply an analogy from a civil case, and vice versa. Berachoth 19a; Baba Metzia 20a; Kiddushin 3b.

2. ממונא מקנסא לא ילפינן

In a case concerning pecuniary restitution we do not apply an analogy from a case concerning fine. Kethuboth 46b; Kiddushin 3b.

3. חולין מקדשים לא גמרינן

In a case concerning profane things we do not apply an analogy from laws concerning sanctified things. Pesachim 45a; Shebuoth 26b; Nazir 36b.

4. מחדוש לא גמרינן

From an extraordinary, exceptional case we make no analogy.[1] Pesachim 44b; Moed Katon 7b; Chullin 98b.

C. LIMITED OR UNLIMITED EFFECT OF AN ANALOGY.

§ 55.

When provisions of one law (A) are to be applied to another law (B) by virtue of a traditional analogy (the constructional Gezera Shava, compare above § 24), the question arises whether those laws are to be treated alike in every respect, so that all particulars found in A are applicable to B or whether the consequences of such an analogy are to be restricted to the main provision only. Concerning this question two different opinions are expressed.

[1] A similar rule is also laid down in modern law interpretation; compare Fr. Lieber, Legal and Political Hermeneutics, p. 276: "An exceptional case can of itself sustain no analogy, since the instance from which we reason, the analogon, must always be one which implies the rule".

One opinion, represented by R. Meir, holds: דון מנה ומנה "deduce from it, and again from it", that is to say, any further provision connected with A may be transferred to B.

But the other opinion is: דון מנה ואוקי באתרא "deduce from it, and (as for the rest) leave it in its place", that is to say, after having transferred the main provision of A to B, we are to let B retain its own character and the provisions expressly connected with it.

The difference between these two opinions may be illustrated by the following example.

In Deut. XXIII, 3, the law provides that a *Mamzer*, that is, one born of incest, "shall not enter the congregation of the Lord, *even to the tenth generation.*" A similar provision has another law concerning an Ammonite and a Moabite: "*Even to the tenth generation* they shall not enter into the congregation of the Lord, *for ever.*" By a Gezera Shava the conclusion is made that also in the former law concerning Mamzer the phrase "even to the tenth generation" is to be understood "for ever". (See above p. 150).

But while the term *Mamzer* implies the female as well as the male, the masculin form of the words עמוני ומואבי is taken by tradition strictly, referring to males only, but not to females (עמוני ולא עמונית).

According to the opinion of דון מנה ומנה, a female *Mamzer*, after the tenth generation, might be admitted to enter the congregation; her case being then, in all respects, analogous to that of a female Amonite who is exempted from the prohibition.

But according to the opinion of דון מנה ואוקי באתרא, the two laws are analogous only in respect to the meaning of the phrase "even to the tenth generation", while the expression *Mamzer* always retains its comprehensive meaning, including females as well as males. See Yebamoth 78b. Another example Shebuoth 31a.

D. REFUTATION AND REINSTATEMENT OF HERMENEUTIC ARGUMENTS.

§ 56.

The generalization of a Special Law (above Chapter III) may be refuted by the objection that a particular circumstance is connected with that special law which renders it unfit to be generalized or to be applicable to other cases.

The phrase used in such a refutation is the same as that which is used in refuting the premise of an inference of Kal Vechomer (see above p. 137), namely:..... מה לפלוני שכן

"Why is that special provision made for the case A? Because that certain peculiarity is connected with this case"....

After such a refutation, the attempt is usually made to defend the Binyan Ab by a reference to case B having the same provision, though not connected with that peculiarity. If then also the generalization of case B is objected to, on account of an other peculiarity connected with its provision, this objection is again removed by a reference to case A in which that peculiarity is not found. The common provision of A and B is then generalized according to the usual method of בנין אב משני כתובים. (See above p. 160). The procedure of this combined generalization is usually introduced by the following phrase:

וחזר הדין לא הרי זה כהרי זה הצד השוה שבהן...

"The conclusion returns (that is, the former argument is to be reinstated), for A is not like B, and vice versa, but the common point of both is....." Examples: Maccoth 2b; Sanhed rin 66a.

Remark. The same dialectic procedure and the same phrases are also applied where a refuted inference of Kal Vechomer is to be reinstated by a combination of two similar cases, as in Berachoth 35a; Kiddushin 5 b; B. Metzia 4a, and often.

E. THE THEORY OF EXTENSION AND LIMITATION.

§ 57.

The term רבוי means *extension*; מיעוט *limitation.* The idea connected with each of these two terms when applied separately, was explained in the introductory chapter § 6 and § 7. We have here to consider their meaning when applied conjointly רבוי ומיעוט to signify a theory in contradistinction to that of כלל ופרט (chapter IV).

In as much as a general term (כלל) denotes an indefinite number of individuals having something in common, it may also be regarded as רבוי, an extension of the meaning; and in as much as a particular, singular term (פרט) restricts the meaning to definite individuals, it may be regarded as מיעוט, a limitation.

That which in the theory of R. Ishmael is called כלל ופרט, is according to the theory of R. Eliezer and R. Akiba regarded as רבוי ומיעוט.

There is the following difference between these two theories.

a) In a combination of כלל ופרט, the particular is regarded as the *explanation* of the preceding general, so as to narrow down its comprehension to the strict contents of the particular, excluding even that which is similar to this (אין בכלל אלא מה שבפרט, see above § 42).

According to the other theory, the מיעוט merely limits the extension of the preceding רבוי, so as to include everything similar. and exclude that only which is not similar to it.

רבוי ומיעוט, רבה הכל. ומיעט שאינו דומה

b) In a combination of פרט וכלל the general following a particular includes everything falling under the general (comp. Rule V. § 43). But according to the other theory, the רבוי following the מיעוט includes that only which is similar to that מיעוט.

c) In a combination of כלל ופרט וכלל we include only that which resembles the particular (comp. Rule VI. § 44).

But, according to the other theory, the rule for רבוי ומיעוט ורבוי is, that the רבוי includes everything, even that which is not similar to the מיעוט, the effect of the latter being, however, to exclude merely one single thing which has the least similarity to it. To define this one thing to be excluded, is entirely left to the judgment of the expounding Rabbis.[1]

רבוי ומיעוט ורבוי רבה הכל, ולא מיעט אלא דבר אחד

The theory of רבוי ומיעוט, being not as clear and exact as that of כלל ופרט, is rejected by most of the Tanaim, and admitted only in some special cases.[2]

The difference between these two theories is illustrated by the following example.

In Levit. V, 21-23, the law provides that if an embezzler without having been convicted before a court, but prompted by his conscience, wants to expiate the sin of his injury to some person in respect to property, then he has to restore the fraudulently acquired property, with the addition of one fifth of its value, and besides bring a trespass-offering. The law introduces the case by the words:

"If a person commits a misdeed, and *lies to his neighbor* (General) concerning a *trust or a deposit* (Particulars), etc. etc. or *whatever it may be about which he has sworn falsely* (General), then he shall restore etc".

According to the theory of כלל ופרט וכלל, these expressions are to be construed in a way that the mulct of one fifth of the original amount is required for such embezzled objects only which are *movables*, and have an *intrinsic value*, the former excluding *real estate*, and the latter excluding *bills* or *notes*.

But according to the theory of רבוי ומיעוט, the law refers to any kind of embezzled property, *including real estate*, excluding, however, *bills* or *notes* which have merely a representative value.

The argumentation according to these two theories is expressed in the following way:

---

[1]See Rashi on Talm. Kiddushin 21b, and on Shebuoth 4b.

[2]See B. Kamma 64b; Shebuoth 5a; Chullin 67a.

A

רבנן דרשי כללי ופרטי:

וכחש בעמיתו — כלל
בפקדון או בתשומת יד — פרט
או מכל אשר ישבע — חזר וכלל
כלל ופרט וכלל אי אתה ד; אלא כעין הפרט
מה הפרט מפורש דבר המטלטל וגופו ממון
אף כל המטלטל וגופו ממון
יצאו קרקעות שאין מטלטלין
יצאו שטרות שאין גופן ממון

B

ר' אליעזר דריש רבויי ומיעוטי:

וכחש בעמיתו — רבוי
בפקדון או בתשומת יד — מיעט
או מכל אשר ישבע — חזר וריבה
ריבוי מיעוט וריבוי רבה הכל
מאי ריבי ריבי כל מילי
ומאי מיעט, מיעט שטרות

Talm. B. Kamma 117b; Shebuoth 37b. Other examples:Succah 50b; Kiddushin 21b; Shebuoth 26a.

F. "MIKRA" or "MASORA"?

§ 58

Although our vowel-signs of the Biblical text were not yet introduced at the Talmudic period, still the correct pronunciation according to the vowels was fixed by oral tradition.

The reading of the text according to the established pronunciation was called מקרא (reading). The proper spelling of the words of the sacred text as fixed by tradition, letters without vowels, is termed *Masora* (מסורת or מסורה).

The peculiar spelling of many words sometimes admits a meaning somewhat different from that which is expressed by the established pronunciation or our present vocalization. The question then arises whether in such a case the law is to be interpreted according to the vowel reading or rather according to the letters with which the word is spelled in the Masora.

In this respect two opposite opinions are expressed in the Talmud. One holds: יש אם למקרא "The source of law is in the reading" i. e. the reading of a word according to its established vocalization is essential to decide its meaning. The other opinion is: יש אם למסורת "the source is in the *Masora*," that is, the spelling of the word as fixed by the Masora is more material in defining its meaning.

Example: Speaking of the cities of refuge to which he who unintentionally killed a fellow-man was to flee, the law illustrates the case of such an unintentional homicide by the following words: As when a man goeth into the the woods with his neighbor to hew wood, and his hand fetcheth a stroke with the axe to cut down the tree, ונשל הברזל מן העץ *and the iron slippeth from the wood*, and findeth his neighbor, that he die, etc." (Deutr. XIX, 5.)

According to the opinion of אם למקרא, this passage refers only to the case where the killing happened by the iron of the axe slipping from the helve. But according to the opinion of אם למסורת the letters of the word ונשל admit that word to be read ונשל in the Piel form, so as to give the sense "and the iron splints a piece from the tree", hence this passage refers only to a case where the killing happened by a piece of wood which the axe cut from the tree.

רבי סבר יש אם למסורת, וְנִשֵּׁל כתיב,
ורבנן סברי יש אם למקרא, וְנָשַׁל קרינן

Maccoth 7b; other examples Pesachim 86a, and Sanhedrin 4a.

In this, as in most of other cases, the opinion of אם למקרא prevailed. The opposite opinion was accepted only where it served to support a traditional interpretation of a law; for instance, that the expression of כפות תמרים (Levit XXIII, 40) which the Masora spells כפת (without ו) refers only to *one* branch of the palm tree (Talm. Succah 32a).

CLOSING REMARK.

Concluding this exposition of the principal rules of Talmudical Hermeneutics, we must remind the student that this system of artificial interpretation was mainly calculated to offer the means of ingrafting the tradition on the stem of Scripture, or harmonizing the *oral* with the *written* law.

Modern scientific exegesis, having no other object than to determine the exact and natural sense of each passage in Scripture, must resort to hermeneutic rules fitted to that purpose, and can derive but little benefit from that artificial system.

Thus already the great Jewish Bible commentators in the Middle Ages, Ibn Ezra, Kimchi, and others who are justly regarded as the fathers of that thoroughly sound and scientific system of exegesis that prevails in modern times, remained in their interpretation of the Bible entirely independent of the hermeneutic rules of Hillel, R. Ishmael and R. Akiba. Nevertheless, this system deserves our attention, since it forms a very essential part of the groundwork on which the mental structure of the Talmud is reared. It must be known even in its details, if the Talmudic discussions, which often turn on some nice point of the rules of that system, are to be thoroughly understood.

PART III

TALMUDICAL TERMINOLOGY AND METHODOLOGY.

TALMUDICAL TERMINOLOGY AND METHODOLOGY

Prefatory

Like any other branch of science and literature, the Talmud has its peculiar system of technical terms and phrases adapted to its peculiar methods of investigation and demonstration. To familiarize the student with these methods and with the terms and phrases most frequently used in the Talmud is the object of the following chapters. As the Mishna is the text on which the Gemara comments, we begin with the explanation of some of the terms in reference to certain features in the structure of the Mishna. We shall then proceed to the various modes and terms used by the Gemara in explaining and discussing the Mishna. This will be followed by an exposition of the ways in which the Talmud generally discusses the reports and opinions of the Amoraim. Finally, the methods and processes of Talmudical argumentation and debates as well as the terms and stereotyped phrases connected therewith, will be set forth.

A. THE MISHNA

CHAPTER I

TERMS AND PHRASES REGARDING THE STRUCTURE OF A MISHNA PARAGRAPH.

סתם

§ 1.

The Mishna very often simply lays down the law without mentioning its author or any conflict of opinions that existed in regard to it. Such a Paragraph of the Mishna is termed סתם, an anonymous and undisputed Mishna. Examples: Berachoth I, 4; III, 1-3.

Such anonymous and undisputed Mishna paragraphs are generally regarded as authoritative. They are mostly of a very ancient origin, having been incorporated into the work of R. Jehuda Hanasi from older Halacha collections made by former teachers, especially that of R. Meir. סתם מתניתין ר' מאיר Sanhedrin 86a.

מחלוקת

§ 2.

Often also the Mishna reports a conflict of opinions in regard to a certain law. Such a conflict is termed מחלוקת a division or difference of opinion.

The conflicting opinions are set forth in different ways:

a. After having laid down the anonymous rule of law, the dissenting opinion of a certain teacher is added by: ר' פלוני אומר, Rabbi A says.... In such cases, the anonymous author of the first opinion is termed in the Gemara תנא קמא *the former teacher*. Example: Berachoth IV, 1.

Remark. As the anonymous opinion represents that of the teachers in general, the Gemara sometimes calls it also דברי חכמים the *words* (the collective opinion) *of the sages*; f. i. Sanhedrin 31a.

b. A rule of law is laid down with the addition דברי ר'

פלוני א' these are the words of Rabbi A, and then the dissenting opinion is introduced by :ור' פלוני ב' אומר but Rabbi B says...; or the question of law is propounded, and then the dissenting opinions concerning it are introduced by ר' פלוני א' אומר ור' פלוני ב' אומר. Examples: Berachoth II, 1 and 3.

Such a difference of opinion in which the opposite views are represented by single teachers is termed in the Gemara מחלוקת יחיד ויחיד a difference between individuals.

c. The opinion of a single teacher concerning a question of law having been set forth, the collective opinion of other contemporary teachers differing therefrom is introduced by: וחכמים אומרים but the (other) sages say.... Example: Berachoth VI, 4.

Such a conflict of opinions between an individual and a majority of other teachers is termed in the Gemara מחלוקת יחיד ורבים *a conflict between an individual and the majority.* Generally, the opinion of the majority prevails. This rule is phrased: יחיד ורבים הלכה כרבים where an individual and the majority differ from each other, the opinion of the majority is Halacha (the accepted law). Berachoth 9a.

d. The conflicting opinions are represented by different schools, especially those of Shamai and Hillel.

Examples: Berachoth I, 1; VIII, 1. 5. 7. 8.

Remark. In a conflict between those two schools the opinion of the School of Hillel generally prevails. ב"ש במקום ב"ה אינה משנה Berachoth 36b.

רישא, סיפא, מציעתא

§ 3.

Where a Mishna paragraph contains provisions for two or more cases, the former case is signified by רישא (the case at the beginning), and the following or last case by סיפא (the case at the end). The case between these two is termed מציעתא the middle case.

Example for a Mishna paragraph with two cases: B. Metzia I, 3; for one with three cases: B. Metzia I, 4. See also Gemara Kiddushin 63a; Kerithoth 11b; Chullin 94b.

In a paragraph divided into two main parts, A and B, each containing two cases, a and b, the case of A b is termed סיפא דרישא, and that of B, a רישא דסיפא.

Example: Shebuoth VI, 7. Compare Talmud Shebuoth 43b; B. Metzia 34b.

Remark. A part of a Mishna paragraph referring to a separate case or proposition is also termed בבא (gate, section, clause); hence the terms בבא דרישא the clause of the first proposition, בבא דסיפא the clause of the subsequent proposition. Sabbath 3a; Yebamoth 18b.

טעם

§ 4.

The Mishna, in general, simply lays down the rule of law without stating its reason. At times, however, the reason is added. The reason of a law is termed טעם. It is either based a) on a biblical passage (קרא) and its interpretation, and is then usually introduced by שנאמר; or b) on common sense (סברא); or c) on a general principle (כלל).

Examples: a) Berachoth IX, 5; B. Metzia II, 7.10. b) B. Metzia I, 7; II, 11. c) B. Kamma III, 10.11.

Remark. The Gemara generally investigates the reason of the law where it is not stated in the Mishna.

פלוגתא

§ 5.

Also the different opinions of the teachers concerning a point of the law are generally set forth in the Mishna without the reason of the difference being added. Occasionally, however, not only the reason of one or both of the contradictory opinions is stated, but even a shorter or longer controversy is recorded in which the teachers argue in opposition to each other on some questions of law. Such a controversy is termad in the Gemara פלוגתא. The elaborate argumentation pro and con is also termed משא ומתן or in Aramaic שקלא וטריא (literally, a taking and giving of arguments, i. e., a *discussion*). Examples of controversies in the Mishna: Berachoth I, 3; Pesachim VI, 2; Taanith I, 1; B. Kamma II, 5.

מעשה

§ 6.

The Mishna sometimes adds to its rule of law or to its

opinions of the contesting teachers the report of a certain case in which a celebrated anthority gave a decision either 1) in accordance with or 2) in contradiction to the rule just laid down or the opinion just expressed. Such a report is usually introduced by the word מעשה it is a reported fact that...., it once occured that...

Examples ad 1: Berachoth I, 1; Bechoroth IV, 4; ad 2: B. Metzia VIII, 8; Gittin I, 5.

כלל אמרו

§ 7.

The word כלל, often occurring the Mishna, signifies a general rule, a guiding principle of a law. Such a general rule either precedes or follows the details of a law.

Where it precedes the details, it is usually introduced by the words כלל אמרו they (i. e. the former teachers) established the following rule concerning....

Examples: Pea I, 4; Shebiith VII, 1. 2; Maaseroth I, 1. Sabbath VII, 1.

Where the general law follows the details, it is introduced by זה הכלל this is the general rule.....

Examples: Berachoth VI, 7; Pesachim III, 1; B. Metzia IV, 1.

Remark. The Gemara usually investigates the necessity of this general rule by asking: לאתויי מאי what is this to add? i. e; which new cases is this general rule to imply besides those explicitly stated in the details of the law?

כל, הכל, חוץ

§ 8.

Paragraphs of the Mishna containing a generalizing or comprehensive provision are introduced by כל or הכל "all", "every", "whatever". Mostly some exceptions from such a generalizing provision are added by the word חוץ "except"..

Examples: Chagiga I, 1; Kiddushin I, 6. 7. 9; Gittin II, 5.; Chullin I,1.

Remark. The Gemara finds that such comprehensive provisions are not always exact, as they often admit of exceptions besides those expressly stated in the Mishna. Erubin 27a; Kiddushin 34a.

מניינא

§ 9.

Without laying down a general rule, the Mishna sometimes states the exact number of cases to which a certain law refers and then specifies those cases more fully, f. i. "there are four main kinds of damages to property, namely...." B. Kamma I, 1; or: "Marriage may be contracted in three ways, namely..." Kiddushin I, 1. Such a stated number is termed מניינא.

Remark. The Gemara finds that such a number is intended to limit the law exactly to those cases mentioned in the Mishna, so as to exclude certain other cases, and the question is generally made: מניינא למעוטי מאי what cases are excluded by this limiting number?

אלו, זו היא

§ 10.

Another limitation of the Mishna occurs, where certain cases are enumerated by the introductory words אלו "these are..." or זו היא "this is..."

Examples: Pea I, 1; Pesachim II, 5; Yebamoth III, 3. 5.

Remark. Also where these limiting words are used in the Mishna the Gemara usually asks: למעוטי מאי what cases are excluded by this limitation?

אין בין.... אלא..

§ 11.

Still another limitation admitting of no other exceptions than those expressly mentioned, is found, where the Mishna points out the only difference that in certain legal respects exists between two things, by the limiting phrase: אין בין...אלא... "there is no difference between...and....except in regard..."

Examples: Megilla I, 4-11.

תנא ושייר

§ 12.

Where the Mishna enumerates different cases to which a

certain law applies without fixing their number and without using any of those limiting terms mentioned above, the enumerated cases do not always exclude other cases to which the same law applies. The Gemara uses in this case the phrase: תנא ושייר "the Mishna teaches concerning certain cases, and leaves others to be added".

Examples: Taanith 14a; B. Kamma 10a; Maccoth 21b.

לא זו אף זו

§ 13.

Where in enumerating certain cases of a law a subsequent case is more unexpected than the preceding, the Gemara uses the phrase לא זו אף זו קתני "the Mishna teaches not only that, but even this," that is, the Mishna intended to arrange the cases in a climax, starting from that which is plain, and adding that which is more unexpected.

Examples: B. Metzia III, 4 and 5. See Talm. B. Metzia 38a.

Remark. The climax in the arrangement of several cases is also expressed by the Talmudical phrase: לא מבעיא קאמר, לא מיבעיא אלא אפילו.. the author of the Mishna states here a case of "not only"; not only as to...but even..., i. e., the Mishna adds here to that which is unquestionable (plain and obvious enough) that which is more unexpected.

Examples: Betza 37a; B. Kamma 54b; Kiddushin 78b.

זו ואין צריך לומר זו

§ 14.

On the other hand, the Mishna sometimes arranges the cases of a law in an anticlimax, so that the subsequent case is self-evident from the preceding. This is expressed in the Gemara by the phrase: זו ואין צריך לומר זו "that, and it is unnecessary to say this" i. e. after having stated the law in the former case, it applies the more to the following case.

Example: Rosh Hashana IV, 8; see Talm. R. Hashana 32b, 33a.

לכתחילה, דיעבד

§ 15.

Of these two antithetical terms the Gemara makes frequent use in the interpretation of the Mishna, especially in questions of the ritual law. לכתחלה means, literally, *as for the beginning*, at the outset, beforehand, previously. The term denotes the question of law concerning an act to be done, whether it may properly be done in that certain manner or not.

דיעבד (contraction of דאי עבד) means *if he has done.* In contradistinction to the former, this term denotes the question of law concerning an act *already done*, whether it is valid and acceptable or not.

The phrases in connection with these two terms are:

1. אפילו לכתחילה or לכתחילה נמי *even directly*, i. e. the expression of the Mishna indicates a direct permission to do the act under consideration, so that it may be done unhesitatingly.

Example: Tal. Chullin 2a.

2. בדיעבד אין לכתחילה לא *if done, yes, but directly not* i. e. only if it has already been done, it is acceptable and legitimate, but directly permissible it is not.

Example: Chullin 13b; 15b.

3. לכתחילה לא, דיעבד שפיר דמי *directly not, but if done it is right*, i. e. it ought not to be done, but if already done, it is acceptable and valid[1].

Examples: Mishna Berachoth II, 3. Terumoth I, 6; Talm. Berachoth 15a b.

4. דיעבד נמי לא even if done, it is not accepted as valid.

Examples: Berachoth 15a; Megilla 19b.

---

[1] Compare the phrase in the civil law: Fieri non debet, sed factum valet.

B. THE GEMARA EXPLAINING AND DISCUSSING THE MISHNA

CHAPTER II.

Modes of Treating an Anonymous Mishna Paragraph.

§ 16.

The Gemara uses a great variety of modes in commenting the Mishna and discussing its contents. Generally, the comments are introduced by a query which is intended to call attention to the point that requires elucidation. This method of introducing a statement or explanation by queries is to some extent already found in the Mishna itself, as מאימתי from what time on may we read....? Berachoth I, 1. 2; Taanith I, 1;..כיצד how are benedictions to be recited..? Berachoth VI, 1; VII, 3;...במה....ובמה with what...and with what...? Sabbath II, 1; IV, 1 ; VI, 1;... מניין whence is it derived...?.. איזהו...ואיזהו which are...and which are...? B. Kamma II, 4; B. Metzia V, 1, and many other similar interrogative phrases. But in the Gemara this method is more commonly applied.

The following is an outline of the different modes and phrases mostly used in the Gemara at the outset of its commentation and discussion on the Mishna.

1. Explaining Words and Phrases of the Mishna.

§ 17.

Such explanations are mostly introduced by the question: ....מאי *what is...?* or, *what means....?*

Examples: Berachoth 59a; Pesachim 2a; Kiddushin 29a.

In answer to this query, the explanation is generally given in the name of a certain Amora. Sometimes, two teachers differ in the answer; f. ex. Berachoth 29a; Pesachim 2a. Where the schools of Babylonia and Palestine differ in the interpretation, that difference is usually expressed by ... הכא תרגומו

התם אמרו *here* (in Babylon) they explain..., but *there* (in Palestine) they say...; or...הכא תרגומו *here* they explain,.. ור' פ' אמר, but a certain (Palestinian) Rabbi says....; f.ex. R. Hashana 30b, Sanhedrin 25a; B. Metzia 20a. Sometimes, however, הכא refers to *Sura* in opposition to other Babylonian schools; f. ex. Pesachim 42b; B. Bathra 61a.

Remark. Where the question מאי is followed by... אילימא *if to say..? is it to say....?* an anticipated explanation is to be rejected as wrong; f. ex. Berachoth 9b; Kiddushin 29a.

2. ASKING FOR THE MEANING OR CONSTRUCTION OF A WHOLE SENTENCE OR OF A STATEMENT IN THE MISHNA

§ 18.

a. מאי קאמר what does he (the author of this Mishna) intend to say here?

The answer to this question is generally introduced by: הכי קאמר thus he says.... Example : Sabbath 41a; Taanith 27a.

b. מאי משמע what does he let us hear?

Examples: Sabbath 84b; Sanhedrin 46b.

Remark. Different is the meaning of the question מאי משמע, when followed by....ד, in which case it is to be translated by: What proves that....? f. ex. R. Hashana 21b; 22b.

3. ASKING FOR THE OBJECT OF A SEEMINGLY INDIFFERENT OR SUPERFLUOUS STATEMENT.

§ 19.

a. למאי הלכתא for what practical purpose is this (statement)?

Examples: R. Hashana 2a; Yebamoth 39a; Kethuboth 82a.

b. מאי קמשמע לן (abbr. מאי קמ"ל) What does he intend to let us hear? What does he want to teach us, here?

The answer to the latter question is mostly introduced by ...הא קמ"ל This he intends to teach us, that...

Examples: Pesachim 89a; Sebachim 85b; Meilah 21a.

c. מאי למימרא What is this to say? Why teach this?

Example: Nazir 13a.

4. INVESTIGATING THE PARTICULAR CIRCUMSTANCES OF A CASE REFERRED TO IN THE MISHNA.

§ 20.

a. במאי עסיקינן Of what case, of what circumstances do we treat here?

Examples: Betza 2a; B. Metzia 12b; Gittin 37b.

b. היכי דמי (abbr. ה״ד) How shall we imagine this case?

Examples: Megilla 18a; Gittin 78a; B. Kamma 28b.

Both of these two interrogative phrases are mostly followed either by ...אילימא *if to say..; is it to say...?* anticipating an answer which is rejected at once; or by a dilemma...אי....אי, *if...? and if...?* presenting two anticipated alternatives to either of which the law under consideration cannot well refer.

The answer to such questions is introduced either by הכא במאי עסקינן Here we treat of the case...., or by... לא צריכא, *no* (i. e. not as you anticipated, but) *necessarily....* (we have to imagine the case under the circumstances that...), or by.... לעולם, *however, still* (i. e. notwithstanding your objection) *I say....*

This last phrase is especially used when one of the alternatives is defended against the objection made to it.

5. INVESTIGATING THE BIBLICAL SOURCE OF A LAW LAID DOWN IN THE MISHNA.

§ 21.

The question introducing such an investigation is either:

מנא לן, contr. מנלן (abbr. מנ״ל) Whence do we have this?

Example: Kidd. 14b; 22b and very often.

Or מנא הני מילי, contr. מנהני מילי (abbr. מה״מ) Whence are these words (laws)?

Examples: Berachoth 30b; 35a a. v. o.

Both of these questions correspond to the Mishnic מנין, whence is it derived?

Correctly the question מנ"ל is applied where the source of only one single point of the law is to be investigated, while מה"מ is used where several points or provisions are under consideration. But this distinction is not always strictly regarded.

In answer to this question either an Amora is quoted who points to the source, by the phrase: דאמר קרא for Scripture says...., or reference is made to a Baraitha in which the law in question is artificially derived from a biblical passage. This reference is introduced by: דת"ר for the Rabbis have taught..

Remark 1. Instead of answering the question of מנלן, the Gemara sometimes repeats the same question with astonishment: מנלן?!, as if to say, How can you ask such a question, since the source of the law under consideration is obvious enough from a plain biblical passage? The original question is then set forth in a modified form by the phrase: אנן הכי קאמרינן We mean to say (ask) thus:...; f. ex. Megilla 2a; Sanhedrin 68b; Sebachim 89a.

Remark 2. In answering the question of מנלן, the Amoraim often differ, one deriving the law from this, and another from another passage. After having investigated the merits of their different derivations, the Gemara sometimes adds another biblical basis given by a Tana in a Baraitha. In this case, the phrase is used : ותנא מייתא לה מהכא but a Tana derives it from this passage...

Example: Betza 15b; Chagiga 9a; Kiddushin 4b; see Rashi on the first mentioned passage.

6. INVESTIGATING THE REASON OR THE UNDERLYING PRINCIPLE OF A LAW.

§ 22.

Such an investigation is generally introduced by the query מאי טעמא (abbr. מ"ט) What is the reason?

Examples: Berachoth 33a; R. Hashana 32b; Megilla 24a; B. Metzia 38a.

This query is especially made in regard to such anonymous Mishna paragraphs where the law contained therein is evidently not based on scriptural grounds, but merely on a rabbinical institution or principle. But in regard to a Mishna containing a difference of opinion, the question:... מאי טעמא דר׳ "What is the reason of the dissenting Rabbi A?" is often also answered by a reference to a biblical passage; f. ex. Berachoth 15a.

Remark 1. Exceptionally the question מ"ט is found in Moed Katon 19a in the sense of לענין מאי "in what respect?" See Rashi on that passage.

Remark 2. Where the reason of one of two cases or one of two opinions contained in a Mishna paragraph is clear enough, but not the other, the query is usually set forth in the following phrase:

בשלמא..... משום.... אלא.... מאי טעמא?

It is all right (in the one case)...., there it is on account of...., but in the case of... what is there the reason?

Examples: Berachoth 33b; 52b; Yebamoth 41b.

Remark 3. Sometimes, both questions מ"ט and מנה"מ are made. In this case the former asks for the underlying principle, and the latter for the biblical basis of that principle; for ex. Sabbath 24b. The reversed order is found in Betza 15b; see Rashi on that passage.

7. INVESTIGATING THE GENERAL BASIS OF THE PARTICULARS OF A LAW.

§ 23.

The Mishna sometimes starts with the particulars of a law without having stated the principal law to which those particulars refer. In this case the Gemara asks:

תנא היכא קאי דקתני.... Where (on what basis) does the author of this Mishna stand, that he here teaches....? i. e. to what general law does he refer? or where is the principal law of these particulars?

Examples: Berachoth 2a; Taanith 2a; see also Shebuoth 17b.

The answer is introduced by the phrase: התם קאי "he refers to the passage there".... (in which the required basis is stated).

8. INVESTIGATING THE AUTHORSHIP OF AN ANONYMOUS MISHNA

§ 24.

The Gemara often endeavors to trace an anonymous Mishna to its author, i. e. to find out whether or not that anonymous Mishna represents the opinion of a certain Tana expressed elsewhere in another Mishna or in a Baraitha. Such an investigation is introduced by one of the following phrases.

a. מאן תנא... Who is that Tana (author)?..., Berachoth 40a; Yoma 14a; Megilla 19b.

b. מני מתניתן... or מתניתן מני... Whose opinion represents our Mishna?... B. Kamma 33a; Gittin 10a; Nedarim 87a.

c. הא מני? ר׳ פ׳ היא Whose opinion is this? It is that of Rabbi A... B. Metzia 40b.

d. מתניתן דלא כפלוני Our Mishna does not represent the opinion of.... B. Kamma 32a.

Remark 1. Where the investigation is merely problematical with a negative result, it is generally preceded by לימא (or נימא), is it to say...? The answer is then usually: אפילו תימא..., you may even say... (our Mishna agrees with the opinion of that Tana); as: לימא מתניתן דלא כי האי תנא, Is it to say that our Mishna does not represent the opinion of that certain Rabbi in the Baraitha? B. Kamma 30a; B. Metzia 2b; Kiddushin 52b. Sometimes, it is also phrased: לימא תנן סתמא..כר׳ (דלא) Is it to say, that that which is taught here anonymously does (or does not) agree with the view of that Rabbi? Berachoth 25b; Betza 27b; Bechoroth 28a.

Remark 2. Also where the Mishna records a dissenting opinion of the sages collectively by וחכמים אומרים, the Gemara often investigates מאן חכמים, Who is the representative of these sages? f. ex. Gittin 22a; B. Metzia 60b; Sanhedrin 66a.

9. INVESTIGATING THE FORCE OF A COMPREHENSIVE OR A LIMITING TERM.

A. COMPREHENSIVE TERMS.

§ 25.

As stated above chapter I, 7. 8, the Mishna often introduces the provisions of law by general and comprehensive terms, as כל, הכל, זה הכלל, כלל אמרו which terms are assumed to imply other cases in addition to those expressly mentioned. Investigating the force of such a comprehensive term, the Gemara usually asks : לאתויי מאי What is this to include? What is this term to add?

Examples: Pesachim 8a ; Chagiga 2a ; Gittin 19a. See Erubin 2a–3b.

B. Limiting Terms.

§ 26.

Where the Mishna is making use of a limiting term (see above I. 9. 10), the question of the Gemara is: למעוטי מאי What is this to exclude?

Examples: Pesechim 76b; Kiddushin 3a; B. Kamma 13b.

10. INVESTIGATING THE REFERENCE OF A CERTAIN STATEMENT IN THE MISHNA.

§ 27.

After having laid down certain provisions of the law, the Mishna sometimes adds either a modification or a dissenting opinion without clearly stating to which of the preceding provisions this addition refers. Investigating such a case the Gemara usually asks: אהייא *to which* ? i. e. to which of the preceding provisions or cases does this addition refer ? This question is generally followed by:....אילימא *shall I say....* (it refers to the latter or to the former case)?

Examples: Berachoth 34b; Kiddushin 46a; Sanhedrin 79a.

11. QUALIFYING A PROVISION OF THE MISHNA.

§ 28.

Without an introductory question, the Gemara often qualifies a provision of the Mishna by limiting its application to certain circumstances. The phrases used for this purpose are:

a. לא שנו אלא....אבל....לא *they only taught this in reference to....* (a case under that certain circumstance), *but ..* (under the different circumstance of...) *not.*

Examples: Berachoth 42b; Succah 32a; B. Kamma 28a.

b. ודווקא....אבל....לא *only....but... not.*

Examples: Yebamoth 98b; B. Bathra 146a; Aboda Zara 74b.

c. The shortest phrase for this purpose is : ....והוא ש *provided that....*

Examples: Sabbath 53a; B. Metzia 11a; Maccoth 6a.

Remark. The phrase לא שנו אלא corresponds to the Mishnic phrase במה דברים אמורים or אימתי.

12. EXTENDING A PROVISION OF THE MISHNA.

§ 29.

Opposite to the preceding case, the Gemara often also extends the effect of a provision above the limits or circumstances indicated in the Mishna. The usual phrase for such an extension is: .... לא....ממש אלא אפילו *not strictly..* (to the circumstance stated in the Mishna refers this law) *but even...*

Examples: Berachoth 53b; Kethuboth 23a; B. Metzia 34a.

Remark. This phrase introducing an extension of the law is often shortened to the simple word: ... אפילו or ואפילו *and even...*; f. i. B. Metzia 22b; 26b; Aboda Zara 41a.

13. MAKING CONCLUSIONS AND DEDUCTIONS FROM THE MISHNA.

§ 30.

A conclusion or deduction made either from the contents or from the wording of the Mishna is termed דיוקא (B. Metzia 8a) or דוקיא (Kethuboth 31b). Such conclusions at the outset of the Gemara form generally the basis of a subsequent question and are introduced by one of the following technical terms and phrases:

a. .... אלמא hence..., consequently..., f. ex. Yoma 14b; Betza 9b; B. Metzia 37a.

b. ...טעמא ד...אבל... the reason (of the decision given in this Mishna) is...., but... (under different circumstances the decision must be different) ; f. ex. Pesachim 9a ; B. Kamma 47b; B. Metzia 18a; 25a.

Remark. This latter phrase is especially used where a conclusion is made from a positive statement to the negative, or vice versa. Such conclusions are sometimes also phrased: ...אין (הא) ..לא (in this case) yes, but... (in the opposite case) not; f. ex Berachoth 17b; Nazir 34b; Chullin 13a.

c. ...שמע מיניה (abbr. ש"מ) *hear from this*, conclude from this that ... f. ex. Berachoth 13a. Interrogatively it is phrased שמעת מינה do you not conclude from this...? Yoma 37b; Sanhedrin 71a; B. Metzia 97b.

Remark. ש"מ is mostly used in deductions by which a legal principle is finally to be established. At the end of an argument the phrase ש"מ expresses the acceptance of the preceding conclusions as proved and correct, and is then to be translated by: you may hear it herefrom, it is proved herefrom.

d ....מכלל in this is implied that..,from this follows that...; f. ex Pesachim 45a, Sanhedrin 66a. This term of inference is often preceded by:... מדקתני since the Mishna teaches.., as : מדקתני... מכלל since he teaches...., it follows....; f. ex. Berachoth 43a, B. Kamma 2a; or... מדקתני... ולא קתני...מכלל since he teaches....and not...., it follows...; f. ex. Kethuboth 90a.

e. .... זאת אומרת this tells, this teaches that .... This phrase introduces deductions of a general principle from a special case in the Mishna, f. ex. Berachoth 20b; Rosh Hashana 22a; B. Kamma 35b.

CHAPTER III

THE GEMARA CRITICISING THE MISHNA

Another kind of questions with which the Gemara introduces its comments on the Mishna are those of astonishment and surprise at finding therein either an incongruity or an inconsistency, a superfluity or an omission, or another difficulty. The following are the different modes in which questions and objections of this kind are set forth and answered.

1. Finding an incongruity of Expressions.

§ 31.

A. Incongruity in one and the same Mishna paragraph.

פתח ב... וסיים ב ... "Why begin with... (this term or expression) and then end with...(a different one)?"

Example: פתח בכד וסיים בחבית B. Kamma 27a. Other examples: Moed Katon 11b, B. Bathra 17b.

The answer is usually....היינו....היינו *it is this...it is the same*; i. e. both expressions are identical, mean the same thing.

B. Incongruity of Expressions in Different Parts of the Mishna.

מאי שנא הכא דתני.... ומאי שנא התם דתני ... (abbr. מ"ש) "Why is the Mishna using here.... (this expression), and there.. (a different one)?"

Examples: Sabbath 2b; Kiddushin 2a; Shebuoth 5a.

Remark. The answer to this question is sometimes: הכא רבותא קמ"ל והתם רבותא קמ"ל "by that change of expression it was intended to add something new and unexpected here as well as there": f. ex. Kidd. 59b.

2. Finding a Tautology in the Mishna.

§ 32.

The technical phrase used in the objection to a tautology is:

...היינו ....היינו "Is not.... (this expression or case) the same as... (that other one)?"; why then this repetition?

Examples: Rosh Hashana 23b; B. Kamma 17b; Shebubuoth 12b.

3. Objecting to the Order of the Stated Cases.

§ 33.

מאי שנא דתנא....ברישא ליתני....ברישא Why does the Mishna just teach the case of.... first, instead of teaching that other case of...first?

Examples: Berachoth 2a; B. Bathra 108a; Bechoroth 13a.

4. Objecting to a Certain Mode of Expression.

§ 34.

a. למה ליה למיתני .... ליתני... Why does the author of the Mishna use the expression...., instead of using.... (that other expression)?

Examples: Sabbath 90b; B. Metzia 2a; B. Bathra 98b.

b. מאי איריא דתני....ליתני... What does he intend to teach in using this expression, instead of....?

Examples: Yebamoth 84a; Kiddushin 69a.

Remark. The answer to such an objection is often: מלתא אגב אורחיה קמ"ל (In using this expression) he lets us hear something by the way, namely... ; f. ex. Berachoth 2a.

5. Objecting to a Certain Limitation of a Provision in the Mishna.

§ 35.

מאי איריא ....אפילו נמי Why just teaching....since the law applies also to....?

Examples: Pesachim 50b; Gittin 34b; B. Bathra 59b.

6. Finding an Omission of a Distinction between two Cases.

§ 36.

The objection to such an omission is generally phrased in the following way;

קא פסיק ותני לא שנא...ולא שנא...
בשלמא... אלא...אמאי

"The Mishna decides here....without distinguishing between....and...;it is right... (concerning the one case), but why should the law apply also to....(the other case)?"

Examples: Succah 29b; Gittin 10b; Sanhedrin 18b.

7. FINDING AN EXPRESSION TO BE INCORRECT OR TOO INDEFINITE.

§ 37.

סלקא דעתך (abbr. ס"ד) Does this enter your mind? i. e., do you indeed mean to say this?

Examples; Yoma 67b; Pesachim 42b; Kiddushin 29a.

The corrected version is then usually introduced by: אלא אימא.. but rather say....

8. FINDING A TERM OR PROVISION TO BE OUT OF PLACE.

§ 38.

מאן דכר שמיה Who mentioned the name of this? i. e. what has this to do here? how is this to be mentioned in this connection?

Examples. Sabbath 57a, Pesachim 8b, Nazir 4a.

The answer to this question is generally introduced by the phrase: הכי קאמר thus he means to say, or by: חסורי מיחסרא והכי קתני something is omitted here which must be supplied by construction, namely....

9. FINDING A CERTAIN PROVISION OF THE MISHNA UNNECESSARY, BEING TOO PLAIN AND OBVIOUS TO BE EXPRESSLY MENTIONED.

§ 39.

פשיטא "this is too plain!" i. e., why make this provision for a case which is so plain? why state that which is a matter of course?

Examples: Berachoth 20b; 47b; Pesachim 21b; Megilla 25a.

The full phrase of this elliptical expression is פשיטא מאי

למימרא it is too plain, why then expressly say (teach) it? f. ex. Nedarim 16a.

In answer to this objection, the Gemara generally tries to show that under certain circumstances the provision under consideration is not as plain and self-evident as it appears to be ; or that it was needed in order to prevent some possible misunderstanding in the application of the general law. Such an answer is mostly phrased either:

.... (כגון) לא צריכא אלא it is not so (plain), as it is needed for the case...;or:... איצטריך סלקא דעתך אמינא it was necessary to state this, since you might have misunderstood me to say...; or: מהו דתימא....קמ"ל what you might have supposed is that....; therefore the author informs us (of this provision).

Remark. Different from this meaning of the word פשיטא, as an elliptical expression of astonishment and objection is that, when the word precedes a propounded question of problem, where two cases are set forth one of which is plain and obvious enough, but not the other. In such a connection the word is simply a statement of self-evidence, and is to be translated by: this case is clear and plain, but (my question concerns that other case); f. ex. Berachoth 12a; B. Kamma 8b; Kiddushin 8b. This kind of פשיטא is generally explained in Rashi's commentary by the remark בניחותא "in calmness" i. e. to be read here not as a question but in a calm manner as a plain statement, while the other kind of פשיטא is explained by בתמיה "in astonishment". As a simple statement preceding a question of doubt and problem, the term פשיטא is sometimes supplied in the Talmud by the word לי "this case is plain to me"; f. ex. Sabbath 3b; Megillah 3b.

10. FINDING AN UNNECESSARY REPETITION OF THE SAME PROVISION ALREADY STATED ELSEWHERE.

§ 40.

The question objecting to such a repetition is phrased:

a. (חדא זימנא) מאי קמ"ל תנינא What does he inform us here, since I have already once before been informed thereof in another passage of the Mishna?

Examples: Berachoth 50a; Kethuboth 42a; 65b.

b. (הא) תנינא חדא זימנא But I learned this already once before....

Examples: Sabbath 89b; B. Metzia 55a; Sanhedrin 20b.

c. הא תו למה לי הא תנא ליה... Why do I need this again, since he taught this already once before? Example: Gittin 15a.

The answer is introduced in different ways according to its different nature:

a. הא קמ"ל... this he intends to inform us here, that....

b. סיפא אצטריכא ליה.... on account of the addition to be made here, this repetition was necessary.

c. צריכא... it was necessary (to repeat here this provision), since....

d. אי מהאי הוה אמינא.. קמ"ל if to derive it from that other Mishna, 1 might have supposed that...., therefore here the additional information.

Remark. Where a similar provision is found in two Masechtoth concerning different, though analogous, cases, the question of unnecessary repetition is not raised, but the Gemara simply states:

ותנן נמי גבי....כי האי גוני וצריכא.... also in reference to....the Mishna provides for a case similar to this, but both of these provisions are necessary, for....

Examples: Kiddushin 50a; Gittin 74a; B. Metzia 119a.

11. FINDING IN A MISHNA AN UNNECESSARY ABUNDANCE OF ANALOGOUS CASES.

§ 41.

a. כל הני למה לי Why are all these cases needed?

Examples: Succah 17a; Kethuboth 23b; Bechoroth 2a.

b. הא תו למה לי (היינו הך) Why is this case still added (since both cases are identical)?

Examples: Yebamoth 23b; Kiddushin 65a; Shebuoth 27b.

c. למה ליה למתני... ולמה ליה למתני... Why does he need to teach...and then teach again...?

Examples: B. Metzia 33b; Shebuoth 27b; Kiddushin 60b.

The answer, always introduced by צריכא "it is necessary"

or צריכי "all the mentioned cases are necessary", generally attempts to show that with each of the stated cases a peculiar circumstance is connected on account of which the analogy with the other case might have been objected to, hence the express statement of all cases. The phraseology of this answer is mostly: דאי תנא ... הוה אמינא ... קמ"ל for if the author had only taught... (that other case) I might have supposed....; therefore he lets us hear this.

Remark. The question "why are all these cases needed?" is sometimes omitted and the Gemare starts with the explanation: וצריכא it was necessary (to state all these cases), since...; f. ex. Sabbath 122a; Kiddushin 50b; B. Kamma 32b.

12. FINDING ONE OF TWO CASES SUPERFLUOUS, SINCE *a fortiori* IMPLIED IN THE OTHER.

§ 42.

The question based on the argument *a fortiori* is generally phrased: השתא (ומה התם) ... אמרת ... (הכא) ... מבעיא (לא כל שכן) if (there in the one case) you say... (that the decision is...) can it here (in our case) be questionable ? i. e., is it not here the more so, why then state the other case?

Examples: Rosh Hashana 32b; Pesachim 55b; Yebamoth 30a; Shebuoth 32b.

Remark. The answer to this objection is sometimes, that the Mishna intended to arrange cases in a climax (לא זו אף זו, Rosh Hashana 32b), or in an anticlimax (זו ואין צריך לומר זו, Kethuboth 58a). Concerning these two phrases see above § 13 and § 14.

13. FINDING AN OMISSION OF CASES WHERE THE MISHNA EXPRESSLY LIMITS THEIR NUMBER.

§ 43.

a. ולתני נמי... (or ונתני) should not the author also have added the case of....?

Examples: B. Metzia 55a; Yebamoth 53a; Zebachim 49b.

b. .... ותו לא (ליכא) והא איכא .... are there not more cases? but behold. there is the case of.... (which is not mentioned).

Examples: Gittin 9b; 86a; Chullin 42a; Menachoth 74b.

14. FINDING A GENERAL RULE OF LAW NOT COVER G ALL CASES.

§ 44.

וכללא הוא הרי.... Is this a general rule? behold the case of... (to which it does not apply.)

Examples: Kiddushin 34a; 66b; Temurah 14a; Chullin 59a.

15. FINDING A DECISION OF THE MISHNA NOT IN ACCORDANCE WITH AN ESTABLISHED PRINCIPLE.

§ 45.

ואמאי or אמאי והא.... Why so? How is this? Is this not against the principle of...?

Examples: Berachoth 47b; Betza 31b; B. Metzia 94a.

Remark. The question אמאי is sometimes omitted, and must be supplied, f. ex. in B. Metzia 99a; Gittin 22b.

16. FINDING A DIFFERENT DECISION REGARDING TWO CASES WHICH OUGHT TO HAVE BEEN TREATED ALIKE.

§ 46.

מאי שנא רישא ומאי שנא סיפא What difference is there between the former and the latter case? i. e., since the two cases mentioned in the Mishna are seemingly alike, why does the decision in the one case differ from that in the other?

Examples: B. Metzia 65b; B. Bathra 20a; Kiddushin 64a.

17. FINDING AN INCONSISTENCY OF PRINCIPLES IN ONE AND THE SAME MISHNA PARAGRAPH.

§ 47.

The phraseology mostly used in such objection of inconsistency is:

הא גופא קשיא, אמרת....אלמא...ואמרת.... אלמא .... is this not self-contradictory? you say...hence.... and then you say.... hence...? i. e., the underlying principle or the consequence of one part of this Mishna contradicts that of the other part.

Examples: Berachoth 50a, B. Kamma 39, B. Metzia 31a.

When the self-contradiction is more obvious, the objection is simply phrased:

והא אמרת רישא.... but did you not say in the first part...?

Examples: Betza 31b; Moed Katon 13a; Gittin 21b.

Remark. In answer to such an objection, the Gemara usually attempts to reconcile the contradictory members of the Mishna. Sometimes, however, the contradiction is admitted by the phrase: תברא מי ששנה זו לא שנה זו verily, (or, here is a break!) he who taught this part did not teach the other; i. e., this Mishna does not represent the opinion of one author, but the opposite opinions of two different teachers; f. ex, Sabbath 92b; B. K. 47b.

18. FINDING A LAW REPORT QUOTED IN THE MISHNA TO BE CONTRARY TO THE PRECEDING LAW.

§ 48.

As stated above § 6, the Mishna, after having laid down a rule of law, occasionally adds the report of a certain case (מעשה) in which a celebrated authority gave a decision in accordance with that law. Sometimes, however, that decision is just contrary to the preceding law. In this case, the Gemara starts with the question: מעשה לסתור is this report to contradict (the preceding)? i. e., instead of corroborating the preceding law, it just conflicts with it.

Examples: Betza 24a; Gittin 66a, B. Metzia 102b.

This question is generally answered by: חסורי מחסרא והכי קתני something is missing here, and thus the Mishna ought to read.... i. e., the Mishna evidently omitted here a dissenting opinion which must be supplied by construction, and to this opinion the report refers.

19. FINDING A CONFLICT OF AUTHORITATIVE PASSAGES.

§ 49.

Anonymous and undisputed paragraphs of the Mishna and of the Baraitha are generally regarded to be authoritative (See above § 1). But the Gemara often finds such a paragraph of the Mishna to be in conflict with another passage of the Mishna or of a Baraitha. This objection of contradiction is usually introduced by: ... ורמינהי (contraction of ורמי אנא אהי) I raise against this the question of a conflict of authorities, i. e. I find this Mishna in conflict with the following passage in another Mishna or in a Baraitha....

Examples: Berachoth 26a; Taanith 4b, Sanhedrin 33a,

The answer, mostly introduced by : לא קשיא *this is no difficulty*, generally removes the contradiction by showing either, that the conflicting passages treat of different cases or circumstances (כאן....וכאן...), or that those passages represent the opposite views of different teachers (הא ר'א' והא ר' ב').

Remark 1. Where not the plain Mishna, but its underlying principle or its consequence is in disharmony with an other Mishna or a Baraitha, there the question ורמינהו is preceded by an argument pointing out that principle or consequence. Examples: Berachoth 17b; Yoma 14b; B. Metzia 18a.

Remark 2. The introductory phrase ורמינהי is often omitted and the question of a conflict of authorities is started simply by ...והתנן but are we not informed in another Mishna ...? or ...והתניא is it not stated in a Baraitha (differently)? Examples: Rosh Hashana 27a; B. Kamma 61a; Gittin 23b.

CHAPTER IV

TREATMENT OF A MISHNA CONTAINING A DIFFERENCE OF OPINION

1. Asking for the Reason of the Dissenting Teacher.

§ 50.

מאי טעמא דר'.... what is the reason of Rabbi.... (the dissenting teacher)?

The answer is usually followed by the further question ותנא קמא and the first anonymous teacher? or ורבנן and our other teachers? i. e., what have they to say against this reason?

Examples: Berachoth 15a; 44a; R. Hashana 22a; B. Kamma 23b.

2. Asking for a Counter-argument.

§ 51.

The Mishna sometimes records an argument of one of the dissenting teachers against his opponent which is neither accepted nor refuted by the latter. In this case, the Gemara usually asks for the probable counter-argument of that opponent, in the following way:

שפיר קאמר ליה ר' (א) לר' (ב) ור' (ב)? Very well did Rabbi A argue against Rabbi B, What then had the latter to say?

Examples: R. Hoshana 26a; Megilla 27b; Kiddushin 61a.

3. Finding two of Several Opinions to be Identical.

§ 52.

After having laid down an opinion concerning a case, the Mishna sometimes adds two dissenting opinions, one of which does not at all seem to differ from that which had been laid down first. The Gemara then usually asks:

ר'.... היינו תנא קמא (or חכמים) Is not the opinion of R. So and So (or of the sages) identical with that of the first mentioned teacher?

Examples: Berachoth 30a; Sanhedrin 15b; Aboda Zara 7b.

The answer to this question is generally...איכא בינייהו there is a difference between them concerning....

4. INVESTIGATING THE PRINCIPLE UNDERLYING THE DIFFERENCE OF OPINION.

§ 53.

במאי קמיפלגי? ר' (א) סבר...ור' (ב) סבר In what (principle) do they differ? R. A holds... and R. B holds....

Examples: Succah 16a; Betza 26a; Gittin 64b.

Remark. Where such an investigation is problematic only, it is introduced by: לימא בהא קמיפלגי דמר סבר...ומר סבר.,. is it to say, that they differ concerning the principle of...., so that one holds that ..., and the other holds that....? The answer is then generally: לא דכולא עלמא סברי... No, both of them agree concerning this principle, but they differ concerning another principle, namely.....

Examples: Pesachim 46b; Nazir 62b; Sanhedrin 23a.

5. LIMITING THE POINT OF DIFFERENCE BETWEEN THE DISSENTING TEACHERS.

§ 54.

מחלוקת ב... אבל....דברי הכל.... the difference concerns only...., but regarding.... all agree that....

Examples: Berachoth 41a, Betza 9a, B. Kamma 61a.

Remark. Where such a limitation of the difference between Tanaim is to offer a basis for a subsequent question, it is usually phrased as follows:

עד כאן לא פליגי אלא...אבל...ד"ה . so far only they differ that...., but concerning....both of them agree that...etc.

Examples: Sabbath 132a; Yebamoth 50b; B. Metzia 28b.

6. INQUIRING WHY THE DISSENT OF THE TEACHERS IN ONE CASE DOES NOT EXTEND ALSO TO THE OTHER.

§ 55.

מאי שנא רישא דלא פליגי ומ"ש סיפא דפליגי

What difference is between the former and this case, that

they dissent here and not also there (though both cases are seemingly alike)?

Examples: Yebamoth 38a; Kethuboth 78a; Gittin 65a.

Remark. Sometimes that question is phrased shorter : ולפלוג נמי בהא(ברישא) Ought not this teacher also to differ in the other case? Ex. Sabbath 39a; Nazir 11a; Yeb. 118a.

7. FINDING AN INCONSISTENCY OF OPINION IN ONE OF THE CONTESTING TEACHERS.

§ 56.

a. וסבר ר'.. .... והתנן (והתניא).... Does this teacher hold the opinion....? but in that other Misbna (or in that Baraitha) he expresses the opposite opinion?

Examples; Yebamoth 44a; 122a; Kethuboth 56a; Chullin 100b.

b. ולית ליה לר'....והתנן... Does this teacher not hold that ..., but in that other Mishna he expresses himself differently?

Examples: B. Kamma 61b; Aboda Zara 6b.

8. FINDING AN INCONSISTENCY OF OPINION IN BOTH OF THE CONTESTING TEACHERS.

§ 57.

למימרא דר'.. (א) סבר .... ור'.. (ב) סבר....
והא איפכא שמעינן להו דתנן (דתניא) ....

Is this to say that Rabbi A holds that ...., and Rabbi B that....; but from that other Mishna (or Baraitha) we understand just the reverse...?

Examples: Berachoth 17b; Pesachim 49b; Kiddushin 64b; Sanhedrin 21a.

Remark. The contradiction is generally removed by the answer that in one of the conflicting passages מוחלפת השיטה "the position of the contesting teachers is to be reversed", or shorter איפוך "I reverse", that is, I correct the Mishna or Baraitha by placing Rabbi A instead of Rabbi B and vice versa. To such a correction suggested by one of the Amoraim, another sometimes objects: לא תיפוך "you do not need to reverse", as I have to offer another way of reconciling these two passages.

9. HYPOTHETICAL CONCLUSION FROM THE OPPOSITE OPINIONS OF DISSENTING TEACHERS.

§ 58.

כשתמצא לומר לדברי ר' (א)…. לדברי ר' (ב)….

If you should find (conclude) that according to the opinion of Rabbi A…. (a certain case must be decided in a certain way), then according to the opinion of Rabbi B…. (that case must be decided differently).

Examples: Pesachim 11b, 121a; B. Metzia 40b; Sanhedrin 78a.

CHAPTER V

THE GEMARA QUOTING THE MISHNA AND KINDRED WORKS.

1. Terms Used in Referring to the Mishna.

§ 59.

In contradistinction to the extraneous Mishna or Baraitha, also called מתניתא, the authorized Mishna of R. Jehuda Hanasi is termed מתניתין or משנתנו *our Mishna*, and the author of a teaching contained in a paragraph of this Mishna, is designated as תנא דידן *our teacher*, in contradistinction to תנא ברא *the teacher in the Baraitha*; f. ex. Moed Katon 17b; B. K. 61a.

Quotations from the Mishna are introduced by:

a. תנן (contraction of תני אנן we learn, study) *we are taught* (in a Mishna).

b. תנן התם *we are taught there*. This phrase is mostly used when a Mishna belonging to another Masechta is to be quoted; f. ex. Yoma 2a; B. Metzia 9b. Exceptionally, however, it refers also to a passage in the same Masechta; f. ex. Pesachim 4b; Maccoth 16a.

c. תנינא (=שנינו) *we have learned*, we have been taught in a Mishna (rarely referring also to a Baraitha).

This term is used only in certain phrases as מאי קמ״ל תנינא What does he inform us here, since we have already been taught thereof in that Mishna? f. ex. Berachoth 50a, or אף אנן נמי תנינא we have also a Mishna to the same effect, f. ex. Berachoth 27a.

2. Terms Used in Quoting the Tosephta and Baraitha.

§ 60.

a. תנא *one has taught*, without adding any subject, mostly quotes a passage from the Tosephta, f. ex. Pesachim 53b; B. Metzia 28a.

b. תנו רבנן (abbr. ת״ר) *our Rabbis taught*, refers to a well known Baraitha, especially to passages from the Mechilta, Siphra and Siphre.

c. תניא *it is a teaching*, refers to a Baraitha in general.

Remark. Two or more Baraithoth contradicting each other are generally introduced by:....תני חדא....תניא אידך....ותניא אידך in one Baraitha it is taught...; in the other.... and again in another....; f. ex. Maccoth 7b.

3. DIFFERENT PURPOSES OF SUCH QUOTATIONS.

§ 61.

1. תנן or תנן התם, at the outset of the Gemara, introduces another Mishna which directly or indirectly has some bearing upon the passage of the Mishna under consideration;or it is intended to use the latter as an argument in a discussion on the quoted Mishna.

Examples: Sabbath 2a; Pesachim 11b: B. Metzia 9b.

Remark. והתנן at the outset of the Gemara as well as under a discussion in the same, raises a question of contradiction or incongruity from the cited Mishna ; דתנן or ותנן or מי לא תנן adduces a support from that Mishna.

2. תנא, at the outset of the Gemara, usually introduces a brief quotation from the Tosephta explaining or qualifying a certain point in the Mishna under consideration.

Examples: Berachoth 50b; Yoma 19a; B. Metzia 28a.

3. תניא, at the outset of the Gemara, introduces a passage from a Baraitha in which a difference of opinion mentioned in the Mishna is more fully set forth with the addition of some arguments.

Examples: Berachoth 12b; Pesachim 27b; Maccoth 7b.

Remark 1. והתניא raises a question of contradiction from that Baraitha.[1] ותניא or דתניא or כדתניא refers to the Baraitha as an ar-

[1] Exceptionally, והתניא is sometimes used not as a question of contradiction, but as an argument in support of a statement, in the sense of ותניא. In this case, Rashi in his commentary generally remarks: בניחותא "in calmness", or סייעתא "a support", i. e., the phrase והתניא is here not a question, but a calm statement in support of the preceding; f. ex. Moed Katon 19b in the first line; Gittin 74b; Kidd. 60b.

gument tn support of something stated in a discussion. The phrase: תניא נמי הכי *we have also a Baraitha to the same effect,* is used to show that an explanation or opinion just expressed by an Amora is corroborated by that Baraitha, while the phrase: ...תניא כותיה ד we have a Baraitha coinciding with .... is a reference in support of an opinion of one Amora against that of his opponent.

Remark. 3. In quotations following after the phrases ורמינהי "I raise a question of contradiction against this" and מיתיבי "they object to this by appealing to a higher authority" the terms תנן as well as תניא are always omitted, thus leaving it uncertain whether the quotation is from the Mishna or from the Baraitha. In most cases, however, this can be ascertained by looking up the parallel passages which are marked in the marginal glosses of the Talmud.

4. תנו רבנן (abbr. ת״ר) introduces longer passages from a well known Baraitha, mostly from the Tosephta, Mechilta, Siphra and Siphre which stand in some connection with the Mishna-paragraph under consideration. Such quoted passages are then usually explained and discussed in the Gemara in the same way as a Mishna-paragraph.

Examples: Berachoth 16a; Sabbath 19a; B. Kamma 9b.

Remark. דת״ר "for the Rabbis taught" usually introduces the answer to the question of מנלן or מנא ה״מ. (See above § 21.) ת״ר is never used as a question or objection, hence not והא ת״ר, but instead thereof, והתניא is used.

5. תנינא להא דת״ר "what we read in this Mishna has reference to that which the Rabbis taught". The meaning of this often used phrase is, the Mishna before us supports the following Baraitha, so as to make it authoritative.

Examples: B. Metzia 25a; Maccoth 8b; Kiddushin 29a.

4. REFERRING BACK TO A PRECEDING QUOTATION.

§ 62.

There are, besides, two peculiar terms of reference which are often used in the Gemara for the purpose of indicating that a quotation incidentally made in a preceding discussion is now to be taken up as a main subject of investigation and discussion. The terms indicating this are:

a. אמר מר *the master* (teacher) *said above....*

Examples. Berachoth 2a; Pesachim 5b; B. Kamma 33b.

b. גופא (the body, the substance, the subject) meaning, that which was mentioned above incidentally is now to to be the main subject. This term is usually translated by: *it was stated above*; *our text says*; *returning to our subject.*

Examples: Berachoth 40b; Pesachim 16a; Sanhedrin 24a.

The difference between these two terms is that, as a rule, the former is used in reference to a quotation from the Mishna or Baraitha, and גופא in regard to a quoted saying of an Amora.

Remark 1. This rule admits, however, some exceptions, as on the one hand, אמר מר is occasionally also applied to a saying of an Amora; f. ex. Rosh Hashana 20b; Yoma 21b; Gittin 12b; on the other hand, גופא is sometimes found as a reference to a Baraitha and even to a Mishna, especially a Mishna belonging to those sections to which no Gemara is extant; f. ex. Berachoth 18a; Succah 14a; Kiddushin 4a. See Rashi on Succah 14a, s. v. משום הכי. In B. Kamma 13a, both terms are used as references to the same Baraitha.

Remark 2. Different from אמר מר, in ihe above mentioned sense, are the phrases דאמר מר "for the teacher said" and והאמר מר "but did not the teacher say?" which are used where in an argument, reference is made to a well known saying of an anonymous author; f. ex. Berachoth 4a; B. Metzia 6a.

C. MEMRA

CHAPTER VI

DEFINITION OF AND PHRASES CONCERNING MEMRA

§ 63.

In contradistinction to the teachings, opinions and decisions of the Tanaim, contained in the Mishna and Baraitha, a reported teaching, opinion or decision of the Amoraim is termed *Memra* (מימרא), a saying.

This term, like that of Amora, is derived from the verb אמר to say, which verb is mostly used in reference to the expounders of the Mishna; while the verbs שנה and תני are more restricted to references to Mishna and Baraitha.[1]

As a characteristic term designating a reported teaching of the Amoraim, the word Memra is but rarely met with in the Talmud; f. i. Gittin 42b; B. Bathra 48a. More frequently it occurs in the post - Talmudic literature. In the Gemara such reported opinions and decisions of Amoraim, especially concerning legal matters are generally termed *Sh'maattha*(שמעתתא that which was heard by tradition, f. ex. Berachoth 42a; Sabbath 24b; Chullin 46a), in contradistiction to *Agadatha*, a reported homiletical teaching.

A Memra is generally introduced by the word אמר a certain Amora said, related; sometimes also this word is preceded by the term אתמר (contraction of אתאמר) it has been said, it is reported.

---

[1] Compare, for instance, the two modifying phrases: ..לא שנו אלא and לא אמרן אלא, the former exclusively used in reference to a statement of the Mishna, and the latter to a teaching af an Amora. In connection with a Memra the verb תנא is used only in certain phrases as: ...איכא דמתני להא דפלוני...אהא "some report the just quoted saying of that Amora in reference to the following case...."; f. ex. Berachoth 8b; Sanhedrin 28b; Aboda Zarah 3b.

A. אמר

§ 64.

a. אמר preceding the name of a teacher, as אמר רב, generally introduces an interpretation, opinion, principle or decision of law originated or reported by that Amora, and not disputed by another, while אמר following the name, as רב אמר indicates at once that he is to be contradicted by another teacher, holding a different view on that subject, as רב אמר...ושמואל אמר.

b. אמר פלוני א' אמר פלוני ב' refers to a report which a disciple or a contemporary makes concerning a teaching which he received orally from its author, as אמר רב יהודה אמר שמואל Rab Juda said that Samuel said (Berachoth 12a).

But (משמיה ד' or) אמר פ' משום פ' refers to a report concerning a teaching which he indirectly received from an authority of a former generation, as: אמר ר' יוחנן משום ר' יוסי R. Jochanan reported in the name of R. Jose (Berachoth 7a).

Where a different version existed concerning the teacher who reported or in whose name something is reported, that different version is conscientiously added either by ואמרי לה and some say it was.... (Berachoth 4a); or ואיתימא (contracted of ואי תימא) there are some who say it was.... (Berachoth 5a), or ומטו בה משום and some differ therefrom, saying it was in the name of... (Rosh Hashana 10a).

d. פלוני א' ופלוני ב' דאמרי תרווייהו Both of the two teachers A and B said... This phrase introduces an opinion concerning which two Amoraim fully agree, though they mostly differ from each other, as רב ושמואל דאמרי תרווייהו Both Rab and Samuel said.. (Berachoth 36b).

B. אתמר

§ 65.

The word אתמר *it was said, it is reported*, especially at the beginning of a passage in the Gemara, generally introduces a Memra containing a difference of opinion or a controversy (פלוגתא) between two or more Amoraim. Such differences ana controversies concern either:

a. The proper reading of a passage in the Mishna, as

אתמר רב זביד אמר ואינו מועד תנן

רב פפא אמר אינו מועד תנן B. Kamma 37a.

Other examples: Pesachim 64b; B. Metzia 80a; Shebuoth 16a.

b. The reason of a law laid down in the Mishna.

Examples: Gittin 17b; B. Kamma 22a; B. Metzia 38a.

c. The meaning of an expression used in the Mishna, as

אתמר מנסך רב אמר מנסך ממש

ושמואל אמר מערב Gittin 52b.

Other examples: Kiddushin 60a; B. Bathra 106a.

d. The final decision in a case concerning which the Tanaim expressed opposite opinions, as:

אתמר רב אמר הלכתא כת"ק ושמואל אמר הלכתא כרבי

B. Kamma 48b; B. Metzia 33a; Sanhedrin 28b.

e. A principle of law not clearly stated in the Mishna, as:

אתמר שומר אבידה רבה אמר כשומר חנם דמי

רב יוסף אמר כש"ש דמי B. Kamma 56b.

Other examples: Pesachim 30b, B. Metzia 21b, Sanhedrin 27a.

f. A case not provided for in the Mishna.

Examples: Berachoth 25a; Kiddushin 43a; B. Kamma 9a.

Remark. There are also Memras containing a controversy without being introduced by the term אתמר, f. ex. Gittin 2a; B. Kamma 3b; Aboda Zara 2a. On the other hand, this term is occasionally applied also to a Memra containing no controversy, for instance Kiddushin 45a; especially, where reference is made to such a Memra in order to corroborate or correct the opinion of a later Amora by the phrase:... אתמר נמי we have also a Memra of a former authority to the same effect, f. ex. Gittin 13b; or...הא אתמר עלה is not a certain Amora reported having remarked concerning this...? f. ex. Gittin 16b; B. Metzia 29b. Besides, this word is used in certain phrases, as : הא דפלוני לאו בפירוש אתמר אלא מכללא אתמר the opinion ascribed to Amora A was not expressly stated by him, but it is merely implied in an occasional decision given by him; f. ex. Berachoth 9a; Sabbath 29a; B. Kamma 20b.

CHAPTER VII

TREATMENT OF A MEMRA CONTAINING A SINGLE OPINION.

1. Questioning the Authenticity of the Reported Memra

§ 66.

The correctness of the Memra is questioned, since the same author expressed elsewhere an opinion which is in conflict with that contained in this Memra. Such a question is always phrased : ומי אמר פ' הכי והא אמר.....(איפכא) Did that Amora really say so ? But is he not reported as having said.... (something implying just the opposite opinion)?

Examples: Berachoth 24b; Pesachim 30a; B. Kamma 29b.

In answer to such a question, the Gemara generally tries to show, that in one or the other way the two contradicting Memras can be reconciled.

Remark. All Amoraim being regarded as having equal authority, the objection that another Amora expressed an opinion conflicting with the Memra under consideration is generally not admitted. Where such an objection is attempted, it is rejected by the phrase : גברא אגברא קא רמית how will you raise an objection from the opinion of one man (teacher) against that of another (who has the same authority and is entitled to have an opinion of his own)? Taanith 4b; Sanhedrin 6a; B. Kamma 43b.

Sometimes, however, such an objection is admitted, especially in the case where the opinion of an Amora is in conflict with the generally accepted decision of a former leading authority among the Amoraim. In this case, the objection is phrased: ....איני? והא Is that so ? but that other Amora (expressed an opinion which conflicts with that under consideration). Examples: Berachoth 14a; Moed Katon 20a; Betza 9a ; compare Rashi's remark on the last mentioned passage.

2. FINDING THE MEMRA TO BE COLLIDING WITH A MISHNA OR A BARAITHA.

§ 67.

The objection is raised against the author of the Memra that the latter is in conflict with an undisputed Mishna or Baraitha, the authority of which is superior to that of an Amora. Such an objection is generally introduced either by the phrase מיתיבי they (i. e. the members of the academy) refuted it, they raised a point of contradiction from the higher authority of a Mishna or Baraitha, or איתיביה he raised against this a point of contradiction from a higher authority, or מתיב פלוני a certain teacher refuted this, or simply by והתנן but are we not taught in the Mishna? והתניא are we not taught in the Baraitha....(differently)?

Examples: Berachoth 10b; Rosh Hashana 6b; B. Metzia 10a.

Remark. Such an objection or refutation from a higher authority is termed תיובתא. The argument of the objection often closes with the phrase תיובתא דפלוני this is a refutation of that Amora; or תיובתא דפלוני? תיובתא is this not a refutation of that Amora? It is a refutation! (i. e., the point of refutation is well taken). Mostly however the objection is removed by showing that the Mishna or Baraitha referred to treats of a different case or different circumstances, and such a defense is introduced by the phrase: ...אמר לך פ' that Amora might say (in answer to this objection) that...; f. ex., Berachoth 34a; B. Kamma 14a.

3. FINDING THE MEMRA TO BE SUPERFLUOUS.

§ 68.

The Memra is shown to be unnecessary, since the same opinion which the Amora expresses therein is already stated in a Mishna. This objection is phrased: מאי קמ"ל תנינא what does that Amora let us hear, since we have already been taught that in the following Mishna..?

Examples: Berachoth 45b; Taanith 10a, B. Kamma 35b.

Remark 1. This objection is mostly removed by showing that the Memra contains something in addition to the Mishna.

Remark 2. The question מאי קמ"ל is not raised where the opinion of the Memra is not expressly but merely impliedly contained in the Mishna. In this case the Mishna is referred to just to corroborate the Memra by the phrase אף אנן נמי תנינא we have also a Mishna to the same effect; f. ex. Berachoth 27a; Yoma 26b; Aboda Zara 8a.

4. CORROBORATING THE MEMRA BY A BARAITHA.

§ 69.

Such a corroborating Baraitha is generally introduced by the phrase: תניא נמי הכי (abbr. תנ"ה). a Baraitha, too, teaches thus; or, we have also a Baraitha to the same effect.

Examples: Berachoth 9b; Taanith 10a; Sanhedrin 23a.

Remark. The question: "Why does the Amora need to teach that which is already stated in the Baraitha?" is never raised, since the Amora was expected to know every Mishna, but not every Baraitha.

5. CORROBORAITING THE MEMRA BY ONE OF ANOTHER AUTHORITY.

§ 70.

Sometimes one Memra is corroborated by another one which is introduced by ...אתמר נמי we have also another Memra to the same effect. Such is especially the case where the Memra of a Babylonian Amora is supported by one of a Palestinian authority.

Examples: Chagiga 24a; Gittin 13b; Sanhedrin 29a.

6. A DIFFERENT REPORT.

§ 71.

After a Memra has been treated in the above stated ways, a different report (איכא דאמרי some say, some report....) is sometimes introduced in which the Amora referred to just expresses the opposite opinion. The discussion then turns the tables, so that every objection which was made to the former report, becomes now a support, and every former support an objection.

Examples: Berachoth 10b; Betza 13a; Maccoth 3b.

7. CORRECTING THE MEMRA.

§ 72.

Strong objections having been raised against a Memra, it is sometimes re-established in a rectified form by the phrase:

...אלא אי אתמר הכי אתמר but if such Memra was reported, it must have been reported in the following way....

Examples: Berachoth 15b; Yoma 28a; Kiddushin 11b.

CHAPTER VIII

TREATMENT OF A MEMRA CONTAINING A DIFFERENCE OF OPINION.

1. The Difference concerning the Correct Reading of a Mishna Paragraph.

§ 73.

Each of the contesting teachers argues for the correctness of his way of reading; the argument being based either on the context of the Mishna under consideration, or on a common sense reason. The question is then finally settled by referring to another Mishna or to a Baraitha in support of one of the two ways of reading.

Examples: B. Kamma 37a; B. Metzia 80a; Shebuoth 16a.

Remark. Sometimes, both ways of reading are declared to be admissible by the phrase: מאן דתני....לא משתבש, ומאן דתני.... לא משתבש.

"He who reads the Mishna in this way is not wrong, and he who reads it in the other way is neither wrong, for..."

Examples: Succah 50b; Yebamoth 17a; Aboda Zara 2a.

2. The Difference concerning the Explanation of a Term or Passage in the Mishna.

§ 74.

The supposed arguments for and against each of the different explanations are investigated in the following way:

Question 1: פלוני א' מ"ט לא אמר כפלוני ב' Why does the Amora A not explain as Amora B?

Answer: ....אמר לך he might say... (I have the following objection to his explanation..)

Question 2: ?ואידך and the other (teacher B)? i. e., how will he remove this objection?

The answer having been given, question 1 is again directed to B: why does he not explain as A? This question is then treated in a similar way as the former.

Examples: Gittin 17a; B. Kamma 22a; Sanhedrin 25a.

3. THE DIFFERENCE CONCERNING THE REASON OF A LAW.

§ 75.

The practical consequence of adopting either of the two reasons assigned to the law by the contesting Amoraim is investigated by asking:

מאי בינייהו what is the difference between them? i. e., in what respect does it make a difference in the application of the law, whether this or the other reason be assigned to it?

The answer is always introduced by the phrase: איכא בינייהו... there is (it makes) a difference concerning....

Examples: Gittin 2b; B. Metzia 15b; Sanhedrin 24b.

4. INVESTIGATING THE PRINCIPLE UNDERLYING THE DIFFERENCE OF OPINION.

§ 76.

Where the difference between the contesting Amoraim involves a principle of law, that principle is investigated by the question: במאי קמיפלגי in what do they differ? Or, What is the point of difference? On what general principle do they disagree?

Examples: Pesachim 63b; Gittin 34a; B. Metzia 15b.

Remark. Before defining the difference, sometimes the points are stated in which both sides agree, and which therefore are excluded from the discussion. This is usually done in the following phrase: כל היכא....(כולי עלמא) לא פליגי כי פליגי.... As regards....they (both of the contesting teachers) do not disagree, but they differ concerning....

Examples: Yoma 6b; Pesachim 30b; B. Metzia 21b.

5. SHOWING CONSISTENCY OF OPINIONS IN BOTH OF THE CONTESTING TEACHERS.

§ 77.

After having stated the difference, the Gemara shows that

the divergence of opinions in this case is in full accordance with the opposite views or principles expressed elsewhere by the same teachers. The phrases used in showing such consistency of opinion in both of the contesting Amoraim are:

a. ואזדו לטעמיהו they go according to their principles, i. e., they differ, each following his own principle.

Examples: Sabbath 34b; Pesachim 29a, Shebuoth 15b.

b. ....פליני א' לטעמיה ופלוני ב' לטעמיה Amora A follows his principle, and also Amora B follows his principle....

Examples: Pesachim 29b; Gittin 24b; B. Kamma 53a.

Remark. The phrase ואזדו לטעמיהו is used where reference is made to another dispute between the same teachers, while פ' לטעמיה refers to a principle laid down by either of the two teachers independently from each other.

6. Discussing the Difference of Opinion.

§ 78.

By the introductory phrase: תא שמע (abbr. ת"ש) *Come and hear*, or : איתיביה or: מיתיבי *a certain teacher* or *they* (the members of the academy) *objected* (by appealing to a higher authority), a Mishna or a Baraitha is referred to in suport (סיוע or סיעתא)of the opinion of one, and as a refutation (תיובתא) of that of the other of the contesting Amoraim. A discussion then usually follows with the object of rejecting the support or repelling the attack. The result of that discussion is either that the question at issue remains undecided, or it is decided against one and in favor of the other of the contesting Amoraim. The usual phrase in the latter case is:

(והלכתא כוותיה דפלוני ב'.) ! תיובתא ? תיובתא דפלוני א' "Is this not a refutation of the opinion of Amora A? It is a refutation! And the decision is according to the opinion of Amora B."

Examples : Sanhedrin 27a; B. Metzia 21b-22b; Chullin 28a. Examples of not distinctly decided discussions: Pesachim 30b-31b; B. Kamma 56b-57b; B. Metzia 38b.

Remark. Commenting on a Mishna-paragraph which has some bearing on a well known difference of opinion between Amoraim, the Gemara sometimes starts with the question, whether, or not this Mishna offers an argument in favor of, or against, the opinion of one of these Amoraim. The phrases used in such an investigation are:

a. לימא מסייע ליה לפ'... is it to say, that this Mishna supports the Amora A?

Examples: Succah 15b; Betza 11a; B. Kamma 62b.

b. לימא תהוי תיובתא ד.... is it to say, that this Mishna is a refutation of Amora B?

Examples: Sabbath 9b; Succah 15a; Yoma 19a.

7. TRACING BACK THE DIFFERENCE BETWEEN AMORAIM TO ONE BETWEEN TANAIM.

§ 79.

After having treated a Memra in accordance with the above stated methods, the Gemara often attempts to show that the same difference of opinion between the two Amoraim is already found among two Tanaim. For this purpose a Mishna or a Baraitha is quoted containing a difference between Tanaim concerning a subject which has some bearing upon the difference under consideration. The point of discussion becomes now whether or not the principle underlying the difference between those two Tanaim is identical with that under consideration, so that Amora A agrees with Tana A, and Amora B with Tana B. The phrases introducing this investigation are:

a. לימא כתנאי (or, נימא) is it to say, that this difference is like that between Tanaim?

Examples: Pesachim 31a; Gittin 14b; Sanhedrin 27a.

b. לימא בפלוגתא ד... (תנאים א' וב') קמיפלגי is it to say, that these Amoraim differ according to the difference of opinion between those Tanaim A and B?

Examples: Shebuoth 25a; Maccoth 11b; Nedarin 5b.

Remark. Like other investigations of the Gemara introduced by לימא or נימא, also this attempt leads generally to a negative result, as it is finally shown that the principle implied in the difference between the Tanaim does not at all concern the case under consideration. But where after a discussion between Amoraim the Gemara simply states: כתנאי "this is like the difference between Tanaim", or תנאי היא "this difference is identical with that of the Tanaim", (f. i. Berachoth 22a; R. Hashana 15a; B. Metzia 54a) that statement is generally not disputed.

8. SUPPORTING EACH OF TWO CONTESTING TEACHERS BY A BARAITHA.

§ 80.

Two anonymous Baraithoth are referred to, one of which agrees with the opinion of one, and the other with that of the other of the contesting Amoraim. The phrase used in this case is,

תניא כוותיה דפלוני א' תניא כוותיה דפלוני ב' there is a Baraitha agreeing with the opinion of Amora A, and a Baraitha agreeing with the opinion of Amora B.

Examples: Yoma 4a; Betza 6a; Gittin 18a.

9. ASCERTAINING THE AUTHORSHIP OF TWO OPPOSITE OPINIONS.

§ 81.

There are Memras reporting that, concerning a certain question, two Amoraim A and B differed from each other, one holding one, and the other the opposite opinion, without clearly stating which is which, that is, who of the contesting Amoraim holds the one, and who the other opinion, as:

אתמר.. פלוני א' ופלוני ב' חד אמר...וחד אמר... it is reported, that concerning....the Amora A and Amora B expressed different opinions, one holding....and the other...

In treating such a Memra, the Gemara usually tries to find

out the representative of each opinion by referring to another case in which one of these two teachers expressed a certain view which coincides with one of the two opinions under consideration.

Such an investigation is always introduced by the phrase: תסתיים דפלוני הוא דאמר... it may be ascertained that it is the Amora A who holds....If the argument is accepted, this is indicated by the closing term תסתיים it is correctly ascertained, or ש"מ, hear it from this.

Examples: Berachoth 45a; Megillah 27a; B. Kamma 29b.

CHAPTER IX

D. ASKING AND ANSWERING QUESTIONS

Classification of Questions

§ 82.

According to their different nature, the questions asked in the Talmudic discussions may be divided into the following classes:

1. Questions of investigation.
2. Questions of astonishment.
3. Questions of objection.
4. Questions of problem.

Remark. The Talmud, besides, often makes use of the *rhetoric interrogation*, that is, that figure of speech which puts in the form of a negative question what is meant to be strongly affirmative, and in the form of a positive question what is meant to be a decided negation, as: אלא לאו is it then not—? = it is certainly so.

מי לא תנן are we not taught in the Mishna ? = we are certainly taught so.

מי אמר הכי did he say so ? = he cannot have said so.

מי סברת do you think..? = you can not think so

1. Questions of Investigation.

§ 83.

As already stated above (§ 16.), the Talmud mostly introduces its explanations and investigations by a query, the object of which is to call attention to the point which requires elucidation, as מאי what is the meaning of....? מאי טעמא what is the reason....? מנלן whence do we have this?

Such questions are generally asked anonymously, while the answer is mostly given in the name of a certain teacher, אמר פ' the teacher....said (in answer to this question)...

Remark. To investigate a subject by questioning is sometimes termed הוי בה פ' a certain teacher asked investigatingly concerning this matter (B. Kamma 7a; Kethuboth 58b; Nedarin 38b); הווינן בה we asked investigatingly concerning it (Berachoth 45b; Sabbath 6b; Gittin 4b and frequently). This latter phrase is especially used where reference is made to investigating questions asked in another passage of the Talmud. Also the noun of this verb הוי is occasionally used, as הויות דרב ושמואל the investigating questions of Rab and Samuel (Berachoth 20a) הויות דאביי ורבא (Succah 28a; B. Bathra 134a).

2. QUESTIONS OF ASTONISHMENT.

§ 84.

A question of astonishment, termed תמיהה, expresses wonder and surprise at an unexpected statement or argument just heard; as: איני is this so? ולא is this not the case? סלקא דעתך does this enter thy mind? i. e., do you really mean to say this? ותסברא how can you understand (explain) it in this way? האי מאי what is this! how can you say this?

Such a question does in general not expect an answer, though the latter mostly follows the question.

To this kind of questions belongs also the counter-question in which a question asking for information, instead of being answered, is repeated with surprise, as if to say, how can you ask such a strange question, as: מנלן? מנלן! (Megilla 2a; Sanhedrin 68b), מניין? מניין! (Chullin 42b.).

Remark. A peculiar phrase expressing a question of astonishment is: ודקארי לה מאי קארי לה he who asks (or objects) this, what does he ask (object) here? i. e., why ask a question where the answer is obvious enough? or, why raise an objection so easily removed? Yoma 30b; Yebamoth 11a; B. Bathra 2b. [1]

---

[1]According to a tradition mentioned by Joshua b. Joseph Halevi (Halichoth Olam p. 9a; compare *Frankel*, Monatsschrift 1861, p. 267), all passages of the Talmud introduced by this peculiar phrase of question belong to the additions made by the Saburaim.

3. QUESTIONS OF OBJECTION

§ 85.

These are questions in which a point of difficulty, disagreement, incongruity or contradiction is raised against a statement, construction or argument. The Gemara uses different terms for such questions:

The general term for a question of this kind is קושיא *a difficulty*, also used as a verb אקשי to ask an objecting question, to raise a point of objection, to show a difficulty. The question is mostly introduced by the interjection: והא but lo! which is often prefixed to the following word, as והתנן but lo! are we not taught in the Mishna...? והתניא is it not taught in the Baraitha...? והאתמר was it not said by an Amora....? והאמרת but did you not say....?

The answer to such a question is termed תירוץ *a reconciliation, a satisfactory answer*, and is usually introduced by the phrase: לא קשיא there is no difficulty. Where no satisfactory answer can be found, it is indicated by the closing term קשיא the difficulty remains, the point of objection is well taken, f. ex. Moed Katon 22b, Maccoth 5b.

Remark 1. When two different questions are raised at the same time, the second is introduced by ותו and again... (I further ask...); f. ex. Berachoth 2a.

Where the same question is answered by the Gemara in two different ways, the second answer is introduced by: ואיבעית אימא and if you wish, you may say....; f. ex. Berachoth 3a. In this case the second answer has generally more force than the former. Sometimes, however, both answers are introduced by this phrase, as ...איבעית אימא ...ואיבעית אימא you may either answer.... or you may answer...; f. ex. Berachoth 4b. In this case both answers are of equal force.

The same question is often answered by two or more teachers, by each in a different way. In this case, the former teacher is introduced by אמר פ׳, and each of the following by פ׳ אמר; f. ex., Sanhedrin 32 a. b, where four teachers belonging to different generations (R. Chanina, Raba, Rab Papa and Rab Ashe) offer different answers to the same question. Great ingenuity is in this respect displayed by some of the teachers, especially by the rivaling contemporaries Abaye and Raba, in showing that a question already answered by the other teacher might also have been answered in a different way; f. ex., Pesachim 5b; Kiddushin 5a; B. Metzia 52a.

Remark 2. The answer to a question or an objection is often refuted, and a new answer is then offered either by the refuter, or by another. In this case, the new answer is generally introduced by אלא אמר פ׳, the word אלא *but* indicating that the point of refutation against the former answer was well taken. Examples: Berachoth 30b; Pesachim 9b; B. Metzia 31a.

Where of two answers given, the latter is refuted, the acceptance of the former is indicated either by the phrase אלא מחוורתא כפלוני but more correct is the answer of the first teacher (f. ex. Taanith 4b; Chullin 117a), or in case that answer had been given anonymously, by the phrase אלא מחוורתא כדשנינן מעיקרא more correct is as we answered at first (f. ex. Pesachim 17b; Maccoth 2b; B. Metzia 3a).

Remark 3. In questions of investigation as well as of objection, the questioner sometimes anticipates an answer which he shows to be inadmissible. Such anticipation (termed in rhetoric *prolepsis*) in questions of investigation is introduced by:... אילימא is it to say...? f. ex. Berachoth 9b; Kiddushin 29a; Gittin 9a. In questions of objection it is introduced by:...וכי תימא and if you will say (answer)..., f. ex. Sanhedrin 6a; Kiddushin 3b; Gittin 3b. On the other hand, where in giving an answer or explanation, an objection is anticipated which is to be removed, it is introduced by ואם תאמר (abbr. וא״ת) but if you will say (object).... f. ex. Succah 16b; Gittin 11b; B. Metzia 10a: וא״ת משנתנו.

SOME SPECIAL KINDS OF OBJECTION.

§ 86.

The terms רומיא and תיובתא are but species of the general term קושיא a question of objection.

a. Where the objection consists in raising a point of contradiction between two statements of equal authority, as between two passages of Scriptures or between passages of the

Mishna and the Baraitha, it is termed רומיא (of the verb רמי to cast, to throw against, to bring in opposition) setting authority against authority, bringing authorities in opposition to each other. Such a question of objection or contradiction is generally introduced by the phrase : ...פלוני רמי a certain teacher asked the following question of contradiction between two passages....; or by : ...ורמינהי I raise against this the question of a conflict of authorities, i. e., I find this Mishna to be in conflict with the following passage in an other Mishna or in a Baraitha.... Omitting this introductory phrase, such a question is often set forth simply by : ...והתנן but are we not taught in (another) Mishna...? והתניא are we not taught in a Braitha...? (See above § 49)

b. תיובתא (the Aramaic form of the Hebrew word תשובה an answer, gainsaying, objection, refutation) signifies an objection raised against an Amora as being in conflict with the superior authority of a statement in a Mishna or Baraitha. It is generally introduced by מתיב פלוני a certain teacher raised the following objection from a higher authority...; or איתיביה he objected to him from a higher authority ; or : מיתיבי they (the teachers of the Academy) raised the following objection (See above § 67)

The answer to such a point of objection is termed שינויא a *difference* or *distinction*, in as much as it mostly attempts to remove the contradiction by showing that the two statements, seemingly in conflict with each other, actually refer to different cases or circumstances. The answer is generally introduced by : ...שאני הכא here is a different case, or by : ....כאן.... התם here... there..., or ....הא ....הא in this case..., but in the other case...., or by : ....הכא במאי עסקינן here we treat of the special case that.....

Remark 1. These distinctions for the purpose of removing a contradiction are often very strained, and are in this case sometimes characterized by the Talmud itself as שינויא דחיקא a forced or strained answer, f. ex. : B. Kamma 43a. ; 106a. ; Kethuboth 42b.

Remark 2. The answer to an objection is also termed פירוקא (from פרק to redeem, to rescue, to unload; hence, to free one from the burden of an objection); as פירוקא דאביי B. Kamma 14a. More frequently used is the verb, as הוא מותיב לה והוא מפרק לה he asked a question of objection, and he answered it, Kiddushin 44b; Gittin 53a. B. Kamma 43b.; or מקשי לי ומפרקינה לה he asked me questions of objection, and I answered them, B. Metzia 84a.

THE DILEMMA.

§ 87

Objections are sometimes set forth in the form of a dilemma (termed ממה נפשך), presenting two or more alternatives of a case or an opinion, and showing it to be equally objectionable whichever alternative we may choose, as:

a. מה נפשך אי...(קשיא) ואי...(קשיא) *what is thy wish?* i. e., which alternative do you choose? *if*.... (then my objection is: ....) *and if*.... (then my objection is: ....).[1]

Examples: Sabbath 46a; B. Kamma 38a; Chullin 12a.

b. היכי דמי אי....(קשיא) ואי....(קשיא) *how shall we imagine this case? if*.... (then my objection is....) *and if*.... (then I have to object....).

Examples: Kethuboth 72a; B. Metzia 21a; B. Bathra 78b.

c. במאי עסקינן אי.... ואי.... *of what circumstance do we treat here? if*.... (objection), *and if*.... (objection).

Examples: Sabbath 30a, Gittin 37b, B. Metzia 12b.

d. מאי קסבר אי.... ואי.... *what is his opinion?* If he holds that.... (then I object....), and if he holds.... (I also object....).

Examples: Berachoth 3a; Sanhedrin 2b; Kiddushin 6b.

The answer to a dilemma either shows a middle ground between the two alternatives, or defends one of the alternatives against the objection made to it. In the first case, it is introduced by

---

[1] The phrase of מה נפשך is also used in introducing an argument in defense, proving that a decision or opinion is equally correct whichever of the two alternatives we may choose. Examples: Betza 10b; Gittin 43b; B. Metzia 6b.

the phrase ...לא צריכא ד it is not necessary so (namely to choose just one of the presented alternatives), for....(a third alternative is imaginable to which none of your objections applies). In the second case, the answer is generally introduced by the word לעולם which in this connection stands for לעולם אימא לך *still I maintain* (one of the alternatives with some modifications).

REJOINDER.

§ 88.

Where the answer to an objection or to a refutation is found to be insufficient, the weak points thereof are set forth in a rejoinder. The phrases mostly used in such a rejoinder are:

a. ....סוף סוף (literally: the end of the end...) *anyhow, at all events*, that is, however extreme my concession to the supposition of your answer may be, my former objection still remains...

Examples: Megilla 3a; Gittin 24a; B. Metzia 16a.

b. Where the rejoinder goes to demonstrate that the answer does not cover all cases the following phrase is used:

תינח ב.... ב.... מאי איכא למימר you may be right... (i. e., your defense is acceptable concerning one case), but concerning... (that other case of....) what have you to say?

Examples: Pesachim 11a; Gittin 4b; B. Metzia 3a.

c. Where the answer is found to be based only on a disputed principle, the rejoinder is phrased:

הניחא למאן דאמר... אלא למאן דאמר... מאי איכא למימר

That is all right according to him who holds...,but according to him who holds....(the opposite opinion), what is there to say? Examples: Berachoth 12a; Yoma 3a; Sanhedrin 3a.

4. QUESTIONS OF PROBLEMS.

§ 89.

Problem is a question proposed for solution concerning a matter difficult of settlement. The pages of the Talmud are full of such questions. The doubt involved in those questions concern there either the correct reading, or the proper construction and meaning of the Mishna, or the decision of a case not provided for in the Mishna.

Such questions are termed בעיות problems, questions of doubt, and are generally introduced by בעי פלוני a certain teacher asked the following difficult question, he propounded a problem for solution, or בעי פלוני מפלוני A asked B to solve the following question; or when such a question was asked anonymously in a school, it is introduced by: איבעיא להו the following problem was proposed by them (i. e. by the members of the academy).

The point of the question is generally followed by the interrogative מהו how is it? The two sides of the question are usually set forth by: ....מי אמרינן .... או דלמא shall we say.... or perhaps..... Sometimes, however, the phrase מי אמרינן is omitted, and must be supplied.

Examples of problems: 1. Concerning the proper reading or construction of the Mishna: Sabbath 36b; Yoma 41b; B. Kamma 19a.

2 Concerning the source or reason of a law: Taanith 2b; Aboda Zara 6a; Gittin 45a.

3 Concerning cases not provided for in the Mishna: Sabbath 3a Pesachim 4b Kiddushin 7b; B. Bathra 5b.

Remark. Where the propounded problem appears to be merely theoretical, the practical consequence of its solution is investigated by the query: למאי נפקא מינה for what case will it be of consequence? Examples: Pesachim 4a; B. Kamma 24a; Gittin 36b.

SOLUTION OF THE PROBLEM.

§ 90

The solution of a problem (the verb is פשט) is introduced by the phrase תא שמע (abbr. ת"ש) come and hear. When rejected, another solution introduced by the same phrase is generally attempted. The final acceptance of a solution is indicated by the closing phrase שמע מיניה hear it therefrom, i. e., this settles the question, this is the correct solution.

Where no solution is found, it is indicated by the term תיקו (=תיקום) it stands, i. e., the question remains unsolved.

Where the questioner himself finds a solution, the phrase is: בתר דבעי הדר פשטה after having propounded this question, he again solved it. Examples: Sabbath 4b; Kiddushin 9b; Sanhedrin 10a.

If out of several problems only one can be solved, the solution is introduced by the phrase פשוט מהא חדא you may solve, at least, one of them: f. ex. B. Metzia 25a; Gittin 44a.

A SERIES OF PROBLEMS LINKED TOGETHER.

§ 91

Sometimes, a series of problems concerning imaginary cases of a certain law are set forth by a teacher, and so arranged that if one of them be solved, the following one would still remain doubtful. Each problem, except the first one, is then generally introduced by the phrase...ואם תמצא לומר and if you should be able to say.... (to solve it in one way) I still ask... (the following case).

Examples: Pesachim 10b; Kiddushin 7b; Kethuboth 2a; B. Metzia 21a; 24a.

Remark. Some of the Babylonian teachers, especially Raba, R. Jirmiah, Rab Papa, were noted for having indulged in propounding such problems concerning imaginary cases in order to display their ingenuity. R. Jirmiah was at a certain occasion even expelled from the academy for having troubled his colleagues by his imaginary and trifling problems (B. Bathra 23b). Of Raba and some other teachers it is expressly stated that they occasionally propounded such problems, merely for the purpose of examining the ability and acuteness of their pupils; Erubin 51a; Menachoth 91b; Chullin 133a.

QUESTIONS LAID BEFORE HIGHER AUTHORITIES FOR DECISION.

§ 92.

Different from the questions of problem just spoken of are

those questions which were directed to a higher authority, either to a celebrated teacher or to an academy, especially of Palestine, to consider and decide upon a difficulty or a dispute. Such questions are usually introduced by the phrase: שלחו ליה לפלוני ילמדנו רבנו.... they sent to a certain teacher (asking): may our teacher instruct us concerning..... The answer is then introduced by: שלח להו.... he sent to them (the answer)....

Examples: Sanhedrin 8a; B. Kamma 27b; Gittin 66b.

Remark. Also the phrase שלחו מתם they sent from there (i. e. from Palestine to Babylon) means, they sent an answer to a question directed to them; f. ex., Betza 4b; Gittin 20a; Sanhedrin 17b.

CHAPTER X

E. ARGUMENTATION

1. Terms and Phrases Introducing an Argument

§ 93

An argument, that is. the reason offered to prove or disprove any matter of question, is termed טעם (the reason).

In the Talmudic discussion, arguments are mostly introduced by one of the following phrases:

a. מאי טעמא what is the reason? Berachoth 3b, a. elsewhere.

b. תא שמע come and hear, i. e., you may derive it from the following...; Berachoth 2b, a. elsewhere.

c תדע you may know (infer) it from the following. Berachoth 15a; B. Metzia 5b, a. elsewhere.

d. מנא אמינא לה whence do I maintain this? on what do I base my opinion? Berachoth 25a; Sabbath 11b, a. elsewhere.

e. ומנא תימרא and whence may you say (prove) that....? Sabbath 23a; B. Metzia 11a.

f. נחזי אנן let us see (into the subject), let us argue on the subject. Berachoth 27a; B. Kamma 51b; B. Metzia 8b.

g. מסתברא it is reasonable, it is in accordance with common sense. Berachoth 2b; Sabbath 25a; Kiddushin 5a.

h. הכי נמי מסתברא so it is also reasonable; this may be proved by the following reasoning. Yoma 16a; B. Kamma 26a; B. Metzia 10a.

i. דיקא נמי it is also proved by a conclusion. Berachoth 26a, a. elsewhere.

The last-mentioned phrase is especially used where the argument is based on a conclusion drawn from the wording of a passage.

2. CLASSIFICATION OF ARGUMENTS

§ 94

Arguments are either *direct* or *indirect.* In the first case, the grounds or reasons are laid down, and the correctness of the proposition to be proved is inferred from them. In the second case, the thesis is not proved immediately, but by showing the falsehood of its contradictory.

In the Talmud, the arguments mostly used in direct as well as indirect reasoning, are the following:

a. The argument from common sense.
b. The argument from authority.
c. The argument from construction and implication.
d. The argument from analogy.
e. The argument *a fortiori.*

a. ARGUMENT FROM COMMON SENSE.

§ 95

A common sense argument is termed סברא, so in the phrases: סברא הוא it is a common sense reasoning; Pesachim 21b; Sanhedrin 15a, B. Metzia 27b. אי בעית אימא סברא ואב"א קרא if you wish, I refer to common sense, and if you wish, I refer to a biblical passage; Berachoth 4b, Yebamoth 39b, Kiddushin 35a.

Common sense reasons are generally introduced by the conjunctives: ....דהא for behold..., ...הואיל ו because, כיון ....ד since, ...לפי because, ...משום ד on account of, מפני ....ש for..., because....

b. ARGUMENT FROM AUTHORITY.

§ 96.

An argument from authority, termed ראיה the proof, the evidence, is that which appeals to the authority of the Bible (דאמר קרא for Scripture says; דכתיב for it is written; שנאמר for it is said), or to the authority of the Mishna (דתנן for it is taught in the Mishna), or to that of the Baraitha (דתניא; דת"ר), or to the accepted teaching of an Amora (דאמר

פלוני), or to an accepted tradition (גמירי we have learned by tradition, Berachoth 28a, Succah 5b; נקטינן we have received it by tradition, Erubin 5a, Gittin 32b, Maccoth 10b), or to a settled rule and established principle of law (דקיימא לן for it is established among us, it is a generally accepted opinion or maxim, Yebamoth 6a, Gittin 28b; דאמרינן for we generally say, hold the opinion, Yebamoth 3b, B. Metzia 25b).

The Talmud being occupied chiefly with questions of law, arguments from authority are there of supreme importance.

The inference from the cited authority is generally introduced by אלמא hence, consequently (Pesachim 2a-3a), or by מכלל in this is implied, from this follows, or by שמע מיניה hear from this, i. e. you may infer herefrom....

Remark 1. The phrase שמע מיניה is also used to express the final approval of the preceding argument, and is then to be translated by: It follows therefrom the argument is accepted; Pesachim 3a a. elsewhere.

Remark 2. Where the argument from authority is based merely on the supposition of a certain interpretation of the quoted passage or on a supposed circumstance to which it refers, that supposition is introduced by ....מאי לאו is it not (to be supposed) that....? In answering such an argument, the opponent generally denies that supposition by ...לא it is not so, but... ; f. ex., Pesachim 16b; Sanhedrin 24b; B. Kamma 15b.

c. ARGUMENT FROM A CLOSE CONSTRUCTION OF A PASSAGE.

§ 97.

This is an argument which draws conclusions from a careful consideration of the words in which a law is framed. Such an argument is termed דיוקא (from the verb דוק to examine minutely, to consider a thing carefully), and is mostly introduced by the phrase: ....דיקא נמי דקתני it is also proved by a conclusion from the expression used in this Mishna or Baraitha.

Examples: Succah 3a; Kiddushin 3a; Shebuoth 29b.

Remark. Hereto belongs also that argument in which conclusions are drawn from a positive statement to the negative, and vice versa, by emphasizing either the subject or the predicate or the modification in the clause of a law under consideration. The phrase used in such conclusions is either: ....טעמא ד.... הא the reason (the force, stress) of this law is in the expressly stated case of.... but.... (in the opposite case, the decision of the law is the reverse); f. ex., Kiddushin 5b; B. Kamma 48b; B. Meztia 25a. Sometimes the phrase is: אין...אבל, ...לא... strictly in this case yes, but...(otherwise) not; f. ex., Yoma 85b; B. Metzia 30a; 34a.

Such arguments resting merely on the emphasis of an expression are often very arbitrary and fallacious, and are in this case promptly refuted in the Talmud.

d. ARGUMENTS FROM ANALOGY.

§ 98.

An argument from analogy, termed היקש or דומיא, is that which infers from the similarity of two cases that, what has been decided in the one, applies also in the other.

Such arguments are introduced by one of the following phrases:

a. ....דומיא ד in similarity with the case of...; Kiddushin 12a; B. Bathra 28b.

b. ....הא לא דמיא אלא להא this is rather like that other case of...; Sabbath 12a; Kiddushin 7a; B. Metzia 30a.

c. ....כדאשכחן גבי as we find concerning...; Berachoth 20b.

d. ....מידי דהוה א something which is found concerning..., i. e., just as in the case of...; Sabbath 6a; Kiddushin 4a; Gittin 8b.

Also the phrase: (תניא) מי לא תנן are we not taught in the Mishna (or Baraitha)? mostly introduces an argument from analogy; Pesachim 7a, 9a; Kiddushin 7a.

The application of the analogous case to the case under consideration is generally introduced by מאי התם... הכא נמי as there... so here, too.

e. ARGUMENT *a Fortiori*

§ 99.

The argument *a fortiori*, termed קל וחומר, is a kind of argument from analogy, and consists in proving that a thing being true in one case is more evidently so in another in which the circumstances are more favorable.

In regard to Biblical interpretation, this argument was treated in Part II of this book as the first rule of the Talmudical Hermeneutics. Its application in the discussions of the Gemara is less artificial than there. The phraseology used in setting forth this argument is:

a. השתא (ומה) התם.... אמרת.... הכא מבעיא now, (since) there... (in that other case of...) you say...., could it here be questioned?

Examples: Gittin 15b; B. Bathra 4a; Maccoth 6b.

b. השתא ומה התם.... הכא לא כל שכן now, if there...., how much the more (or the less) here.

Examples: Yoma 2b; B. Metzia 2b; Yebamoth 32a.

Remark. In the Agadic passages of the Talmud, the final conclusion of such an argument is generally expressed by על אחת כמה וכמה; f. ex. Gittin 35a; Nedarim 10b; Maccoth 24a.

3. INDIRECT ARGUMENTATION.

§ 100.

The mode of proceeding in indirect argumentation is to assume the denial of the point in question or a hypothesis which is the contradictory of the proposition to be proved, and then to show that such a denial or hypothesis involves some false principle, or leads to consequences that are manifestly absurd. The assumed contradictory thus shown to be false, the original proposition must consequently be true.

This method is very frequently applied in the Talmudic discussion. The phrases used in indirect argumentation are:

a. דאי לא תימא הכי....(קשיא) for if you do not say so (i. e. if you deny my proposition), the difficulty or the objection is....

Examples: Berachoth 26b; Yoma 15a; B. Metzia 5b.

b. (קשיא)....דאי אמרת for if you say... (the contrary), then... (objection).

Examples: Berachoth 2b; Yoma 24b; Gittin 35b; B. Metzia 28b.

c. (קשיא)....דאי סלקא דעתך for if it should enter your mind, (i. e., if you should assume the contrary...), then... (it will lead to the following objectionable consequence).

Examples: Berachoth 13a; Sanhedrin 6a; B. Metzia 5b.

Indirect arguments are often introduced by the phrase מסתברא it is proved by the following reasoning... or הכי נמי מסתברא it may thus also be proved by reasoning.....

The conclusion from an indirect argument is generally expressed by אלא לאו is it then not...? or אלא לאו שמע מיניה is it then not to be concluded herefrom... (the correctness of the proposition which was to be proved)? In direct arguments, the phrase is simply: שמע מיניה.

Remark. Arguments introduced by הכי נמי מסתברא or by דיקא נמי are generally regarded conclusive. As to the exceptions, see Tosaphoth Yoma 84a, s. v. הנ"מ and Tosaphoth Sebachim 13a and Chullin 67b, s. v. דיקא נמי.

4. DIRECT AND INDIRECT ARGUMENTS COMBINED.

§ 101.

To support a proposition against the contrary view of an opponent, the Talmud often uses a combination of direct and indirect arguments, by referring to an authority, and showing it to be in harmony with the proposition and in disharmony with the contradictory. The phrases used in such argumentations are:

a. (בשלמא אי אמרת=) אי אמרת בשלמא.... (שפיר)
אלא אי אמרת..... (קשיא)

it is well, if you say... (if you accept my proposition), then every thing is all right; but if you say... (the contradictory), then... (you meet some difficulty).

Examples: Berachoth 26b; Sabbath 23a; B. Metzia 3a.

b. (היינו or) שפיר .....בשלמא לדידי

קשיא ....אלא לדידך

it is well according to my view....; but according to your view... (there is a difficulty).

Examples: Yoma 4a; Pesachim 46b; Moed Katon 2b.

c. (היינו) שפיר ....בשלמא למאן דאמר

קשיא ....אלא למאן דאמר

it is well according to him who holds....; but according to him who holds....(the contrary view)....(there is the diffiiculty).

Examples: Berachoth 41a; Yoma 40a; B. Kamma 22a.

CHAPTER XI

REFUTATION

DEFINITION AND TERMS

§ 102.

A refutation consists either in proving that a given proposition is false, or in overthrowing the arguments by which it has been supported. In the first case, it is termed: תיובתא (the Aramaic word for the Hebrew תשובה an answer, gainsaying, refutation), and in the second case: פירכא (from the verb פרך to break into pieces, to crumble; hence, to destroy, to invalidate), or: דחיה (from the verb דחי to push aside, to overthrow to supersede).

A. THE REFUTATION OF A PROPOSITION.

§ 103.

The strongest argument against a proposition advanced by an Amora is to show that it conflicts with the authoritative decision laid down in a Mishna or a Baraitha. Such a refutation is generally introduced by: איתביה, or מתיב פלוני, or מיתיבי; see above § 86b.

A proposition is refuted indirectly by showing that, assuming it to be true, a certain passage of a Mishna or Baraitha bearing on that subject ought to have been expressed differently or could not well be explained. The phrases mostly used in such negative argumentation after quoting such a passage are:

a. ואי אמרת..... (מיבעי ליה) (קשיא) now, if you say.. (maintain your proposition), then... (we meet with a difficulty).

Examples: Gittin 53a; Kiddushin 32a; B. Metzia 10a.

b. ואי סלקא דעתך... (קשיא) now, if you assume... (your proposition to be true), then...

Examples: Sabbath 7b; Betza 9b; B. Metzia 10b.

c. ואם איתא... (קשיא) now, if it were so.. (as you maintain), then....

Examples: R. Hashana 3b; Pesachim 25a, Betza 18a.

Remark. A proposition is also refuted indirectly by proving the truth of its contradictory. The confirmation of one of two antagonistic opinions is thus the virtual refutation of the other, and vice versa. Hence the Talmudic phrases: מסייע ליה לפלוני (א) ותיובתא דפלוני (ב) this Mishna is a support (confirmation) of the opinion of A, and a refutation of the (opposite) opinion of B; f. ex, Yebamoth 53a, and: מתיב לפלוני (א) לסיועי לפלוני (ב) he refuted A in support of B; f. ex., Yoma 42b; B. Bathra 45b; Chullin 10a; Zebachim 10a.

B. REFUTATION OF ARGUMENTS.

§ 104.

Such refutations are very often introduced by the phrase: מתקיף לה פלוני a certain teacher asked a strong question against this (argument)....; (f. ex., Sabbath 4a; R. Hashana 13a; Sanhedrin 4a; Maccoth 3a). Occasionally, it is introduced by: ...פריך פ' a certain teacher refuted this argument (f. ex. Kiddushin 13a; Yebamoth 24a; Shebuoth 41b), or...מנדף בה פ' a certain teacher ridiculed this argument, in showing its absurdity (Sabbath 62b: Kidd. 71b; Sanhedrin 3b; Aboda Zara 35a; Zebachim 12a).[1]

---

[1]) The term מתקיף (from תקף *to overpower*, to attack; hence, to overthrow. to confute an argument,) is mostly used only in reference to refuting questions asked by the later Amoraim from the time of Rabba and Rab Joseph, though in Temura 7a it is exceptionally applied to a question raised by Resh Lakish.

פרך meaning, literally, to *break into pieces*, to *crumble*; hence, to invalidate an argument, to *refute*, is by the earlier Amoraim used as a term of refuting especially a *Kal vechomer* or a *Binyan Ab* (in the phrase איכא למפרך, and as a noun פירכא). As a term of refuting any argument it is mostly used by Rab Acha. The Talmud commentators Rashi and Tosaphoth often use the verb פרך in the general sense, to ask a question.

The term מנדף is mostly used by R. Abuha, and only once by R. Jirmija and once by R. Chanina.—Tosaphoth Yebamoth 2b, s. v. פשיט calls attention to the circumstance that some of the Amoraim used their own peculiar terms in setting forth a question. See *Kohut's* Aruch Completum s. v. נדף.

The procedure of refuting a particular argument varies with the nature of the latter, as will be shown in the following paragraphs.

§ 105.

1. An *argument from common sense* (see above § 95) is overthrown by showing that good common sense rather sides with the opposite view.

The phrase used in such counter-argument is: אדרבה (also spelled אדרבא) *on the contrary*, or more emphatically: אדרבה איפכא מסתברא on the contrary, the reverse is more reasonable.

Examples: Sabbath 3b; Pesachim 28a; Gittin 23b.

Remark 1. The term אדרבה or אדרבא (a contraction of the words על די רבה, literally, on that which is greater or stronger, i. e., on the contrary side is a stronger argument) must not be confounded with the words אדרבה and אדרבא meaning *against the view of Rabba* or *of Raba*, in the phrases: קשיא דרבה אדרבה Gittin 27a, and קשיא דרבא אדרבא B. Bathra 30a.

Remark 2. A similar meaning as the term אדרבה *on the contrary*, is expressed by the phrase כלפי לייה, literally: where does this turn? i. e., on the contrary, the opposite view is more reasonable; f. ex. Pesachim 5b; B. Metzia 58b.

§ 106.

2. *An argument from authority*, (see above § 96) is defeated in different ways:

a. By showing that the whole argument is based on a misapprehension of the passage referred to. In demonstrating this, either of the following phrases is used:

ותסברא how do you reason? How can you understand that passage in this way?

Examples: Pesachim 26a; Yebamoth 15a, B. Kamma 14a.

מי סברת...לא do you think...,do you understand the passage in this way? It is not so, but....

Examples: Pesachim 29a; Kiddushin 7a, B. Metzia 32b.

b. By showing that the authority referred to does not

necessarily concern the case under consideration. This is phrased either: (הכא or) שאני התם there (or, here) the case is different, for....

Examples: Pesachim 5a; Shebuoth 15a; B. Metzia 10a.

Or: ...הכא במאי עסקינן here we treat of the special case of...

Examples; Gittin 12a; B. Kamma 8a; B. Metzia 10b.

c. By showing that the passage referred to is not authoritative, as it only expresses the individual opinion of one Mishna Teacher, disputed by another authority.

הוא דאמר כי האי תנא he holds it with that other teacher ...;f. ex., Maccoth 10b; 12a.

Or: הא מני פלוני...היא whose opinion is here accepted? that of....; f. ex., Sabbath 11b; Pesachim 32a; B. Kamma 10a.

Or: תנאי היא concerning this matter, the Tanaim differ.

Examples: R. Hashana 19b; Betza 9a; B. Metzia 62a.

§ 107.

3. *An argument from a close construction* or from implication (see above § 97) is refuted by showing it to be too arbitrary, as the same construction, if applied to another clause of the same passage, would result in a contradiction of the conclusions from the two clauses.

This refutation is mostly introduced by: (רישא) אימא סיפא *tell me the other clause...* (and apply to it the same construction)....

The result of this counter-argument is often added in the phrase:

אלא מהא ליכא למשמע מינה hence nothing can be proved herefrom.

Examples: Kiddushin 5b; Yebamoth 76b; B. Metzia 26b.

§ 108.

4. *An argument from analogy* (see above § 98) is refuted by impugning the premise, in showing that the resemblance

between the two cases is merely superficial, or that points of difference have been overlooked which vitiate the analogy. The phrases used in such refutations are:

a. ....מי דמי התם....הכא are the two cases alike? there.... here....

Examples: Sabbath 6a; Kiddushin 7a; Gittin 3a.

b. ...הכי השתא התם...הכא *now, is this so?* i. e., is this analogy correct? There....; but here....

Examples: Berachoth 21a; R. Hashana 28a; Kiddushin 7a.

Remark. The phrase מי דמי is used in refuting an analogy which was intended to *support* a proposition, while that of הכי השתא in refuting the analogy on which an *objection* to a proposition was based. In other words, the former phrase is mostly applied in *attacking* a proposition, and the latter in *repelling* such an attack.

c. מידי אריא הא כדאיתא והא כדאיתא *does this prove anything? This case as it is, and the other case, as it is* ; i. e., the two cases are not as analogous as you presume, since the circumstances are quite different.

Examples: Succah 43b; Gittin 33a; B. Metzia 14b.

Remark. This phrase is applied especially in refuting an analogy based on the parallelism or the juxtaposition of two cases in one and the same Mishna paragraph (רישא וסיפא).

§ 109.

5. An indirect argument (see above § 100) is often refuted by a counter-argument, showing that a similar objection, as had been raised against the contradictory proposition, might also be raised against the original proposition. To remove the latter objection, a distinction must necessarily be made, but this distinction at the same time removes the objection against the contradictory proposition, and thus destroys the whole indirect argument.

The phrases used in introducing such a counter-argument are:

a. (...תקשי נמי) (מי ניחא ?) ...ולטעמך but according to your own opinion... (does it agree with the passage referred to?) (is there not also an objection to be raised?..)

Examples: Yoma 8b; Posachim 19b; Betza 8a.

b. (נמי קשיא) (כדקאמרת ?) ...ואלא מאי and what then?.. (shall it be so as you say? i. e. do you want me to accept your proposition?) but also against this the objection is....

Examples: Berachoth 27a; Betza 13a; B. Metzia 3a.

Remark. The words אלא מאי introducing such a counter-argument must not be confounded with the same words in a different connection in which they are to be translated by: *what then is...? what then means?* as: אלא מאי אותו "but what means the expression אותו "(Rosh Hashana 22b), or in the frequent phrase: אלא מאי איח לך למימר "but what then remains for you to say? (Yoma 8b). In Rosh Hashana 13a, we find on the same page the words אלא מאי in three different connections and meanings.

§ 110.

6. A mode of refutation very frequently applied in the Talmudical discussions, consists in showing that the advanced argument, if admitted at all, would prove too much, that is, it proves, besides the intended conclusion, another which is manifestly inadmissible. The characteristic phrases used in this mode of invalidating an argument are:

a. אי הכי אפילו... נמי *if so, even... also,* i. e. if that argument (or conclusion) were correct, its consequences ought also to extend to that other case of... to which, however, they do not extend.

Examples: Berachoth 13a; Pesachim 7b; Betza 8b.

b. אי הכי מאי איריא... אפילו... נמי *if so, why just teaching...* (this case)? since it ought to apply also to the case of...

Examples: Berachoth 16b; Betza 8a; Gittin 10a.

§ 111.

7. A similar but more effective mode of overthrowing an argument is, to introduce another analogous case where the

application of that argument would lead to a palpable absurdity.

The phraseology of this kind of refutation is:

אלא מעתה... הכי נמי but now (according to your argument or conclusion), can it apply also to that other case of...?

Examples: Berachoth 13a; Pesachim 5a; Gittin 23a.

§ 112.

8. Propositions as well as arguments are often refuted by the objection that the advanced opinion is without parallel and example, and against common sense, or against the established principles in law.

מי איכא מידי ד.... is there anything like this, that...?

Examples: Yoma 2b; Betza 13b; Sanhedrin 55a.

§ 113.

9. A mild and polite mode of refuting an argument is that which, instead of a decided objection, merely intimates a certain possibility which would invalidate the argument under consideration. Such refutations are introduced either by. ....ואימא but I might say...; f. ex. Yoma 2b, or, by... ודילמא but perhaps....; f. ex. Sabbath 5a; B. Metzia 8b.

The answer to such a mild objection or refutation is often: לא סלקא דעתך this cannot enter thy mind, i. e., you can impossibly think so, since...; f. ex., R. Hashana 13a.

CHAPTER XII

THE DEBATE

1. Definition and Terms

§ 114.

Besides the minor discussions to be found almost on every page of the Talmud, and consisting either of a query, an answer, and a rejoinder, or of an argument, an objection, and a defense, the Talmud contains also numerous more elaborate discussions or debates in which two or more teachers holding different opinions on a certain question contend with each other in mutual argumentation. Such an interchange of arguments between opposing parties is termed שקלא וטריא (literally, *taking up and throwing back*, namely, arguments). A debate displaying great dialectical acumen is termed פלפול. These debates generally concern either the interpretation and application of a provision of the Mishna, or a new principle of law advanced by an Amora.

2. The Principal Debaters.

§ 115.

The debates recorded in the Talmud are generally between the associate members of an academy, or between a teacher and his prominent disciples. The most noted among them are the following:

R. Jochanan with Resh Lakish.

Rab Huna with Rab Nachman; also with Rab Shesheth and Rab Chisda.

Rab Nachman with Rab Shesheth; also with Raba.

Rab Chisda with Rab Schesheth; also with Rab Nachman b. Isaac.

Rabba with Rab Joseph; also with Raba and with Abaye.

Raba with Abaye, and both of them also with Rab Papa and with Rabina I.

Abaye with Rab Dime.

Rab Ashe with Amemar, also with Rabina, with Mar Zutra and Rab Acha.

Of most of the other numerous Amoraim only opinions, remarks, traditions and occasional discussions, but no formal debates are recorded in the Talmud.

Some contemporary authorities, as Rab and Mar Samuel, though widely differing from each other in many legal questions, are rarely (f. i., B. Kamma 75a; Aboda Zarah 36a) mentioned as having been personally engaged in debates with each other. But their differences of opinion are frequently quoted, and made a basis of academical discussions between the teachers of later generations.

3. ILLUSTRATION OF DEBATES.

§ 116.

The following synopsis of a debate between Rabba and Rab Joseph, the former being seconded by Abaye, may serve to illustrate the usual procedure in the Talmudical controversies.

In Baba Kamma 56b the question is as to the degree of legal responsibility of שומר אבידה, that is, of the keeper of a lost object waiting for its owner to claim it.

Rabba maintains that the responsibility of that keeper is only that of a *gratuitous* depositary (שומר חנם) who is not liable for the loss of the object entrusted to his care, except in the case of gross negligence.

Rab Joseph holds that he has the greater responsibility of a *paid* depositary (שומר שכיר) who is liable for all losses except those caused by inevitable accident.

The reasons for each of these two opinions are stated.

Rab Joseph opens the debate with the attempt to refute the opinion of his opponent (איתביה רב יוסף לרבה) by showing it to be in conflict with a passage in the Mishna.

Rabba parries this attack by construing that Mishna passage differently.

R. J. objects to this construction

Rabba removes the objection.

R. J. renews his attack by appealing to a Baraitha from which he infers that the keeper of a lost object has the greater responsibility of a paid depositary.

Rabba admits the correctness of this inference in the special case mentioned in that Baraitha, but denies its general application to the question at issue.

After having thus far been successful on the defensive, Rabba assumes the offensive (איתביה רבה לרב יוסף), by calling attention to another Baraitha which he dialectically interprets in such a way as to be a refutation of his opponent's opinion.

R. J. overthrows the refutation by showing that there was no necessity for construing this Baraitha just in the way as done by his opponent.

Now, Abaye, a disciple of Rabba, enters the arena to second the opinion of his master. Addressing himself to the opponent of the latter, he quotes a reported decision of the acknowledged authority of one of the former Amoraim in Palestine (R. Jochanan) from which decision he, by indirect reasoning, draws the conclusion that the keeper of a lost object has only the responsibility of a gratuitous depositary.

Rab Joseph rejects this conclusion by restricting the decision of the quoted authority to certain circumstances which alter the case.

Abaye denies that the case is altered even under the supposed circumstances, and the discussion continues without leading to a definite result. But later authorities decided in favor of Rab Joseph's opinion which is adopted in the Rabbinical codes.

Other examples of such debates are furnished: Yoma 6b—7b; Pesachim 46b—47a; Moed Katon 2b; Kiddushin 59a; Gittin 32b—33a; Nedarim 25b—27a; B. Kamma 61a—62a; B. Metzia 43a; B. Bathra 45a—46a.

Remark. Different from these debates in which two Amoraim holding opposite opinions argue personally against each other, are the discussions of the Gemara on a reported difference between authorities of a former generation (f. ex. Gittin 2a sqq.) in which discussions, arguments for and against either of those authorities are advanced, refuted or defended. See above §§ 74—80.

4. ANONYMOUS DISCUSSIONS AND DEBATES.

§ 117.

Dicussions and debates are, as a rule, reported very carefully with the names of those engaged therein. But in numerous instances, the names are omitted, so that either a question or an answer, or both of them are reported anonymously. Sometimes, a lengthy discussion carried on anonymously is interrupted by an answer made by an authority mentioned by name. At other times again, a debate started by named authorities is continued anonymously.

The omission of names in a discussion is probably indicative that this was a general discussion among the members of the academy, while only the questions and answers of the prominent teachers were recorded with the names of their authors.

In consequence of the succinct and elliptical mode of expression, so prevalent in the Talmud, and in the absence of all punctuation marks, the anonymous discussions especially, often offer great and perplexing difficulties to the inexperienced student, as question and answer are there sometimes so closely connected that it requires a considerable practice in Talmud reading to discern where the one ends and the other begins.

PART IV

OUTLINES OF TALMUDICAL ETHICS

OUTLINES OF TALMUDICAL ETHICS

Ethics is the flower and fruit on the tree of religion. The ultimate aim of religion is to ennoble man's inner and outer life, so that he may love and do that only which is right and good. This is a biblical teaching which is emphatically repeated in almost every book of Sacred Scriptures. Let me only refer to the sublime word of the prophet Micah: "He hath showed thee, O man, what is good, and what doth the Lord require of thee, but to do justice and to love kindness and to walk humbly with thy God." (Micah vi, 8).

As far as concerns the Bible, its ethical teachings are generally known. Translated into all languages of the world, that holy book is accessible to every one, and whoever reads it with open eyes and with an unbiased mind will admit that it teaches the highest principles of morality, principles which have not been surpassed and superseded by any ethical system of ancient or modern philosophy.

But how about the Talmud, that immense literary work whose authority was long esteemed second to that of the Bible? What are the ethical teachings of the Talmud?

Although mainly engaged with discussions of the Law, as developed on the basis of the Bible during Israel's second commonwealth down to the sixth century of the Christian era, the Talmud devotes also much attention to ethical subjects. Not only are one treatise of the Mishna (*Pirke Aboth*) and some Baraithoth (as, *Aboth d'R. Nathan*, and *Derech Eretz*) almost exclusively occupied with ethical teachings, but such teachings are also very abundantly contained in the Aggadic (homiletical) passages which are so frequently interspersed in the legal discussions throughout all parts of the Talmud.[1]

[1] Also the *Midrash*, a post-Talmudic collection of extracts from popular lectures of the ancient teachers on Biblical texts, contains an abundance of ethical teachings and maxims advanced by the sages of the Talmud, which must likewise be taken into consideration, when speaking of Talmudical Ethics.

It must be borne in mind that the Talmudical literature embraces a period of about eight centuries, and that the numerous teachers whose ethical views and utterances are recorded in that vast literature, rank differently in regard to mind and authority. At the side of the great luminaries, we find also lesser ones. At the side of utterances of great, clear-sighted and broad-minded masters with lofty ideas, we meet also with utterances of peculiar views which never obtained authority. Not every ethical remark or opinion quoted in that literature can, therefore, be regarded as an index of the standard of Talmudical ethics, but such opinions only can be so regarded which are expressed with authority and which are in harmony with the general spirit that pervades the Talmudic literature.

Another point to be observed is the circumstance that the Talmud does not treat of ethics in a coherent, philosophical system. The Talmudic sages made no claim of being philosophers; they were public teachers, expounders of the Law, popular lecturers. As such, they did not care for a methodically arranged system. All they wanted was to spread among the people ethical teachings in single, concise, pithy, pointed sentences, well adapted to impress the minds and hearts, or in parables or legends illustrating certain moral duties and virtues. And this, their method, fully answered its purpose. Their ethical teachings did actually reach the Jewish masses, and influenced their conduct of life, while among the Greeks, the ethical theories and systems remained a matter that concerned the philosophers only, without exercising any educating influence upon the masses at large.

Furthermore, it must be remembered that the Talmudical ethics is largely based on the ethics of the Bible. The sacred treasure of biblical truth and wisdom was in the minds and hearts of the Rabbis. This treasury they tried to enrich by their own wisdom and observation. Here they develop a principle contained in a scriptural passage, and give it a wider scope and a larger application to life's various conditions. There they crystallize great moral ideas into a pithy, impressive maxim as guide for human conduct. Here they give to a jewel of biblical ethics a new lustre by setting it in the gold of their own wisdom. There again they combine single pearls of biblical wisdom to a graceful ornament for human life.

Let us now try to give a few outlines of the ethical teachings of the Talmud. In the first place, concerning

MAN AS A MORAL BEING.

In accordance with the teaching of the Bible, the rabbis duly emphasize man's dignity as a being created in the likeness of God.[1] By this likeness of God they understand the spiritual being within us, that is endowed with intellectual and moral capacities. The higher desires and inspirations which spring from this spiritual being in man, are called *Yetzer tob*, the good inclination; but the lower appetites and desires which rise from our physical nature and which we share with the animal creation, are termed *Yetzer ha-ra*, the inclination to evil.[2] Not that these sensuous desires are absolutely evil; for they, too, have been implanted in man for good purposes. Without them man could not exist, he would not cultivate and populate this earth[3], or, as a Talmudical legend runs: Once, some overpious people wanted to pray to God that they might be able to destroy the *Yetzer ha-ra*, but a warning voice was heard, saying: "Beware, lest you destroy this world!"[4] Evil are those lower desires only in that

[1] Aboth III, 14: R. Akiba used to say: "How distinguished is man, since created in the image of God, and still more distinguished by the consciousness of having been created in the image of God!"

[2] Mishna Berachoth IX,5: בשני יצריך ביצר טוב וביצר רע

[3] Midrash R. Bereshith IX: והנה טוב מאד זה יצר רע שאילולי יצ"הר וכו'

[4] Yoma 69b: חזו דאי קטליתו ליה כליא עלמא.

they, if unrestrained, easily mislead man to live contrary to the demands and aspirations of his divine nature. Hence the constant struggle in man between the two inclinations.[1] He who submits his evil inclination to the control of his higher aims and desires, is virtuous and righteous. "The righteous are governed by the *Yetzer tob*, but the wicked by the *Yetzer ha-ra*.[2] "The righteous have their desires in their power, but the wicked are in the power of their desires."[3]

FREE-WILL.

Man's free will is emphasized in the following sentences: "Everything is ordained by God's providence, but freedom of choice is given to man."[4] "Everything is foreordained by heaven, except the fear of heaven"[5] or, as another sage puts it: Whether man be strong or weak, rich or poor, wise or foolish depends mostly on circumstances that surround him from the time of his birth, but whether man be good or bad, righteous or wicked, depends upon his own free will.[6]

GOD'S WILL, THE GROUND OF MAN'S DUTIES.

The ground of our duties, as presented to us by the Talmudical as well as the biblical teachings, is that it is the will of God. His will is the supreme rule of our being. "Do His will as thy own will, submit thy will to His will".[7] "Be bold as a leopard, light as an eagle, swift as a roe, and strong as a lion, to do the will of thy Father, who is in heaven".[8]

MAN ACCOUNTABLE TO GOD FOR HIS CONDUCT.

Of man's responsibility for the conduct of his life, we

---

[1] Kiddushin 30b: יצרו של אדם מתחדש עליו בכל יום. Berachoth 5b: לעולם ירגיז אדם יצר טוב על יצר הרע.

[2] Berachoth 61b. [3] Midrash Bereshith XXXIII.

[4] Aboth III, 15. [5] Berachoth 33a. [6] Nidda 16b.

[7] Aboth II, 4. [8] Ibid. V, 20.

are forcibly reminded by numerous sentences, as: "Consider three things, and thou wilt never fall into sin; remember that there is above thee an all-seeing eye, an all hearing ear, and a record of all thy actions".[1] And again, "Consider three things, and thou wilt never sin; remember whence thou comest, whither thou goest, and before whom thou wilt have to render account for thy doings."[2]

HIGHER MOTIVES IN PERFORMING OUR DUTIES.

Although happiness here and hereafter is promised as reward for fulfillment, and punishment threatened for neglect of duty, still we are reminded not to be guided by the consideration of reward and punishment, but rather by love and obedience to God, and by love to that which is good and noble. "Be not like servants, who serve their master for the sake of reward."[3] "Whatever thou doest, let it be done in the name of heaven"[4] (that is, for its own sake).

DUTY OF SELF-PRESERVATION AND SELF-CULTIVATION.

As a leading rule of the duties of *self-preservation* and *self-cultivation*, and, at the same time, as a warning against selfishness, we have Hillel's sentence: "If I do not care for myself, who will do it for me? and if I care only for myself, what am I?"[5]

The duty of *acquiring knowledge*, especially knowledge of the divine Law (Thora) which gives us a clearer insight in God's will to man, is most emphatically enjoined in numerous sentences: "Without knowledge there is no true morality and piety."[6] "Be eager to acquire knowledge, it does not come to thee by inheritance".[7] "The more knowledge, the more spiritual life."[7] "If thou hast acquired knowledge, what doest thou lack? but if thou lackest knowledge, what

[1] Ibid. II, 1. [2] Ibid. III, 1.
[3] Aboth I, 3. [4] Ibid. II, 12. [5] Ibid. I, 14.
[6] Ibid. II, 5. [7] Ibid. II, 12, [8] Ibid. II, 7.

hast thou acquired?"[1] But we are also reminded that even the highest knowledge is of no value, as long as it does not influence our moral life. "The ultimate end of all knowledge and wisdom is man's inner purification and the performance of good and noble deeds."[2] "He whose knowledge is great without influencing his moral life, is compared to a tree that has many branches, but few and weak roots; a storm cometh and overturneth it."[3]

LABOR.

Next to the duty of acquiring knowledge, that of *industrious labor* and *useful activity* is strongly enjoined. It is well known that among the ancient nations in general, manual labor was regarded as degrading the free citizen. Even the greatest philosophers of antiquity, a Plato and Aristotle, could not free themselves of this deprecating view of labor.[4] How different was the view of the Talmudic sages in this respect! They say: "Love labor, and hate to be a lord."[5] "Great is the dignity of labor; it honors man."[6] "Beautiful is the intellectual occupation, if combined with some practical work."[7] "He who does not teach his son a handicraft trade, neglects his parental duty."[8] "He who lives on the toil of his hands, is greater than he who indulges in idle piety."[9]

In accordance with these teachings, some of the most prominent sages of the Talmud are known to have made their living by various kinds of handicraft and trade.

CARDINAL DUTIES IN RELATION TO FELLOW-MEN.

Regarding man's relation to fellow-men, the rabbis consider *justice*, *truthfulness*, *peaceableness* and *charity* as cardinal duties. They say, "The world (human society) rests on three things—on justice, on truth and on peace."[10]

---

[1] Midrash Levit. I: דעה קנית מה חסרת, דעה חסרת מה קנית
[2] Berachoth 17a. [3] Aboth III, 17.
[4] Arist. Polit. VIII, 3. [5] Aboth I, 10. [6] Gittin 67a; Nedarim 49a.
[7] Aboth II, 2. [8] Kiddushin 29a. [9] Berachoth 8a.
[10] Aboth I, 18.

JUSTICE

The principle of *justice* in the moral sense is expressed in the following rules: "Thy neighbor's property must be as sacred to thee, as thine own."[1] "Thy neighbor's honor must be as dear to thee, as thine own."[2] Hereto belongs also the golden rule of Hillel: "Whatever would be hateful to thee, do not to thy neighbor."[3]

TRUTH AND TRUTHFULNESS.

The sacredness of *truth* and *truthfulness* is expressed in the sentence: "Truth is the signet of God, the Most Holy."[4] "Let thy yea be in truth, and thy nay be in truth."[5] "Truth lasts forever, but falsehood must vanish."[6]

Admonitions concerning *faithfulness* and *fidelity* to given promises are: "Promise little and do much."[7] "To be faithless to a given promise is as sinful as idolatry."[8] "To break a verbal engagement, though legally not binding, is a moral wrong."[9] Of the numerous warnings against any kind of deceit, the following may be mentioned: "It is sinful to deceive any man, be he even a heathen."[10] "Deception in words is as great a sin as deception in money matters."[11] When, says the Talmud, the immortal soul will be called to account before the divine tribunal, the first question will be, "hast thou been honest and faithful in all thy dealings with thy fellow-men?"[12]

PEACEFULNESS.

Peace and harmony in domestic life and social intercourse as well as in public affairs are considered by the Talmudic sages as the first condition of human welfare and happiness, or as they express it: "Peace is the vessel in which all God's blessings are presented to us and preserved

---

[1] Ibid. II, 12. [2] Ibid. II, 10. [3] Sabbath 30a.
[4] Sabbath 45a. [5] B. Metzia 45a.. [6] Sabbath 104a. [7] Aboth I, 15.
[8] Sanhedrin 92a. [9] B. Metzia 48a. [10] Chullin 94a. [11] B. Metzia 58b.
[12] Sabbath 28b.

by us."[1] "Be a disciple of Aaron, loving peace, and pursuing peace."[2] To make peace between those in disharmony is regarded as one of the most meritorious works that secure happiness and bliss here and hereafter.[3]

As virtues leading to peace, those of *mildness* and *meekness*, of *gentleness* and *placidity* are highly praised and recommended. "Be not easily moved to anger"[4] "Be humble to thy superior, affable to thy inferior, and meet every man with friendliness."[5] "He who is slow to anger, and easily pacified, is truly pious and virtuous."[6] "Man, be ever soft and pliant like a reed, and not hard and unbending like the cedar."[7] "Those who, when offended, do not give offence, when hearing slighting remarks, do not retaliate—they are the friends of God, they shall shine forth like the sun in its glory."[8]

CHARITY.

The last of the principal duties to fellow-men is *charity*, which begins where justice leaves off. Prof. Steinthal in his work on General Ethics, remarks, that among the cardinal virtues of the ancient philosophers, we look in vain for the idea of *love* and *charity*, whereas in the teachings of the Bible, we generally find the idea of love, mercy and charity closely connected with that of justice.[9] And we may add, as in the Bible so also in the Talmud, where charity is considered as the highest degree on the scale of duties and virtues. It is one of the main pillars on which the welfare of the human world rests.[10]

The duty of *charity* (Gemilath Chesed) extends farther than to mere *almsgiving* (Tzedaka). "Almsgiving is practiced by means of money, but charity also by personal services and by words of advice, symphaty and encouragement. Almsgiving is a duty towards the poor only, but charity towards

---

[1] Mishna Oketzin III, 12. [2] Aboth I, 12.
[3] Mishna Peah I, 1. [4] Aboth II, 10. [5] Ibid. III, 12. [6] Ibid. V, 11
[7] Taanith 20b. [8] Yoma 23; Gittin 36b.
[9] Allgemeine Ethik. p. 108. [10] Aboth I, 2.

the rich as well as the poor, nay, even towards the dead (by taking care of their decent burial)"[1]

By works of charity man proves to be a true image of God whose atributes are love, kindness and mercy.[2] "He who turns away from works of love and charity turns away from God".[3] "The works of charity have more value than sacrifices; they are equal to the performance of all religious duties."[4]

Concerning the proper way of practicing this virtue, the Talmnd has many beautiful sentences, as: "The merit of charitable works is in proportion to the love with which they are practiced."[5] "Blessed is he who gives from his substance to the poor, twice blessed he who accompanies his gift with kind, comforting words".[6] "The noblest of all charities is enabling the poor to earn a livelihood".[7] He who is unable to give much, shall not withhold his little mite, for "as a garment is made up of single threads, so every single gift contributes to accomplish a great work of charity".[8]

DUTIES CONCERNING SPECIAL RELATIONS.

Besides these principal duties in relation to fellow-men in general, the Talmud treats also very elaborately of duties concerning the various relations of life. Not intending to enter here into all details, we shall restrict ourselves to some of its ethical teachings in reference to the domestic relations, and regarding the relation to the country and the community.

THE CONJUGAL RELATION.

"First build a house and plant a vineyard (i. e., provide for the means of the household), and then take a wife".[9] "Let youth and old age not be joined in marriage, lest the purity and peace of domestic life be disturbed"[10] "A man's home means

---

[1] Succah 49b.
[2] Sotah 14a. [3] Kethuboth 61a. [4] Succah 49a; B. Bathra 9a.
[5] Succah 49a. [6] B. Bathra 9b. [7] Sabbath 63a. [8] B. Bathra 10b.
[9] Sotah 44a. [10] Sanhedrin 76a.

his wife."[1] "Let a man be careful to honor his wife, for he owes to her alone all the blessings of his house".[2] "If thy wife is small, bend down to her, to take counsel from her".[3] "Who is rich ? He who has a noble wife."[4] "A man should be careful lest he afflict his wife, for God counts her tears."[5] "If in anger the one hand removed thy wife or thy child, let the other hand again bring them back to thy heart."[6] "He who loves his wife as his own self, and honors her more than himself, and he who educates his children in the right way, to him applies the divine promise: Thou shalt know that there is peace in thy tent."[7] "Tears are shed on God's altar for the one who forsakes the wife of his youth."[8] "He who divorces his wife, is hated before God".[9]

PARENTS AND CHILDREN.

"Parental love should be impartial, one child must not be preferred to the other".[10] "It is a father's duty not only to provide for his minor children, but also to take care of their instruction, and to teach his son a trade and whatever is necessary for his future welfare".[11] "The honor and reverence due to parents are equal to the honor and reverence due to God".[12] "Where children honor their parents, there God dwels, there He is honored"[13].

COUNTRY AND COMMUNITY.

Regarding duties to the country and the community, the Rabbis teach: "The law of the country is as sacred and binding as God's law".[14] "Pray for the welfare of the government; without respect for the government, men would swallow each other".[15] "Do not isolate thyself from the community and its interests".[16] "It is sinful to deceive the government regard-

---

[1] Yoma 2a. [2] B. Metzia 59a. [3] Ibid. [4] Sabbath 25b.
[5] B. Metzia 59a. [6] Sota 47a. [7] Yebamoth 62b. [8] Gittin 90b.
[9] Ibid. [10] Sabbath 10b. [11] Kiddushin 29a. [12] Ibid 29b.
[13] Ibid 30a. [14] Gittin 10b; Nedarim 28a; B. Kamma 113a; B. Bathra 54b. [15] Aboth III, 2. [16] Ibid II, 4.

ing taxes and duties".[1] "Do not aspire for public offices"[2]; "but where there are no men, try thou to be the man".[3] "Those who work for the community shall do it without selfishness, but with the pure intention to promote its welfare".[4]

GENERAL CHARACTERISTICS.

To these short outlines of Talmudical ethics let us add only a few general remarks. Being essentially a development of the sublime ethical principles and teachings of the Bible, the Talmudical ethics retains the general characteristics of that origin.

It teaches nothing that is against human nature, nothing that is incompatible with the existence and welfare of human society. It is free from the extreme excess and austerity to which the lofty ideas of religion and morality were carried by the theories and practices of some sects inside and outside of Judaism.

Nay, many Talmudical maxims and sayings are evidently directed against such austerities and extravagances. Thus they warn against the monastic idea of obtaining closer communion with God by fleeing from human society and by seclusion from temporal concerns of life: "Do not separate thyself from society."[5] "Man's thoughts and ways shall always be in contact and sympathy with fellow-men."[6] "No one shall depart from the general customs and manners."[7] "Better is he who lives on the toil of his hand, than he who indulges in idle piety."[8]

They strongly discountenance the idea of *celibacy*, which the Essenes, and later, some orders of the Church regarded as a superior state of perfection. The rabbis say: "He who lives without a wife is no perfect man."[9] "To be unmarried

---

[1] Pesachim 112b: ואל תבריח עצמך מן המכס also B. Kamma 113a אסור להבריח את המכס.

[2] Aboth I, 10. [3] Ibid. II, 5. [4] Ibid. II, 2.

[5] Aboth II, 4. [6] Kethuboth 11a. [7] B. Metzia 86b.

[8] Berachot 8b. [9] Yebamoth 63a.

is to live without joy, without blessing, without kindness, without religion and without peace."[1] "As soon as man marries, his sins decrease."[2]

While, on the one hand, they warn against too much indulgence in pleasures and in the gratification of bodily appetites and against the insatiable pursuit of earthly goods and riches, as well as against the inordinate desire of honor and power, on the other hand, they strongly disapprove the ascetic mortification of the body and abstinence from enjoyment, and the cynic contempt of all luxuries that beautify life. They say: "God's commandments are intended to enhance the value and enjoyment of life, but not to mar it and make it gloomy."[3] "If thou hast the means, enjoy life's innocent pleasures."[4] "He who denies himself the use of wine is a sinner."[5] "No one is permitted to afflict himself by unnecessary fasting."[6] "The pious fool, the hypocrite, and the pharisaic flagellant are destroyers of human society."[7] "That which beautifies life and gives it vigor and strength, just as riches and honor, is suitable to the pious, and agreeable to the world at large."[8]

Finally, one more remark: The Talmud has often been accused of being illiberal, as if teaching its duties only for Jews towards fellow-believers, but not also towards fellowmen in general. This charge is entirely unfounded. It is true, and quite natural, that in regard to the *ritual* and *ceremonial* law and practice, a distinction between Jew and Gentile was made. It is also true, that we occasionally meet in the Talmud with an uncharitable utterance against the heathen world. But it must be remembered in what state of moral corruption and degradation their heathen surroundings were, at that time. And this, too, must be

---

[1] Ibid. 62a. [2] Ibid. 63b.

[3] Yoma 85b: וחי בהם ולא שימות בהם. [4] Erubin 54a: אם יש לך היטב לך. [5] Taanith 11a. [6] Ibid. 22b. [7] Mishna Sota III, 4.

[8] Baraitha, Aboth VI, 8: הנוי והכח והעושר והכבוד... נאה לצדיקים ולעולם.

remembered, that such utterances are only made by individuals who gave vent to their indignation in view of the cruel persecutions whose victims they were. As regards *moral* teachings, the Talmud is as broad as humanity. It teaches duties of man to man without distinction of creed and race. In most of the ethical maxims, the terms *Adam* and *Beriyot*, "man," "fellow-men," are emphatically used; as: "Do not despise any man."[1] "Judge every man from his favorable side."[2] "Seek peace, and love fellow-men."[3] "He who is pleasing to fellow-men is also pleasing to God."[4] "The right way for man to choose, is to do that which is honorable in his own eyes (i. e., approved by his conscience) and at the same time, honorable in the eyes of his fellow-men."[5] In some instances, the Talmud expressly reminds that the duties of justice, veracity, peacefulness and charity are to be fulfilled towards the heathen as well as to the Israelites; as: "It is sinful to deceive any man, be he even a heathen."[6] It is our duty to relieve the poor and needy, to visit the sick and bury the dead without distinction of creed and race."[7]

"Thou shalt love thy neighbor as thyself" (Lev. XIX, 18); this is, said R. Akiba, the all embracing principle of the divine law. But *Ben Azai* said, there is another passage in Scriptures still more embracing; it is the passage (Gen., v, 2): "This is the book of the generations of man; in the day that God created man, he made him in the likeness of God."[8] That sage meant to say, this passage is more embracing, since it clearly tells us who is our neighbor; not, as it might be misunderstood, our friend only, not our fellow-citizen only, not our co-religionist only, but since we all descend from a common ancestor, since all are created in the image and likeness of God, every man, every human being is our brother, our neighbor whom we shall love as ourselves.

---

[1] Aboth IV, 3. [2] Ibid. I, 6. [3] Ibid. I, 12. [4] Ibid. III, 10.

[5] Ibid. II, 1. [6] Chullin 94a. [7] Gittin 61a. [8] Siphra on Lev. XIX, 18.

The liberal spirit of Talmudic ethics is most strikingly evidenced in the sentence: "The pious and virtuous of all nations participate in the eternal bliss,"[1] which teaches that man's salvation depends not on the acceptance of certain articles of belief, nor on certain ceremonial observances, but on that which is the ultimate aim of religion, namely, *Morality*, purity of heart and holiness of life.

---

[1] Tosephta Sanhedrin ch. XIII; Maimonides Yad Hachezaka, Teshuba III, 5; Melachim VIII, 11.

ADDITIONAL NOTES, CORRECTIONS, Etc

The initial in parenthesis following a note indicates the author: (M.) for Mielziner; (B.) for Dr. Joshua Bloch; (F.) for Dr. Louis Finkelstein.

PAGE

4. As to the opinions of Hoffmann, Lerner and Halevy concerning the origin of Mishna, see Strack, Einl., p. 19 f. Ginzberg (in *Journal of Jewish Lore and Philosophy,* Vol. I, p. 33 ff.) has proven that Tamid was the oldest treatise of the Mishna. Tamid and Middot, however, do not belong to the Mishna. The Mishna of the Tannaim consisted of only 58 tractates. (*B.*)

5. When R. Jehuda Hanasi arranged the final collection of the Mishna, he entrusted it to the memory of R. Isaac b. Abdimi (or Roba)) who made some changes in it, introducing the opinions of his master. See Lewy, Jahresbericht, Breslau Seminary, 1905, p. 25, and Marx *JQR* N. S., Vol. 13, p. 353. (*B.*)
Paragraph 3.
Since several of the colleagues of R. Jehuda Ha-Nasi had arranged their own Mishna-systems, each of those works was distinguished by being called after its author. Thus the *Mishna of Bar Kappara* was the work of that scholar, the *Mishna of R. Hiyya,* was the work of another scholar of the same period. Some parts of these works are preserved in quotations in the Talmud, and have been incorporated into other books. The Mishna of *R. Jehuda Ha-Nasi,* being the generally accepted code, was called *Mishna,* without further description. (*F.*)
Note.
The question of whether the *Mishna* was actually committed to writing or not has further been discussed by the following authors: Jacob Bruell, *Mebo Ha-Mishna,* II, 10-13; Jawitz, *Toledot Israel,* p. 340ff.; and J. S. Bloch, Einblicke in der Gesch. der Entstehung der Talmud. Literatur, Vienna, 1884. The first two hold that it was committed to writing, the last that it was not. It is now generally believed that the *Mishna* was not committed to writing till a much later date, but that the scholars used private notes as an aid to their memory. See Marx, *JQR* N. S., XIII, 353. (*F.*)

7. The six divisions of the Mishna are sometimes also termed Shesh Erke Hamishna. See Pesikta d. R. Kahana 7a and Cant. R. 6, 4. (*B.*)

8. As to the names of the Masechtoth and the order of their ar-

PAGE

rangement, some important notes are given by Prof. Louis Ginzberg in his remarkable study *Tamid the Oldest Treatise of the Mishna;* in Neumark's *Journal of Jewish Lore and Philosophy,* Vol. I, pp. 33-44, 197-209, and 265-295. (*B.*)

9. As to the particulars concerning each Masechta listed herewith, consult the respective articles in the *JE.* (*B.*)

11. *Baba Kama.* As to particulars concerning this and the two following Masechtoth, see the articles Baba Kamma, Baba Mezia and Baba Batra, in the Jewish Encyclopedia, Vol. II. (*M.*)
On Kethuboth cf. D. Kaufmann, Zur Geschichte der K. in *MGWJ* 41 (1897), 213-221; E. N. Adler in *JE* 7, 472-478; S. Krauss, Archeol. 2, 44; M. Gaster, Die K. bei den Samaritanern, *MGWJ* 54 (1910), 174 ff; M. Gaster, The Kethubah, Berlin, 1923. (*B.*)

12. *Eduyoth.* See Herman Klueger, Ueber die Genesis und Composition der Halachasammlung Edujoth, Berlin, 1898.
Aboda Zara. See article Abodah Zarah in Jewish Encyclopedia, Vol. I,
Aboth. See article Abot in Jewish Encyclopedia, Vol. I.
Arachin. See article Arakin in Jewish Encyclopedia, Vol. II. (*M.*)
Eduyoth. See J. H. Duenner, Ueber Ursprung u. Bedeutung des Tracktates Edojoth, *MGWJ* 20 (1871), 33-42, 59-77; H. Klueger, Genesis u. Composition der Halacha-Sammlung Edujot, Breslau, 1895. Cf. *MGWJ* 41 (1897), 278-283, 330-333; D. Feuchtwang, Der Zussammenhang der Mischna im Tractat Edujoth, Hoffmann-Festschr. 92-96.
Aboda Zara. See P. Fiebig, *ZDMG* 57 (1903), 581-604; N. Blaufuss, Roemische Feste und Feiertage nach den Traktaten ueber fremden Dienst, Nuernberg, 1909. (*B.*)

13. *Middoth.* See I. Hildesheimer, Die Beschreibung des herodianischen Tempels im Tractate Middoth u. bei Flavius Josephus, Berlin, 1877.
Khelim. See D. Graubart, Le véritable auteur du traité Kèlim, *REJ* 32 (1896), 200-225. (*B.*)

15. Addition to Bibliography in the foot note: F. Hillel, Die Nominal bildungen in der Mischna. Frankf. a. M., 1891.
H. Sachs, Die Partikel der Mischna, Berlin, 1897. (*M.*)
Note 1.
To the list of works on the language of the *Mishna,* must now be added Segal, Mishnaic Hebrew and its Relation to Biblical Hebrew, *JQR* XX, 617-737. (*F.*)

17. Chapter II.
The sixty treatises of the Tosefta are not identical with those

PAGE

of the Mishna. There is no Tosefta to *Abot, Tamid, Middot,* or *Kinnim.* As there are 63 treatises in the Mishna (as at present divided) that would leave only 59 treatises in the Tosefta. But as the Tosefta of Kelim is divided into three parts (called *Baba Kamma, Baba Mezia* and *Baba Bathra*) there are 61 treatises in the Tosefta. In the Erfurt Ms. which is the basis of Zuckermandel's edition the treatise *Arlah* is omitted, and there remain therefore in that edition but 60 treatises.

The nucleus of the Tosefta as now extant, is probably that of R. Hiyya. But the redactor has made use of several other sources. It is clear that very often the order of the laws in the Tosefta presupposes an earlier arrangement of the *Mishna,* than that found in our texts of that work. A complete discussion of the various theories advanced as to the nature of the Tosefta, is given by Malter, *JQR* 11, 75. (*F.*)

The various theories bearing on the origin and composition of the Tosephta and its relation to the Mishna are well summarized by Strack. See his Einl. p. 75 ff., and bibliography given there.

In the Tosephta, as we have it, are to be found side by side statements and supplements to the Mishna which cannot be understood without the latter and enlarged Mishnas including both the text of our Mishna and additions to it. The Tosephta frequently follows the arrangements of an earlier form of the Mishna, perhaps that of R. Meir. (See Brüll, Central Anzeiger, p. 75. Cf. Marx, *JQR* N. S., Vol. 13, p. 354.) The Amoraim made frequent use of the Tosephta texts in statements which, later, were quoted in their own names by their pupils. See Horowitz, Magazin, 1891, pp. 145-154. (*B.*)

18. Section 8.

The Tannaitic Midrashim are the various works consisting mainly of the explanations given by the *Tannaim* on the Pentateuch. These works were developed primarily in the second century, when the Rabbinic world was divided in two great schools, the School of Ishmael, and the School of R. Akiba. There were therefore two groups of such *midrashim* or commentaries. Each group consisted originally of four books, commentaries on Exodus, Leviticus, Numbers and Deuteronomy. There was no such commentary on Genesis because the main legal portions of the Pentateuch begin with Exodus XII, and it was in the legal portions of the Scriptures that these Sages were primarily interested.

It so happens that of the eight works that were extant only four have survived in a complete form. Two of these are from the School of R. Ishmael and two from that of R. Akiba. In modern times, however, scholars have succeeded in reconstructing partially on the basis of quotations in early books and manuscripts recovered from the Genizah, a large part of the lost books. We therefore now have the following books:

On the book of	From the school of R. Ishmael	From the school of R. Akiba
Exodus.......	Mechilta of R. Ishmael	*Mechilta of R. Simeon b. Johai.*
Leviticus......	Sifre	Sifra
Numbers.....		*Sifre Zuta*
Deuteronomy..	*Mechilta on Deuteronomy*	Sifre

The works marked in italics have only partially been recovered in modern times. It is somewhat confusing to the student that the two parts of the Sifre (that on Numbers and that on Deuteronomy) should be from two different schools. It is especially confusing since they are usually printed together. But it is only within the last generation that the true facts about these Midrashim have been discovered, mainly through the efforts and wide learning of the late Professor David Hoffmann.

The Mechilta of R. Ishmael is sufficiently described in the text. The Mechilta of R. Simeon b. Johai, has been published by Dr. D. Hoffmann, Frankfurt-a-M., 1905. It is ascribed to R. Simeon b. Johai, the disciple of R. Akiba, but has been revised at a later time, by Hezekiah, the son of the R. Hiyya who is mentioned in connection with the Tosefta. The methods of study in the two schools were quite different and this is reflected in a difference in the methods of interpreting the Biblical verses. In general it may be said that the school of R. Ishmael adhered to the thirteen hermeneutic rules laid down by their founder, while the school of R. Akiba, besides using some additional rules of interpretation laid special emphasis on the redundancy of words and letters. Naturally each school had its technical terms by means of which it is easy to distinguish the works of the one from those of the other.

For further studies on the Mechilta of R. Simeon b. Johai, see D. Hoffmann, Einleitung in d. Hal. Midrashim, 45-51; J. Lewy, Ein Wort u. d. Mechilta d. R. Simon, Breslau, 1889, and Ginzberg, in Lewy Festschrift, p. 403-436.

Mechilta or *Mechilta de R. Ishmael* are designations for the Halachic or Tannaitic Midrash on Exodus. According to Lauterbach (*JQR* n.s. Vol. II., 1920-21, pp. 169 ff.) Mechilta is a later name for the older, original name Sifre, which included the Midrash on Exodus. He also finds no proof from Talmudic and post-Talmudic literature in support of the interpretation of the term Mechilta to mean a Midrashic collection. Hence he assumes that Mechilta, originally meant, like Me-

PAGE

sichta, Tractates, and its correct pronunciation is Mechilata in the plural, since the Midrash so named is composed of many (9) tractates. The original arrangement according to tractates has been slightly changed later on and adopted to another arrangement according to Sidras. See J. Z. Lauterbach, The Arrangement of the Mekilta in Hebrew Union College Annual, Vol. 1, 1924, p. 427. The views as to the meaning of the name Mechilta expressed by J. Z. Lauterbach in *JE* 8, 444 f., are abandoned by him in the above mentioned article. (*B.*)

Of the Sifra, it must merely be added, that while it originates in its present form mainly from the school of R. Akiba, it contains large parts of the lost commentary of the school of R. Ishmael on Leviticus. The name *Sifra d'be Rab* may mean merely that these were school text books rather than they were primarily redacted in the academy of Rab. (*F.*)

20. Of the Sifre it must be remarked that since that on Numbers comes from the school of R. Ishmael while that on Deuteronomy comes primarily from the School of R. Akiba, they must be discussed separately. The Sifre on Numbers is more Halakic in character than the Mechilta of R. Ishmael, as has been pointed out by the author, but otherwise its earmarks are those of the works of that school. The authorities mentioned are those of that group, the technical terms are the same, and the methods of interpretation are the same. The latest edition of this work is that of Horovitz, Leipzig, 1917. At the end of that book is also published what remains of the *Sifre Zuta*, the commentary to Numbers from the school of R. Akiba.

The Sifre on Deuteronomy is the work to which the Talmud refers when it says that the Sifre is mainly the work of R. Simeon b. Johai. That is evident from the fact that a number of statements that occur anonymously in this book are elsewhere quoted as those of R. Simeon. But as the names of later authorities occur in it, it must have been redacted at a later time. According to Hoffmann (Einleitung z. d. Hal. Midraschim) its final redactor was R. Johanan.

As was the case with other books, there existed also a Midrash on Deuteronomy from the school of R. Ishmael. Fragments of this work have been found in the Genizah and were published by Dr. S. Schechter in the Jewish Quarterly Review. These fragments together with extracts from the *Midrash Ha-Gadol*, in which the Sifre and this work were found side by side, have been published by Dr. D. Hoffmann as the *Midrash Tannaim* to Deuteronomy (1908). (*F.*)

Baraita.

The *Baraitot* were traditions which were not included in the standard collections of Tannaitic statements studied in the academies. When the Mishna of R. Judah Ha-Nasi was ac-

PAGE

cepted by all groups as the authoritative basis for academic study, other traditions which had not been included, were studied "without" the academy. Some of these have been shown by Professor Ginzberg to have been of high antiquity. See his article *Baraita* in Jewish Encyclopedia, II., 513b.

Baraita is generally understood to be the technical term whereby Tannaitic traditions not found in the Mishna are designated. Such traditions are scattered in the Talmuds and Midrashim such as Sifra, Sifre, Mekilta, Tosefta, etc. In post-Talmudic times it became the general designation of those works which either originated or were claimed to have originated in the time of the Tannaim. See Ginzberg, *JE* 2, 514-516; Zunz, Gottesd. Vortr. 2nd ed., p. 52; Strack, Einl., p. 2. (*B.*)

22. On the Zugoth, see Frankel, Monatschrift, 1852, pp. 405-421. (*M.*)

The literature dealing with the important teachers of the Mishna and Gemara is surveyed by Strack, Einl., p. 116 f. (*B.*)

24. The differences between the School of Shamai and that of Hillel have been discussed by several scholars, e. g., Ad. Schwarz, Die Controversen der Schammaiten u. Hilleliten, Wien, 1893. Cf. D. Feuchtwang, *MGWJ* 39 (1895), 370-379; S. Mendelsohn, *JE* 3, 115 f.; Rosenthal, Entst. 2, 16-48; Strack, Einl., pp. 119-120. (*B.*)

Akabia b. Mahalalel was the subject of a study by J. Kaempf, *MGWJ* 5 (1856), pp. 146-158. See also S. Mendelsohn *REJ* 41 (1900), 31-44; *JE* 1, 302; Strack, Einl., p. 120.

Rabban Gamaliel the Elder (Spoken of as the teacher of the Apostle Paul. See Acts of the Apostles, 22, 3 and cf. 5, 34 ff.; see also Weiss Dor. II., 6) was the son of Hillel. The assumption that he was Hillel's grandson rests on a single prayer in the Talmud which states that Simon, the son of Hillel, must have been Gamaliel's father (Sab. 15a). See S. J. Kaempf, *MGWJ* 3 (1854), 39 ff., 98 ff.; Zipser in Ben Chananja, 1886, supplement 4; *JE* 5, 528-550; Strack, Einl., p. 120. As to his ordinances, cf. Hollander, Die Institutionen des Rabban Gamaliel, Halberstadt, 1869. (*B.*)

25. Paragraph 5.

The story that R. Simeon b. Gamaliel was executed by the Romans is found only in very late sources, such as *Masseket Semahot,* chapter 8. There is no historical corroboration of the legend and it is extremely doubtful. (*F.*)

R. Jochanan b. Zaccai. See Rosenthal Entst. 2, §25-30; A. Schlatter, Jochanan b. Zakkai, der Zeitgenosse der Apostel, Guetersloh, 1899. Cf. L. Blau, *MGWJ* 43 (1899), 548-561. (*B.*)

Rabban Gamaliel II. Cf. Landau, *MGWJ* 1 (1851-52), pp. 283-295, 322-335; A. Scheinin, Die Hochschule zu Jamnia u. ihre

PAGE

bedeutendsten Lehrer mit besonderer Ruecksicht auf Rabbi Gamaliel II., Halle, 1878; H. Reich, Zur Genesis des Talmud, Wien, 1892; *JE* 5, 560-562; A. Sulzbach, Gamaliel u. Josua, in Jeschurun 4 (1917), pp. 75-90. (*B.*)

26. *R. Eliezer b. Hyrkanos.* Cf. *REJ* 60, pp. 107 f; Ch. Oppenheim, Beth Talmud 4 (Wien, 1885), 311 ff., 332 ff., 359 ff.; Zarkes in Suwalski's Keneseth Hagedolah 4 (1891), pp. 65-71; Wassertrilling, Die halachische Lehrweise des Eliezer b. Hyrkanos in *JLB*, 1877, No. 22, f. 26; Halevy, Dorot 1e, 293-296; S. Mendelsohn, *JE* 5, 113-115; J. Bassfreund, *MGWJ* 42, (1898), pp. 49-57. The view of C. A. R. Tötterman (R. Eliezer ben Hyrkanos, Leipzig, 1877) that R. Eliezer leaned towards Christianity is without foundation or proof.

R. Joshua b. Chanania. Cf. Graetz, Geschichte, 4th ed. 4, 47-50, and Note 6; Halevy, Doroth le, 317-318, 386-392. See also L. J. Mandelstamm, Horae Talmudicae I., Berlin, 1860; Br. Meissner, *ZDMG* 1894, 194 f.; M. Guedemann, Religionsgeschichtliche Studien, Leipzig, 1876, pp. 131-144; Brüll, *Jhb* 3, 180. (*B.*)

27. *R. Elazar b. Azaria.* See J. Derenbourg in *MGWJ* 37 (1893), 395-398; *JE* 5, 97 f.; Halevy, Dorot 1e, 362-368. (*B.*)

28. *R. Tarphon* is said to have witnessed, while a youth, the temple and was strongly opposed to the Judeo-Christian worship (Sab. 111a). His permanent home was Lydda where an academy existed already three decades prior to the destruction of the Temple. See S. Klein, Die Beschluesse zu Lod, in Jeschurun, 5 (1918), 522-535 and *JE* 12, 56 f. As to the mention of Tarphon in early church literature cf. Freimann, *MGWJ* 55 (1911), 565 ff.; and S. Krauss, *JQR* 5 (1892-93), 123-134. (*B.*)

R. Ishmael (*b. Elisha*) and his academy are frequently mentioned in Midrashic literature such as the Mechilta, Siphra and Siphre. See Hoffmann, Einleitung in d. hal. Midr., p. 87 f.; M. Petuchowski, Der Tanna Rabbi Ismael, Frankfurt, 1894; *JE* 6, 648-650. (*B.*)

29. *R. Akiba.* As to fuller characteristics of this teacher, see L. Ginzberg's article, Akiba ben Joseph, in *JE* 1, pp. 304-310, and cf. Landau, *MGWJ* 3 (1854), 45-51, 81-93, 130-148; Is. Gastfreund, Toldoth R. Akiba, Lemberg, 1871; Halevi, Dorot 1e. 455-467, 620-629, 659-664; S. Funk, Ein palaestinenischer Gelehrter aus dem zweiten nachchristl. Jahrhundert, Jena, 1896; J .Hirsch, Religionsgeschichtl. Bedeutung R. Akibas, Prag, 1912; L. Stein, R. Akiba u. seine Zeit, Berlin, 1913; P. Billerbeck, R. Akiba, Leben u. Wirken eines Meisters in Israel. in Strack's "Nathanael," 1916-1918; G. J. Horowitz, Menorah Journal 1 (1915), pp. 227-236; Witkind, Chut Hameshulash,

PAGE

Vilna, 1877, pp. 9-60. (*B.*)

R. Jochanan b. Nuri. See *JE* 7, 213. (*B.*)

30. *R. Jose the Galilean.* See *JE* 7, 240 f. Cf. Ch. Oppenheim, Beth Talmud 5, 138-145, 172-176. (*B.*)

R. Jochanan b. Broka was the pupil of R. Joshua b. Chanania. See Frankel, Darke, p. 131; Brüll, Mebo, 137 f; *JE* 7, 210. (*B.*)

Ben Zoma who belonged to the second generation of Tannaim was a famous Darshan (expounder) who became absorbed in theosophic and mystic speculations and as a result, he is said to have become demented. (*B.*)

31. *R. Meir.* Cf. M. Joel, *MGWJ* 4 (1855), 88 ff., 125 ff.; Isaac Broyde, *JE* 8, 432-435. (*B.*)

Of R. Meir's origin little is known. It is by no means certain that he was not a native Palestinian. As to the story of his dying in Asia Minor, that forms the subject of a controversy between Weiss and Graetz on the one hand, and Halevy on the other. See Halevy, *Dorot Ha-Rishonim,* Ie, p. 790-6, and Weiss II., p. 132 and note. (*F.*)

Ben Azai really belonged to the second generation of Tannaim and flourished in the second century C.E. His untimely death is ascribed to the fact that he, too, was absorbed in the theosophic speculations of his time. (*B.*)

32. *R. Jehuda b. Ilai.* See M. Joel, *MGWJ* 6 (1857), 125-134; Lauterbach, *JE* 7, 343 f. As to his controversies with R. Nehemiah (see p. 35) and anonymous scholars, see Bacher, Rabbanan, Budapest, 1914, pp. 23-30. (*B.*)

33. *R. Jose b. Chalafta.* Cf. M. Joel, *MGWJ* 6 (1857), 83-91; M. Seligsohn, *JE* 7, 341 f.; Halevi, Dorot 1*e*, 781-788. (*B.*)

R. Simon b. Jochai. Cf. M. Joel, *MGWJ* 5 (1856), 365 ff., 401 ff.; M. Seligsohn, *JE* 11, 359-363; L. Lewin, R. Simon ben Jochai, Frankfurt, 1893. (*B.*)

34. *R. Elazar b. Shamua* was born in Alexandria and was a loyal disciple of R. Akiba whom he visited even while in prison in order to receive instruction. See *JE* 5, 94 f. Halevi, Dorot 1*e*, 806-809. (*B.*)

R. Jochanan the Sandelar. Cf. *JE* 7, 213 f. (*B.*)

35. *R. Elazar b. Jacob.* S. Horovitz (Siphre, p. xviiif.) is inclined to attribute to this school the authorship of Siphre Zutta. Cf. *JE* 5, 116. (*B.*)

R. Joshua b. Korcha. Cf. *JE* 7, 293. (*B.*)

R. Simon b. Gamaliel. Cf. Ph. Bloch, *MGWJ* 13 (1864), 81 ff., 121 ff.; Lauterbach, *JE* 11, 347 f.; Ad. Büchler, La conspiration de R. Nathan et R. Meir contre le Patriarche Simon ben Gamaliel, *REJ* 28, 60-74. (*B.*)

PAGE

36. *R. Nathan* usually called the Babylonian, because he had emigrated from Babylon to Palestine. *JE* 9, 176 f.; Halevi, Dorot le, 819-830; Bacher, Tannaiten 2, 437-453. (*B.*)

37. *R. Jehuda Hanasi,* also spoken of as Rabbenu (Yeb. 45a) or Rabbenu Hakadosh (Pes. 37a, Sab. 156a) because of his strict ethical conduct, was born in 135 C.E. Scholars differ as to the date. See Abr. Krochmal, Hechaluz, 2 (1853), 63-93; 3 (1854), 118-146; A. Bodek, Marc Aurel. Antoninus als Zeitgenosse und Freund des Rabbi Jehuda ha-Nasi, Leipzig, 1868; H. W. Schneeberger, The Life and Works of Rabbi Jehuda ha-Nasi, Berlin, 1870; S. Gelbhaus, Rabbi Jehuda Hanassi u. die Redaktion der Mischna, Wien, 1876; A. Büchler, Der Patriarch R. Jehuda u. die griechisch-roemischen Staedte Palaestinas; *JQR* 13 (1901), 683-740; Die Maultiere u. die Wagen des Patriarchen Jehuda I., *MGWJ* 48 (1904), 193-208; *JE* 7, 333-337; J. Fürst, Antoninus u. Rabbi, in Mag. 1889, 41-45; R. Leszynsky, Die Loesung d. Ant. Ratsels, Berlin, 1910; S. Krauss, Ant. u. Rabbi, Wien, 1910; La lagende de la naissance de Rabbi, *REF* 58 (1909), 65-74; Zifronowitz in Hashiloah 23 (1910), pp. 246-255; Strack, Einl., 133. (*B.*)
The most important of the teachers of R. Judah Ha-Nasi seems to have been R. Jacob b. Korshai (Jer. Sabbath 12.5, 10c). (*F.*)
Bar Kappara was actually named R. Elazar b. Elazar Hakappar and was the teacher of Hoshaya and of R. Joshua b. Levy. His academy was located in Ceasarea. See Halevi, Dorot 2, 114 ff., 123-126; Bacher, Tann. 2, 503-520; L. Ginzberg, *JE* 2, 503-505. (*B.*)

38. *R. Jose b. Juda* (*b. Ilai*) *I.* See Rosenthal, Entst. 3, §64; Bacher, Tann. 2, 417-421; *JE* 7, 243. (*B.*)
R. Elazar b. Simon. See *JE* 5, 104 f.; S. Krauss, R. Elazar ben Simon als roemischer Befehlshaber, *MGWJ* 38 (1894), 151-156. (*B.*)
R. Simon b. Elazar is often mentioned in Tosephta. See *JE* 11, 349. (*B.*)

39. *R. Elazar b. Jose* (*b. Chalafta*). *JE* 5, 99 f. (*B.*)
R. Chiya was also one of the editors of the Siphra. See Bacher, Tann. 2, 520-530; Baer, Mag. 1890, 28-49, 119-135; Is. Broyde, *JE* 6, 430 f. (*B.*)
R. Oshaya was also a disciple of Bar Kappara. He collected Mishnayoth. See Bacher, Pal. Am. 1, 89-108; Halevi, Dorot 2, 253-258; *JE* 6, 475 f. Cf. Bacher, The Church Father Origen and Hoshaya, *JQR* 3 (1890-91), 357-360. (*B.*)

40. *Expounders of the Mishna.* See the article Amora in Jewish Encyclopedia, Vol. I. (*M.*)

41. The question as to whether the Babylonian Amoraim knew the

Palestinian Talmud is still unsettled. Rabbi H. Hirschenson in Hamisderona II. (1888), pp. 97-120, is against such an assumption while Jerushalimski in Hakerem (1887), pp. 144-154, and Halevi, Dorot, Vol. 3, pp. 111-113, favor such a view. (*B.*)

R. Chanina b. Chama, succeeded R. Ephes in Sephoris. See Bacher, Pal. Am. 1, 1-34; Halevi, Dorot 2, 258 ff.; *JE* 6, 216 f. (*B.*)

R. Hanina b. Hama was a man of considerable importance even during the life of R. Judah Ha-Nasi. That scholar on his death-bed commanded that R. Hanina should succeed him as chief lecturer at the academy, while his son, Gamaliel, was to succeed to the Patriarchate. Thus for the first time since the days of Hillel was the office of the head lecturer separated from the Patriarchate. R. Hanina refused to accept the office, withdrawing in favor of the older R. Efes. (*F.*)

R. Gamaliel III. See Weiss, Dor. 3, 42-44; Bacher, Tann. 2, 554; Halevi, Dorot, 2, 19-23; *JE* 5, 562. (*B.*)

R. Judah II. See Bacher, Pal. Am. 3, 581; *JE* 7, 337 f; Halevi, Dorot, 2, 23-52. Cf. A. Marmorstein, L'opposition contre le patriarche R. Juda II., *REJ* 64, 59-66. (*B.*)

R. Judah III, the Patriarch, was likewise an Amorah but of a later date. It was he who commissioned R. Ame and R. Ashi to establish schools for children. See Graetz, Gesch, 4 ed., 4, 276 f.; Halevi, Dorot, 2, 333 ff.; Bacher, *JE* 7, 338 f. (*B.*)

42. *R. Ephes* was also Rabbi's successor as head of the Academy in Sephoris. See *JE* 5, 50 f. (*B.*)

Levi b. Sissi generally quoted as R. Levi. He should not be confused with another Amora bearing the same name who was a disciple of R. Johanan and a friend of R. Abba b. Kahana. See Bacher, Pal. Am. 2, 296-436; Tann. 2, 536-539; *JE* 8, 21; Halevy, Dorot, 2, 119-121; B. Ratner, Die Mishna des Levi b. Sissi, in Harkavy Festschrift, 117-122; A. M. Padua, Chut Hameshulash, Vilna, 1877, pp. 61-104. (*B.*)

R. Jochanan b. Napacha is said, by Sherira Gaon, to have been the head of the Academy for about eighty years. Halevi, Dorot, 2, 298-332, endeavored to prove that he was born in 175-180 C.E., and died in 290. See Bacher, Pal. Am. 1, 205-339; Graetz, Gesch. 4th ed., 4, 234-238, and Note 26; J. Bondi, *JLG* 1, 233-268; S. Mendelsohn, *JE* 7, 211-213; Loewenmayer, *MGWJ* 4 (1855), 285-294; 321-328; Horowitz, Literaturblatt d. jud. Presse, Berlin, 1871-1873; S. A. Jordan, Rabbi Jochanan bar Nappacha, Budapest, 1895; S. J. Zuri, R. Jochanan, Berlin, 1918; Witkind, Chut Hameshulash, Vilna, 1877, pp. 105-142. (*B.*)

R. Simon b. Lakish. See Bacher, Pal. Am. I, 340-418; Graetz, Gesch. 4 ed., 238-240; Halevi, Dorot, 2, 317-327; *JE* 11, 354 f. (*B.*)

PAGE

Note 1. To the list of books mentioned must be added now Halevi, *Dorot Ha-Rishonim,* the Jewish Encyclopedia, Hyman's *Toledot Tannaim v'Amoraim,* Bacher's *Agada der Pal. Amoraer.* (*F.*)

43. *R. Joshua b. Levi.* I. H. Weiss, in his Dor Dor III., p. 60, proves that Levi, the father of this Amora, was not the celebrated Levi bar Sissi, and that there were two teachers by the name of Joshua b. Levi.

R. Joshua b. Levi, one of the most prominent Palestinian Amoraim. A pupil of Bar Kappara, Judah b. Pedaya and R. Phineas b. Jair, he flourished during the first half of the third century C.E. He organized the communities in Southern Judea and visited Rome as collector of revenues for the patriarch. See Bacher, Pal. Am. 1, 124-194; Halevi, Dorot, 2, 293-296; *JE* 7, 293 f.; J. Rachlin, Toldoth R. Joshua b. Levy, N. Y., 1906.

R. Simlai b. Abba had frequent controversies with Christian dogmatists. Bacher, Pal. Am. 2, 552-566; Graetz, Gesch. 4 ed., 4, 241-246. (*B.*)

Abba Areca was called Areca because of his bodily form. See *JE* 1, 29 f.; Graetz, Gesch. 4 ed., 4, 256-261; Halevi, Dorot, 2, 210-223, 400-410; Funk, Jud. in Bab. I., 42-56; Umanski, in Graeber's Ozar Hasifruth (Krakau 1896), 159-212; J. S. Zuri (Schesak), Rab, sein Leben u. seine Anschauungen, Zürich, 1918; J. E. Melamed, Raban shel kol bene hagolah, Wilna, 1914. (*B.*)

44. *Mar Ukba I,* was Exilarch 210-240 C.E. See Hoffmann, Mar Samuel 74 ff.; Felix Lazarus in Brüll's Jhb., 10, 74-84; S. Funk, Jud. in Bab. I. 44, 63, and Note 4; *JE* 5, 589. Cf. Graetz, Gesch. 4 ed., 4, Note 27; Halevi, Dorot, 2, 246-252. (*B.*)

Mar Ukba II. was, like his grandfather, also Exilarch. See Funk, Ib. 107-109, and Note 4; *JE* 5, 289. (*B.*)

45. *R. Abbahu.* See S. Perlitz' monograph on Rabbi Abahu in Monatschrift XXXVI (1887); also article Abbahu in Jewish Encyclopedia, Vol. I. (*M.*)

R. Elazar b. Pedath. Bacher, Pal. Am. 2, 1-87; Halevi, Dorot, 2, 327-332; Bondi, *JLG* 1, 253-256; *JE* 5, 95 f. (*B.*)

R. Ame. See *JE* 1, 522 f.; Bacher, Pal. Am. 2, 143-173. (*B.*)

R. Assi. See Halevi, Dorot, 2, 232; *JE* 2, 231. (*B.*)

The R. Assi who lived his whole life in Babylon is said to have been inferior to Rab in knowledge of traditional teachings, but his equal in dialectic ability (Sanhedrin 36b). It can hardly be maintained therefore that he was in any real sense a disciple of Rab's. When Rab came to Babylonia he found this Rab Assi and Rab Kahana in Nahardea. Rab treated him with respect as an equal (Baba Kamma 80b, Kiddushin 44b). (*F.*)

PAGE

R. Chiya bar Abba and *Simon bar Abba.* See Graetz, Gesch. 4 ed., 4, 280 f.; Bacher, Bab. Am. 86 f.; Pal. Am., 2, 174-204; *JE* 11, 348. (*B.*)

R. Abbahu. See Perlitz, *MGWJ* 36 (1887), 60-88, 119-126, 177-183, 269-274, 310-320; Graetz, Gesch. 4 ed., 4, 282-287; Bacher, Pal. Am., 2, 88-142; K. Kohler, *JE* 1, 36 f. (*B.*)

46. There is no evidence to point to the election of R. Judah to the presidency of the Sura academy after the death of R. Huna. It is known, however, that while R. Hisda, who occupied toward R. Huna the relation of *Talmid-Haber,* i. e. a pupil who afterward had developed into a colleague, remained at Sura, most of R. Huna's other pupils left that city to continue their studies under R. Judah b. Ezekiel after the death of their master, R. Huna. When R. Judah died two years later, a number of the students of Sura returned and re-organized the academy under the presidency of R. Hisda. (*F.*)

R. Zeira I. (Must not be confused with a later Palestinian Amora who bore the same name and who was a pupil of R. Jeremiah.) L. Bank, *REJ* 38, 47-63, points out that there were three Amoraim bearing this name, two of whom were Babylonians. Cf. Graetz, Gesch. 4 ed., 4, 300-302; Bacher, Pal. Am. 3, 1-34; Halevi, Dorot, 2, 242 ff.; *JE* 12, 651 f. (*B.*)

R. Zeira. See JE 12, 652b; S. Berman in Luach Erez Yisrael X, 145-154.)

R. Huna. See Bacher, Babl. Am., 52-60; Graetz, Gesch. 4 ed., 4, 289-292; Halevi, Dorot, 2, 411 ff., 417 ff.; *JE* 6, 492 f. S. Funk, Jud. in Bab. 1, 111-116; A. Lapiduth in Rabinowitz's Keneseth Yisrael III., 297-303. Another R. Huna, son of R. Joshua was, like his contemporary, R. Papa (see above p. 51), a disciple of Raba and was rather rich as well as scholarly. See Bacher, Babl. Am., 141; Halevi, Dorot, 2, 505 ff.; *JE* 6, 493.

46. *R. Chisda.* A distinguished Casuist (Er. 67a); Bacher, Babl. Am., 61-71; Graetz, Gesch. 4 ed., 4, 297; Halevi, Dorot, 2, 421 f.; *JE* 6, 422 f.; Funk,, Jud. in Bab., 1, 116-123. (*B.*)

R. Shesheth. Graetz, Gesch. 4 ed., 4, 289; *JE* 11, 285 f.; Bacher, Bab. Am. 76-79. (*B.*)

47. *Rab Nachman b. Jacob..* I. H. Weiss, in his Dor Dor, contradicts the generally accepted statement that Rab Nachman had an academy in Shechan-Zib. (*M.*)

It is now generally agreed that while R. Abba b. Abuha, the father-in-law of R. Nahman, was a member of the family of the exilarch, and because of that fact and through his wealth very influential, he was not himself the Exilarch. (See Halevy, *Dorot Ha-Rishonim* II. 207a.) (*F.*)

R. Nachman b. Jacob made the Masora a subject of study in

PAGE

his home. See J. Mann, *JQR* ns. 8, 352 f.; Graetz, Gesch. 4 ed., 4, 298-300; Halevi, Dorot, 2, 412 ff.; Bacher, Bab. Am. 79-83; Funk, Jud. in Bab. 1, 123-132; *JE* 9, 143 f. (*B.*)

Rabba bar Chana was a nephew of R. Chiya. See Bacher, Bab. Am. pp. 87-93; Heilprin, Seder Hadorot II., 331; J. Z. Lauterbach, *JE* 10, 290 f. (*B.*)

Ulla. See Bacher, Bab. Am. 93-97; *JE* 12, 340. (*B.*)

48. *Hillel II*. Patriarch 330-365 was the son of Patriarch Judah III. See Graetz, Gesch. 4 ed., 4, 316-318; *JE* 6, 400; Bacher, Pal. Am., 3, 203 f. (*B.*)

R. Jeremiah. See Bacher, Pal. Am., 3, 95-106; Halevi, Dorot 2, 356-366; *JE* 7, 108 f. (*B.*)

R. Jonah and *R. Jose* were at 350 C.E. heads of the academy in Tiberias. See Bacher, Pal. Am., 3, 220-237; Halevi, Dorot 2, 366 ff.; *JE* 7, 230 f. (*B.*)

49. *Rabba bar Huna*. See Heilprin, Seder Hadorot, pp. 167b, 168a; Weiss, Dor III, 195; Bacher, Bab. Am., pp. 62-63; J. Z. Lauterbach, *JE* 10, 291. (*B.*)

Rabba bar Nachmani. See Heilprin, Seder Hadorot II., 332-334; Weiss, Dor III., 190-191; Graetz, Gesch. 4 ed., 4, 320-325; Bacher, Bab. Am., 97-101; Halevi, Dorot 2, 218-220, 435-440; Funk, Jud. in Bab. 2, 25-33; Lauterbach, *JE* 10, 292 f. (*B.*)

R. Joseph (*bar Chiya*). The redaction of the Targum on the Prophets is attributed to him. Bacher, Bab. Am., 101-107; Graetz, Gesch. 4 ed., 4, 325 f. Halevi, Dorot, 2, 440 ff.; Funk, Jud. in Bab. 2, 25-34. (*B.*)

Abaye. There was another Amora by that name who flourished in a former generation, and is characterized as Abaye the elder; see Jebamoth 24 a. (*M.*)

Abaye. See Graetz, Gesch. 4 ed., 4, 327-329; Bacher, Bab. Am., 107-113; *JE* 1, 27 f.; Halevi, Dorot, 2, 473-480; Funk, Jud. in Bab. 2, 34-40. (*B.*)

50. §5.

Raba is stated in the Talmud to have been born when R. Judah died (Kiddushin 72b). Since we know from the letter of R. Sherira Gaon (ed. B. Levin, p. 85) that R. Judah died in the year 299, it has been assumed by some that Raba was born in that year. But the correct texts of the Talmud read "Raba was born before the death of R. Judah," and that is the sense of the passage as it occurs elsewhere. We may therefore assume that Raba was born before 299. That view is corroborated by the several instances in the Talmud of discussions between Raba and R. Huna who died in 297. On the basis of these facts and others pointing in the same direction, it is now the generally accepted view that Raba was born about 280. (*F.*)

PAGE

Raba. See Bacher, Bab. Am., 108 f., 150, and Proöm, 88; Graetz, Gesch. 4 ed., 4, 329-335; J. A. Joffe, Mag., 1885, 217-224; Halevi, Dorot, 2, 473-480, 494-496; S. Funk, Jud. in Bab. 2, 66-77, and in *JLG* 4, 204-213; *JE* 10, 288 f.; Antokolski in Straschun's Heasif, I., Sect. 2, 194-201; A. Lapiduth, in Rabinowitz' Keneseth Yisroel III., 333-340. (*B.*)

Rab Nachman b. Isaac. See Bacher, Bab. Am., 133-137; Proöm, 88; S. Funk, Jud. in Bab., 2, 86-88; Halevi, Dorot, 2, 499-502; *JE* 9, 143. (*B.*)

51. *Rab Papa.* See Bacher, Bab. Am., 141-143; Graetz, Gesch. 4 ed., 4, 336 f.; Halevi, Dorot, 2, 505-517; *JE* 9, 510; Piyoska in Graeber's Ozar Hasifruth 5, 213-218; S. Funk, Jud. in Bab., 2, 89, 93. His disciple, Huna b. Nathan, who is frequently mentioned by R. Ashi, was, according to Sherira Gaon, Exilarch. See *JE* 6, 493 f. (*B.*)

Rab Ashe (d. 427 C.E.). See Bacher, Bab. Am., 144-147; *JE* 2, 187 f.; Graetz, Gesch. 4 ed., 4, 348-353; Halevi, Dorot, 2, 536-539; S. Funk, Jud. in Bab. 2, 98-110, 140-143. As to his relations to the Exilarch, Huna bar Nathan, see L. Bank, *REJ* 32, 51-55. (*B.*)

Rab Ashe. As to fuller characteristics of this distinguished Amora, see in Jewish Encyclopedia, article *Ashi,* Vol. II. (*M.*)

52. *Rab Zebid.* See *JE* 12, 645. (*B.*)

Rab Dime also called *Abudimi.* See Bacher, Pal. Am., 3, 691-693; *JE* 4, 603 f. Was head of the Academy in Pumbeditha. (*B.*)

Rafram bar Papa was a pupil of R. Chisda (Sab. 82a) in whose name he translated various halachik and haggadic sayings. See Weiss, Dor. 3, 207; Halevi, Dorot, 3, 85-89; J. Z. Lauterbach in *JE* 10, 307. (*B.*)

Mar Zutro who was on friendly terms with R. Ashe, died in 417 C.E. See Bacher, Bab. Am. 147. His successor, *Rab Acha bar Raba,* died in 419 C.E. *JE* 1, 278. (*B.*)

Rab Gebiha. See *JE* 5, 578; Funk, Jud. in Bab., 2, 102. (*B.*)

Amemar. See Bacher, Bab. Am., 146; *JE* 1, 490 f; Halevy, Dorot, 2, 515, 3, 68-73. (*B.*)

53. *Mar bar Rab Ashe.* See Graetz, Gesch. 4 ed., 4, 399 f.; Halevi, Dorot, 3, 93 f.; Bacher, *JE* 11, 665. (*B.*)

Rafram II. was a pupil of R. Ashi to whom he frequently addressed questions (Ket. 95b; Git. 42a). See Halevi, Dorot, 3, 85-89; J. Z. Lauterbach, *JE* 10, 307. (*B.*)

54. *Rabina (II.) bar Huna* was a nephew of Rabina I. See Halevi, Dorot, 3, 5-15, 100-102; J. Z. Lauterbach, *JE* 10, 300. (*B.*)

The period of the Saboraim, which is by most Jewish histo-

PAGE

rians limited to about sixty years, is one of the activities of which we know little, and yet to which we owe very much. According to R. Sherira Gaon in his letter (ed. Lewin, p. 70-1) it is the Saboraim who in many cases fixed the decisions of the law which are found in the Talmud, and added explantory remarks and editorial signs by means of which the study of the Babylonian Talmud has been rendered so much less difficult than the study of the Talmud of Jerusalem in which this editorial work is lacking. We also are told by R. Sherira that it was a tradition of the academy that the long passage in the beginning of Kiddushin 2a-3b dealing with the exact use of the words in that first Mishna and commenting on each of them, is of Saboraic origin. It may perhaps be assumed on the basis of this that the several other passages in the Talmud of like character are of the same origin. Besides those Saboraim mentioned in the text there should be named, R. Simuna, who is said by R. Sherira Gaon to have been the last of the Saboraim, R. Ahai who is mentioned by name several times in the Talmud and who has by some commentators erroneously been identified with the R. Ahai of Shabha of the eighth century, who wrote the *Sheeltot.* The period of the Saboraim was one of persecutions, at one time the academy at Pumbedita had to be closed because of the persecution of the Persian government. A criticism of the views of Weiss and Graetz on this period has been attempted by Halevi in *Dorot Ha-Rishonim* III., 2a-32a, but much of his argument has been refuted by Epstein in the Revue d. Etudes Juives, XXXVI., 222-236. See also Bacher in *JE* X, 610b. (*F.*)

Note 2. As to Rabina I., who died at about 420 C.E., see Halevi, Dorot, 2, 536-550, 3, 74-85. Cf. *JE* 10, 300. (*B.*)

56. *Agada.* The Agada of the Talmud served as a fruitful source for many subsequent collections of Jewish legends For a list of such works, see Strack, Einl. pp. 172-175. Cf. also Ch. 11, pp. 95 f., 100 ff.; H. S. Hirschfeld, Die hagadische Exegese, Berlin, 1847; J. Ziegler, Die haggad. Exegese und der einfache Wortsinn, *MGWJ* 43 (1899), 159-167, 241-250; N. J. Weinstein, Zur Genesis der Agada, Goettingen, 1901. Cf. Leop. Cohn, *MGWJ* 47 (1903), 89-96; Z. Frankel, Geist der palaest. u. babylon. Haggada, *MGWJ* 2 (1853), 388-398, 3 1854), 149-158, 191-196, 387-392, 453-361; Bacher, Rabbanan, Budapest, 1914; Die Prooem.; Leipzig, 1913. Cf. V. Aptowitzer, *MGWJ* 60 (1916), 184-188; J. Bergmann, Geschichte u. Legende, Schwarz-Festschr., 89-108; H. G. Enelow, The Significance of the Agada, Year Book, *CCAR* 24, pp. 283 ff.; Ginzberg, Legends of the Jews, 4 vols., Phila., 1909-13; Rapaport, Tales and Maxims of the Talmud, 2 vols., London, 1912;

PAGE

A. S. Isaacs, Stories from the Rabbis, N. Y., 1911; Berdizewsky, Der Born Judas, 6 vols. (*B.*)

58. Section 27.
As the author has shown above, bottom of p. 48, the statement that the Palestinian Talmud was completed *after* the Babylonian is not to be taken seriously. There can be no doubt whatever that the Talmud of Jerusalem was completed long before that of Babylonia. (*F.*)
The appellation *Talmud eretz Yisrael* is mentioned already by Saadia Gaon, but in later Gaonic literature, the Palestinian Talmud is also called Gemara d'eretz Yisrael and Talmud d'Maarba as well as other appellations. See Harkawi, Teshuboth Hageonim, Berlin, 1885 ff.; Hakedem II, 35; *REJ* 58, 183 f. (*B.*)

59. The *Babylonian Talmud* is so called to distinguish it from the Palestinian. In Gaonic literature it is frequently referred to as *Talmud dilan* "our Talmud." (*B.*)

63. *Aboth d'Rabbi Nathan.* See article under that heading in Jewish Encyclopedia, Vol. I. (*M.*)

64. The following are the seven "minor Treatises": (a) Sefer Torah, (b) Mezuzah, (c) Tephillin, (d) Zizith, (e) Abadim, (f) Kuthim, (g) Gerim. English translations of Kuthim are found in Nutt's Samaritan Targum, p. 68-72, and J. A. Montgomery's Samaritans, p. 196-203. (*B.*)

65. For a larger list of commentaries on the Babylonian Talmud, see Strack, Einl., pp. 160-167. (*B.*)

66. Paragraph 3.
The commentary on the last chapter of Pesahim which is ascribed to Rashi, has been shown by Dienemann, Lewy Festscrift, p. 259, not to have been the work of Rashi—at least not in its present form. That the commentary on Nedarim ascribed to Rashi is from another hand is well known. The commentary ascribed to R. Gershom, which is substituted after f. 22b, for that ascribed to Rashi, is by a group of later scholars at Mayence. For references on both these facts, see Freimann in Hoffmann, Festschrift, p. 122, and Epstein in Steinschneider, Festschrift, p. 116. (F.)
Note 4.
The Tosafot to most of the treatises are those of R. Eliezer of Touques. But there are a large number which were written by R. Perez or his pupils. These are the treatises, Bezah, Nedarim, Nazir, Sanhedrin, Maccot and Meila. The Tosafot on Sabbath, Erubin, Sotah and Menahot, are those of R. Samson of Sens, while those on Succah are a reworking of his Tosafot, in many cases preserving the original readings. The

PAGE

Tosafot on Yoma are those of R. Meir of Rothenburg. Besides these Tosafot which have been printed with the ordinary Talmud editions, there are a large number that have been printed separately, and many that are still in manuscript. (*F.*)

The *Tosaphoth* and their authors are described by M. Seligsohn, *JE* 12, 202-207; P. Buchholz, Die Tosaphisten als Methodologen, *MGWJ* 38 (1894), 343-359, 398-404, 450-462, 549-556; Ch. Tschernowitz, Schwarz-Festschrift (Hebrew section), pp. 9-18. (*B.*)

68. For a fuller list of commentaries on the Mishna cf. Strack, Einl., pp. 156-159.

For other commentaries on the Babyl. Talmud, see Strack, Einl., pp. 161-163, and the literature there referred to.

Parts of Moses Maimonides' commentary on the Mishna in Arabic have been published by Edw. Pococke and J. Dernbourg, and formed the subject for quite a number of Doctor dissertations. They have all been listed by Strack in his Einl., p. 157 f. Mention should be made of J. Gorfinkle's Eight Chapters of Maimonides on Ethics N. Y., 1912. Cf. A. Cohen, *JQR* ns. 4, 475-479; Husik, *JQR* ns. Vol. 4, p. 508 f. An earlier effort to translate the Eight Chapters was made in Raphall's Hebrew Review, Vols. 1 and 2 (1834-36). Maimonides' commentary on Pesachim was edited with a Hebrew translation by J. M. Toledano, Safed, 1915, under the title *Yede Moshe*, from a MS. Sassoon which the editor considered as an autograph. See Marx, *JQR* ns. 13, 360. It should be mentioned that Maimonides was not the first to write a commentary on the Mishna. There is extant a Gaonic commentary to Sedar Teharoth, the publication of which J. N. Epstein recently undertook for the Mekize Nirdamim and to which he has already published a critical introduction. See Malter, *JQR* ns. Vol. 13, pp. 102-105. (*B.*)

69. Section 2.

The commentary of R. Meir b. Baruch of Rothenburg on *Negaim, Ahalot, Parah and Mikvaot*, has been printed on the margin of the ordinary Talmud editions. Similarly a commentary ascribed to R. Hai Gaon on the Mishna of the Order *Taharot* has been printed in the late Talmud editions. Both R. Abraham b. David (Rabad) and his contemporary R. Zerahiah Ha-Levi (Provence, twelfth century) wrote commentaries to the treatise Kinnim. On the other hand the commentary on *Eduyot*, ascribed to R. Abraham b. David in the Talmud editions, has been shown not to have been written by him.

To the list of modern commentaries must be added the *Tiphheret Israel*, by R. Israel Lifschitz, a popular commentary which

PAGE

with that of Bertinoro, has been printed in all recent editions of the Mishna. (*F.*)

69. Of R. Asher b. Yechiel's commentary on Zeraim and Teharoth, the last two chapters of Sotah, Kinnim and Middoth is printed besides commentaries on various Talmudic treatises. See A. Freimann, *JLG* 12, 1918, 237-317. (*B.*)

70. Add to the commentaries on the Palestinian Talmud the following: Elijah b. Jehudah Loeb, Zeraim, Amsterdam, 1710; Baba Kama, Meziah and Bathra, Frankfurt, 1742; N. Trebitsch, Shelom Yerushalayim on Moed., Wien; Elijah Wilna, Hagaoth Yerushalmi, Konigsberg, 1858; A. Krochmal, Yerushalayim Habnuyah, Lemberg, 1868; D. B. Ashkenazi, Shaare Yerushalayim, Warsaw, 1866; Joshua Isaac of Slonim, Noam Yerushalayim, 4 vols., Wilna, 1863-1869. (*B.*)

71. Lunz has published part of the Talmud of Jerusalem to the order, *Zeraim,* with a commentary. Even more useful to the student is the *Ahabat Zion v'Yerushalaim,* by B. Ratner, containing numerous references to the early codes, compendia and responsa in which the Talmud of Jerusalem is quoted. This is of very great aid not merely in establishing the correct text, but very often the quotation is accompanied by a clarifying sentence of commentary which is very helpful. Unfortunately the author did not live to complete his work. The part published practically covers the orders *Zeraim* and *Moed.* Of great aid in re-establishing the text of the Talmud of Jerusalem, has proven the discovery of the Genizah. A large number of fragments bearing on the Jerushalmi have been found in that treasure. These have been published as *Jerushalmi Fragments,* by Professor L. Ginzberg (New York, 1909). The most recent edition of the Jerushalmi, that of Wilna, 1923, contains a republication of the commentary of Sirillo on the treatise *Berakot,* and has made use of the *Ahabat Zion v'Yerushalaim* of Ratner as well as of the Jerushalmi Fragments of Ginzberg. (*F.*)

Lehman's edition of Syrileio's commentary on P. Berachoth was severely criticized by R. Kirchheim in Hamagid, 1875, pp. 220 ff. For other commentaries, see Strack, Einl., p. 85. (*B.*)

73. The code of Mordecai b. Hillel, after its author, the *Mordecai,* has most often been published with Alfasi, but there is at least one edition (that of Riva, the text of which differs to some extent from that of the ordinary editions) in which the *Mordecai* is printed separately. It is compendium like that of *Asheri,* but can hardly be described as a commentary on Alfasi. (*F.*)

PAGE

74. Paragraph c.
R. Meir Ha-Cohen, author of the *Hagahot Maimoniot*, was, like R. Asher b. Jehiel and R. Mordecai b. Hillel, a disciple of R. Meir b. Baruk of Rothenburg. (*F.*)

75. Besides the commentary on R. Joseph Caro on the Tur, mention should be made of that of R. Joel Sirkes (Poland, 1561-1640), called *Bet Hadash* (usually abbreviated *BaH*. (*F.*)

77. Besides the MSS. mentioned in the text there should be noted the MS. of treatises *Rosh-Ha-Shanah, Succah and Yoma* in the Elkan Adler Collection (Cat. Adler 850) and that of *Aboda Zara* in the library of the Jewish Theological Seminary of America. The Munich MS. of the Talmud has been published in a photographed edition by Strack, while the Hamburg MS. containing the treatises of *Baba Kamma, Baba Mezia and Baba Bathra* has been published in a similar way by Goldschmidt. (*F.*)

78. Where the text of the Mishna published by Lowe differs from that of the ordinary editions and of the Talmud copies, it is very often supported by the reading of the Mishna in the Talmud of Jerusalem. This did not however justify Lowe in calling his text "that on which the Palestinian Talmud rests." So far as is at present known the Mishna as studied in Palestine and in Babylonia was practically identical.
Regarding the MSS. of the Jerushalmi, the Leyden MS. is one of those that lay at the basis of the first printed edition. Lunz found in the library of the Vatican a MS. of a portion of the Order *Zeraim*, which he utilized in his edition. There are other fragments in the libraries of Oxford, the British Museum and Paris. There is no MS. of the Talmud of Jerusalem known to exist in the Parma library at present. Of the Genizah MSS. which were utilized by Professor Ginzberg in his *Jerushalmi Fragments* mention has been made. (*F.*)

78 f. For additional interesting bibliographical material on the various editions of the Babylonian Talmud, see Strack, Einl., pp. 85-88. (*B.*)

80. End of Section 41. See M. Jastrow, The History and the Future of the Talmudic text. Philadelphia, 1897. (*M.*)

80. Section c.
Since the appearance of the last edition of this book, there have been printed two complete editions of the Palestinian Talmud. They are: The Pietrokow Edition, with all the commentaries that had appeared in the Shitomir edition, and also a new commentary by Ridbaz (R. Jacob David of Slutsk). (*F.*)

PAGE

To the editions of the Palestinian Talmud listed, the following should be added: The Krotoshin edition was reprinted in 1919 by L. Lamm, Berlin. A new edition of the text with all MSS., variants and commentaries was published in Wilna, 1922. The Shitomir edition was reprinted in Petrokow, 1900-02. (*B.*)

81. On the *Aruch* and its author, see Dr. H. G. Enelow's illuminating article, Nathan ben Jehiel, in *JE* 9, pp. 180-183. (*B.*)

LEXICONS.

Dr. D. G. H. Dalman, Aramaisch-Neuhebraisches Handworterbuch zu Targum, Talmud und Midrasch, Frankfurt, 1922.

S. J. Fuenn, Ozar Leshon Hamikra Wehamishnah, 4 vols., Warsaw, 1912-1913.

Jul. Fuerst, Glossarium Graeco-Hebraeum oder der griech. Woerterschatz der jued. Midrasch werke, Strassburg, 1891. Cf. Jos. Cohn, *MGWJ* 37 (1893), 283-285, 341 f., 429-434, 485-488, and J. Furst, Zur Erklaerung grieschischer Lehnworter in Talmud u. Midrasch, *MGWJ* 38 (1894), 305-311, 337-342.

Samuel Krauss, Griechische und lateinische Lehnwoerter in Talmud, Midrasch und Targum, Berlin, 1898. Cf. also his Zur griech. u. latein. Lexikographie aus jued. Quellen, in Byzantinische Zeitschrift 2 (1893), 493-548. (*B.*)

82. GRAMMARS.

Margolis, Max L. A Manual of the Aramaic Language of the Babylonian Talmud. München, 1910. Cf. Bacher in *JQR*, Vol. 1, n.s. pp. 265-273.

Albrecht, K. Neuhebraeische Grammatik auf Grund der Mischna. München, 1913.

I. H. Weiss, Mishpat Leshon Hamischna. Wien, 1867.

Abraham Geiger, Lehr-und Lesebuch zur Sprache der Mischna, Breslau, 1845. Cf. Graetz, Der Orient, Literaturblatt, 1844, No. 52; 1845, Nos. 1, 2, 4-6, 41, 42, 46, 48-50; J. Levy, Ibid, 1844, No. 51.

D. G. H. Dalman, Grammatik des juedisch-palaestinischen Aramaeisch nach den Idiomen des pal. Talmud, des Onkelostargum, etc. Second ed., Leipzig, 1905. (*B.*)

W. B. Stevenson, Grammar of Palestinian Jewish Aramaic. Oxford, 1924.

C. Chrestomathies.

S. A. Wolff, Mishna-Lese oder Talmud Texte religioes-moralischen Inhalts 2 Parts, Leipzig, 1866.

O. Lipschuetz, Mishnath Samuel. Lehr und Uebungsbuch fuer den ersten Unterricht in der Mischnah, I., Hamburg, 1867. II., Berlin, 1871.

Ch. D. Rosenstein, Mishna Berurah, Warsha, 1910. Beth Midrash, Wilna, 1907.

PAGE

Chananiah. *E. H. Kohen,* Sefer Sofoh Ahath Ragionamento sulla linqua del testo misnico. Reggio, 1819-22.
J. Goldmann, Gemarah lemathhilim, Wilna, 1902.
N. Lewin, Mebo Hatalmud, 15th edition, Wilna, 1913.
Ch. Tschernowitz, Kizzur Hatalmud I., Lausanne, 1919. II., Berlin, 1922. III., Leipzig, 1923. (*B.*)

83. The *Kelale Ha-Talmud,* by R. Bezalel Ashkenazi (Egypt, 17th century), has recently been published by Professor A. Marx (Hoffmann Festschrift, pp. 179-217). (*F.*)
I. H. Weiss in Beth Talmud, Vol. I. (1881), pp. 26-31, 53-60, 85-89, 115-122, 153-159, 181-184, and Vol. II. (1882), pp. 1-8, gives a fine bibliographical survey of the various introductory works to the Talmud. See also Strack, Einl., pp. 150-154. (*B.*)

84. The latest work on the history of Talmudic times in Hebrew, is Halevy, *Dorot Ha-Rishonim,* Berlin, 1901. 4 vols.
Of articles on the Talmud in modern languages, the most important are that by Schechter in Hastings Dictionary of the Bible, and that by Bacher in the Jewish Encyclopedia. The *Einleitung in den Thalmud,* by Herman L. Strack, which is mentioned in previous editions, has now been revised in the fifth edition, as Strack's *Einleitung in Talmud u. Midrasch,* Munich, 1921.
For an appreciation of that important work and for important additions, see a review of it by Professor A. Marx, *JQR* N.S. IX, 352 ff. (*F.*)

WORKS AND ARTICLES IN MODERN LANGUAGES.

84. *J. Bassfreund,* Zur Redaktion der Mischna, *MGWJ* 51 (1907), 291-322, 429-444, 590-608, 678-606.
L. Ginzberg, Zur Entstehungsgeschichte der Mischna, in Hoffmann, Festschrift, 311-345.
Z. L. Lauterbach, JE 8, 609-619.
S. Schechter, Talmud, in Hastings Dictionary of the Bible, 5 (1904), pp. 57-66. Reprinted in his Studies in Judaism, Third Series, Philadelphia, 1924.
W. Bacher, JE 12, 1-37.
M. Rodkinson, The History of the Talmud, N. Y., 1903.
W. Bacher, Traditionen u. Tradenten, Leipzig, 1914. (*B.*)

85. *H. Graetz.* An English translation of the whole work of this historian has been published by the Jewish Publication Society of America. The Talmudical period is treated especially in Vol. II. Philadelphia, 1893. (*M.*)

ENCYCLOPEDICAL WORKS.

86. *M. Guttmann,* Mafteah Hatalmud, Vol. I., Budapest, 1908. Vol. II., Budapest, 1917. An encyclopedical work in Hebrew. (*B.*)

PAGE

87. Similar to Zionim, but more complete is the book Ozar Leshon Chakamim by *Kalman Perla.* Warsaw, 1900. (*M.*)

88. Translations of the Talmud. See *E. Bischoff* Kritische Geschichte der Talmuduebersetzungen. Frankf. o. M., 1899. (*M.*)
The treatise *Abot* has been most recently translated into English by B. Halper, printed together with the Hebrew text and a Yiddish translation by Yehoash, New York, 1922. (*F.*)
R. T. Herford, Pirke Abot, in Charles' Apocrypha and Pseudepigrapha, Vol. II., Oxford, 1913, pp. 686-714.
C. Taylor, The Sayings of the Jewish Fathers, appeared in a second edition, 2 vols., Cambridge, 1897. (*B.*)
To the list of Mishna translations, the following should be added: Mischnajoth Hebr. Text mit Punktation, deutscher uebersetz., u. Erklaerung. Berlin-Frankfurt. Seraim von A. Sammter, 1887. Moed v. Ed. Baneth, 1920. Naschin v. Petuchowski 189 (incomp.). Nesikin v. D. Hoffmann, 1898. Kadoschim, J. Cohen, 189 (incomp.). Die Mischna Text, Uebersetzung u. ausf. Erklaerung, von G. Beer u. O. Holtzmann. Giessen, 1912 ff. Carelessly done, see Halper, *JQR* ns. Vol. 5, pp. 99-103, Vol. 6, 209-215; Vol. 7, pp. 408-414;. Aptowitzer, *MGWJ* 57 (1913), pp. 1-23, 129-152, 272-283; 58 (1914), 386-394.
H. L. Strack, Ausgewaehte Mischna-traktate nach Handschriften u. alten Drucken. Aboth 4 ed. (1915), Berakoth (1915), Joma 3 (1912), Sanhedrin Makkoth (1910), Aboda Zara (2nd edition, 1909), Pesahim (1911), Schabbath (1890).
J. Rosenfeld, Der Mischna-tractat Berachot uebs. u. erlautert. Pressburg, 1886.
P. Volz, Das Neujahrfest Jahwes (Laubhüttenfest), Tübingen, 1912. (*B.*)

ENGLISH TRANSLATIONS.

88c. *H. Danby,* Tractate Sanhedrin, Mishna and Tosefta...... translated with brief annotations. London, 1919.
W. A. L. Elmslie, The Mishna on Idolatry. Aboda Zara. Edited with translation and notes. Cambridge, 1911.
Greenup, A. W. The Mishna Tractate Taanith...with brief annotations. London, 1918.
—— Tractate Sukkah Mishna and Tosephta. London, 1921.
A. Lukyn Williams, Tractate Berakot, Mishna and Tosefta. London, 1922. (*B.*)

90. Latin Translations of single Masechtoth. *H. S. Hirchfield* Tractatus Maccoth cum Scholiis hermeneuticis, etc. Berlin, 1842.
German Translations, add: *Laz. Goldschmidt.* Der Babyl. Talmud herausgegeben nach der ersten Zensurfreien Bom-

PAGE

bergschen Ausgabe...uebersetzt und mit kurzen Anmerkungen verschen. Vols. I.-VIII. Berlin, 1897-1922.

M. Rawicz. Der Tractat Kethuboth uebersetzt. Frankf. o. M., 1898, 1900. (*M.*)

GERMAN TRANSLATIONS.

90b. *H. Georg F. Loewe.* Der erste Abschnitt des ersten Traktats von Babylonischen Talmud betitelt Brachoth....uebers. nebst Vorrede u. Einl. Mit drei Anhangen. Hamburg, 1836.

M. Rawicz, Der talmud. Traktat Chulin....nach der Wiener Ausgabe von Jahre 1865 uebertragen und kommentiert. Offenburg, 1908.

——, Der Tractat Kethuboth....uebertragen und kommentiert. Frankfurt, 1898, 1890.

W. Rothstein, Der Mischnatractat Megilla....uebersetz.... mit Anm. Tuebingen, 1912.

H. Bahr und *L. A. Rosenthal,* Der Mischna-tractat Sotah. Einl., Textausgabe und Uebersetz, Berlin, 1916.

G. Hoelscher, Sanhedrin und Makkot, uebers. und....mit Anm., Tuebingen, 1910.

G. Beer, Mischnatractat Sabbath uebers. u. mit Anm., etc., Tuebingen, 1908.

Wünsche, Bab. Talmud has been completed in four volumes, of which Vol. 3 and 4 appeared in 1889. (*B.*)

FRENCH TRANSLATIONS.

91. *L. Chiarini,* Le Talmud de Babylone traduit....et complété par celui de Jérusalem. 2 vols., Leipzig, 1831. (Only Berachoth.) (*B.*)

ENGLISH TRANSLATIONS.

92d. *Michael L. Rodkinson* is publishing The Babylonian Talmud, translated into English (partly abridged), of which the following volumes appeared: Volumes I. and II., Sabbath; Volume III., Erubin; Volume IV., Shekalim and Rosh-Hashana; Volume V., Pesachim; Volume VI., Yomah and Hagigah; Volume VII., Betzah, Succah and Moed Katon; Volume VIII., Megillah and Ebel Rabbathi; Volume IX., Aboth, Aboth de Rabbi Nathan and Derech Eretz; Volume X., Baba Kama; Volumes XI. and XII., Baba Metzia; Volumes XIII. and XIV., Baba Bathra. New York, 1896, 1902. (*M.*)

92. Palestinian Talmud.
Greenup, A. W. A Translation of the Treatise Taanith from the Palestinian Talmud. London, 1918. (*B.*)

93. Agada. Of his "Agada der Palastinischen Amoraer," *W. Bacher* published 1896, Volume II., Die Schueler Jochanan's, and 1899, Vol. III., Die letzten Amoraer des heiligen Landes.

PAGE

Archaelogical. *P. Rieger*, Technologie u. Terminologie der Handwerke in der Mischnah. Berlin, 1895.

H. Vogelstein. Die Landwirthschaft in Palestina zur Zeit der Mischna. Berlin, 1894. (*M.*)

ARCHAEOLOGICAL.

S. Meyer, Arbeit und Handwerk im Talmud, Berlin, 1878.

Gust. Loewy, Die Technologie u. Terminologie der Mueller u. Baecker in den rabbin. Quellen. Leipzig, 1898.

J. Krengel, Das Hausgeraet in der Mischnah, Frankfurt, 1899.

M. Winter, Die Koch-u. Tafelgeraete in Palestina zur Zeit der Mischnah, Berlin, 1910.

A. Sch. Herschberg, Cemer u. Pista zur Zeit der Mischna u. d. Talmuds. Hakedem 2 (1908), 57-80; 3 (1912), 7-29.

A. Rosenzweig, Das Wohnhaus in der Mischnah, Berlin, 1907.

Siegfr. Schemel, Die Kleidung der Juden im Zeitalter der Mischnah, Rostock, 1914.

S. Krauss, Baden u. Badenwesen im Talmud. Hakedem 1 (1907), 87-110, 171-194; 2 (1908), 32-50.

A. Sch. Herschberg, Yofi wehithyafutha shel haishah bizman ha-Talmud. Heathid 4 (1912) 1-56; 5 (1913), 102-4.

S. Krauss, Hakrah Hair we'hakfar batalmud. Heathid, 3 (1911), 1-50.

A Sch. Herschberg, Habarsauth bime ha Mishna wehatalmud. Hakedem, 3 (1909), 93-106. (*B.*)

94. Biographical. *M. D. Hoffmann.* Biographie des Elischa ben Abuya. Vienna, 1870.

F. Kanter.. Beitraege zur Kenntniss des Rechtsystems und der Ethik Mar Samuels. Bern, 1895.

A. Kisch. Hillel der Alte, Lebensbild eines jued. Weisen Prag 1889.

L. Lewin, R. Simon b. Jochai. Frankf. o. M., 1893. (*M.*)

To biographical literature on Hillel add:

Alex. Kisch, Hillel der Alte. Lebensbild eines juedischen Patriarchen, Prag, 1889.

G. Goitein, Mag. 1884, 1-16, 49-87.

Fr. Delitzsch, Jesus und Hillel, 3 Aufl. Erlangen, 1879. (*B.*)

95. Customs. *I. M. Cassanowicz.* Non-Jewish religious ceremonies in the Talmud (in proceedings of the American Oriental Society). New York, 1894.

Education. *E. Van Gelden.* Die Volkeschule des juedischen Alterthums nach Talmudischen Quellen. Berlin, 1872.

J. Lewit. Darstellung der theoretischen und practischen Paedagogik im juedischen Alterthum. Berlin, 1896.

Ethics. *M. Lazarus.* Die Ethik des Judenthums. Franf. o. M., 1898. Translated into English (the Ethics of Judaism) by Henriette Szold, 2 volumes. Philadelphia, 1900-1901. (*M.*)

PAGE

CUSTOMS.

W. Bacher, Zur Geschichte der Ordination. *MGWJ* 38 (1894), 122-127.

L. Loew, Die Horaa (Schriften 4, 158-166).

——, Der Titel Rabbi u. Rabban. Ib. 210-216. (*B.*)

EDUCATION.

Ad. Buechler, Learning and Teaching in the Open Air. *JQR* ns. 4, 485-491.

N. H. Imber, Education in the Talmud, in Report of the U. S. Commissioner of Education for 1894-5, pp. 1795-1820. Washington, 1896.

Sal. Stein, Schulverhaeltnisse, Erziehungslehre und Unterrichtsmethoden im Talmud. Berlin, 1901.

L. Wiesner, Die Jugendlehrer in der talmudischen Zeit. Wien, 1914.

B. Strassburger, Geschichte der Erziehung u. der Unterrichts bei den Israeliten. Von der vortalm. Zeit bis auf die Gegenwart. Stuttgart, 1885.

J. Ster, Die talmudische Paedagogik, Breslau, 1915.

E. van Gelder, Die Volkschule d. jued. Altertums nach talmud. u. rabb. Quellen. Berlin, 1872.

Jul. Lewit, Darstellung der theoret. u. prakt. Paedagogik in jued. Altertum. Berlin, 1896.

W. Bacher, Das altjuedische Schulwesen. Jhrb. *JGL* 6, 48-81.

B. Spiers, School System of the Talmud. London, 1898.

H. Gollancz, Padagogics of the Talmud and that of modern times. London, 1924. (*B.*)

ETHICS.

Salo Stein, Materialen zur Ethik des Talmud, Frankfurt, 1894. Cf. *MGWJ* 41 (1897), 239 f.

Albert Katz, Der Wahre Talmud-jude. Berlin, 1893.

M. Guedemann, Moralische Rechtseinschraenkung in mosaisch-rabb. Rechtssystem. *MGWJ* 61 (1918), 422-443.

J. Günzig, Pessimistische Gedanken in Talmud u. Midrasch. Maybaum-Festsch. 148-156.

Felix Perles, Zur Wurdigung der Sittenlehre des Talmuds in his Jued. Skizzen, pp. 100-110.

J. Z. Lauterbach, The Ethics of the Halakah in Year Book C.C.A.R. 1913.

S. Stein, Das Problem d. Notluege im Talmud. *JLG* 5, 206-224. (*B.*)

96. Exegesis and Bible Criticism. *W. Bacher*. Ein Woerterbuch der bibelexegetischen Kuntsprache der Tannaiten. Leipzig, 1899.

M. Eisenstadt. Ueber Bibelkritik in der talmud. Literatur. Berlin, 1894. (*M.*)

PAGE

GEOGRAPHY AND HISTORY.

Is. Levi, Les sources talmudiques de l'histoire juive. *REJ* 35 (1897), 213-223.

M. Weinberg, Die Organisation der jued. Ortsgemeinden in der talmud. Zeit. *MGWJ* 41 (1897), 588-604, 639-660, 673-691.

S. Krauss, Die Versammlungstätten der Talmud. Gelehrten. Levy-Fest. 17-35. (*B.*)

LAW (*a*) IN GENERAL.

97. *Ch. Tschernowitz,* Zur Erforschung der Geschichte des jued. Rechts. *Zeitsch f. verg. Rechtswissenschaft* 27, 404-424. (*B.*)
Law in General. *M. Mielziner.* Legal Maxims and Fundamental Laws of the Civil and Criminal Code of the Talmud. Cincinnati, 1898.

M. W. Rapaport. Der Talmud und sein Recht (In Zeitschrift fuer vergleichende Rechtswissenschaft, XIV. Band. Stuttgart, 1900.

Judicial Courts. *Adolf Buechler,* Das Synhedrion in Jerusalem. Vienna, 1902.

J. Klein. Das Gesetz ueber das gerichtliche Beweisverfahren nach mosaisch talmudischem Rechte. Halle, 1885. (*M.*)

(*b*) JUDICIAL COURTS.

H. P. Chajes, Les juges juifs en Palestine d l'an 70 a l'an 500. *REJ* 39 (1899), 39-52.

M. Waxman, Civil and Criminal Procedure of Jewish Courts. *JTS* Students' Annual I., N. Y., 1914, pp. 259-309.

(*c*) EVIDENCE IN LAW.

Z. Frankel, Die Eidesleistung der Juden, Dresden und Leipzig, 1840. 2nd edition, 1847. (*B.*)

CRIMINAL LAW.

J. Wohlgemuth, Das. jued. Strafrecht u. die positive Strafrechtsschule. Berliner-Fest. 364-376.

Joel Blau, Lex Talionis. Year Book, C.C.A.R., 26, p. 336 ff.

M. Aron, Histoire de l'excommunication juive. Nimes, 1882.

D. W. Amram, Retaliation and Compensation. *JQR* ns. 2, 191-211.

—— The Summons, a Study in Jewish and Comparative Procedure. Reprint from Univ. of Penna. Law Review, 1919. 18 pp. (*B.*)

98. Civil Law. *M. Bloch.* Der Vertrag nach mosaisch-talmud. Rechte Budapest, 1892.
Inheritance and Testament. *M. Bloch.* Das mosaisch-talmud. Erbrecht. Budapest, 1890.

M. Mielziner. The Rabbinical Law of Hereditary Succession. Cincinnati, 1900.

M. W. Rapaport. Grundsaetze des (talmudischen) Intestater-

PAGE

brechts und Schenkungen (in Zeitschrift fuer vergleichende Rechtswissenschaft XIV. Band, pp. 33-148). Stuttgart, 1900.

LAW OF MARRIAGE AND DIVORCE, ETC.

D. W. Amram. The Jewish Law of Divorce. Philadelphia, 1896. (*M.*)

Lewi Freund, Genealogien und Familienreinheit in biblischer u. talm. Zeit. Schwarz-Fest., pp. 163-192.

L. Blau, Die jued. Ehescheidung u. der jued. Scheidebrief, Budapest, 1911-12.

Is. Unna, Die Aguna-Gesetze, Jeschurun 3 (1916), 347-366.

Jacob Neubauer, Beitraege zur Geschichte des biblisch-talmudischen Eheschliessungsrechtes. Leipzig, 1920.

A. Sch. Herschberg, Minhage Haerusin Wehane'suim bizman hatalmud in Heathid 5 (1913), pp. 75-102.

W. Leiter, Die Stellung der Frau im Talmud. Amsterdam, 1918. (*B.*)

LAWS CONCERNING SLAVES, MINORS AND DEFECTIVES.

99. Laws Concerning Slavery. *D. Farbstein.* Das Recht der freien und der unfreien Arbeiter nach Juedish-talmudischem Recht. Frankf. o. M., 1896.

Is. Lebendiger, The Minor in Jewish Law. *JQR* ns. 6, 459-493; 7, 89-111, 145-174.

M. Bloch, Die Vormundschaft nach mosaisch-talmudischen Recht. Budapest, 1904.

J. Blau, The Defective in Jewish Law and Literature. N. Y., 1916.

R. Kirsch, Der Erstgeborene nach mosaisch-talmud. Recht. Frankfurt, 1901.

S. Rubin, Der naseiturus als Rechtsubject im talmud u. romischen Rechte. Zeitschr. f. vergl. Rechtwiss., 20 (1907), 119-156. (*B.*)

R. Grunfeld, Die Stellung der Sklaven bei den Juden nach bibl. u. talm. Quellen. 1886.

M. Olitzski, Der juedische Sklave nach Josephus u. der Halacha. Mag. 1889, 73-83.

D. Farbstein, Das Recht der unfreien u. der freien Arbeiter nach jued.-talm. Recht, etc. Frankfurt, 1896.

S. Rubin, Ein Kapitel aus der Sklaverei im Talmud. u. roem. Rechte. Schwarz-Fest. 211-229, 572-574. Das Talmudische Recht I. Buch: Die Sklaverei, Wien, 1920. (*B.*)

LINGUISTICS.

S. Mannes, Ueber den Einfluss des Aramaeischen auf den Wortschatz der Mishnah. Posen, 1899.

L. Dukes, Die Sprache der Mischna, lexikographisch u. grammatisch betrachtet. Esslingen, 1846.

PAGE

H. Rosenberg, Das Geschlecht der Hauptwoerter in der Mischna. Berlin, 1908.

Sal. Stein, Das Verbum der Mischnasprache. Berlin, 1888.

F. Hillel, Die Nominalbildungen in der Mischnah. Frankfurt, 1891.

H. Sachs, Die Partikeln der Mischna. Berlin, 1897.

C. Siegfried, Beitraege zur Lehre von dem zusamengesetzten Satze im Neuhebraeischen. Kohut Studies, Berlin, 1897, 543-556.

M. H. Segal, Mishnaic Hebrew and its Relation to Biblical Hebrew and to Aramaic. *JQR* 20 (1908), 647-737.

Felix Perles, Nachlese zum neuhebr. u. aram. Woerterbuch. Schwarz-Fest. 293-310.

J. N. Epstein, Zur Babylonisch-Aramaischen Lexikographie. Schwarz-Fest. 317-327.

Louis Ginzberg, Beitraege zur Lexikographie des Aramaeischen. Schwarz-Fest. 329-360.

S. u. M. Bondi, Or Esther oder Beleuchtung der im Talmud von Babylon und Jerusalem in d. Targumim u. Midraschim vorkomenden fremden bes. lateinischen Woerter. Dessau, 1812.

M. Schlesinger, Das aramaeische Verbun im Jerusalemischen Talmud. Berlin, 1889.

A. Liebermann, Das Pronomen u. das Adverbium des Babylonisch-talmud. Dialekts. Berlin, 1895.

I. Rosenberg, Das aramaeische Verbum im Babylonischen Talmud. Marburg, 1888.

M. Lewin, Aramaische Sprichwoerteh u. Volksspraeche. Berlin, 1895.

Z. Rabbiner, Beitraege zur hebr. Synonymik in Talmud u. Midrasch. Berlin, 1899. (*B.*)

100. Proverbs, Maxims. *Henry Cohen.* Talmudic Sayings. Cincinnati, 1895.

G. Taubenhaus. Echoes of Wisdom or Talmudic Sayings. Part I. Brooklyn, 1900. (*M.*)

MEDICINE, SURGERY, ETC.

M. Steinschneider, Schriften ueber Medizin in Bibel u. Talmud, etc. Wiener Klinische Rundschan, 1896, No. 25-26. Cf. J. Preuss, *ZHB* 1 (1896), 22-28.

Isr. M. Rabbinowicz, Einl. in die Gesetzbung u. die Medizin des Talmuds. Leipzig, 1883.

G. Nobcl, Zur Geschichte der Zahnheilkunde im Talmud. Leipzig, 1909.

NATURAL HISTORY AND SCIENCES.

Imm. Loew, Die Flora der Juden. Wien, 1924.

M. Z. Taksin, Yediath Hateba Shebatalmud. Warsaw, 1907.

PAGE

S. Alexander, Beitraege zur Ornithologie Palaestina's auf Grund der alten hebraeischen Quellen. Berlin, 1915. (*B.*)

101. Popular Treatises. *Arsene Darmstetter.* The Talmud (translated from the French by Henriette Szold). Philadelphia, 1897.
H. Goitein. Anklaeger und Vertheidiger des Talmud. Frankf. o. M., 1897.
J. Eschelbacher. Zwei Reden ueber den Talmud. Frankf. o. M., 1897. (*M.*)

123. On Halacha l'Moshe Mi-Sinai, see also Schorr in Hechaluz, Vol. IV., pp. 28-49. In the Mishna this term occurs only three times, namely: Peah, ii, 6; Eduyoth, viii, 7; and Yedayim, iv, 6. (*M.*) See also Bacher in Studies in Jewish Literature...in honor of K. Kohler, pp. 56-70. (*B.*)

128. The earliest commentary on the thirteen rules of R. Ishmael of which we know, is that by Saadia Gaon (tenth century). It was published by Schechter in *Bet Talmud,* IV., 237, and in the Oeuvres Completes, IX., 73-83. The most important recent work on the subject has been that of A. Schwartz, in his books, *Die Hermeneutische Analogie,* Vienna, 1897, and *Die Hermeneutische Syllogismus,* ib. 1901. (*F.*)

129. Add to Literature on Hermeneutic Rules the following:
Adolf Schwarz. Die Hermeneutische Analolgie in der Talmudischen Literatur. Vienna, 1899. Cf. L. Blau, *REJ* 36, 150-159.
Adolf Schwarz. Der Hermeneutische Syllogismus in der Talmudischen Literatur. Vienna, 1901. Cf. Wachstein, *MGWJ* 1902, 53-62. (*M.*)

140. Instead of the last eight lines of this and the first three lines of page 141, read the following:
The fallacy of this inference is obvious. It postulates that one may enter marriage only with such a woman in whose place he can marry her mother, hence when that mother is either a widow or a divorced woman. But according to this postulate the high priest could not enter marriage at all, since he was forbidden to marry either a widow or a divorced woman. Rabbi Gamaliel therefore answered the questioner: "Go thou and take care of the high priest in regard to whom it is written, 'Only a virgin from among his people he shall marry;' I shall then take care of all Israel." (*M.*)

PART III.

191. Chapter 1.
The best work of reference on the subject of the Terminology of the Talmud for the advanced student is Bacher's "Die

PAGE

Exegetische Terminologie der Judischen Traditions-literatur. (*F.*)

195. Section 11.

In Hoffmann Festschrift (p. 311) Professor Ginzberg has pointed out that the words "en ben" which occur as the beginning of a number of Mishnayot in *Megillah* are a trace of the time when rules of law were arranged not always in accordance with their subject but often in accordance with the terms of their formulation . There are a number of other such collections still preserved in our Mishna. (*F.*)

197. Section 15.

The terms *lakathillah* and *b'diabad* require somewhat further elucidation. They are usually mentioned in connection with ritual law. Some of the details of a ceremony are essential to its performance, and some ought to be observed but are not absolutely essential. For instance, in slaughtering fowl, one ought to cut both the esophagus and the trachea; nevertheless if one has cut either of them, the fowl may be eaten. The manner in which the ceremony ought to be performed is called *lakathillah;* those elements of the ceremony without which it cannot be performed at all are called *b'diabad.* (*F.*)

220. Sections 59, 60 and 61.

For a further discussion of these terms see Bacher, *Exeg. Termin.*, II., 238-240. T'nan is to be translated "We have studied." *Tnena* is an older form of the same word; *Tania* is a passive participle of the same root, and is to be translated "It is studied" or "It is handed down by tradition." (*F.*)

Chapter IX.

The expression "hewe" has been discussed by Bacher, *op. cit,* II., 49, and by Ginzberg in Schwarz Festschrift, p. 347. (*F.*)

ADDITIONAL BIBLIOGRAPHY

A list of the important commentaries on the Talmud that have thus far been printed is given by Freimann, in the Hoffmann Festschrift, pp. 115 ff. He also gives a list of the MSS. of commentaries to the Talmud and the various libraries in which they are to be found.

English.

A. Cohen, The Babylonian Talmud, Tractate *Berakot,* translated into English for the first time, with Introduction, Commentary, Glossary and Indices, Cambridge, 1921.

S. Krauss, The Mishnah Treatise Sanhedrin, with Introduction, Notes and Glossary, Leyden, 1909.

AGADA.

W. Bacher, Rabbanan. Die Gelehrten der Tradition, Budapest, 1914.

W. Bacher, Die Proömien der alten jüdischen Homilie, Leipzig, 1913.

In Hebrew (Compendia, Collections, Indices).

En Jacob, by R. Jacob Ibn Habib, translated in part into English by J. Glick, 5 vols., New York, 1918-1922.

Sefer Ha-Agadah, by J. Ravnitski and Ch. N. Bialik, Vols. I., II., III., Cracow, 1908-10.

Ozar Ha-Midraschim, by J. D. Eisenstein, New York, 1915.

Ozar Kol, by K. W. Perla, Vol. I., Lublin, 1909.

Ozar Agadot, by G. Muller, Vols. I., II., III., Pressburg, 1877; Vol. IV., Paks, 1901.

Bet Vaad La-Hakamim, by A. Hyman, London, 1902.

Zikron Torath Mosheh, by Moses Figo, Constantinople, 1552.

Yefeh Mareh, by S. Jaffe (a collection of the aggadic statements of the Palestinian Talmud), Constantinople, 1587, Amsterdam, 1727.

Asher Feldman, The Parables and Similes of the Rabbis. Cambridge, 1924.

M. Gaster, The Exempla of the Rabbis. London-Leipzig, 1924.

Yalkut Eliezer, by E. Z. Sofer, Pressburg, 1874.

Mafteah Ha-Aggadot, by Mordecai b. Benjamin, Wilna, 1880.

Zion Lidaresh, by S. P. Frankel, Krotoschin, 1858.

Rab Pe'alim, by Abraham Wilna, Warsaw, 1894.

Z. Fränkel, Geist der paläst. u. babyl. Haggada, *MGWJ* 1853, 1854.

M. Grünbaum, Neue Beitrage zur semit. Sagenkunde, Leyden, 1893.

M. Grünbaum, Aufsätze zur Sprach u. Sagenkunde, Berlin, 1901.

H. S. Hirschfeld, Die Halachische Exegese, Berlin, 1847.

S. Hurwitz, Pygmy Legends in Jewish Literature, *JQR,* NS, VI.

N. J. Weinstein, Zur Genesis der Agada, Vol. II., Die Alexandrinische Agada, Göttingen, 1901.

I. Ziegler, Die Königsgleichnisse des Midrasch beleuchtet durch die römische Kaiserzeit, Breslau, 1903.

Smaller Collections.

B. Beer, Leben Abrahams nach Affassung der jüdischen Sage, Leipsic, 1859.

P. Billerbeck, Abrahams Leben u. Bedeutung...nach Auffassung der alteren Haggada, Strack's Nathanel, 1899-1900.

R. Faerber, König Salomon in der Tradition, Vienna, 1902.

R. Fischer, Daniel u. seine Drei Gefährten in Talmud u. Midrasch, Frankfort-am-M., 1906.

J. S. Renzer, Hauptpersonen des Richterbuches in Talmud u. Midrasch, Vol. I., Samson, Berlin, 1902.

A. Rosner, Davids Leben u. Charakter nach Talmud u. Midrasch, Oldenberg, 1908.

G. Salzberger, Die Salomo-Sage in der semit. Literatur, Berlin, 1907.

G. Salzberger, Salomos Tempelbau u. Thron in der semit. Sagen literatur, Berlin, 1912.

ARCHAEOLOGY.

General.

S. Krauss, Talmudische Archäologie, Vols. I., II., III., Leipzig, 1910-1912. Hebrew translation, Wien, 1923.

Particular Phases.

J. Krengel, Das Hausgerät in der Mishnah, Vol. I., Frankfort-am-M., 1899.

Adolph Rosenzweig, Kleidung u. Schmuck in biblischen u. Talmudischen Schrifttum, Berlin, 1905.

Arthur Rosenzweig, Das Wohnhaus in der Mishnah, Berlin, 1907.

M. Winter, Die Koch- u. Tafelgeräte in Palästina zur Zeit der Mishna, Berlin, 1911.

BIOGRAPHICAL AND HISTORICAL.

Hebrew Works.

Seder Ha-Dorot, by Jehiel Hailperin, Warsaw, 1882.

Mebo Ha-Mishna, by J. Brull, Frankfort-am-M., 1876.

Darke Ha-Mishna, by Z. Frankel, Leipsic, 1859.

Mebo Ha-Jerushalmi, by Z. Frankel, Breslau, 1870.

Dor Dor Ve-Dorshav, by I. H. Weiss, Vienna, 1871, and later.

Dor Jesharim, by J. Lifschitz, Petrokow, 1907.

Dorot Ha-Rishonim, by I. Halevi, Pressburg, 1896-1918.

Toledot Israel, by W. Yavitz, Vol. VI., Cracow, 1907; VII. and VIII., Berlin, 1909-12; IX., London, 1922.

IN MODERN LANGUAGES.

Bacher's works on the Agada mentioned above.

M. Braunschweiger, Die Lehrer der Mishnah, Frankfort-am-M., 1903.

S. Funk, Die Juden in Babylonien, Berlin, 1902.

H. Tj. de Graaf, De Joodsche Wetgeleerden in Tiberias van 70-400 n.c., Groningen, 1902.

Jewish Encyclopedia, Under the names of the individual scholars.

H. Kottek, Die Hochshulen in Palastina u. Babylonien, *JJLG*, 1905.

CHRONOLOGY AND CALENDAR.

J. von Gumpach, Üben den altjüdischen Kalendar, Brussels, 1848.

A. Kistner, Der Kalender der Juden, Karlsruhe, 1905.

D. Sidersky, Étude sur l'origine astronomique de la chronologie juive, Paris, 1914. Cf. *MGWJ* 1914, 382-384.

E. Mahler, Handbuch der jüdischen Chronologie, Leipzig, 1916.

CUSTOMS.

F. I. Grundt, Die Trauergebräuche der Hebräer, Leipsic, 1868.

S. Klein, Tod u. Begräbnis in Palästina zur zeit der Tannaiten, Berlin, 1908. Cf. *REJ* LX., 110-113.

J. L. Palache, Das Weinen in jüd. Literatur, *ZDMG* 1916, 251-6.

J. Rabbinowicz, Der Todtenkultus bei den Juden, Frankfort-am-M, 1889.

Adolph Büchler, Das Ausgiessen von Wein u. Öl als Ehrung bei den Juden; *MGWJ*, 1905, 12-40.

A. Wünsche, Der Kuss in Bibel, Talmud u. Midrasch, Breslau, 1911.

EDUCATION.

W. Bacher, Das altjüdische Schulwesen, *JJLG* VI., pp. 48-81.

E. van Gelder, Die Volksschule des jüd. Altertums nach talmud u. rabbinischen Quellen, Berlin, 1872.

J. Lewit, Darstellung der theoret. u. prakt. Pädagogik im jüd. Altertum, Berlin, 1896.

GEOGRAPHY.

W. Bacher, Rome dans le T. et Midrash, *REJ*, Vol. XXXIII., 187-196.

P. Berto, La temple de Jérusalem, *REJ*, Vol. LIX., 14-35, 161-187; LX., 1-23.

I. Goldhor, Admat Kodesh, Jerusalem. 1913.

S. Klein, Beiträge zur Geographie u. Geschichte Galiläas, Leipsic, 1909.

S. Krauss, Les divisions administratives de la Palestine à l'époque romaine, *REJ*, Vol. XLVI., 218-236.

ETHICS.

H. G. Enelow, *Kawwana*, The Struggle for Inwardness in Judaism, in Studies in Jewish Literature....in honor of Kaufmann, Kohler. pp. 82-107.

M. Güdemann, Moralische Rechtseinschränkung im mosaisch-rabbinischen Rechtssytem, *MGWJ* 1917, pp. 422-443.

A. Katz, Der Wahre Talmudjude, Berlin, 1893.

K. Kohler, Die Nächstenliebe in Judentum, Cohen Festschrift, pp. 469-480.

A. Kohut, The Ethics of the Fathers. A series of lectures, New York, 1885. New edition edited by Dr. B. A. Elzas, New York, 1920.

J. Z. Lauterbach, The Attitude of the Jew, etc. Yearbook C. C. A.R., 1921.

Luzzatto, Israelitische Moraltheologie, deutsch von L. E. Igel, Breslau, 1870.

S. J. Moscoviter, Het nieuve Testament en de Talmud, Rotterdam, 1884.

PAGE

H. Oort, Evangelie en Talmud uit het oogpunt der zedelijkheid vergeleken, Leyden, 1881.

H. Oort, The Talmud and the New Testament, London, 1883.

F. Perles, Zur Würdigung der Sittenlehre des Talmuds, in his Jüdische Skizzen, Leipsic, 1912, pp. 114-124.

J. Scheftelowitz, Grundlagen einer Jüdischer Ethik, *MGWJ* 1912, pp. 129-146, 359-378, 478-495.

M. Steckelmacher, Etwas über die "leichten u. schweren" Gebote, Schwarz Festschrift, pp. 259-268.

S. Stein, Materialen zur Ethik des Talmuds, Vol. I., Die Pflichtenlehre, Frankfurt-am-M., 1894.

S. Stein, Das Problem d. Notlüge im Talmud, *JJLG*, V., pp. 206-224, 384.

INDUSTRY AND ECONOMICS.

F. Goldmann, Der Ölbau in Palästina in der tannäit. Zeit; *MGWJ* 1906, 563-580, 707-728; 1907, 17-40, 129-141.

S. Klein, Weinstock, Feigenbaum u. Syckomore in Palästina in Schwarz Festschrift, 389-402.

E. Lambert, Les changeurs et la monnaie en Palestine, *REJ*, Vol. LI., 217-244; LII., 24-42.

J. Z. Lauterbach, Weights and Measures, *JE* XII., 483- 490.

M. Mainzer, Der Jagd, Fischfang u. Bienenzucht bei den Juden in der tannäit. Zeit, Frankfort-am-M., 1910.

S. Meyer, Arbeit u. Handwerk im Talmud, Berlin, 1878.

P. Rieger, Technologie u. Terminologie der Handwerke in der Mischnah, Vol. I.: Spinnen, Färben, Weben, Walken, Berlin, 1894.

M. Salmonoski, Gemüsebau u. Gewächse in Palästina zur Zeit der Mishnah, Berlin, 1911.

M. B. Schwalm, L'Industrie et les artisans juifs à l'epoque de Jésus, Paris, 1909.

H. Voglestein, Die Landwirtschaft in Palästina zur Zeit der Mishnah, Berlin, 1894.

LAW.

a. In General.

M. Eschelbacher, Recht und Billigkeit in der Jurisprudenz des Talmuds, Cohen Festschrift, pp. 501-514.

S. Gandz, Recht (Monumenta Talmudica, Vol. II.), Vienna, 1913.

J. Kohler, Darstellung des talmudischen Rechtes, Zeitschrift fur vergleich. Rechtswissenschaft, Vol. 20, 1908, pp. 161-264. Cf. V. Aptowitzer, *MGWJ*, 1908, 37 ff.

M. Mielziner, Legal Maxims and Fundamental Laws of the Civil and Criminal Code of the Talmud, Cincinnati, 1898.

A. Perls, Der Minhag im Talmud, Lewy Festschrift, pp. 66-75.

M. W. Rappaport, Der Talmud u. sein Recht, Berlin, 1912.

Courts.

PAGE

L. Fischer, Die Urkunden im Talmud, zugestellt, erklärt, und mit den Ausgrabungen verglichen. Berlin, 1912; *JJLG,* IX, 47-197.

S. Funk, Die Gerichtshofe in nachexil. Judentum, *MGWJ,* 1911, pp. 33-42, 699-712. Cf. A. Karlin, *MGWJ,* 1913, 24-31; Funk, pp. 501-506.

H. Heinemann, Das Königtum nach biblisch-talmudischer Rechtsauffassung, *JJLG,* X., 115-190.

Evidence.

J. Blumenstein, Die Verschiedenen Eidesarten nach mosaisch-talmudischen Rechte u. die Fälle ihrer Anwendung, Frankfurt-am-M., 1883.

Z. Frankel, Die Eidesleistung der Juden, Dresden, 1840.

J. Horovitz, Zur rabb. Lehre von den falschen Zeugen, Frankfurt-am-M., 1914.

J. Klein, Das Gesetz uber das gerichtliche Beweisverfahren nach mosaisch-thalmudischen Rechte. 1885.

A. Gulak, Yesode hamishpat haibri. 4 vols., Berlin, 1922.

J. S. Zuri, Mishpat hatalmud. Warsaw, 1921.

CRIMINAL LAW.

D. W. Amram, Retaliation and Compensation, *JQR,* NS, II., pp. 191-211.

M. Bloch, Das mosaisch-talmud. Strafgerichtsverfahren, Budapest, 1901. Cf. *MGWJ,* 1902, 381-388.

A. Buchler, Die Todesstrafen der Bibel u. der jüdischen nachbiblischen Zeit, *MGWJ,* 1906, pp. 539-562, 644-706.

A. Buchler, L'enterrment des criminels d'après le Talmud et le Midrasch, *REJ* 46: 74-88.

A. Buchler, Die Strafe der Ehebrecher in der nachexilischen Zeit, *MGWJ,* 1911, pp. 196-219.

J. Goitein, Das Vergeltungsprinzip im bibl. u. talmud. Strafrechte, Mag. 1892-3.

J. Horovitz, Auge um Auge, Zahn um Zahn, Cohen Festschrift, pp. 609-658.

S. Mandl, Der Bann, Brunn, 1898. Cf. *MGWJ,* 1898, 524 f.

S. Ohlenburg, Die Bibl. Asyle in talmud. Gewande, Munich, 1895.

A. Perls, Der Selbstmord nach der Halakha, *MGWJ,* 1911, 287-295.

I. Steinberg, Die Lehre vom Verbrechen im Talmud, Stuttgart, 1910. Cf. *MGWJ,* 1916, 429-431.

Ch. Tschernowitz, Der Einbruch nach bibl. u. talmud. Rechte: Zeitschrift für vergleichende Rechtswissenschaft, XXV., pp. 443-458.

Ch. Tschernowitz, Der Raub nach bibl. talmudischem Recht, *Zeitschrift für Vergleichende Rechtswissenschaft,* XXVII., 187-196.

H. Vogelstein, Notwehr nach mosaisch.-talmud. Recht, *MGWJ,* 1904, pp. 513-533.

J. Weismann, Talion u. öffentliche Strafe im mosaisch. Rechte, Leipzig, 1913.

CIVIL LAW.

L. Auerbach, Das jüdische Obligationenrecht, Berlin, 1871.

M. Bloch, Das mosaisch-talmud. Erbrecht, Budapest, 1890.

M. Bloch, Der Vertrag nach mosaisch-talmud. Rechte, Budapest, 1893.

H. B. Fassel, Das mosaisch-rabbin. Civilrecht, 2 vols., Grosskanischa, 1852.

N. Hurewitsch, Die Haftung des Verwahrers nach talmud. Recht, Zeitschrift für vergleichende Rechtswissenschaft, XXVIII., 425-439.

I. Lewin, Die *Chasaka* des talmud. Rechts, Stuttgart, 1912.

J. Marcuse, Das Biblisch-talmud. Zinsenrecht, Konigsberg, 1895.

N. A. Nobel, Studien zum talmud. Pfandrecht, Cohen Festschrift, pp. 659-668.

A. Wolff, Das jüdische Erbrecht, Budapest, 1890.

JEWISH LAW OF MARRIAGE AND DIVORCE.

David W. Amram, The Jewish Law of Divorce, Philadelphia, 1896.

J. Bergel, Die Eheverhältnisse der alten Juden im Vergleiche mit den griechishen u. römischen, Leipsic, 1881.

A. Billauer, Grundzüge des biblisch-talmud. Eherechts, Berlin, 1910.

L. Blau, Zur Gesch. des jüd. Eherechts, Schwarz Festschrift, pp. 193-209.

A. Büchler, Familienreinheit u. Familienmakel in Jerusalem vor dem Jahre 70, Schwarz Festschr., pp. 133-162.

L. Fischer, Die Urkunden im T. Eherechtliche Urkunden, *JJLG,* IX, pp. 103-197.

S. Krauss, Die Ehe zwischen Onkel u. Nichte, in Studies in Jewish Literature in honor of K. Kohler. pp. 165-175.

L. G. Lévy, La famille dans l'antiquite israélite, Paris, 1905.

L. Löw, Eherechtliche Studien (in Schriften, III., Szegedin, 1893, pp. 13-334).

Israel Mattuck, The Levirate Marriage in Jewish Law, in Studies in Jewish Literature in honor of K. Kohler. pp. 210-222.

Ch. Tschernowitz, Das Dotalsystem nach der mos.-talmud. Gesetzgebung, *Zeitschrift für vergleichende Rechstwissenschaft,* XXIX, pp. 445-473.

E. Weill, La femme juive. La condition légale d'après la Bible et la Talmud, Paris, 1874.

K. Weissbrodt, Gattenpflichten nach Bibel u. Talmud, Berlin, 1891.

LINGUISTICS.

Z. Rabbiner, Beiträge zur hebräischen Synonymik in T. u. Midrasch, Vol. I., Synonyme Nomina, Berlin, 1899.

MEDICINE.

W. Ebstein, Die Medizin im N.T. und im Talmud, Stuttgart, 1903.

M. Grunwald, Die Hygiene der Juden, Dresden, 1911.

J. L. Katzenelson, Die Normale u. die Pathelogische Anatomie in der althebr. Literatur u. ihr Verhältnis zur altgriech. Medizin, St. Petersburg, 1889; trans. into German, by R. Kirshberg, Historische Studien aus dem pharmakolog. Institut zur Dorpat, Vol. 5 (1896), pp. 164-296.

L. Kotelmann, Die Opthalmologie bei den alten Hebräern, Hamburg, 1910.

L. Löw, Zur Medizin u. Hygiene, Shriften, Vol. III., pp. 368-406, Szegedin, 1893.

J. Preuss, Biblisch-talmud. Medizin, Berlin, 1911. Cf. Imm Loew, *MGWJ*, 1912, 167-115; H. Illoway, Jewish Review, Vol. 4, pp. 175-185.

M. Rawitzki, Die Lehre vom Kaiserschnitt im Talmud; Virchow's Archiv für patholog. Anatomie, Vol. 80 (1880), pp. 494-503.

A. Rosenzweig, Das Auge in Bibel u. Talmud, Berlin, 1892.

D Schapiro, Obstétrique des anciens Hébreux d'apres la Bible, les Talmuds et les autres sources rabbiniques, comparée avec la tocologie gréco-romaine, Paris, 1904.

PHILOSOPHY AND PSYCHOLOGY.

R. Wohlberg, Grundlinien einer talmud. Psychologie, Berlin, 1902.

L. L. Mann, Freedom of the Will in Talmudic Literature. C.C.A.R. Year Book, Vol. 27, pp. 301-337.

THEOLOGY.

J. Abelson, The Immanence of God in Rabbinical Literature, London, 1912.

G. Dalman, Der leidende u. sterbende Messias der Synagoge im erst. nachchristl. Jahrtausend, Berlin, 1888.

M. Duschak, Biblisch.-talmud. Glaubenslehre, Vienna, 1873.

J. Klausner, Die Messianischen Vorstellungen des jüd. Volkes im Zeitalter der Tannaiten, Berlin, 1904.

M. J. Lagrange, Le Mesianisme chez les Juifs, Paris, 1909.

Israel Lévi, Le péché originel dans les anciennes sources juives, Paris, 1909.

PAGE

L. Löw, Die talmud. Lehre vom Göttlichen Wesen, Schriften, Vol. I., pp. 177-186, Szegedin, 1889.

C. G. Montefiore, Rabbinic Conceptions of Repentance, *JQR,* 1904, pp. 209-257.

F. C. Porter, The Yeçer Hara: A Study in the Jewish Doctrine of Sin, Biblical and Semitic Studies, Yale University, N. Y., 1901.

Solomon Schechter, Some Aspects of Rabbinic Theology, London, 1909.

F. Weber, Jüdische Theologie auf Grund des Talmud u. verwandter Schriften, Leipsic, 1897.

INDEX TO SUBJECTS AND NAMES

B

E

F

G

T

U

SPECIAL BIBLICAL, MISHNAIC AND TALMUDIC REFERENCES

BIBLICAL

MISHNAIC

HORAYOTH, BABYLONIAN

KETHUBOTH, BABYLONIAN

KHERITHOTH BABYLONIAN

KIDDUSHIN BABYLONIAN

ZEBACHIM
BABYLONIAN

INDEX OF EXPLAINED TECHNICAL TERMS AND PHRASES.

KEY TO THE ABBREVIATIONS USED IN THE TALMUD AND ITS COMMENTARIES.

א.

א"א. אברהם אבינו. או אינו
" אי אמרת. אי אפשר
" אשת איש
אא"ב. אי אמרת בשלמא
אא"כ. אלא אם כן
א"ב. איכא בינייהו. אין בו (בה)
אב"א. אי בעית אימא
אב"ד. אב בית דין
אב"ע. אלעזר בן עזריה
א"ר. איכא דאמרי
אד"הר. אדם הראשון
אדר'. אדרבה
א"ה. אי הכי. אפילו הכי
" אומות העולם
אה"נ. אין הכי נמי
א"וא. אב ואם
א"וא. אחד ואחד
אוה"ע. אומות העולם
או"נ. אוכל נפש
א"ז. את זה
א"ח. אינו חייב. אורח חיים
אח"ז. אחר זה
אח"כ. אחר כך
א"י. ארץ ישראל
איב"א. איבע"א. } אי בעית אימא
א"כ. אם כן
אכה"ג. אנשי כנסת הגדולה
אכ"כ. אין כתיב כאן
אכ"ע. אכולי עלמא
א"ל. אמר ליה (להו)
" אי לימא. אית ליה (להו)
" איכא למימר
אלת"ה. אי לא תימא הכי
א"מ. אמר מר
אמ"ה. אבר מן החי
אמ"ה. אלהינו מלך העולם
א"נ. אי נמי
א"ע. את עצמ
אע"ג. אף על גב
אע"פי. אף על פי
אעפ"כ. אף על פי כן
אפ"ה. אפילו הכי
אפי'. אפילו
א"צ. אינו צריך
אצ"ל. אין צריך לומר
א"ק. אמר קרא
א"ר. אמר רבי
אר"ת. אמר רבינו תם (in Tosaphoth)
א"ש. אמר שמואל. אתי שפיר
א"ת. אם תאמר
את"ל. אם תמצא לומר.

ב.

ב"א. בנין אב. בני אדם
בא"ד. באותו דבר
בא"י. בארץ ישראל
" ברוך אתה י"י
ב"ב. בבא בתרא. בעל בית
בב"ח. בר בר חנה. בשר בחלב
ב"ד. בית דין
בד"א. במה דברים אמורים
ב"ה. בית הלל. בית המקדש
" בעל הבית. ברוך הוא
בה"א. בית הלל אומרים
בה"ג. בהלכות גדולות (in Tosaphoth)
בה"כ. בית הכנסת
בה"מ. ברכת המזון
בהמ"ד. בית המדרש
בהמ"ק. בית המקדש
ב"ו. בשר ודם
ב"ח. בעל חוב. בעלי חיים
בחש"מ. בחולו של מועד
בכ"מ. בכל מקום

בלא"ה. בלאו הכי
ב"מ. בבא מציעא
במ"מ. במה מצינו
" בורא מיני מזונות
בנ"ד. בנידון דידן
בס"ד. בסיעתא דשמיא
בע"ה. בעל הבית
בע"ה. בעזרת השם (in Tosaph.)
בעה"ז. בעולם הזה
בע"כ. בעל כרחו
בע"פ. בעל פה
בפ"א. בורא פרי אדמה
בפ"נ ובפ"נ. בפני נכתב ובפני נחתם
ב"ק. בבא קמא
ב"ש. בית שמאי
בש"א. בית שמאי אומרים
בש"ר. בשם ר'.

ג.

ג"א. גירסא אחרינא (in Rashi)
ג"ד. גזר דין
גה"נ. גיד הנשה
ג"ז. גם זה
גז"ש. גזירה שוה
" גם זה שם (in Marginal Notes)
ג"ח. גמילות חסדים
גי'. גירסא, גירסת
ג"כ. גם כן
גמ'. גמרא
ג"נ. גטי נשים
ג"ע. גן עדן. גלוי עריות
ג"פ. ג' פעמים
גר'. גרס. גרסה
ג"ש. גזירה שוה

ד.

ד"א. דבר אחר
דא"א. דאי אפשר
דאל"כ. דאם לא כן
דאלת"ה. דאי לא תימא הכי
דאת"ל. דאם תמצא לומר
דבלא"ה. דבלאו הכי
ד"ה. דבור המתחיל (in Marginal Notes)
דה"א. דהיה אמינא
דה"ה. דהוא הדין
דה"ל. דהוה ליה
דהל"ל. דהוה ליה למימר
דה"מ. דהוה מצי
דהמ"ל. דהוה מצי למימר
דה"ק. דהכי קאמר
דכ"ע. דכולי עלמא
ד"מ. דיני ממונות
דמ"ד. דמאן דאמר
דמה"ט. דמהאי טעמא
דמ"מ. דמכל מקום
ד"נ. דיני נפשות
דנ"מ. דנפקא מיניה
ד"ס. דברי סופרים
דע"כ. דעל כרחך
דעכ"פ. דעל כל פנים
דקי"ל. דקימא לן
דקס"ד. דקא סלקא דעתך
ד"ת. דבר תורה, דין תורה
דת"ר. דתנו רבנן.

ה.

ה"א. הוה אמינא
הב"ע: הבא בעבירה
הב"ה. הקדוש ברוך הוא
הב"ע. הכא במאי עסקינן
ה"ג. האי גוונא
" הכי גרסינן (in Rashi)
" הלכות גדולות
ה"ד. היכי דמי
ה"ה. הוא הדין. הרי הוא
הה"ד. הרא הוא דכתיב
הו"מ. הוה מצי
ה"ז. הרי זה
הז"ג. הזמן גרמה
ה"ט. האי טעמא
ה"ל. הוה ליה
הל'. הלכה
הל"ל. הוה ליה למימר
הל"מ. הלכה למשה מסיני
ה"מ. הני מילי. הוה מצי
המד"א. היך מה דאת אמר
המ"ל. הוה מצי למימר

המע"ה. המוציא מחבירו עליו הראיה

ה"נ. הכי נמי

" הכא נמי

הנ"ל. הנכתב לעיל

" הנאמר למעלה

הנ"מ. הני מילי

" הכי נמי מסתברא

הע"הב. / העו"הב. } העולם הבא

העוה"ז. העולם הזה

ה"פ. הכי פירושו. הכי פריך

הפ"נ. הפרת נדרים

הק'. הקשה. הקטון

ה'ק. הכי קאמר

הקב"ה. הקדוש ברוך הוא

הר"ב. הרב ברטנורה

הרע"ב. הרב עובדיה ברטנורה

הש"י. השם יתברך.

ו.

וא"א. ואי אמרת

ואב"א. ואי בעית אימא

וא"ו. ואם תאמר

וגו'. וגומר

וג"ח. וגמילת חסדים

ודו"ק. ודייק ותמצא קל (in Commentaries)

וה"ה. והוא הדין

והה"נ. והוא הדין נמי

והנ"מ. והני מילי

וח"א. וחכמים אומרים

וי"ל. ויש לומר

וי"מ. ויש מפרשים

וכו'. וכולו

וכ"ת. וכי תימא

ולכ"ע. ולכלו עלמא

ומ"ד. ומאן דאמר

ומ"ה. ומשום הכי

ומ"ס. ומר סבר

ומ"ש. ומה שכתב

וע'. ועיין

ועי"ל. ועוד יש לומר

" ועיין לעיל. ועיין לקמן

וע"ע. ועיין עוד

וע"ק. ועוד קשה (in Tosaphoth)

וצ"ע. וצריך עיון (in Tosaphoth)

וקי"ל. וקיימא לן

וק"ל. וקל להבין

וש"נ. ושם נסמן (in Marginal Notes)

ז.

ז"א. זה אינו. זה אומר

זא"ז. זה אחר זה. זה את זה

זב"ז. זה בזה

זו"ז. זה וזה

זוז"ג. זה וזה גורם

ז"ל. זכרונו (זכרונם) לברכה

" זה לשונו

זלש"ב. זכין לאדם שלא בפניו

זמ"גר. זמן גרמה

זע"ז. זה על זה. זה עם זה

זש"ה. זה שאמר הכתוב

ח.

ח"א. חד אמר

ח"המ. חול המועד

ח"ו. חס ושלום

חו"ל. חוצה לארץ

חוש"מ. חולו של מועד

חז"ל. חכמינו זכרונם לברכה

חכ"א. חכמים אומרים

ח"ל. חל להיות

" חוץ לארץ

ח"מ. חושן משפט

חמוה"ק. חסורי מחסרא והכי קתני

ח"נ. חצי נזק

חש"ו. / חשו"ק. } חרש שוטה וקטן

חש"מ. חולו של מועד.

ט.

ט"ב. ט' באב (תשעה באב)

טבו"י. טבול יום

ט"הנ. טומאת הגוף
טוש"ע. טור ושולחן ערוך (in Marg. Notes)
ט"מ. טעמא מאי
ט"ס. טעות סופר.

י.

י"א. יש אומרים
י"ש. יש בו (בה)
י"נ. יש נורסין
יד"ח. ידי חובתו
יר"ש. ידי שמים
י"ה. / יה"כ. / יוה"כ. } יום הכפורים
יהר"מ. יהי רצון מלפניך
י"ח. ידי חובתו
י"ט. / יו"ט. } יום טוב
יי"נ. יין נסך
י"ל. יש לומר. יש לישב
י"מ. יש מפרשים
י"ס. יש ספרים
יע"ש. יעוין שם
יצה"ר. יצר הרע
יצ"ט. יצר טוב
יצ"מ. יציאת מצרים
יקנה"ז. יין קדוש נר הבדלה זמן
יר"מ. יהי רצון מלפניך
י"ש. ירי שמים
ית"ש. יתברך שמו

כ.

כ"א. כי אם. כל אחד
כאו"א. כל אחד ואחד
כ"ג. כהן גדול
" כך גרסינן
כה"ג. כהאי גוונא
" כהן הגדול
" כנסת הגדולה
כו'. כולו
כ"ז. כל זה. כל זמן
" כלאי זרעים
כ"י. כתב יד (ידו ידם)
כיו"ב. כיוצא בו
כ"כ. כל כך. כמו כן
" כלאי כרם
" כך כתב
כ"מ. כל מקום
" כן משמע. כך מצאתי
" כסף משנה (1
כמ"ד. כמאן דאמר
כמ"ש. כמו שכתוב (שנאמר)
כנ"ל. כן נראה לי
כ"ע. כולי עלמא
כעל"פ. כולי עלמא לא פליגי
כ"פ. כי פליגי. כמה פעמים
כצ"ל. כן צריך להיות
כ"ש. כל שכן. כל שהוא
כת"י. כתב יד

ל.

ל"א. לישנא אחרינא
ל"נ. לא נרסינן
להד"מ. לא היו דברים מעולם
לכ"ע. לכולי עלמא
לכ"ש. לא כל שכן
ל"ל. למה לי. לית ליה
ל"מ. לא מיבעיא
למ"ד. למאן דאמר
לעה"ב. לעולם הבא
לע"ז. לשון עם זר
לעי' לעיל
לע"ל. לעתיד לבא
ל"פ. לא פליגי
לפע"ד. / לפענ"ד. } לפי עניות דעתי (in Commentaries)
לק'. לקמן
ל"ק. לא קשיא
לק"מ. לא קשיא מידי
ל"ש. לא שנא (שנו)
" לא שמיה
לשה"ר. לשון הרע
לש"ש. לשם שמים
ל"ת. לא תעשה.

1) Name of Joseph Karo's Commentary on the code of Maimonides.

מ.

מ'. משנה
מ"א. מי אמרינן
מא"ל. מאי איכא למימר
מבע"י מבעוד יום
מ"ד. מאן דאמר. מאי דכתיב
מד"ס. מדברי סופרים
מ"ה. מדינת הים. משום הכי
מה"ד. מידת הדין
מה"מ. מנא הני מילי
מה"ס. מהר סיני
מה"ש. מלאכי השרת
מה"ת. מן התורה
מומ'. מומר
מו"מ. מקח וממכר
" משא ומתן
מ"ז. מחק זה (in Marginal notes)
מח"ל. מחוצה לארץ
מ"ט. מאי טעמא
מ"ס. מר סבר
מ"ע. מצות עשה
מע"ל. מעת לעת
מ"ק. מועד קטן
מ"ר. מדת רחמים
" מדרש רבות
מרע"ה. משה רבנו עליו השלום
מ"ש. מאי שנא. מה שכתב
" מעשר שני. מוצאי שבת
מש"ה. משום הכי
משו' משום
משי"ח. מורי שיחיה (בתוספות)
מ"ת. מתן תורה
מתני'. מתניתן

נ.

נ"א. נוסחא אחרינא
נ"ב. נכתב בצידו
נ"ח. נר חנוכה
נ"ט. נותן טעם
נ"י. נטילת ידים
" נימוקי יוסף [1]
נ"ל. נאמר למעלה. נכתב לעיל
" נראה לי
נ"מ. נפקא מינה
נ"ש. נזק שלם
" נר שבת. נושא שכר.

ס.

ס"א. סוגיא אחרינא.
" ספרים אחרים
ס"ד. סלקא דעתך
סד"א. סלקא דעתך אמינא
סד"ה. סוף דבור המתחיל
סו"מ. סורר ומורה
סי'. סימן
ס"ל. סבירא ליה
סמ"ג. ספר מצות גדול (in Marginal Notes) [2]
ס"נ. ספק נפשות
ס"ס. סוף סוף. ספק ספקא
סעי' סעיף
ס"פ. סוף פרק
ספ"ב. סוף פרק בתרא
ספ"ק. סוף פרק קמא
ס"ת. ספר תורה
סת"מ. ספרים תפילין מזוזות

ע.

ע'. עיין. עמוד
ע"א. עבודת אלילים
" עמוד א'
עאכ"ו. על אחת כמה וכמה
ע"ב. עמוד ב'.
ע"נ. על נב
ע"ד. על דרך
ע"ה. עם הארץ. עליו השלום
עה"ב. / עוה"ב. } עולם הבא

[1]) Name of annotations to Alfasi's Talmudical compendium by R. Joseph b. Chabiba, often referred to in Tosaphoth Yomtov (Heller).

[2]) Name of the rabbinical code by R. Moses of Coucy. It is divided into עשין commendatory, and לאווין prohibitory laws.

עה"ז.	עולם הזה
ע"ז.	על זה. עבודה זרה
ע"ח.	ערובי חצרות
ע"י.	על ידי
"	עין יעקב [1]
עיו"ט.	ערב יום טוב
עי"ל.	עוד יש לומר
ע"כ.	עד כאן, על כל
"	על כרחך
"	עבד כנעני
עכ"ד.	עד כאן דבריו
עכו"ם.	עובד כבבים ומזלות
עכ"ל.	עד כאן לשונו
עכ"פ.	על כל פנים
ע"ל.	עיין לעיל
ע"מ.	על מנת
ע"ע.	עבד עברי. עיין עוד
עע"א.	עובדי עבודת אלילים
ע"פ.	על פי, ערבי פסחים
ער"ה.	ערב ראש השנה
ער"ח.	ערב ראש הודש
ע"ש.	ערב שבת, עיין שם
ע"ת.	ערובי תחומין

פ.

פ'.	פרק. פרשה
פ"א.	פעם אחת. פרק א'.
פ"ב.	פרק בתרא. פרק ב'.
פ"ה.	פירוש הקונטרוס (in Tosaphot referring to Rashi)
פי'.	פירש
פס'.	פסוק
פס"ד.	פסק דין
פ"ק. פ-"ק.	פרק קמא
פר"ח.	פירש רבנו חננאל (in Tosaphoth)
פר"ת.	פירש רבנו תם (in Tosaphoth)

צ.

צב"ח.	צער בעל חיים
צ"ה.	צד השוה
צה"ש.	צד השוה שבהן
צ"ל.	צריך לומר. צריך להיות
צ"ע.	צריך עיון.

ק.

קה"ת.	קריאת התורה
ק"ו. קו"ח.	קל וחומר
קי"ל.	קיימא לן
ק"ל.	קל להבין
קמ"ל.	קא משמע לן
קס"ד.	קא סלקא דעתך
קצ"ע.	קצת צריך עיון
ק"ק.	קדשי קדשים
"	קצת קשה (in Tosaph.)
ק"ש.	קריאת שמע.

ר.

ר'.	רבי. רב
ר"א.	רבי אליעזר. ר' אלעזר
ראב"ע.	רבי אלעזר בן עזריה
ר"ב.	רבנו (מ)ברטנורה [2]
רבב"ח.	רבה בר בר חנא
רביש'ע.	רבונו של עולם
ר"ג.	רבן גמליאל
ר"ה.	ראש השנה. רב הונא
רה"י.	רשות היחיד
רה"ר.	רשות הרבים
ר"ח.	ראש חדש
"	רבי חייא, רבי חנינה.
"	רב חסדא
"	רבנו חננאל (בתוספות)
רחב"א.	רבי חייא בר אבא
ר"ט.	רבי טרפון
ר"י.	רבי יהודה. ר' יהושע
"	ר' יוחנן. ר' יצחק

[1]) En Jacob to which sometimes references are made in the marginal notes to the Talmud is the name of a collection of all Agadic passages of the Talmud. See above p. 76.

[2]) Frequently occurring in Tosaphoth Yom Tob (Heller) and referring to the Mishna Commentary by R. Obadja Bertinoro.

ריב"ז	ר' יוחנן בן זכאי
ריב"ל.	ר' יהושע בן לוי
ר"כ.	רב כהנא
ר"ל.	ריש לקיש
ר"מ.	ר' מאיר
ר"נ.	ר' נתן. רב נחמן
ר"ע.	ר' עקיבא
ר"פ.	ר' פפא. ריש פרק
ר"ש.	ר' שמעון
רשב"א.	ר' שמעון בן אלעזר
"	רבנו שמשון בן אברהם (בתוספות)
רשב"י.	ר' שמעון בן יוחאי
רשב"ג.	ר' שמעון בן גמליאל
רשב"ם.	ר' שמואל בן מאיר (בתוספות)
רש"י.	רבנו שלמה יצחקי
ר"ת.	ראשי תיבות
ר"ת.	רבנו תם, (בתוספות)

ש.

שא' א.	שאי אפשר
שא"ב.	שאין בו
שאב"מ.	שאין בו מעשה
שאל"כ.	שאם לא כן
שא' צ.	שאינו צריך
שבע"פ.	שבעל פה
ש"ד.	שפיר דמי. שפיכת דמים
שהז"נ.	שהזמן גרמה
שה"ש.	שיר השירים
שו"ת.	שאלות ותשובות
שח"ל.	שחל להיות
שט"ח.	שטר חוב
שי"ב.	שיש בו
ש"מ.	שמע מיניה
"	שכיב מרע
שמ"מ.	שמכל מקום
שנ'. שנא'.	שנאמר
ש"ס.	ששה סדרים = **תלמוד**
ש"ע.	שחרורי עבדים
"	שלחן ערוך
ש"ע א"ח.	שלחן ערוך אורח חיים
ש"ע אה"ע.	שלחן ערוך אבן העזר
ש"ע יו"ד.	שלחן ערוך יורה דעה
ש"ע ח"מ.	שלחן ערוך חושן משפט
שפ'.	שפירש
ש"פ.	שוה פרוטה
ש"צ.	שליח ציבור
שרצ"ל.	שרצונו לומר
ש"ש.	שם שמים. שומר שכיר
"	שטר שחרור
ש"ת.	שומע תפילה

ת.

ת"א.	תניא אידך
"	תרגום אונקלוס
ת"ב.	תשעה באב
ת"ה.	תחיית המתים
"	תפלת הדרך
תו"מ.	תרומה ומעשר
תוס'.	תוספות
ת"ח.	תלמיד חכם. תני חדא
ת"י	תרגום יהונתן
"	תוספות ישנים
תי"ט.	תוספות יום טוב
ת"כ.	תורת כהנים
"	תשלומי כפל
תכ"ד.	תוך כדי דיבור
תנ"ך	תורה נביאים כתובים
ת"ל.	תלמוד לומר
תנ"ה.	תניא נמי הכי
ת"ק.	תנא קמא
תק"ס.	תנא קמא סבר
ת"צ.	תענית ציבור
ת"ר.	תנו רבנן
ת"ש.	תא שמע. תחום שבת
תשבע"פ.	תורה שבעל פה
ת"ת.	תלמוד תורה.

TALMUD and MIDRASH

A Selected Bibliography: 1925-67

by Alexander Guttmann

CONTENTS

I. *Bibliography. History of Literature. Printing.*

Shunami, S., מפתח המפתחות *Bibliography of Jewish Bibliographies.* Second ed., enlarged (See particularly pp. 172 ff), Jerusalem, 1965.

Berliner, A., כתבים נבחרים (Essays). Vol. II. Translation with notes by Haberman, A. M. Jerusalem, 1949.

Cohen, B., *Bibliography of the writings of Louis Ginzberg,* New York, 1945.

Eisenstadt, B., עין משפט *Eyn Mishpat: Repertorium Bibliographicum Litteraturae totius iurisprudentiae hebraicae.* Jerusalem, 1931.

Feldman, L. Ḥ., *Scholarship on Philo and Josephus* (1937-1962). Studies in Judaica, 1. New York, 1963.

Halevy, S., הספרים העברים שנדפסו בירושלים תר"א — תרנ"א Jerusalem, 1963.

Kohn, P. J., אוצר הבאורים והפירושים *Thesaurus of Hebrew Halachic* (including Talmudic) *Literature.* London, 1952.

Malachi, E. R. פרי עץ חיים *Bibliography of the works of Chaim Tchernowitz.* New York, 1946.

Marcus, J. R. and Bilgray, A. T., *Index to Jewish Festschriften.* Cincinnati, 1937.

Marcus, R., *A Selected Bibliography (1920-1945) of the Jews in the Hellenistic-Roman Period.* PAAJR, XVI. New York, 1947.

Metzger, B. M., *Index of articles on the New Testament and the Early Church published in Festschriften.* Philadelphia, 1961. (See particularly "The Jewish Background," pp. 40 ff).

Rabinowitz, R. N., מאמר על הדפסת התלמוד *History of the printing of the Talmud,* ed. Haberman, A. M. Jerusalem, 1952.

Roth, E., *Hebräische Handschriften.* Hrsg. von H. Striedl unter Mitarbeit von L. Tetzner beschrieben von E. Roth. Wiesbaden, 1965.

Scheiber, A., *List of writings of Michael Guttmann.* Budapest, 1946.

Slatkine, M. M. שמות הספרים העבריים Neuchatel, 1950.

Wachstein, B., *Literatur über die jüdische Frau.* Wien, 1931.

Waxman, M., *A History of Jewish Literature.* Second ed. New York, 1938-47. Reprint: 5 vols. New York 1960.

Zuckrow, S., ספרות ההלכה מחתימת התלמוד עד הש"ע ונושאי כליו New York, 1932.

II. *Introductions. Literary Problems. Problems of Text.*

Albeck, H., מבוא למשנה Jerusalem-Tel-Aviv, 1959.

———*Untersuchungen über die halakischen Midraschim.* Berlin, 1927.

Chajes, Z. H., *The Student's Guide Through the Talmud.* Translated and annotated by Shachter, J., London, 1952.

Epstein, J. N., מבוא לנוסח המשנה Jerusalem, 1948.

——— מבואות לספרות התנאים. *Introduction to Tannaitic Literature.* Tel-Avive, 1957.

——— מבואות לספרות האמוראים *Introduction to Amoraitic Literature.* Jerusalem, 1962.

Finkelstein, L., *The Transmission of Early Rabbinic Tradition.* HUCA XVI. (1941).

Guttmann, A., *Das redaktionelle und sachliche Verhältnis zwischen Mischna und Tosephta.* Breslau, 1928.

———*Tractate Aboth—Its place in Rabbinic Literature.* JQR XLI, No. 2, (1950).

———*The Problem of the Anonymous Mishna.* HUCA XVI. (1941).
Hyman, A. B. ed., *The Sources of the Yalkut Shimeoni on the Prophets and Hagiographa* (Hebrew). Jerusalem, 1965.
Hyman, M. A., דיקדוקי סופרים על נדרים ונזיר Chicago, 1943.
Melamed, E. Z. מבוא לספרות התלמוד Jerusalem, 1954.
Mielziner, M., *Introduction to the Talmud.* Third. ed. New York, 1925.
Kaplan, J., The Redaktion of the Babylonian Talmud. New York, 1933.
Karl, Z., מחקרים בספרי Tel-Aviv, 1954.
Schachter, M., המשנה הבבלי והירושלמי *The Babylonian and Jerusalem Mishnah Textually Compared.* Jerusalem, 1959.
Strack, H. L., *Introduction to the Talmud and Midrash.* Philadelphia 1931 and New York, 1959.
Weiss, A., התהוות התלמוד בשלמותו *The Babylonian Talmud as a Literary Unit.* New York, 1943.
——— לחקר הספרותי של המשנה HUCA XVI. (1941).
——— על היצירה הספרותית של האמוראים New York, 1962.

III. *Editions* of Hebrew and Aramaic Texts (mostly primary sources). *Some with translations.*

A. Tannaitic texts, including Halakhic Midrashim:

Brody, A., *Der Mischna-Traktat Tamid.* Uppsala, 1936 (with translation).
Greenup, A. W., *Sukkah, Mishnah and Tosefta.* London, 1925.
Higger, M. אוצר הברייתות 6 vols. New York, 1938.

Kafah, J., *Mishnah with Maimonides' commentary,* translated from the Arabic. (Hebrew) Jerusalem, 1963.
Kahle, P. and Weinberg, J., *The Mishnah Text in Babylonia.* HUCA X. (1935), and XII-XIII. (1937-1938).
Lichtenstein, H. *Die Fastenrolle. Eine Untersuchung zur jüdisch-hellenistischen Geschichte.* Introduction, text and interpretation. HUCA VIII-IX. (1931-32).
Lurie, B. Z., *Megillath Ta'anith with Introductions and Notes.* Jerusalem. 1964.
Epstein, J. N., completed by Melamed, E. Z., *Mekilta de Rabbi Shimeon (facs).* מכילתא דרבי שמעון בן יוחאי. Jerusalem, 1955.
Finkelstein, L., *Sifra According to Codex Assemani LXVI.* Facsimile ed. with Hebrew introduction. New York, 1956.
Horovitz, H. S., completed by Rabin, I. A., *Mechilta D'Rabbi Ismael.* Breslau, 1930 (Jerusalem, 1960).
Horovitz, H. S.—Finkelstein, L. *Sifre Deuteronomy.* Berlin, 1935-1939.
Rabinowitz, M. D., ed. of and commentary on הקדמות לפירוש המשנה 2nd revised ed., Jerusalem, 1961.
Lauterbach, J. Z., *Mekilta de-Rabbi Ishmael.* With translation. 3 vols. Philadelphia, 1933-1935.
Lieberman, S., *The Tosefta Zeraim According to Codex Vienna with Commentary* (Hebrew) 3 vols., New York, 1955.
———*The Tosefta Moed* . . . (Hebrew) 3 vols., New York, 1962.
Melamed, E. Z., מדרשי הלכה של התנאים בתלמוד בבלי Jerusalem. 1943.

B. Talmud and Minor Tractates:

Goldschmidt, L. B., *Talmud.* Text and German translation. Berlin, 1897-1933. 8 vols. 9th vol. Haag, 1935. Index vol. ed. by Edelman, R. Copenhagen, 1959.

Higger, M., edited a number of *Minor Tractates,* some with translation, such as: *Sefer Torah and Seven minor tractates* (Mezuzah; Tefillin; Zizit; 'Abadim; Kutim; Gerim, and treatise SoferimII.). New York, 1930. *Treatise Semahot.* New York, 1931. *The Treatises Derek Erez.* (with translation). New York, 1935. *Masektot Kallah.* New York, 1936. *Masseket Soferim,* New York, 1937.

Malter, H., *The Treatise Ta'anith of the Babylonian Talmud.* New York, 1930.

Zlotnik, D., *Massekhtot qetanot. Massekhet semahot. The tractate* "Mourning." Text from Manuscripts. Translated. New Haven (Yale), 1966.

C. Midrash (Aggadic):

Midrash Rabbah with commentary by Mirkin, M. A. Vocalized. 9 vols. Tel-Aviv, 1956- 1964.

Bereshith Rabbah. Theodor—Albeck. Berlin 3 vols. 1912-1936; 1965 (reprint).

Wayyikra Rabbah. Margulies, M. 5 vols. Jerusalem, 1953-1960.

Debarim Rabbah. Ed. Lieberman. S., Jerusalem, 1940 and 1964.

Pesikta de Rav Kahana, ed. Mandelbaum, B., 2 vols. New York, 1962.

Midrash Ha-Gadol. Genesis. Ed. Margulies, M., Jerusalem, 1947. *Exodus.* Jerusalem, 1956.

Midrash Ha-Gadol. Leviticus. Ed. Rabinowitz, E. N., New York, 1932.

בתי מדרשות Ed Wertheimer, S. A. Second ed. enlarged and amended by Wertheimer, A. 2 vols. Jerusalem, 1950-1953.

מדרשי גאולה; פרקי האפוקליפסה היהודית מחתימת התלמוד ועד ראשית האלף הששי
Ed. with notes and commentaries by Judah Ibn-Shmuel (Kaufman). Jerusalem, 1954.

The Mishnah of Rabbi Eliezer or the Midrash of Thirty Two Hermeneutic Rules משנת רבי אליעזר או מדרש שלשים ושתים מדות
Ed. Enelow, H. G., New York, 1933.

D. Commentaries. Novellae: Misc.

Ashkenaizi, B. ben Abraham שטה מקובצת on many tractates. Tel-Aviv and Brooklyn. Incomplete. Last vol. 1966-67.

Judah Berabbi Kalonymus of Speier יחוסי תנאים ואמוראים
Ed. by Maimon, J. L. 2 vols. Incomplete. Jerusalem, 1962-1963.

Lewin, B. M., *Otzar ha-Geonim. Thesaurus of the Gaonic Responsa and Commentaries.* 13 vols., Haifa-Jerusalem, 1928-1962. Vol. on Sanhedrin ed by Taubes, Ch. Z., Jerusalem, 1966.

Löwinger, S., *Gaonic Interpretations on the Tractates Gittin and Qiddushin.* HUCA XXIII, Part One (1950-51).

Meiri, Menahem ben Solomon. בית הבחירה on several tractates. In various places and at various times. Last vol. 1966. Incomplete.

Trani, Isaiah the Elder, ben Mali di. תוספות רי"ד on a number of tractates. New York, 1952—Jerusalem, 1959. Incomplete.

Israel Ibn Al-Nakawa, *Menorat Ha-Maor* מנורת המאור
Ed. Enelow, H. G., 4 vols. New York, 1929-1932.

She'eltoth, ed. Mirsky, S. K. 3 vols. Jerusalem, 1959-63. Incomplete.

IV. *Translations (See also section III).*

Danby, H., *The Mishnah.* London, 1933.
Blackman, Ph., *Mishnah,* with vocalized text. 7 vols. New York, 1963.
Cohn, J., *Mischnajot: Kodaschim.* Text, German translation and commentary. Berlin, 1925.
Petuchowski, M. and Schlesinger, S., *Mischnajot:Naschim.* Text, German translation and commentary. Wiesbaden, 1933. (This vol. completes the Itzkowski ed. of the Mishnah begun in 1887.)
Kittel, G. and Rengstorf, K. H., editors: *Tosefta.* Text and German tr. with commentary. Stuttgart, 1933-67. Incomplete.
Goldin, J., *The Fathers According to Rabbi Nathan.* New Haven, 1955.
Epstein, I., editor. *The B. Talmud.* (Soncino ed.). 34 vols. and Index vol. London, 1935-1952; and 1959 (Small ed.).—*Minor Tractates.* 2 vols. 1965.
Goldschmidt, L., *Der Babylonische Talmud.* 12 vols. Berlin, 1929-1936. (See also section III, ed. of text with translation).
Horowitz, Ch., *Talmud Yerushalmi, Nedarim.* German translation and commentary. Düsseldorf—Benrath, 1957. *Sukkah.* Bonn, 1963.
Kuhn, G. K., *Sifre zu Numeri.* Stuttgart, 1959.
Levertoff, P. P., *Midrash Sifre on Numbers.* London, 1926.
Freedman, H. and Simon, M., editors, *Midrash Rabbah.* 10 vols. London, 1951.
Braude, W. G., *The Midrash on Psalms.* (Yale Judaica Series). 2 vols. New Haven, 1959.
Oberman, J. and Nemoy, L., editors: *Maimonides, Mishneh Torah.* (Yale Judaica Series.) New Haven, 1949-1965. Incomplete.
Chavel, Ch. B., *Maimonides, The Book of Divine Commandments (Sefer Ha-Mitzvoth).* Vol. I. *The Positive Commandments.* London, 1940.

Maccabees, First Book, Translated by Tedesche, S., Introduction and Commentary by Zeitlin, S., New York, 1950.
Maccabees, Second Book, Translated by Tedesche, S., Edited by Zeilin, S. New York, 1954.
Maccabees, Third and Fourth Books, Edited and translated by Hadas, M., (Greek text included in all four books). New York, 1953.
Philo, Loeb Classical Library ed. in 10 vols. Translated by Colson, F. H.: Vols. I, II, VI—IX. By Colson, F. H. and Whitaker, H.: Vols. III—V. By Colson, F. H. and Earp, J. W.: Vol. X. (Greek text included). London, 1929-62.
Josephus, Loeb Classical Library ed. in 9 vols. Translated by Thackeray, H. St. J.: Vols. I—IV. By Thackeray and Marcus, R.: Vol. V. By Marcus, R.: Vols. VI—VII. By Marcus, R. and Wikgren, A.: Vol. VIII. By Feldman, L. H.: Vol. IX. (Greek text included). London, 1926-65.

V. *Commentaries (See also section I) and Talmudic Exegesis* (modern).

Abramski, J., תוספתא חזון יחזקאל Wilna, London, Jerusalem, 1925-1963. Incomplete.
Albeck, H., *Mishnah.* Also text, vocalized by Yallon, H., 6 vols. Tel-Aviv, 1953-1959.

Levi, E., משנה מפורשת Also text. Tel-Aviv, 1951-1958.
Lieberman, S., תוספת ראשונים 4 vols. Jerusalem, 1937-1939.
Epstein, J. N., editor: תלמוד בבלי עם תרגום עברי ופרוש חדש Jerusalem. 1925-1963. Incomplete.
Ginzberg, L., פירושים וחדושים בירושלמי *A Commentary on the Palestian Talmud.* Berakboth, chapters I—IV. 3 vols. New York, 1941. (Hebrew. Introduction also in English). Vol. IV posthumously edited by Halivni, D., New York, 1961.
Lieberman, S. הירושלמי כפשוטו on Sabbath, Erubin, Pesachim, Jerusalem, 1935.

VI. *Linguistics.*

Epstein, J. N., דקדוק ארמית בבלית Dikduk Aramit Bavlit. Ed. by Melamed, E. Z., Jerusalem, 1960.
Jerusalmi, I., *The Talmud is in Aramaic.* Cincinnati 1966.
Krauss, S., תוספות הערוך השלם *Addimenta Ad Librum Aruch Completum Alexandri Kohut.* New York, 1955.
Krupnik, B. and Silbermann, A. M., *A Dictionary of the Talmud, the Midrash and the Targum*, London, 1927.
Margolioth, R., לחקר שמות וכנויים בתלמוד Jerusalem, 1960.
Orlinsky, H. M., *Studies in Talmudic Philology.* HUCA XXIII. Part One. (1950-1951).
Schlesinger, M., *Satzlehre der Aramäischen Sprache des Babylonischen Talmuds.* Leipzig, 1928.
Segal, M. H., *A Grammar of Mishnaic Hebrew.* Oxford, 1927.
Spicehandler, E., בי דואר and דינא דמגיסתא *Notes on Gentile Courts in Talmudic Babylonia.* HUCA XXVI. (1955.)
Yalon, H., מבוא לניקוד המשנה Jerusalem, 1964.

Ashkenazi, S. and Jarden, D., *Thesaurus of Hebrew Abbreviations.* Jerusalem, 1965.
Bader, G., *Cyclopedia of Hebrew Abbreviations.* New York, 1951.
Stern, A., ראשי תיבות Sighetul-Marmatiei, 1926.

VII. *Encyclopedical works. Concordances. Indices. Ozaroth.*

Assaf, D., *Concordance of the Mishneh Torah.* Haifa, 1960. Incomplete.
Berlin, M. and Zevin, J., editors: אנציקלופדיה תלמודית *Talmudic Encyclopedia.* 12 vols. Jerusalem, 1955-67. Incomplete.
Bloch, Ch., with Geier, M., היכל לדברי חז"ל ופתגמיהם, New York, 1948.
Essrig, I. D., פרי עץ הדר. אוצר כללי התלמוד והפוסקים New York, 1952-1960. 3 vols. Incomplete.
Gross, M. D., אוצר האגדה 3 vols. Jerusalem, 1954.
Gulak, A., אוצר השטרות Jerusalem, 1926.
Guttmann, M., מפתח התלמוד *Clavis Talmudis.* 4 vols. Csongrad, Budapest, Breslau, 1906-1930. Incomplete.
Hasidah, I. I., אוצר מאמרי הלכה Jerusalem, 1959-1960. 3 vols.
Horowitz, I. S. D., ירושלים בספרותנו; אנציקלופדיה Jerusalem, 1964.
Hyman, A., תורה הכתובה והמסורה 3 vols., Tel-Aviv, 1936-1939.
——— אוצר דברי חכמים ופתגמיהם Tel-Aviv, 1933.
Kasher, M. M., תורה שלמה Encyclopedia of Biblical interpretation. Hebrew ed. Jerusalem, 1927-67. 22 vols. Incomplete. English ed., editor Friedman, H., New York, 1953-67. 7 vols. Incomplete.

Kassovsky, H. J., אוצר לשון המשנה *Concordantiae Totius Mischnae.* Frankfurt/M., 1927. 2 vols., 2 ed. 4 vols. Jerusalem, 1956-60.

——— אוצר לשון התוספתא Thesaurus Thosephtae. 6 vols. Jerusalem, 1932-1961.

——— אוצר לשון התלמוד *Thesaurus Talmudis Concordantiae Verborum.* Jerusalem, 1954-1967. 17 vols. Incomplete.

Kosovsky, B., *Concordance to the Mekhilta of R. Jishmael.* 4 vols. Jerusalem, 1965-66. *Sifra,* 1967. Incomplete.

——— אוצר השמות של מכילתא דרבי ישמעאל. שמות פרטיים... Jerusalem, 1965.

Konovitz, I., *Akiba.* Tel Aviv, 1955-56. - *Beth Shammai, Beth Hillel. Judah ben Ilai. Simeon ben Yohai. Judah ha-Nasi.* (Hebrew). Jerusalem, 1965.

Lerinman, Z., אוצר אמרי אבות 4 vols. Jerusalem, 1959-66.

Orenstein, A., אנציקלופדיה לתארי כבוד בישראל 4 vols., Tel-Aviv, 1958-63.

Schechter, J., אוצר התלמוד; ביאורי מונחים ומושגים, ענינים וכללים בתלמוד בבלי Tel Aviv, 1962.

Sever, M., מכלול המאמרים והפתגמים 3 vols. Jerusalem, 1961-62.

Tarshish, P., אישים וספרים בתוספות New York, 1942.

Umanski, J., חכמי התלמוד; רשימת כל התנאים והאמוראים שבתלמוד ירושלמי... כל המקומות שבהם נזכרו שמותיהם Tarnow, 1928-31; Jerusalem, 1948-52. Incomplete.

Yemini, M., תורת ההשגחה והבטחון. אוסף מאמרי חז"ל מש"ס ומדרשים Jerusalem, 1961.

Zeligman, I., אוצר המספרים The Treasury of Numbers . . . from the Bible, Talmud, Midrash etc., New York, 1942.

VIII. *Law, Development of the Halakhah* (including *Custom*). (*See also II*).

Abramowitz, A. I., וחי בהם: פקוח נפש בהלכה Jerusalem, 1957.

Albeck, S., פשר דיני הנזיקין בתלמוד *General Principles of the Law of Tort in the Talmud.* (Hebrew.) Tel-Aviv, 1965.

Albeck, H., האירוסין ושטרותיהן in Studies in Memory of Moses Schorr. New York, 1944.

Allom, G., *The Sociological Method in the Study of Jewish Law.* In Tarbiz, X. 1939.

Aptowitzer, V. השפעת המשפט העברי על התפתחות המשפט במזרח הנוצרי Gulak-Klein Memorial Vol., Jerusalem, 1942.

——— פוליטיקה חשמונאית ונגד חשמונאית בהלכה ובאגדה in Poznanski Memorial Vol., Warsaw, 1927.

Ashkenazi, S., האשה באספקלרית היהדות 3 parts. Tel Aviv, 1953-1955.

Assaf, S., לשאלת הירושה של הבת in *Festschrift* in honor of Jakob Freinmann. Berlin, 1937.

Atlas, S., להתפתחות הסוגיא וההלכה in HUCA XVII. (1942-1943.)

——— להתהוות הסוגיא in HUCA XXIV. (1952-1953.)

——— הערמה משפטית בתלמוד in Ginzberg Festschrift, New York, 1946.

——— הרצון הצבורי בתחוקה התלמודית in HUCA XXVI. (1955.)

Auerbach, Ch., *The Talmud: A gateway to the common law,* Cleveland, 1942.

Bamberger, B. J., *Qetanah, Na'arah, Bogereth.* HUCA XXXII (1961).

Blau, L., גופו של גט. פרוש למשנה גטין פ"ט, מ"ג in the Hevesi, S. Jubilee Volume. Budapest, 1934.
Cohen, B., *Letter and Spirit in Jewish and Roman Law,* in M. M. Kaplan Jubilee Volume, New York, 1953.
———*Law and Tradition in Judaism.* (Essays). New York, 1959.
———*Jewish and Roman Jurisprudence.* PAAJR, v. 17, 1949.
———*Jewish and Roman Law.* 2 vols. New York, 1966.
Daube, D., *Collaboration with Tyranny in Rabbinic Law.* London, 1965.
——— *Texts and Interpretation in Roman and Jewish Law.* In The Jewish Journal of Sociology, June 1961.
De Vries, B., תולדות ההלכה התלמודית Tel Aviv, 1962.
Dykan, P., *Criminal Law With Special Reference to the History of Jewish Law and the Law of Israel.* 6 vols., Tel Aviv, 1955-1962.
Elias (אליאש), M. and Dikstein, P., *editors*: המשפט העברי (Essays by many scholars). 5 vols. Tel-Aviv, 1926-1937.
Elon, M., מבוא למשפט העברי 3 vols., Jerusalem, 1964.
Epstein, L. M., *Marriage Laws in the Bible and the Talmud.* Cambridge, Mass., 1942.
———*Sex laws and customs in Judaism.* New York, 1948. Hebrew translation: Tel Aviv, 1959.
———*The Jewish Marriage Contract.* New York, 1927. Hebrew, New York, 1954.
Federbush, S., בנתיבות התלמוד, (Essays.) Jerusalem, 1957.
——— משפט המלוכה בישראל. Jerusalem, 1952.
Freehof, S. B., *Reform Jewish Practice and its Rabbinic Background.* 2 vols. Cincinnati, 1944, 1952.
Freimann, J., לשנוי דעות בין בבלי וירושלמי בנדון ר"ה שחל להיות בשבת in Hama'or, I.1. Berlin, 1933.
Ginzberg, J., משפטים לישראל A study in Jewish criminal law. Jerusalem, 1956.
Ginzberg, L., *On Jewish Law and Lore.* (Essays). Philadelphia, 1955.
——— על הלכה ואגדה (Essays). Tel-Aviv, 1960.
Gulak, A., לחקר תולדות המשפט העברי בתקופת התלמוד. א. דיני קרקעות Jerusalem, 1929.
———*Das Urkundenwesen im Talmud im Lichte der griechischen und ägyptischen Papyri* etc. Jerusalem, 1935.
Guttmann, A., *Dezisionsmotive im Talmud.* Berlin, 1938.
———*Akiba "Rescuer of the Torah."* In HUCA. XVII. (1942-1943.)
——— לשאלת היחס מחג — הלכה בתקופת התלמוד In Bitzaron VII. (1946.)
———*Foundations of Rabbinic Judaism.* In HUCA XXIII. Part I. (1950-1951.)
Guttmann, M., *The Decisions of Maimonides in his Commentary on the Mishna.* HUCA II. (1925.)
——— ארץ ישראל במדרש ותלמוד בהשקפה פרטית על יחס הארץ לתורה ומצוות Breslau, 1929.
——— בחינת המצוות Breslau, 1928.
——— בחחינת קיום המצוות Breslau, 1931.
Heinemann, I., *Die Lehre vom Ungeschriebenen Gesetz im Jüdischen Schrifttum.* HUCA IV. (1927.)
——— טעמי המצות בספרות ישראל 3rd ed. 2 vols. Jerusalem, 1954, 1956.

Heinemann, J., The Status of the Labourer in Jewish Law and Society in the Tannaitic Period. HUCA XXV. (1954.)
Herr, M. D., ... לבעית הלכות מלחמה בשבת *The Problem of War on the Sabbath in the Second Temple and the Talmudic Periods.* Tarbiz, XXX. 3. (1961.)
Herzog, I., *Main Institutions of Jewish Law.* 2 vols. London, 1936-1939.
Horowitz, G., *The Spirit of Jewish Law; a brief account of Biblical and rabbinical jurisprudence etc.,* New York, 1953.
Kagan, K. K., *Three Great Systems of Jurisprudence.* London, 1955.
Kahana, J. Z., אמנות בית הכנסת בספרות הלכה Jerusalem, 1950.
Kaminka, A., מחקרים במקרא ותלמוד ובספרות הרבנית Tel Aviv, 1938-51.
Karl, Z., תולדות המשפט העברי Tel Aviv, 1953.
Krauss, S., *The Jewish Rite of Covering the Head.* HUCA. XIX. (1945-1946.)
Lauterbach, J. Z., *The Ceremony of Breaking a Glass at Weddings.* HUCA II. (1925.)
———*Tashlik, A Study in Jewish Ceremonies.* HUCA XI. (1936.)
———*The naming of children in Jewish folklore, ritual and practice.* C.C.A.R. Yearbook, XLII. (1932.)
———*The ritual for the Kapparot-ceremony.* In Kohut Memorial vol., New York, 1935.
——— זמן שחיטת הפסח In PAAJR, 1942.
———*The Origin and Development of Two Sabbath Ceremonies.* HUCA XV. (1940.)
——— שבירת עצם בפסח. Hazofeh, Budapest, 1925.
———*Rabbinic Essays.* (Also on laws). Silberman, L. H. editor. Cincinnati, 1951.
Levin, B. M. לתולדות נר שבת In Linda R. Miller Memorial Volume. New York, 1938.
——— אוצר חילוף מנהגים בין בני ארץ ישראל ובין בני בבל. Jerusalem, 1942.
Löwinger, S., *Entwicklung unserer Traditionsliteratur.* In Jewish Studies in memory of Michael Guttmann. Budapest, 1946.
Marcus, R., *Law in the Apocrypha.* New York, 1927.
Maimon, J. L. (vols. 1-4) and Raphael, J. (vols. 5-8), editors, *Torah Sheb'al Pe.* Lectures on the Oral Law (Hebrew). 8 vols. Jerusalem, 1959-66.
Neufeld, E., *Ancient Jewish Marriage Laws.* London, 1944.
Passamaneck, S., *Traces of Rabbinical Maritime Law and Custom. Revue D'histoire Du Droit.* XXXIV (1966).
Rabinowitz, J. J., *Jewish Law. Its influence on the development of legal institutions.* New York, 1956.
Rosenthal, J., רבית מן הנכרי in Talpiyyoth, V, 3-4 (1952); VI, 1-2 (1953).
Roth, E., לתולדות המונוגמיה אצל היהודים In M. Guttmann Memorial Vol. Budapest, 1946.
Rowly, H. H., *Jewish Proselyte Baptism.* HUCA XV. (1940.)
Silberg, M., כך דרכו של תלמוד *Principia Talmudica.* Jerusalem, 1961.
Silberman, L. H., *The Sefirah Season.* HUCA XXII (1949).
Tchernowitz, Ch., תולדות ההלכה *Toledoth Ha-Halakhah.* 4 vols. New York, 1934-1950.
——— תולדות הפוסקים *Toledoth Ha-Poskim,* 3 vols. New York, 1943-1947.

Wacholder, B. Z., *Attitudes towards proselyting in the classical Halakhah.* In "Historia Judaica" XX. (1958).
Weinberg, J. J., מחקרים בתלמוד Berlin, 1937-1938.
——— חקירת מקורות להלכת עידית In J. Freimann Jubilee Vol., Berlin, 1937.
Weiss, A., *The Talmud and its Development,* New York, 1954 (Hebrew).
——— סדר הדיון *Court Procedure, Studies in Talmudic Law.* New York, 1957.
Yaron, R., *Gifts in Contemplation of Death in Jewish and Roman Law.* Oxford, 1960.
Zeitlin, S., *Prosbol. A Study in Tannaitic Jurisprudence.* JQR XXXVII. (1947.)
———*The Halaka: Introduction to Tannaitic Jurisprudence.* JQR XXXIX. (1948.)
———*The Takkanot of Erubin*: JQR XLI. (1951.)
Zevin, S. Y., לאור ההלכה (Essays). Tel-Aviv, 1957.
Zuckrow, S., *Adjustment to Life in Rabbinic Literature.* Boston, 1928.
Zuri J. S., תורת המשפט האזרחי העברי. משפט הנזיקין. חלק ראשון Treatise of Hebrew Civil Law. Tort of Negligence. London, 1937.
——— תולדות המשפט הצבורי העברי Paris, 1941.

VIII-B. *Liturgy.* (See also VIII).

Elbogen, I., *Der Jüdische Gottesdienst in seiner geschichtlichen Entwicklung.* 4th ed. Hildesheim, 1962.
Feldman, M. J., ארשת שפתינו *Concordance to Hebrew Liturgy.* St. Louis, Mo., 1942-1958. 3 vols.
Freehof, S. B., *The Origin of the Tahanun.* HUCA II. (1925.)
Gandz, S., *The Benediction Over the Luminaries and the Stars.* JQR XLIV. (1954.)
Goldschmidt, E. D., הגדה של פסח ותולדותיה Jerusalem, 1960.
Heinemann, J., התפילה בתקופת התנאים והאמוראים Jerusalem, 1964.
Idelsohn, A. Z., *Jewish Liturgy and its Development.* New York, 1932.
Kasher, M. M., הגדה שלמה 2. ed., Jerusalem, 1961.
Levy, E., יסודות התפלה. מחקר על תולדות התפלה... עד עריכתה בימי הגאונים Tel-Aviv, 1955.
Mann, J., *The Bible as Read and Preached in the Old Synagogue.* V. 1, Cincinnati, 1940. V. 2, Mann-Sonne, 1966.
Segal, J. B., *The Hebrew Passover from the earliest times to A.D. 70.* London, 1963.
Wahrmann, N.. מועדים; פרקי הלכה, ותפלה לכל מועדי השנה, 2nd ed. Jerusalem, 1957.
Zeitlin, S., *The Liturgy of the First Night of Passover.* JQR XXXVIII. (1948.)
———*Historical Studies of the Hebrew Liturgy.* JQR XLIX. (1959.)

IX. *Aggadah (See also VII and VIII).*

Ginzberg, L., *Legends of the Jews. Philadelphia, 1909-1938.* Index vol. by Cohen, B., 7 vols.
Heinemann, I., דרכי האגדה *The Methods of the Aggadah* Jerusalem, 1949.

Marmorstein, A., *The Background of the Haggadah.* HUCA VI. (1929.)
Patai, R., אדם ואדמה. מחקר במנהגים, אמונות ואגדות אצל ישראל ואומות העולם 3 vols., Jerusalem, 1942.
Vermes, G., *Scripture and Tradition in Judaism. Haggadic Studies.* Leiden, 1961.
Vilnay, Z., *Legends of Palestine.* Philadelphia, 1932.
——— אגדות ארץ ישראל, ערוכות לפי אזורי הארץ 4th ed. Jerusalem, 1953. 2 vols.
Zunz, L., הדרשות בישראל (Translation). Jerusalem, 1947.

X. *History (See also II, VIII, XIV and XV).*

Allon, G., תולדות היהודים בארץ ישראל בתקופת המשנה והתלמוד 2 vols. Tel-Aviv, 1952, 1955.
——— מחקרים בתולדות ישראל *Studies in Jewish History in the times of the Second Temple, The Mishna and the Talmud.* 2 vols. Tel-Aviv, 1957, 1958.
Aptowitzer, V., *Parteipolitik der Hasmonäerzeit in rabbinischem und pseudepigraphischem Schrifttum.* Vienna and Leipzig, 1927.
Avi-Yonah, M., בימי רומא וביזנטיון ; third ed., Jerusalem, 1962.
———*Geschichte der Juden im Zeitalter des Talmud in den Tagen von Rom und Byzanz* (Translation). Berlin, 1962.
Baron, S., *The Jewish Community, I.* Philadelphia, 1942.
———*A Social and Religious History of the Jews.* Second ed. New York, 1952-67. 12 vols. Index to vols. 1-8, Philadelphia 1960.
Baer, Y. F., ישראל בעמים Jerusalem, 1955.
Baer, M., *The Exilarchs in Talmudic Times* (Hebrew). Ziyyon 28 (1963).
Bickermann, E., *Der Gott der Makkabäer.* Berlin, 1937.
———*From Ezra to the Last of the Maccabees. New York,* 1962.
———*The Maccabees.* (Translation) New York, 1947.
Büchler, A., ed. by Brody, I. and Rabinowitz, J., *Studies in Jewish History.* Oxford 1956.
Dinur (Dinaburg), B. Z., תולדות ישראל. ישראל בגולה 2nd ed., Tel Aviv, 1958-66, vol. 1.
Englander, H., *The Men of the Great Synagogue.* HUCA Jubilee — Special, 1925.
Finkelstein, L., *Akiba.* New York, 1936.
———*The Pharisees.* Third ed., Philadelphia, 1962.
——— הפרושים ואנשי כנסת הגדולה New York, 1950.
Finkelstein, L., ed., *The Jews, Their History, Culture and Religion.* Third ed., Philadelphia, 1960.
Glatzer, N. N., *Untersuchungen zur Geschichtslehre der Tannaiten.* Berlin, 1933.
———*Geschichte der Talmudischen Zeit.* Berlin, 1937.
Gross, M. D., אבות הדורות. מונוגרפיות על אבות המשנה והתלמוד Tel-Aviv, 1957.
Guttmann, A., *Hillelites and Shammaites — a Clarification.* HUCA XXVIII. (1957.)
———*The Patriarch Judah I — His Birth and His Death.* HUCA XXV (1954.)
———*The End of the "Houses."* The Abraham Weiss Jubilee Volume. New York, 1964.
———*The End of the Jewish Sacrificial Cult.* HUCA XXXVIII (1967).

Guttmann, H., *Die Darstellung der jüdischen Religion bei Flavius Josephus.* Breslau, 1928.
Guttmann, M., *The Term "Foreigner"* (נכרי) *Historically Considered.* HUCA III, (1926.)
Hengel, M., Die Zeloten; *Untersuchungen zur jüdischen Freiheitsbewegung in der Zeit von Herodes I bis 70 n. Chr.*, Leiden, 1961.
Hoenig, S. B., *The Great Sanhedrin.* Philadelphia, 1953.
Katz, B., פרושים, צדוקים, קנאים, נוצרים Tel-Aviv, 1947.
Kennard, J. S., Jr., *The Jewish Provincial Assembly.* Zeitschrift für Neutestamentliche Wissenschaft . . . vol. 53, (1962.)
Krauss, S., פרס ורומי בתלמוד ובמדרשים Jerusalem, 1948.
Klausner, J., הסטוריה של הבית השני. Jerusalem, 1941. 5 vols.
Lauterbach, J. Z., *The Pharisees and Their Teachings.* HUCA VI, (1929.)
Leon, H. J., *The Jews of Ancient Rome.* Philadelphia, 1960.
Liver, Y., תולדות בית דויד Jerusalem, 1959.
Luria, B Z., היהדות בסוריה בימי שיבת ציון, המשנה והתלמוד Jerusalem, 1957.
Maimon, J. L., אביי ורבא Jerusalem, 1965.
Mantel, H., *Studies in the History of the Sanhedrin.* Cambridge, Mass., 1961.
————*Herod's Trial* (Hebrew). In Annual of Bar-Ilan University, vol. I., Jerusalem, 1963.
Mazar, B., Davis, M., Sason, B., editors: *The Illustrated History of the Jews.* Jerusalem, New York, 1963. — Hebrew edition: Jerusalem, 1964.
Mommsen, Th., *Judaea und die Juden.* (reprint). Mit einem Nachwort von E. Täubler. Berlin, 1936.
Neher, R. B., *Le Judaisme dans le Monde Romain. Textes commentes.* Paris, 1959.
Neusner, J., *A Life of Rabban Yohanan ben Zakkai.* Leiden, 1962.
————*A History of the Jews in Babylonia. I. The Parthian Period.* Leiden, 1965. *II. The Early Sassanian Period.* Leiden, 1966.
Oesterly, W. O. E., *A History of Israel*, vol. II. Oxford, 1932.
————*Jews and Judaism during the Greek Period.* London, 1941.
Rosenstein, A. M., התנאים ומשנתם: תקופת הבית. רבן יוחנן בן זכאי תקופת יבנה. 3 vols., Tel-Aviv, 1951-1953.
Sandmel, S., *Herod. Profile of a Tyrant.* Philadelphia and New York, 1967.
Schürer, E., *A History of the Jewish People in the Time of Jesus.* (Abridgement). Edited by Glatzer, N. N. (includes bibliography), New York, 1961.
Seaver, J. E., *Persecution of the Jews in the Roman Empire.* (300-438), Lawrence, 1952.
Shalit, A., הורדוס המלך Jerusalem, 1960.
Sonne, I., *The Schools of Shammai and Hillel from Within.* Ginzberg Jubilee Volume. New York, 1945.
Täubler, E., *Palästina in der hellenenistisch-römischen Zeit. In Tyche. Berlin*, 1926.
Tchernowitz, Ch., הזוגות ומקדש חוניו Ginzberg Jubilee Vol., New York, 1946.
Urbach, E., בעלי התוספות *The Tosaphists: Their History, Writings and Methods.* 2nd ed., Jerusalem, 1955.

———*Class-Status and Leadership in the World of the Palestinian Sages.* The Israel Academy of Sciences and Humanities. Proceedings, vol. II, No. 4. Jerusalem, 1966.
Wacholder, B. Z., *Nicolaus of Damascus.* Berkeley and Los Angeles, 1962.
Widengren, G., *The Status of the Jews in the Sassanian Empire.* In Iranica Antiqua, Leiden, 1961.
Zeitlin, S., *The Sadducees and Pharisees.* Philadelphia, 1937. Also in *Horeb.* (Reprint: New York, 1936, Hebrew.)
——— *The History of the Second Jewish Commonwealth. Prolegomena.* Philadelphia, 1933.
———*The Political Synedrion and the Religious Sanhedrin.* JQR XXXVI (1945).
———*The Rise and Fall of the Judaean State.* 2 vols. Philadelphia, 1962, 1967.
Zucker, H., *Studien zur jüdischen Selbstverwaltung im Altertum.* Berlin, 1936.
Zuri, J. S., רב Jerusalem, 1925.

Rostovzeff, M., *The Social and Economic History of the Roman Empire.* Oxford, 1926.
———*Social and Economic History of the Hellenistic World.* Oxford, 1941.

XI. *Chronology and Calendar (See also VIII).*

Akavia, A. A., הלוח ושמושו בכרונולוגיא Jerusalem, 1953.
Feldman, W. M., *Rabbinical Mathematics and Astronomy.* Second ed. New York, 1965.
Frank, E., *Talmudic and Rabbinical Chronology.* New York, 1956.
Gandz, S., *Studies in the Hebrew Calendar.* JQR XI (1949 and 1950.)
Kahana, K., מנין לשמיטין וליובלות Sinai, v. 56, no. 4-5 (1965).
Segal, J. B., *Intercalation and the Hebrew Calendar.* Vetus Testamentum, vol. VII, No. 3 (1957).
Wacholder, B. Z., *How Long Did Abraham Stay in Egypt?* HUCA XXXV (1964).
Zeitlin, S., *The Second Day of Rosh Ha-Shanah in Israel.* JQR XLIV (1954).

XII. *Archaeology. Realia.*

Blau, L., *Early Christian Archaeology from the Jewish Point of View.* HUCA III, (1926.)
Brand, Y., כלי חרס בספרות התלמוד *Ceramics in Talmudic Literature.* Jerusalem, 1953.
Dalman, G., *Arbeit und Sitte in Palästina.* 7 vols. Gütersloh, 1928-1942.
Finesinger, S. B., *The Shofar.* HUCA VIII-IX. (1931-1932.)
Goodenough, Erwin, R., *Jewish Symbols in the Greco-Roman Period.* 12 vols., New York, 1953-1965.
Hollis, F. G., *The Archaeology of Herod's Temple With Commentary of the Tractate Middoth.* London, 1934.

Kindler, A., אוצר מטבעות ארץ ישראל. מבחר מטבעות א"י וכו' *Thesaurus of Judaen Coins From the Fourth Century B.C. to the Third Century A.D.* (With English summary). Jerusalem, 1958.

Krauss, S., קורות בתי התפלה בישראל (trans.) New York, 1955.

Loew, I., *Die Flora der Juden.* 4 vols. Wien, 1924-1934.

Newman, J., *The Agricultural Life of the Jews in Babylonia between the years* 200 *C.E. and* 500 *C.E.*, London, 1932.

Reifenberg, A., *Ancient Jewish Coins.* Third ed. Jerusalem, 1963.

Wirgin, W. and Mandel, S., *The History of Coins and Symbols in Ancient Israel.* New York, 1958.

XIII. *Geography.*

Avi-Yonah, M., גיאוגרפיה היסטורית של ארץ ישראל למן שיבת ציון ועד ראשית הכיבוש הערבי . . . (2nd ed.) Jerusalem, 1951.

————*The Holy Land, from the Persian to the Arab Conquests* (536 B.C. to A.D. 640); *a historical geography.* Grand Rapids, 1966.

———— אטלס כרטא לתקופת בית שני המשנה והתלמוד *Carta's Atlas of the Period of the Second Temple, the Mishnah and the Talmud.* Jerusalem, 1966.

Duensing, H., *Verzeichnis der Personennamen und der geographischen Namen in der Mischna.* Stuttgart, 1960.

Glueck, N., *The River Jordan.* Philadelphia, 1946. 4th ed., Hebrew, Jerusalem, 1956.

Klein, S., *Das Tannaitische Grenzverzeichnis Palästinas.* HUCA V (1928.)

———— ארץ יהודה מימי העליה מבבל עד התימת התלמוד *The Land of Judah from the Babylonian Exile to the End of the Talmudic Period.* Jerusalem, 1939.

———— ארף ישראל Tel-Aviv, 1939.

———— ארץ הגליל Jerusalem, 1946.

Obermeyer, J., *Die Landschaft Babylonien im Zeitalter des Talmuds und des Gaonates.* Frankfurt/M. 1929.

Romanoff, P., *Onomasticon of Palestine — Post Biblical Topography.* Philadelphia, 1937.

XIV. *Philosophy, Theology, Ethics, Hellenism, Sects.* (*See also X and XV*).

Altmann, A., *Gnostic Themes in Rabbinic Cosmology.* In "Essays in Honor of J. H. Hertz." London, 1942.

Baeck, L., *Essence of Judaism* (Translation). London, 1936.

———— *Aus drei Jahrtausenden* (Essays). Berlin, 1938.

————*Die Pharisaeer,* Berlin, 1927 and 1934. English: New York, 1947.

Belkin, S., *Philo and the Oral Law.* Cambridge, Mass., 1940.

————In His Image: *The Jewish Philosophy of Man as Expressed in Rabbinic Tradition.* London, 1960.

————*"Questions and Answers to Genesis and Exodus" by Philo Judaeus — The Earliest Source for the Midrash.* Abraham Weiss Jubilee Volume, New York, 1964.

Büchler, A., *Studies in Sin and Atonement in the Rabbinic Literature of the First Century.* London, 1928.

Bousset, W., *Die Religion des Judentums im späthellenistischen Zeitalter*. 3rd revised ed. by Gressmann, H. Tübingen, 1926.

Bamberger, B., *Proselytism in the Talmudic Period.* Cincinnati, 1939.

———*Revelation of Torah after Sinai.* HUCA XVI, (1941.)

Braude, W. C., *Jewish Proselyting in the First Five Centuries of the Common Era.* Providence, 1940.

Cohen, B., *Law and Ethics in the Light of the Jewish Tradition.* (Essay). New York, 1957.

Cohen, S. S., *The Name of God, a Study in Rabbinic Theology.* HUCA XXIII, Part One. (1950-1951.)

———*The Unity of God, a Study in Hellenistic and Rabbinic Theology.* HUCA XXVI, (1955.)

———*Original Sin.* HUCA XXI, (1948.)

———*Judaism, A Way of Life.* Cincinnati, 1948.

Daube, D., *Rabbinic Methods of Interpretation and Hellenistic Rhetoric.* HUCA XXII, (1949.)

———*Alexandrian Methods of Interpretation and the Rabbis.* Hans Lewald Festschrift, Basel, 1954.

Davies, W. D., *Torah in the Messianic Age and/or the Age to Come.* Philadelphia, 1952.

Esh, S., ה ק (ב ה) *"der Heilige (Er sei gepriesen)"; zur Geschichte einer nachbiblisch-hebräischen Gottesbezeichnung.* Leiden, 1957.

Federbush, S., המוסר והמשפט בישראל Jerusalem, 1947.

Gaster, M., *Die 613 Gebote und Verbote der Samaritaner.* In Festschrift of Breslau Jewish Theological Seminary, 1929.

Guttmann, A., *The Significance of Miracles for Talmudic Judaism.* HUCA XX, (1947.)

———*Pharisaism in Transition.* Essays in honor of Solomon B. Freehof. Pittsburgh, 1964.

Hadas, M., *Hellenistic Culture: Fusion and Diffusion.* New York, 1959.

Heinemann, I., *Philons griechische und jüdische Bildung.* Breslau, 1932.

———*Die Lehre vom ungeschriebenen Gesetz im jüdischen Schrifttum.* HUCA IV, (1927.)

———*Altjüdische Allegoristik.* Breslau, 1936.

Helfgott, B. W., *The Doctrine of Election in Tannaitic Literature.* New York, 1954.

Herford, R. T., *Talmud and Apocrypha*, etc., London, 1933.

———*Pirke Aboth. The Ethics of the Talmud: Sayings of the Fathers.* Last ed. with Preface by John J. Tepfer, New York, 1962.

Jakobovits, I., *Jewish Medical Ethics.* New York, 1959.

Heschel, A. J., תורה מן השמים באספקלריה של דורות London, 1962, 1965.

Jeremias, J., *Die Passahfeier der Samaritaner.* Giessen, 1932.

Kadushin, M., *Aspects of the Rabbinic Concepts of Israel, A Study in the Mekilta.* HUCA XIX, (1945-1946.)

———*The Rabbinic Mind.* Second ed. New York, 1965.

———*Worship and Ethics, a Study in Rabbinic Judaism.* Evanston, 1964.

Katsh, A. I., *Judaism in Islam; Biblical and Talmudic Backgrounds of the Koran*, etc., New York, 1954.

Kaufmann, Y., תולדות האמונה הישראלית מימי קדם עד סוף בית שני 8 vols., Tel-Aviv, 1937-56.
Klausner, J., *The Messianic Idea in Israel, from its Beginning to the Completion of the Mishnah.* (Translation) New York, 1955.
Lieberman, S., *Greek in Jewish Palestine.* New York, 1942.
———*Hellenism in Jewish Palestine.* (2nd ed.). New York, 1962.
———*Light on the Cave Scrolls from Rabbinic Sources.* In PAAJR 20 (1951).
Mach, R., *Der Zaddik in Talmud und Midrasch.* Leiden, 1957.
Marcus, R., *Law in the Apocrypha.* New York, 1927.
Marmorstein, A., *The Old Rabbinic Doctrine of God.* 2 vols. London, 1927-1937.
Mihaly, E., *Religious Experience in Judaism* (Essay). London (World Union for Progressive Judaism), 1957.
Moore, G. F., *Judaism.* 3 vols. Cambridge, Mass., 1927-1930.
Oesterly, W. O. E. and Robinson, T. H., *Hebrew Religion.* 2nd ed. London, 1947.
Petuchowski, J. J., *The Mumar — A Study in Rabbinic Psychology.* HUCA XXX, (1959.)
———*The Controversial Figure of Melchizedek.* HUCA XVIII, (1957.)
Rabin, Ch., *Qumran Studies.* London, 1957.
Reines, Ch. W., תורה ומוסר, Jerusalem, 1954.
Sandmel, S., *Philo's Place in Judaism.* Cincinnati, 1956. (Also in HUCA: Part I XXV, 1954; Part II XXVI, 1955).
Sanders, J. L., *Suffering As Divine Discipline.* Rochester, 1955.
Silberg, M., *Law and Morals in Jewish Jurisprudence.* Cambridge, Mass., 1961, tr. of חוק ומוסר במשפט העברי Jerusalem, 1952.
Stewart, R., *Rabbinic Theology. An introductory study.* Edinburgh, 1961.
Slonimsky, H., *The Philosophy Implicit in the Midrash.* HUCA XXVII, (1956.)
Tcherikover, V., *Hellenistic Civilization and the Jews.* Philadelphia, 1959.
——— היהדות בעולם היווני והרומי Tel-Aviv, 1960.
——— היהודים והיוונים בתקופה ההלניסתית Tel-Aviv, 1963.
Urbach, E., הנבואה והנביאים בעיני חז"ל Jerusalem, 1961.
Wallach, L., *A Palestinian Polemic Against Idolatry.* HUCA XIX, (1945-46.)
Wolfson, H. A., *Philo; Foundations of Religious Philosophy,* etc., 2 vols., Cambridge, Mass., 1947.

XV. *Judaism and Christianity (Including apologetical literature.) (See also X and XIV).*

Baeck, L., *Haggadah and Christian Doctrine.* HUCA XXIII, Part One, (1950-1951).
———*Judaism and Christianity.* Translation with introduction by Kaufmann, W., Philadelphia, 1958.
——— בשלהי בית שני: הפרושים. ספרי הבשורה Jerusalem, 1963.
Added: Flusser, D., הנצרות הקדומה לאור המגילות הגנוזות
———*Paulus, die Pharisäer und das Neue Testament.* Frankfurt/M., 1961.

Bloch, Ch., *Blut und Eros im jüdischen Schrifttum und Leben.* Wien, 1935.

——— דע מה שתשיב Appropriate Replies to Inquiries from the Vatican. New York, 1943.

Bloch, J. S., *Israel and the Nations.* Berlin, 1927. (Translation).

Bonsirven, J. *Textes Rabbiniques Des Deux Premiers Siècles Chrétiens Pour Servir à L'intelligence Du Nouveau Testament.* Roma, 1955.

———*Palestinian Judaism in the Time of Jesus Christ.* Translation. New York, 1964.

Brandon, S. G. F., *Jesus and the Zealots,* Cambridge, 1967.

Cohon, B. D., *Jacob's Well; Some Jewish Sources and Parallels to the Sermon on the Mount.* New York, 1956.

Cohon, S. S., *Why Do the Heathen Rage?* Chicago, 1938.

Daube, D., *The New Testament and Rabbinic Judaism.* London, 1956.

Davies, W. D., *Christian Origins and Judaism.* Philadelphia, 1962.

———*Paul and Rabbinic Judaism,* London, 1948.

Davies, W. D. and Daube, D., *The Background of the New Testament and its eschatology,* ed. Cambridge (England), 1956.

Die Lehren des Judentums. Editors: Bernfeld, S. (I-IV) and Bamberger, F. (V). Contributors: Baeck, L., Bamberger, F., Dienemann, M., Elbogen, I., Guttmann, J., Wiener, M., and others. Second ed., Berlin-Leipzig, 1922-29.

Finkel, A., *The Pharisees and the Teacher of Nazareth.* Leiden/Köln, 1964.

Flusser, D. G., האמונות והדעות של הכנסיה הנוצרית הראשונה Jerusalem, 1964.

Gavin, F., *Rabbinic Parallels in Early Church Orders.* HUCA VI (1929).

Gerhardsson, B., *Memory and Manuscript. Oral Tradition and Written Transmission in Rabbinic Judaism and Early Christianity.* Uppsala, 1961.

Glicksman, S., *The Forgeries and Falsifications in the Antisemitic Literature.* New York, 1939.

Goldstein, M., *Jesus in the Jewish Tradition.* New York, 1950.

Grayzel, S., *The Talmud and the Medieval Papacy.* Essays in Honor of Solomon B. Freehof. Pittsburgh, 1964.

Guignebert, Ch., *The Jewish World in the Time of Jesus.* London, 1939 (and 1951). (Translation).

Guttmann, A., *Enthüllte Talmudzitate.* Berlin, 1930.

Guttmann, M., *Das Judentum und seine Umwelt.* Berlin, 1927.

——— היהדות וסביבתה Jewish Studies in Memory of M. Guttmann. Budapest, 1946.

Herford, R. T., *Judaism in the New Testament Period.* London, 1928.

Hirschberg, H., *Allusions to the Apostle Paul in the Talmud.* JBL, vol. 63. (1943.)

———*Once again the Minim.* Ibid. vol. 67. (1948.)

Jeremias, J., *Jerusalem sur Zeit Jesu.* 3rd ed. Göttingen, 1962.

Judaism and Christianity. Vol. I. *The Age of Transition;* ed. Oesterley, W. O. E., London, 1937. Vol. II. *The Contact of Pharisaism with other Cultures.* Ed. Loewe, H., 1937. Vol. III. *Law and Religion.* Ed. Rosenthal, E. I., 1938.

Klausner, J., *Jesus of Nazareth, His Life, Times and Teachings.* New York, 1927 (Translation).
———*From Jesus to Paul.* (Translation). New York, 1945.
Kosmala, H., Hebräer — Essener — Christen. Leiden, 1959.
Marmorstein, A., *Judaism and Christianity in the Middle of the Third Century.* HUCA X, (1935.)
Mihaly, E., *A Rabbinic Defence of the Election of Israel.* HUCA, XXXV (1964).
Montefiore, C. G., *Rabbinic Literature and Gospel Teachings.* London, 1930.
Parkes, J., *The Conflict of the Church and the Synagogue. A Study in the Origins of Antisemitism.* London, 1934. New York, 1961.
———*The Foundations of Judaism and Christianity.* Chicago, 1960.
Petuchowski, J. J., *The Theology of Haham David Nieto.* New York, 1954.
———*Halakhah in the Church Fathers.* Essays in Honor of Solomon B. Freehof. Pittsburgh, 1964.
Pfeiffer, R. H., *History of New Testament Times.* New York, 1949.
Purinton, C. E., *Christianity and its Judaic Heritage: An Introduction with Selected Sources.* New York, 1961.
Sandmel, S., *Judaism, Jesus and Paul: Some problems of method in scholarly research.* Vanderbilt Studies in the Humanities. I., Nashville, 1951.
———*A Jewish Understanding of the New Testament.* Cincinnati, 1956.
———*Myths, Genealogies, and Jewish Myths and the Writing of the Gospels.* HUCA XXVII, (1956.)
———*The Genius of Paul.* New York, 1958.
———*We Jews and Jesus.* New York, 1965.
Schoeps, H. J., *Theologie und Geschichte des Judenchristentums.* Tübingen, 1949.
———*Aus frühchristlicher Zeit.* Tübingen, 1950.
———*Paul: The Theology of the Apostle in the Light of Jewish Religious History* (Translation). London, 1961.
Smith, M., *Tannaitic Parallels to the Gospels.* Philadelphia, 1951.
Strack H. L.—Billerbeck, P., *Kommentar zum Neuen Testament aus Talmud und Midrasch.* München, 1922-1928. Index vol. by Adolph, K., edited by Jeremias, J., 1956.
Wilde, R., *The Treatment of the Jews in the Greek Christian Writers of the First Three Centuries.* Washington, 1949.
Winter, P., *On the Trial of Jesus.* Berlin, 1961.
Zeitlin, S., *Who Crucified Jesus?* New York, London. 1942.

XVI. *Education.*

Arzt, M., *The Teacher in Talmud and Midrash.* M. Kaplan Jubilee Vol., New York, 1953.
Blau, L., *Lehren und Gruppieren der Gebote in Talmudischer Zeit.* Heinrich Brody Festschrift (Soncino Blätter III), Berlin, 1930.
Drazin, N., *History of Jewish Education from 515 B.C.E. to 200 C.E.*, Baltimore, 1940.

Ebner, E., *Elementary Education in Ancient Israel During the Tannaitic Period* (10-220 C.E.). New York, 1956.
Lauterbach, J. Z., *The Names of the Rabbinical Schools and Assemblies in Babylon.* HUCA Jubilee-Special, 1925.
Mirsky, S. K., לראשית הישיבה ומהותה Horeb 5, 1939.
——— לסדרי הישיבות בבל בתקופת האמוראים Horeb 3-4, 1936-1937.
———*Types of Lectures in the Babylonian Academies.* Essays in Honor of Salo W. Baron. New York, 1959.
Schwabe, M., על בתי הספר היהודיים — רומיים בתקופת המשנה והתלמוד Tarbiz XXI. (1950).
Yudelowiz, M.D., ישיבת פומבדיתא בימי האמוראים Tel-Aviv, 1932.

XVII. *Anthologies. Abridgements. Popular Works.*

Baron, S. W. and Blau, J. L., editors, *Judaism; Postbiblical and Talmudic Period.* New York, 1954.
Bokser, B. Z., *The Wisdom of the Talmud.* New York, 1951.
Cohen, A., *Everyman's Talmud.* New York, 1949.
Ginzberg, L., *Legends of the Bible.* (Shortened from Legends of the Jews). Philadelphia, 1956.
Glatzer, N. N., *The Rest Is Commentary; A Source Book of Judaic Antiquity.* Boston, 1961.
Montefiore, C. G., and Loewe, H., *A Rabbinic Anthology.* London, 1938.
Newman, L. I., and Spitz, S., *The Talmudic Anthology.* New York, 1947.
Trattner, E. R., *Understanding the Talmud.* New York, 1955.
Unterman, I., The Talmud. New York, 1952.

XVIII. *Miscellany.*

Abstracts of papers read at the World Congress of Jewish Studies in Jerusalem quadrennially. Last vol. (abstracts of the Fourth Congress) Jerusalem, 1965. (See sections on Talmud and Rabbinics, Jewish Law, and on Ancient Jewish History). Unabridged papers (Fourth Congress), Jerusalem, 1967.
Blank, S., *The Death of Zechariah in Rabbinic Literature.* HUCA XII-XIII, (1937-1938.)
Ehrlich, E. L., *Kultsymbolik im Alten Testament und im nachbilischen Judentum.* Stuttgart, 1959.
Federbush, S., *The Jewish Concept of Labor.* New York, 1956.
Hirsch, W., *Rabbinic Psychology* . . . London, 1947. Hebrew: Tel-Aviv, 1957.
Jacobs, L., *Studies in Talmudic Logics and Methodology.* London, 1961.
Katz, R., *Empathy in Modern Psychotherapy and in the Aggada.* HUCA XXX, (1959.)
Kohen, P. J., ספר הסימנים השלם London, 1952.
Patai, R., *The "Control of Rain" in Ancient Palestine.* HUCA XIV, 1939.
Petuchowski, J. J., *Ever since Sinai.* New York, 1961.
———*Man and Temple in Ancient Jewish Myth and Ritual.* London . . . 1947.
Trachtenberg, J., *Jewish Magic and Superstition.* New York, 1939.
Waxman, M., גלות וגאולה בספרות ישראל New York, 1952.